INSIGHT GUIDES

IRELAND

www.insightguides.com/Ireland

◉ Walking Eye App

YOUR FREE DESTINATION CONTENT AND EBOOK AVAILABLE THROUGH THE WALKING EYE APP

Your guide now includes a free eBook and destination content for your chosen destination, all for the same great price as before. Simply download the Walking Eye App from the App Store or Google Play to access your free eBook and destination content.

HOW THE WALKING EYE APP WORKS

Through the Walking Eye App, you can purchase a range of eBooks and destination content. However, when you buy this book, you can download the corresponding eBook and destination content for free. Just see below in the grey panels where to find your free content and then scan the QR code at the bottom of this page.

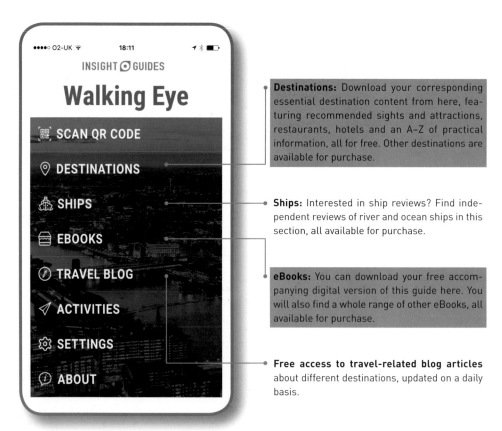

Destinations: Download your corresponding essential destination content from here, featuring recommended sights and attractions, restaurants, hotels and an A–Z of practical information, all for free. Other destinations are available for purchase.

Ships: Interested in ship reviews? Find independent reviews of river and ocean ships in this section, all available for purchase.

eBooks: You can download your free accompanying digital version of this guide here. You will also find a whole range of other eBooks, all available for purchase.

Free access to travel-related blog articles about different destinations, updated on a daily basis.

HOW THE DESTINATION CONTENT WORKS

Each destination includes a short introduction, an A–Z of practical information and recommended points of interest, split into 4 different categories:
• Highlights
• Accommodation
• Eating out
• What to do

You can view the location of every point of interest and save it by adding it to your Favourites. In the 'Around Me' section you can view all the points of interest within 5km.

HOW THE EBOOKS WORK

The eBooks are provided in EPUB file format. Please note that you will need an eBook reader installed on your device to open the file. Many devices come with this as standard, but you may still need to install one manually from Google Play.

The eBook content is identical to the content in the printed guide.

HOW TO DOWNLOAD THE WALKING EYE APP

1. Download the Walking Eye App from the App Store or Google Play.
2. Open the app and select the scanning function from the main menu.
3. Scan the QR code on this page – you will then be asked a security question to verify ownership of the book.
4. Once this has been verified, you will see your eBook and destination content in the purchased ebook and destination sections, where you will be able to download them.

Other destination apps and eBooks are available for purchase separately or are free with the purchase of the Insight Guide book.

Contents

Introduction

The Best of Ireland **6**
The New Ireland...................... **19**
The Irish Character **22**

History

Decisive Dates......................... **30**
Ireland's Invaders.................... **35**
The Making of a Nation **42**
Living with Partition **52**
Ireland Transformed **58**

Features

Music **67**
The Irish Way With Words **72**
Contemporary Art **78**
Food **82**
Pubs **86**
A Sporting Nation **90**
Golf.. **94**
Angling **96**
Walking in Ireland................... **98**

Insights

PHOTO FEATURES

Ireland in the Movies............... **26**
Ireland's Finest Ruins **40**
Dublin at War **50**
Arts Festivals **76**

Ireland's Architecture **102**
Bloomsday **140**
Horse Culture........................ **150**
The Burren **218**

MINI FEATURES

Ireland's Top 10 Walks.......... **101**
Trinity College........................ **120**
Horse-drawn Caravans **169**
The Irish Language............... **199**
The Cliffs of Moher **212**
Rural Bungalows **251**
The Marching Tradition.......... **290**
Belfast's Turbulent History.... **308**

Places

Introduction **111**
Dublin.................................... **117**
Excursions from Dublin **143**
The Southeast **153**
Cork and Surroundings **171**
The Southwest...................... **181**
Limerick and the
    Shannon Region................ **201**
Galway and the West............ **221**
Inland Ireland **237**
The Northwest **253**
Northern Ireland **273**
Belfast................................... **305**

Travel Tips

TRANSPORT

Getting There **324**
 By Air **324**
 By Sea **324**
 By Bus **325**
Getting Around.......................**325**
 Public Transport................**325**
 Private Transport **325**
 Car Rentals **325**
 Cycling................................**325**

A – Z

Accidents and Emergencies ..**326**
Accommodation **326**
Budgeting for Your Trip **326**
Children..................................**327**
Climate...................................**327**
Clothing..................................**327**
Crime and Safety **327**
Customs and
 Entry Regulations **327**
Disabled Travellers **328**
Electricity **328**
Embassies and Consulates ..**328**
Events **328**
Gay and Lesbian Travellers ...**330**
Health and Medical Care **330**
Liquor Laws **330**
Maps **330**

Media **330**
Money **331**
Opening Hours.......................**331**
Postal Services **331**
Public Holidays **331**
Religious Services **331**
Smoking.................................**332**
Telephones **332**
Time Zone **332**
Tourist Information **333**

FURTHER READING

Irish Classics..........................**334**
Contemporary Fiction
 and Poetry.........................**334**
History....................................**335**
Biography...............................**335**
Memoirs and Journalism **335**
Current Affairs.......................**335**
Genealogy..............................**335**
Architecture **335**
Art and Decorative Arts **335**
Cookery **335**
Drama **336**
Folklore **336**
Music **336**
Travel **336**
Landscape and
 Topography **336**
Other Insight Guides **336**

Maps

Ireland....................................**112**
Dublin.....................................**114**
Dublin Suburbs......................**137**
DART and Suburban
 Rail Network **138**
Excursions from Dublin **144**
The Southeast **154**
Cork..**172**
Cork and Surroundings **178**
The Southwest.......................**182**
Around Killarney **191**
Limerick **202**
Shannon Region....................**208**
Galway....................................**222**
The West **228**
Inland Ireland **238**
The Northwest **254**
Northern Ireland **270**
Derry City...............................**274**
Belfast....................................**306**
Greater Belfast **319**
Inside front cover Ireland
Inside back cover Dublin

THE BEST OF IRELAND: TOP ATTRACTIONS

There is a lot of variety packed into a small island, from the slightly faded elegance of Dublin to the wild remoteness of windswept Connemara.

△ **Georgian Dublin**. The city retains some of its Georgian heritage – for example, the characteristic doors – but the real appeal is the Dubliners' vibrancy and sense of fun. See page 117.

▽ **The Giant's Causeway**. This astonishing assembly of more than 40,000 hexagonal basalt columns on the north coast is one of the world's wonders. See page 300.

△ **Glendalough**. Round towers are a striking reminder of Ireland's Golden Age when, after the fall of the Roman Empire and Europe plunged into the Dark Ages, monks in Ireland ('the Land of Saints and Scholars') kept alight a lone beacon of learning and civilization. See page 144.

▷ **The Glens of Antrim**. A goat sculpture at Cusdendun represents the magic of the nine steep valleys, which reminded the novelist William Makepeace Thackeray of 'Switzerland in miniature'. See page 298.

△ **The Wild Atlantic Way**. This scenic drive along the west coast takes in the famous Ring of Kerry - expect a panorama of coastal and mountain scenery, lush vegetation and sandy beaches. See page 193.

△ **Traditional Irish Music**. This has influenced so many styles of music around the world, and can be heard at its authentic best everywhere from street buskers to sessions in city and country pubs. See page 67.

▷ **Connemara**. The far west of Ireland is iconic – a landscape of wild, rocky bog land, its deeply indented coastline covered in autumnal shades of seaweed, its stunted pine trees struggling for a foothold and mirrored in the surprisingly blue water of its many loughs. See page 226.

△ **The Burren**. The moon-like plateau in Co. Clare contains ancient tombs and a remarkable variety of rich flora. See page 214.

▷ **The Aran Islands**. An unspoiled Irish-speaking community, beaten by the Atlantic, the islands echo a much older Ireland. See page 229.

▽ **The Rock of Cashel**. Towering above Tipperary's green plain is a dramatic cluster of romantically ruined stone buildings, dating to the 12th and 13th centuries and the former stronghold of the Kings of Munster. See page 167.

THE BEST OF IRELAND: EDITOR'S CHOICE

Discover the country's best-kept secrets, the best festivals, museums and unique attractions. Here at a glance are our recommendations, plus some tips and tricks that even the locals won't always know.

Bloomsday performer in a James Joyce mask.

BEST FAIRS AND FESTIVALS

Bloomsday. Fans of James Joyce's Ulysses celebrate 16 June (the day on which it is set, in 1904) by proceeding around Dublin in period costume. Alcohol is consumed. See page 140.

Fleadh Nua. Fleadh means festival, and in May Ennis's *Fleadh Nua* (*Nua* means new or modern) attracts thousands of traditional musicians, amateur and professional, with the music continuing at night in bars. See page 210.

The Auld Lammas Fair. The oldest fair in Ireland, dating from 1606, held in Ballycastle, Co. Antrim, still sees traditional horse trading alongside a busy trade in dulse (edible seaweed) and yellowman (hard toffee). See page 299.

ONLY IN IRELAND

Newgrange, Co. Meath. This ancient passage tomb predates the Egyptian pyramids by centuries. See page 147.

Kissing the Blarney Stone. Even if it doesn't bestow the 'gift of the gab', it's a dizzying experience. See page 177.

Trinity College, Dublin. With its cobbled court-yards, elegant Georgian buildings and bustling student population, it has a unique ambience. See page 119.

The Ring of Kerry. A day-long drive around the coastal scenery of Kerry's southwesterly peninsula, renowned for its comb-ination of lush subtropical vegetation, and rugged seascapes. Visit a series of pretty seaside villages while offshore the rugged Skellig Rocks hover mysteriously on the horizon. See page 193.

Cruinniú na mBád. Traditional wooden boats with brown sails, laden with turf, race across Galway Bay in August. See page 217.

Croagh Patrick. Thousands of pilgrims, many of them barefoot, walk up Mayo's 'holy mountain' on the last Sunday in July, as did their grandparents before them. See page 231.

Derry's walls. The last walled city to be built in Europe is the centre of a vibrant cultural life. See page 274.

Dubai Duty Free Irish Derby. Held in June at the Curragh Racecourse in Co. Kildare, this is the most popular event on the colourful horseracing calendar. See page 329.

Kiss the Blarney Stone to gain the gift of the gab.

BEST TRADITIONAL PUBS

Guinness, worth raising a glass to.

The Crown Liquor Saloon. 46 Great Victoria Street, Belfast. Its ornate Victorian interior is cared for by the National Trust. See page 310.

The Auld Shebeen. Abbey Street, Ballina, Co. Mayo. Town-centre bar with music nightly. Good food. See page 234.

Hargadon's. 4–5 O'Connell Street, Sligo.

A great 'brown' pub (furniture, floors, walls, ceilings: brown). Good food, music. See page 255.

MacCarthy's. Main Square, Castletownbere, Beara, Co. Cork. The front is a grocery shop, used by local trawlermen; behind it is MacCarthy's Bar. See page 190.

M.J. O'Neill. Suffolk Street, Dublin 2. An old-style pub, with a warren of 'snugs'. See page 139.

Morrissey's. Main Street, Abbeyleix, Co. Laois (on the N8 Dublin–Cork road). Opened as a grocer's in 1775.

Tigh Neachtain. Cross Street, Galway, has stubbornly retained its old-fashioned painted wooden interior. Music. www.tighneachtain.com.

Traditional pubs showcase traditional music.

TOP MUSEUMS AND GALLERIES

National Museum. A wealth of priceless Irish treasures, including Celtic antiquities, Bronze Age gold jewellery and early Christian crosses. See page 123.

National Gallery. Paintings by Vermeer, Rembrandt, Poussin and Goya: plus a major collection of Irish art. See page 124.

Chester Beatty Library. Exquisite collection of Islamic and Far Eastern art housed in a wing of Dublin Castle. See page 127.

Irish Famine Museum. Strokestown, Co. Roscommon. Visit for a compelling account of 1845's tragic scourge. See page 245.

Hunt Museum. Limerick. Celtic and medieval treasures in

historic Customs House on the River Shannon. See page 204.

The Model. Sligo. Converted 'model school' houses superb collection of paintings by Jack Yeats. See page 256.

Ulster Folk and Transport Museum. Reconstructed houses and cottages bring Ulster c.1910 to life. Transport ranges from huge locomotives to the DeLorean sports car (one of which featured in the film *Back to the Future*). See page 296.

Dublin City Gallery The Hugh Lane. Imposing 18th-century town house in the Palladian style; collection of Impressionists plus 19th- and 20th-century Irish art. See page 132.

BEST BIG HOUSES

Dublin Castle. The State Apartments showcase traditional Irish craftsmanship. See page 127.

Castletown House. Co. Kildare. One of the largest private houses, dating from 1722. See page 148.

Fota House. Co. Cork. Shooting lodge in the classical style. Arboretum. See page 177.

Strokestown Park House. Co. Roscommon. Grandiose Georgian residence. See page 244.

Castle Ward House. Magnificent site overlooking Strangford Lough. Two facades: one classical, one Gothic. See page 293.

Dublin Castle.

National Gallery, Dublin.

RECOMMENDED FOR FAMILIES

Viking Splash Tours. Use amphibious vehicles for a hilarious orientation tour of Dublin by land and water. (Departs St Patrick's Cathedral and St Stephen's Green). www.vikingsplash.com .

The Ark. Eustace Street, Temple Bar, Dublin. This cultural centre for children has a gallery and workshop space. See page 126.

Ulster Folk and Transport Museum.

Carrick-a-Rede Rope Bridge. Ballycastle, Co. Antrim. Spans a 60ft (18-meter) gap between mainland and Carrick-a-Rede Island. Strictly for thrill-seekers. See page 300.

Dublinia. St Michael's Hill, Dublin. A reconstruction of life in medieval Dublin with high-tech displays. See page 128.

Malahide Castle. Escape from the city to 22 acres (9 hectares) of pleasure gardens with playground and pitch and putt course, and sweet treats at the Avoca Café. See page 139.

Cobh Heritage Centre. Cobh, Co. Cork. Compelling recreation of the emigrant experience. See page 178.

Muckross Traditional Farms. Muckross Park, Killarney. Walking tour of three farms inhabited by farming families and their animals, including a friendly pair of giant Irish wolfhounds. See page 192.

Bunratty Castle and Folk Park. Bunratty, Co. Clare. The huge 15th-century castle is authentically furnished, while the village is inhabited by real people and animals. See page 207.

Sheep and Wool Centre. Leenane, Co. Galway. Twenty breeds of sheep graze around the house, where craftspeople show how sheep's fleece is turned into wool. See page 231.

Fota Wildlife Park. Giraffe and wallabies roam free, while the cheetah have a huge run in their cage. See page 177.

Titanic Belfast. Visitor centre built to the same scale as the fated ocean liner, and located beside the dry dock in which it was built: hours of fascinating multimedia exhibits on the ship and the men who built her. See page 312.

Cliffs of Moher. Trails lead to viewing points above the towering cliffs. See page 211.

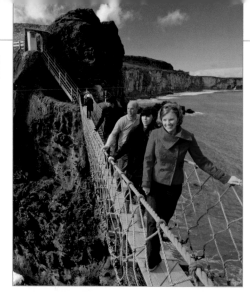

Carrick-a-Rede Rope Bridge.

BEST BEACHES

Irish beaches are generally undeveloped, with free car parking. Beaches are popular with walkers outside July and August.

Banna Strand. Co. Kerry. West-facing beach backed by dunes big enough to get lost on. Fine views over Tralee Bay. See page 198.

Brittas Bay. Co. Wicklow. White sand backed by dunes interspersed with small coves. Popular holiday spot for Dubliners. See page 144.

Curracloe Strand. Co. Wicklow. Stood in for Normandy for the D-Day landing scenes in the 1998 film *Saving Private Ryan*. Stretches for 5.5 miles (9km). Nature trails and birdwatching hides to observe winter migrants. See page 154.

Lahinch. Surfers flock to Lahinch on the west coast of Co. Clare in search of huge waves offshore, but the waves on the beach, which is in the village centre, are ideal for beginners. See page 211.

Inch Strand. Dingle, Co. Kerry. Stretch of golden sand running for 5 miles (8km) on a spit of land protruding into Dingle Bay. See page 196.

Mullaghmore beach, Co. Sligo.

BEST CRAFT SHOPS

Avoca Handweavers. Killmacanogue, Co. Wicklow (also Dublin, Kenmare and Letterfrack). Flagship store of a family-run chain known for their jewel-coloured, handwoven rugs and throws. Also famed for fresh, wholesome food. www.avoca.com.

Blarney Woollen Mills. Blarney, Co. Cork (also Killarney and Tipperary). Amid the leprechaun key rings and Guinness T-shirts is good, Irish-made clothing. www.blarney.com.

Waterford Crystal Experience, The Mall Waterford. A 50-minute tour takes visitors through the various stages of production. Wide range of crystal on sale in the shop. www.waterfordvisitorcentre.com.

The Kilkenny Design Centre. Kilkenny Castle. Well-designed Irish-made ceramics, jewellery, clothing and textiles. www.kilkennydesign.com.

Judy Greene Pottery. Kirwan's Lane, Galway. The best of hand-crafted design: ceramics by Judy Greene, wood, textiles, glass and basket ware. www.judygreenepottery.com.

Belleek Pottery. Co. Fermanagh. Fine bone china. See page 284.

Thomas Ferguson. 54 Scarva Rd, Banbridge, Co. Down. Wide range of goods in Irish linen for sale in Ireland's last remaining linen weaving factory. www.fergusonsirishlinen.com.

Walking in Connemara.

Belleek Pottery.

BEST WALKS

Ireland's scenery can be enjoyed on waymarked paths suitable for all levels of fitness.

The Grand Canal Way. Flat canal-bank walk from the Dublin outskirts to the little-visited Midlands (highest point, Lowtown, 280ft/85 metres). See page 101.

The Kerry Way. Passes through some of Ireland's most beautiful scenery between Glenbeigh and Killarney. See page 99.

The Slieve Bloom Way. Inland route close to the exact centre of Ireland.

Quietly spectacular. See page 101.

The Ballyhoura Way. Easy walking on an inland pastoral route though low hills with views of the Golden Vale. See page 168.

Beara Way. A variety of coastal and mountain scenery on one of the southwest's less frequented peninsulas. See page 190.

The Sperrin Mountains. Sparsely populated area in the northeast of County Tyrone; bog, heather and moorland. See page 279.

MONEY-SAVING TIPS

Heritage Cards An OPW Heritage Card gives you unlimited admission to all 780 sites in the Office of Public Works scheme for one year. At €25 adult (€20 seniors, €60 family) it will quickly pay for itself.

Hostels To save on hotel costs, consider the 100 options listed by Independent Holiday Hostels of Ireland (nine in Northern Ireland), with no curfew or membership needed. Some are in historic buildings, all are friendly and well run. Outside Dublin expect to pay under €20 per night in a double room (in Dublin around €30). www.hostels-ireland.com.

Bed and Breakfast If you are staying for more than one night, ask for a reduction on advertised price. Check online for the amazing special offers available since the downturn.

Early Bird or Special Value/market menus Many restaurants offer cheaper two or three-course menus before 6.30 or 7.30pm. If you are keen to sample some of Ireland's top grade restaurants and hotels but fear it may wreck your budget, go for lunch rather than dinner. A good-value way to enjoy the ambience of Ireland's famous castle hotels is to drop by mid-morning for a coffee.

Bar Food is a thrifty alternative to restaurant food.

Lough Corrib, Connemara.

Giant's Causeway.

*Grattan Bridge over the Liffey,
Dublin.*

The Dark Hedges, Co Antrim.

THE NEW IRELAND

Ireland has changed dramatically in recent years. The Republic has become a secular, multiracial, European state, while Northern Ireland has progressed from terrorism to power-sharing.

Aurora Borealis at Desertegney, Co Donegal.

That quintessentially Irish phenomenon 'Blarney' – talk that aims to charm, flatter or persuade – is a potent sales tool. An alluring brand image has been created for Ireland over the years, portraying an unspoilt green land with hospitable people, a leisurely pace of life and an uncanny ability to have fun. But then it's always been known as a mythical land of leprechauns, fairies and warriors…

A changed society

Today's visitors who enjoy having their preconceptions smashed will indeed have a grand time in Ireland, on both sides of the border.

A dramatic transformation has taken place in the Republic. Branded 40 years ago by Northern Protestants as an economically deprived, priest-ridden country whose most prolific product was emigrants, the Republic has gone full circle economically since joining the European Union (then the EEC) in 1972. Adopting the euro in 2003 distanced the country decisively from its old imperial master, Britain, which clung to sterling. Irish culture, it found, travelled well, whether in the form of the decidedly bogus 'Irish pub', which took root in 42 countries, or as cunningly modernised traditional music and dance epitomised by Riverdance. The global success of stadium rockers U2, and of Bob Geldof's Live Aid gave Dublin a new hip identity, consolidated by its buzzing Temple Bar district.

The Big Fish sculpture, Belfast.

Generous tax breaks and a job market flooded with well-educated, personable graduates encouraged multinationals – from Pfizer and other pharmaceutical companies in the early days, to Google and Facebook – to set up Irish operations, often basing their European headquarters in this hospitable English-speaking Eurozone country. Many of those who had emigrated returned to a new Ireland with a booming economy, and were joined by emigrants from eastern European countries and elsewhere, diluting the former homogeneous population of white, Irish-born Catholics. Embracing globalisation, the Republic took as its model not its fellow European countries, with their emphasis on the welfare state, but the US, with its stress on individual achievement. It was, the saying went, 'more Boston than Berlin'. Tipping its hat to US values, the low-fare airline Ryanair shamelessly modelled itself on America's Southwest Airlines, and became the biggest airline in Europe.

Boom and bust

In more recent years however, the 26-county Republic has endured a dramatic cycle of boom-and-bust. Ireland, like many other countries, has fallen into recession, the legacy being an excess of 15,000 hotel rooms (good news for holiday-makers looking for competitive rates), untenanted office blocks and unsold apartments and houses. Emigration soared, as people travelled abroad in search of work once more.

The country was in a state of shock, as people faced pay cuts, pension cuts and years of negative equity while the huge debts run up by a few irresponsible bankers and developers were paid off. Criminal prosecutions are still awaited. Meanwhile Ireland's austerity measures won praise from the all-important EU and IMF, and there is an increasing sense that the worst is over. Unemployment is falling and the economy has stabilised.

Social upheaval

Social change has accompanied Ireland's economic metamorphosis, but at an uneven pace. Divorce was not decriminalised in the Republic until 1995 and homosexuality until 1993. Most state schools are managed by the Catholic Church. Ireland still has the most restrictive abortion

laws in Europe, with Irish women routinely travelling to the UK for terminations. In 2012, there were huge demonstrations after the death of Savita Halappanavar, an Indian dentist living in Galway, due to complications from a sceptic miscarriage. There is a continuing campaign to repeal the 8th Amendment and legalise abortion, with emotions running high on both sides. Revelations about paedophilia in the church, the cover up of child abuse by Bishops, and the exploitation of women in church-run 'Magdalen Laundries' have led to widespread anger and a sharp decline in attendance at Sunday Mass. In 2015, Ireland voted by a landslide to legalise same-sex marriage.

Ha'penny Bridge, Dublin.

The Northern transformation

Northern Ireland meanwhile, once known chiefly for urban terrorism, broadcast daily on television, is selling itself as a great place to play golf. What caused this transformation? The answer is comparatively straightforward. After three decades of bloodshed, the Republic amended its constitution to abandon all claims of sovereignty towards Northern Ireland, and the IRA agreed to lay down its arms. This created the conditions for a power-sharing Assembly between the Unionist leaders and Sinn Fein, a political party closely linked to the IRA. The British government invested heavily in the province, and tourism in scenic Northern Ireland – home of the Giant's Causeway, the Mountains of Mourne, the Antrim Coast Road, the Fermanagh lakelands, the Glens of Antrim – gathered momentum.

Ireland's continuing allure

Ireland manages to combine modernity with traditional hospitality and unspoilt scenery. The weather may be wet and windy at times and the prices may be steep, but the people still have an outstanding capacity for friendliness and sense of fun that they are more than willing to share with their visitors.

THE IRISH CHARACTER

Take generous portions of charm, wit, congeniality and loquacity. Then mix in melancholy, daydreaming, opportunism and a history of violence. Stir gently and wait for a surprising result...

With a cheerful disregard for political correctness, the Irish take a perverse delight in the universal jokes made against them. Indeed, they even print selections on linen tea towels, which they sell at fancy prices in souvenir shops. That explains the perverse delight, of course: there's money to be made in conforming to a stereotyped image and, by appearing to be dim, the Irish can lull potential opponents into an ill-advised sense of superiority.

The trick works on tourists. In Co. Cork, guileful guides, deploying words like grapeshot, can charm the most sceptical travellers into paying good money to kiss the Blarney Stone, at the same time reassuring them fulsomely that its promised ability to confer eloquence on all who kiss it is, in itself, just a bit of blarney.

Embracing cultural identity

Millions of visitors respond to this captivating charm by falling in love with Ireland at first sight. An increasing number, be warned, choose to consummate this love affair by giving up their life elsewhere, and moving to Ireland full time. Yet many in Ireland consider that the colossal social and economic changes that have taken place in recent decades (see page 19) have eroded the traditional Irish values of courtesy, hospitality, spontaneity, sportsmanship and sense of fun.

These critics argue that Ireland is selling its soul in return for a rootless cosmopolitanism, ruining the attraction of its unspoilt countryside by ill-thought-out and badly designed developments, while ignoring the widening gap between the rich and the poor. Countering these arguments, others – in an echo of Oscar Wilde's dictum 'Those who live within their means suffer from a lack of imagination' – insist that the Irish are bringing to bear on rescuing

Local shop merchant in Dalkey.

the wrecked economy the creativity they have always deployed in literature and the arts.

As usual, the truth lies somewhere in the middle. Certainly, the Republic, with its car-dependent, increasingly suburban commuter lifestyle, and its preference for British and American TV channels, has become more like everywhere else. But enough people have realised the danger of diluting Ireland's unique cultural identity, and are working hard to promote a pride in, and affection for, all things Irish, including the language, the music, even the soccer team, and the (sometimes elusive) idea of a less stressful way of life. Visitors, therefore, once they have recovered from the shock of discovering how expensive everything is, are likely to find that the time-honoured sense of hospitality has survived, sustained by an innate gregariousness.

The two Irelands

After achieving independence from Britain in 1921, an event accompanied by bloody internal strife, the new Republic signalled its priorities in its currency, with coins displaying images not of rulers or tyrants but of emblems evoking a rural idyll and Celtic mythology: pigs, hens, hares and salmon. But only the coins of *the Republic*, of course, for there are two Irelands. One consists of the 26 counties of the Republic, whose citizens

Northern Catholic, who is in turn seen as less outgoing, less impulsive than the Southern Catholic.

Such stereotypes, naturally, soon turn into absurd over-simplifications. An English journalist, for instance, despatched to Northern Ireland in the 1970s to discover why its Protestant and Roman Catholic communities were effectively at war, reported: 'They are incomparably more pleasant to the outsider than any other people in the British Isles. Even the terrorists have excellent manners.'

It was the German writer Heinrich Böll who identified the two turns of speech most

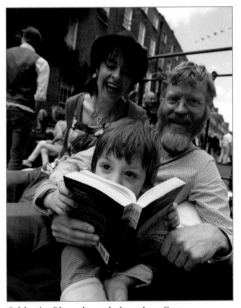

Celebrating Bloomsday at the James Joyce Centre.

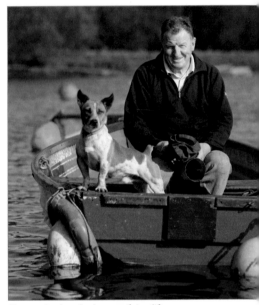

Shannon locals make the most of river life.

English as spoken in Ireland is influenced by the grammar and vocabulary of the Irish language, and is known as Hiberno-English.

are seen as friendly and easy-going. Then there are the Six Counties of Northern Ireland, part of the United Kingdom, a more complex place to characterise, where society is more fragmented and divided, and memories are long.

Britain's colonial involvement with Ireland over many centuries ensured that there are many facets to the Irish character. In terms of personality, the Northern Protestant is generally regarded as being more earnest, more unimaginative than the

characteristic of the Irish as 'It could be worse' and 'I shouldn't worry'. In a world where worries proliferate daily, Ireland retains an insane optimism. One of the most popular posters of recent times, as Ireland was facing up to the economic devastation that followed the boom, and the revelation of the corruption that led to its demise, had the optimistic slogan 'Keep going, sure it's grand', an Irish version of the British wartime advice 'Keep calm and carry on'. It summarised the blind faith in the status quo that had led to this situation, and the average citizen's inability to do anything about the wreckage that ensued, beyond putting a smile on the face, pretending everything was all right, and carrying on regardless.

A strong theatricality

The contradictory and quick changing Irish character can be as elusive as the fairy gold to be sought at the end of Irish rainbows, and the conversation as elliptical as an incomplete jigsaw puzzle.

Unarguably, there is a strong theatricality about the national character. There's a recklessness, a tendency towards exaggeration. This characteristic is a key feature in the much-loved TV sitcom, Father Ted, where all the cast are grotesque exaggerations of one kind or another, to great comic effect. The same could

an erratic brilliance, the convivial mood abruptly changes to one of wistful melancholy.

The Irish are as much at home with sorrow as with laughter. This characteristic, sometimes manifesting itself as a natural pessimism, is the same one that makes Irish sporting fans such good losers. This was much remarked on during Ireland's disastrous performance at Gdansk in Euro 2012, as the Irish side headed for a 4-0 defeat by Spain. In about the 86th minute of the game the fans en masse broke into a beautiful and melodic rendition of 'The Fields of Athenry', one of the saddest songs in the repertoire, recall-

Street performers in Galway.

be said of the darkly funny series Black Books. But there's an introversion, too, the proneness to melancholy captured by George Bernard Shaw in *John Bull's Other Island,* a play set in the land of his birth: 'Your wits can't thicken in that soft moist air, on those white springy roads, in those misty rushes and brown bogs, on those hillsides of granite rocks and magenta heather. You've no such colours in the sky, no such lure in the distance, no such sadness in the evenings. Oh the dreaming! the dreaming! the torturing, heartscalding, never satisfying dreaming, dreaming, dreaming.'

You can sometimes sense this aspect of the Irish character in a pub when, after the talk – once called 'a game with no rules' – has achieved

ing the deporting to Australia of a man who stole to feed his family during the 1845 Great Famine. The intention was to encourage the team, who were outclassed by the eventual champions, but it was also seen as demonstrating the fans' very Irish resignation in the face of an unavoidable defeat.

It is significant that the same sad song is also often sung by fans at rugby matches, where the demographic of the crowd tends to be very different than at a soccer match.

Violence and vendettas

The poet Louis MacNeice, described Ireland as a nation 'built upon violence and morose vendettas.' This less flattering aspect of the Irish personality was nicely summed up by another poet, Seamus

Heaney, writing in 1975 at the height of the sectarian violence generally referred to euphemistically as 'the Troubles' in a poem entitled '*Whatever You Say, Say Nothing*'. The title in fact came from a poster common in Belfast at the time, beginning 'Loose talk costs lives...' warning people to be careful about gossip lest it lead to violent recriminations. As another great Irish poet, W.B. Yeats in the poem '*Remorse for Intemperate Speech*' (1931) reflected on the notorious Irish ability to bear a grudge: Out of Ireland have we come. / Great hatred, little room, / Maimed us at the start. / I carry from my mother's womb / A fanatic heart.

contains an echo of an 18th-century pace of life that has not completely faded away, a psychological climate in which a racehorse attracts more glances than a Rolls-Royce.

It's this attitude to life, never far beneath the surface despite the upheavals that makes Ireland such a rewarding place to visit. As the US-born novelist J.P. Donleavy, an exemplar of the less folksy style of Irish writing, expressed it winsomely in *The Ginger Man*: 'When I die I want to decompose in a barrel of porter (dark beer) and have it served in all the pubs of Dublin. I wonder would they know it was me?'

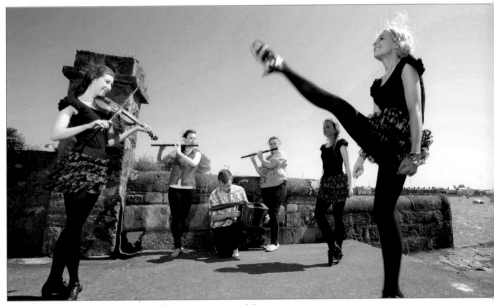

Dungarvan TradFest is a lively gathering of musicians, singers and dancers.

The history of this 'wretched little clod, broken off a bigger clod, broken off the west end of Europe,' as Shaw called it, encouraged it to view itself as a victim of colonialisation, which lies behind the moral authority that singers such as Bono and Bob Geldof assumed when they lectured world leaders face-to-face on the need to get to grips with the causes of world poverty. Enya's easy-listening take on traditional Celtic rhythms, *Only Time*, was judged poignant enough to be used as the soundtrack to TV replays of the collapse of the World Trade Center.

An attitude to life

In an age that esteems brand awareness, Ireland's international image is a potent one. It

WHY DUBLIN IS DIFFERENT

Just as London is not representative of England, nor New York of the US, so the gap has widened between Dublin and the rest of the country. If the whole of Ireland had the same population density as Dublin, there would be more than 300 million people living there. But the Republic's 4.7 million population produces a density of only 57 people per sq km (148 per sq mile). Thirty years ago, almost everyone you met in the capital's streets or pubs would be a Dubliner. Immigration has diluted that homogeneity as Ireland changed into a multiracial society. To get a feel for the 'real' Ireland, you have to travel beyond Dublin.

IRELAND IN THE MOVIES

While Irish films once played on stereotyped images aimed at the lucrative Irish-American market, these days they are more likely to be about rock bands than red-headed colleens.

Ireland's first dedicated cinema, the Volta in Dublin's Mary Street, was opened in 1909 by none other than James Joyce – an indication that the Irish have always valued the word more than the visual. But the country had no film studio until 1958, when Ardmore Studios opened in Bray, Co. Wicklow. It was thus left to Hollywood to portray Ireland to the world, and it did so by peddling whimsicality to the huge audience of Irish-Americans who had a sentimental attachment to the pastoral ideal most potently portrayed in John Ford's *The Quiet Man*. The Irish, who were in reality facing hardship and chronic emigration, didn't object to such a portrayal: indeed, they built a tourist industry on it.

The leprechauns massed in 1959 for *Darby O'Gill and the Little People*, in which a pre-007 Sean Connery sang and danced with Janet Munro and gangs of diminutive actors. No cliché was left unturned and Walt Disney ended up with a pot of gold.

Three decades of terrorism produced a muted response from international film-makers – Neil Jordan's *The Crying Game* was a rare success. The best recent film about the Irish Civil War was made by Englishman Ken Loach: *The Wind That Shakes the Barley* (2006) is set in 1920 and was filmed on location in rural Cork, starring Cillian Murphy.

The movie that did most to cement the image of the Irish as fighting boyos with a pre-feminist outlook was John Ford's 1952 production The Quiet Man, in which John Wayne slugged it out with Victor McLaglen and Maureen O'Hara in a virulently green landscape. Americans loved it – and so did the Irish.

Neil Jordan's 1996 biopic Michael Collins, was dubbed Ireland's first national epic film, though it was US funded. Jordan sacrificed historical detail for dramatic impact, but Liam Neeson conveyed the romanticism and ruthlessness that characterised Ireland's struggle.

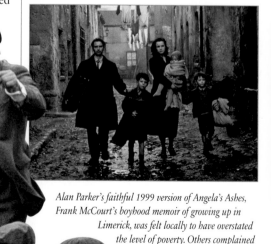

Alan Parker's faithful 1999 version of Angela's Ashes, Frank McCourt's boyhood memoir of growing up in Limerick, was felt locally to have overstated the level of poverty. Others complained that pain was driven out by glossy photography and sentimentality.

Veteran Hollywood director John Huston, who came of Irish stock and had a home in Ireland, captured the country's streak of Chekovian melancholy in his last film, The Dead (1987), adapted from a classic short story by James Joyce.

Once (2006) was funded by the Irish Film Board and cost €130,000. The touching tale of a Dublin busker and his Czech girlfriend has taken over €20m worldwide, and won an Oscar for Best Song. The Broadway musical (2012) won eight Tonys.

The Magdalen Sisters.

FRESH VOICES

Peter Mullan's critically acclaimed 2002 film *The Magdalen Sisters* told the story of the young girls – perhaps 30,000 of them over the years – who had been sent to live-in convent laundries as a punishment for having premarital sex or becoming pregnant out of wedlock. These sadistic labour camps finally closed in the 1990s.

With the Irish box office representing less than 0.5 percent of the global market there was limited scope for purely Irish films. So the government tempted foreign producers with tasty tax breaks. This persuaded Mel Gibson, for instance, that, although his 1995 *Braveheart* portrayed a legendary Scottish hero, the stirring battle scenes would look no less patriotic if they were filmed in Ireland.

Lenny Abrahamson may have a name that sounds American but he is actually one of Ireland's success stories. *Room* (2015) based on the Emma Donoghue film of the same name was nominated for four Academy Awards. His debut film was the darkly comic tale of two hapless Dublin junkies *Adam and Paul* (2004). The heart-wrenching *Garage* (2007) tells the story of a lonely garage attendant in a country town and won a prize at the Cannes Film Festival. *What Richard Did* (2012).starring Jack Reynor focuses on a group of privileged South Dublin teenagers.

John Carney started out as a bassist in an Irish rock band The Frames before moving into filmmaking. *Once* (2006) enjoyed enormous success with an Academy Award for Best Song. *Sing Street* (2016) is a musical comedy set in 1980's Dublin in which a teenage boy meets the girl of his dreams and starts a band in the hopes of impressing her.

The debut feature film of playwright Martin McDonagh (pictured), In Bruges (2008), a black comedy starring Colin Farrell and Brendan Gleeson as a pair of Irish hitmen hiding out in Belgium's medieval city, proved an international triumph and raised the profile of the Irish film industry overseas.

King John's Castle, Limerick.

DECISIVE DATES

An Ogham stone.

c.7000 BC
Archaeological evidence of Mesolithic hunter-fisher people (flints, etc.) along the coast dates from this period.

From c.3000 BC
The Neolithic period sees megalithic tombs appear. Signs of prolonged settlement, agriculture and cultural sophistication (portal tombs) grow more frequent. From around 500 BC, the migration of Celts from Britain marks the start of Ireland's Iron Age.

c.AD 300
Stone-carved inscriptions appear in the 'Ogham alphabet', a rune-like script.

431
The Pope sends Palladius as a bishop to Ireland. This implies that Christian communities existed before St Patrick arrived.

432
St Patrick (later Ireland's patron saint) comes back to Ireland as a missionary around 432. At 16, he had been abducted from Britain and taken to Ireland, but later fled to France.

From c.800
Viking attacks begin. After a series of raids (many monasteries are plundered) the Norsemen found settlements which grew into harbour towns (eg Dublin).

976–1014
Brian Ború, crowned King of Munster in 976, proclaims himself High King of Ireland in 1002 and defeats the Vikings near Clontarf in 1014. After his murder later that same year, the kingdom falls apart again.

From 1169
Anglo-Normans – sent to Ireland by the English King Henry II after a request from Dermot MacMurrough, who is losing the fight for the Irish throne – conquer large areas of the island and settle there. A system of Feudalism is introduced and castles built.

Statue of King Brian Ború at Dublin Castle.

James I was responsible for 'the Plantation of Ulster'.

1366
The Statutes of Kilkenny represent an attempt by the English crown to stop its barons from assimilating, marrying Irishwomen or speaking the Irish language.

From 1541
England's Henry VIII declares himself King of Ireland and begins asserting British supremacy over the Irish clan princes.

1607
The most powerful of the Irish clan princes flee to Spain (called the 'Flight of the Earls'), marking the end of Gaelic supremacy.

1608
James I starts the systematic settlement of Protestant Scots and English (dubbed 'the Plantation of Ulster').

1641–53
A rebellion by Irish Catholics against the English settlement policy is initially successful. In

1649, after his victory in the English Civil War, Oliver Cromwell conquers Ireland in a merciless campaign.

1690
England's Catholic King James II loses his throne to William of Orange at the Battle of the Boyne, and the period of 'Protestant Ascendancy' begins.

1691
The Irish-Protestant parliament in Dublin passes the Penal Laws, which exclude Catholics from public office, deprive them of their property and their right to vote.

1791
Influenced by the revolutions in France and America, the United Irishmen movement is formed in Belfast. Its leading light, Wolfe Tone, is a Protestant coachbuilder's son.

1800
The Act of Union makes Ireland part of the United Kingdom. The parliament in Dublin is dissolved and Ireland is represented by 100 MPs in the House of Commons in London.

1829
A Catholic politician, Daniel O'Connell (known as 'the Liberator'), forces the London parliament to pass a law emancipating Catholics.

From 1840
Nationalist movements gain strength (Irish Republican Brotherhood founded in 1858, Irish National Land League founded in 1879). There is a renewed interest in Gaelic culture (the Gaelic League is formed in 1893).

Daniel O'Connell.

1845–51
The Great Potato Famine deprives more than one-third of the Irish population of their main source of nutrition. An estimated 1 million people die between 1846 and 1851 of malnutrition, typhus and other diseases; approximately 1 million others emigrate.

From 1880
The Land League and the Irish Home Rule Party led by Charles Stuart Parnell employ parliamentary means in their struggle for Irish autonomy and land reform. In 1886, the first of several draft resolutions for Irish independence is rejected.

1905–08
The group known as Sinn Féin (We Ourselves) is formed 'to make England take one hand from Ireland's throat and the other out of Ireland's pocket'.

1912
Almost three-quarters of all Ulster Protestants sign a solemn pledge to stop all attempts at autonomy 'by all necessary means'. The Ulster Volunteer Force is formed in 1913 to enforce the pledge.

1916
On 24 April around 1,800 volunteers, led by Pádraig Pearse and James Connolly, occupy public buildings in Dublin and declare the formation of an Irish Republic. This 'Easter Rising' is put down six days later. Britain's harsh response strengthens the nationalist cause.

1918–23
Sinn Féin wins an overall majority in UK elections and announces the formation of an Irish parliament in Dublin, with Éamon de Valera as president; the British government sends in troops, leading to the Anglo-Irish War of 1919–21. In 1922

Engraving of a family evicted from their farm in the 1880s.

Eamon de Valera, opposing the 1922 treaty that divided Ireland.

the Irish Parliament narrowly accepts the Anglo-Irish treaty for the foundation of an Irish Free State excluding the Six Counties of Ulster with Protestant majorities. Civil war ensues and the pro-treaty Free State government, which wins.

1937

The Free State (now called Éire) adopts its own political constitution.

1939

Éire declares its neutrality during World War II. Germany tries to damage Britain's interests by supporting the IRA.

1949

Éire leaves the British Commonwealth to become the Republic of Ireland.

1969–70

A demonstration by the Northern Irish Civil Rights Movement is attacked by the British army. The IRA splits into two factions in 1970. The Provisional IRA intensifies its armed struggle in Northern Ireland.

1972

Thirteen demonstrators are shot dead by British soldiers on 'Bloody Sunday'. The parliament in Belfast is dissolved and Northern Ireland is ruled directly from London.

1973

The Republic joins the European Economic Community along with Great Britain.

1990

Mary Robinson becomes the first woman president of Ireland.

1997

In the Republic, divorce becomes legal. Mary McAleese, a Northerner by birth, becomes president.

1998

A Northern Ireland peace treaty is signed by all parties, including Sinn Féin. David Trimble and John Hume receive the Nobel Peace Prize. A car bomb in Omagh kills 29.

1999

An all-party Assembly with limited powers sets up in Northern Ireland. The Republic drops its claim to sovereignty over the North.

2002

The Republic adopts the euro. In the North, rule from London is reimposed.

2005

The IRA declares that its war is over and its weapons destroyed. The legendary Irish footballer George Best dies.

2007

In Northern Ireland Ian Paisley's Democratic Unionists and Gerry Adams's Sinn Féin agree to work together.

Unionist mural in the Newtownards Road area of east Belfast.

Mary Robinson.

2008
Taoiseach (Irish Prime Minister) Bertie Ahern, resigns and hands over to Brian Cowen. The effects of the international financial crisis hit home, and the recession begins.

2010
The government decides that Irish tax payers will bail out the banks following irresponsible loans to property developers. Many homeowners are left in negative equity or on reduced pensions. Several bishops resign following revelations of the Catholic Church's failure to protect children from sexually abusive priests.

2011
Fine Gael wins a landslide victory and forms a coalition with the Labour party with Enda Kenny as Taoiseach. Michael D Higgins, a former Labour Party TD, an Irish speaker from Galway and a published poet, is elected President. At Ireland's first-ever Citizenship Ceremony, 73 new citizens from 24 countries are sworn in.

2012
Mass demonstrations follow the death of Savita Halappanavar, an Indian dentist, in a Galway hospital from a sceptic miscarriage, despite her repeated requests for a termination. Emigration of unemployed young people to Canada and Australia grows apace.

2013
Ireland legalises abortion in medical emergencies following calls from the European Court of Human Rights. Taoiseach Enda Kenny apologises publicly to the former inmates of the 'Magdalen Laundries' for their mistreatment. Austerity increases, a property tax is introduced, and banks start to negotiate with mortgage defaulters.

2014
Widespread revulsion at the discovery that 796 babies had been buried in a sceptic tank on the grounds of the Tuam Mother and Baby Home between 1925 and 1961. Tens of thousands march as anti-water charges protests begin. Ian Paisley, former First Minister of Northern Ireland, passes away. Albert Reynolds, former Taoiseach of the Irish Republic dies. The Irish soccer team qualifies for Euro 2016.

2015
Ireland votes yes in same-sex marriage referendum. Rugby fans travelled to Wales to support Ireland in the Rugby World Cup. Anti-water charges protests continue. Dubliner Conor McGregor becomes the UFC featherweight champion of the world in Mixed Martial Arts (MMA).

2016
Massive centenary commemorations for 1916. General Elections show a rise in support for independent candidates, as well as a resurgence in support for Fianna Fail. After two months of negotiations, a minority government is formed with Enda Kenny as Taoiseach, despite his widespread unpopularity.

To universal surprise, former sworn enemies Ian Paisley (left) and Martin McGuinness agree to work together as the Northern Ireland Assembly's first minister and deputy first minister – smiling so much that they are dubbed the Chuckle Brothers.

IRELAND'S INVADERS

First the Celts came, followed by the Vikings and Normans. Then the English decided to stake a strategic claim, and that's when the trouble really began.

The key to much of Ireland's bloodstained history lies in the extraordinary love-hate relationship that it has had with its more powerful neighbouring island to the east. Ireland's history, in a nutshell, is its resistance to England. In this geographically forced marriage, the dominant partner sometimes deliberately abused the weaker, but more often unthinkingly ignored her; yet the Irish, while hating the English for their arrogance and neglect, also admired them for their character and achievements and, until a surprisingly late stage, had no great wish for the marriage to be totally dissolved.

> *The Celts brought with them from mainland Europe a loose tribal structure, the blueprint for building a civilisation, and had little trouble in overcoming the natives, a primitive people known as the Firbolg (Bag Men).*

Prehistoric monument Newgrange, built in the Neolithic period.

The first conquest

Evidence of Ireland's earliest inhabitants survives in the form of thousands of megalithic burial chambers. The Newgrange passage-grave in the Boyne valley, near Dublin, for example, is thought to be 5,000 years old. From the Bronze Age, when Ireland was one of the world's largest metal producers, beautifully crafted leaf-shaped swords and gold ornaments are preserved.

Several centuries before the birth of Christ, the island's first conquerors arrived. The Celts (or Gaels), masters of horsemanship, came not from England but from mainland Europe, mostly France and Spain, to this wild, wet island at the continent's fringes. Europe's next conquerors did not get as far as Ireland. The Roman legions, hard pressed to hold southern Britain against incursions by Picts and Scots, were disinclined to take on more trouble. Their inaction had far-reaching consequences: if Julius Caesar had successfully ventured west, it is unlikely that Ireland's character today would be so distinct from Britain's.

The Golden Age

The divergences between the two cultures widened still further when the fall of the Roman Empire plunged Europe into the Dark Ages. Ireland, in contrast, entered its Golden Age, becoming a lone beacon of learning and civilisation – 'the Land of Saints and Scholars'.

Christianity had been brought to the island by an English-born missionary, St Patrick, who had been kidnapped as a youth and taken to Ireland to tend sheep. Later, he travelled widely in France and Italy, returning to Ireland in 432 to spread the word of Christ. Today, he is fondly thought of as being responsible for having banished snakes from the island.

Viking raids plagued Ireland in the 9th and 10th centuries (see box), but the Norse tyranny was destroyed at the Battle of Clontarf in 1014 by the High King, BrianBorú, who saw himself as Ireland's Charlemagne. Less destructive but no less ambitious visitors were Norman such as Strongbow, an English earl who came looking for land. Having gained a toehold, the Normans built a power base with fortified stone castles. This alarmed England's Henry II, who promptly paid a visit, inaugurating an involvement between the two countries that was to last, with immeasurable bloodshed, for 800 years.

Norman influence

Over the next three centuries, the Normans, intermarrying with the natives, expanded their

St Patrick in military dress on horseback.

SAVED BY THE MONASTERIES

In the absence of a Roman substructure of towns and cities, monasteries became centres of population. The kings kept treasures there, which made the monasteries a target for plundering Vikings, who sailed to Ireland in the 9th century. Tall round towers, many still standing, were built by the monasteries to serve as lookouts, refuges and belfries. Also surviving are some of the monks' exquisite manuscripts, such as the Book of Kells, which the illiterate Vikings ignored. Ireland's tradition of storytelling dates from this period. It can be seen on sandstone High Crosses, designed to teach Bible stories with elaborate carvings.

influence. Many of the country's elaborate castles, such as Blarney in Co. Cork and Bunratty in Co. Clare, date from this time.

But, as the barons thrived, the English Crown's authority gradually shrank to an area around Dublin known as 'the Pale'. It was Henry VIII, determined finally to break the local nobles' power, who proclaimed himself 'King of this land of Ireland as united, annexed and knit for ever to the Imperial Crown of the Realm of England'. When the nobles resisted, Henry seized their lands, resettling them with loyal 'planters' from England and Scotland.

His daughter, Elizabeth I, fought four wars in Ireland. As well as trying to impose the Reformation on the country, she wanted to protect

England's right flank against an invasion from her principal opponent, Spain.

Later, James I defeated a particularly powerful baron, Hugh O'Neill, Earl of Tyrone, at the Battle of Kinsale and planted new settlers on O'Neill's lands in six of the nine counties of the ancient province of Ulster. The new settlers were Protestants, firm believers in the Calvinist work ethic, and the religious mix they created led to strife in Ulster in the 19th and 20th centuries.

An early sign of the troubles ahead came in 1641, when Ulster Roman Catholics, hoping to

1652, about a third of the Catholic Irish had been killed. Much of their land was handed over to Protestants.

When the monarchy was restored, Charles II disappointed Catholics by throwing his support behind the Protestants, on whom he depended for power. His successor, James II, himself a Roman Catholic, raised hopes by introducing an Act of Parliament that would have ousted the Protestant settlers; but, before it could be put into practice, James was defeated in 1690 at the Battle of the Boyne, near Dublin, by William of Orange. William had been

William of Orange, who defeated James II at the Battle of the Boyne in 1690.

recover their confiscated lands, rebelled at Portadown. The facts of the rebellion were rapidly overwhelmed by the legend as lurid tales spread of a drunken Catholic pogrom against the God-fearing settlers, with 12,000 Protestants knifed, shot and drowned, pregnant women raped, and infants roasted on spits.

The Gaelic Irish had further cause to worry when, after Charles I was beheaded, the new Puritan Parliament in England began suppressing the Roman Catholic religion. Fanned by the flames of this resentment, a new Catholic revolt began to spread. This 'Great Rebellion' was ruthlessly suppressed by the English Protector, Oliver Cromwell, whose 20,000 Ironside troops devastated the countryside. By

called in by the English establishment to end James's 'Popish ways' and his success in doing so is still commemorated annually on 12 July with mammoth parades by Protestant Orangemen throughout Northern Ireland. From that day in 1690, Roman Catholics became a persecuted majority in Ireland. New anti-Catholic legislation, the Penal Laws, barred them from all public life and much social activity.

The land problem

Pressure for change was applied by Protestant patriots such as Henry Grattan. The threat of force was added in the shape of the Irish Volunteers, 80,000 strong by 1782. London caved in and agreed to a separate parliament in Dublin.

But a fatal flaw in all this was that the Catholic majority (three-quarters of the population) were still denied a political role and the extensive patronage at the disposal of the English parliament allowed it to manipulate policy in Dublin.

The government in London thought it had done rather well to pass two Catholic Relief Acts giving Catholics limited voting rights and allowing them once more to own or lease land. As so often in Ireland, however, a well-meaning policy gave birth to anarchy. Catholics began buying land in Ulster, forcing up prices and alarming the Protestants, who formed a vigi-

Henry Grattan.

lante outfit, the Peep o' Day Boys, to burn out Catholics in dawn raids. The Catholics set up their own vigilante force, the Defenders. The lines of a long conflict were drawn.

Yet Ulster was the cradle in 1791 for a brave attempt by Protestants and Catholics to fight together for reform. Wolfe Tone, the son of a Protestant coachbuilder, set up the first Society of United Irishmen club in Belfast and a second soon opened in Dublin. It began well, largely as a debating society, but was suppressed within three years when British Prime Minister William Pitt feared an alliance between Ireland and France, with whom Britain was then at war. Tone, condemning England as 'the never-failing source of all our political evils', fled to America.

Government anxiety increased when the United Irishmen, largely a middle-class Protestant group, began forging links with the Defenders, mostly working-class Catholics. And soon an even more threatening alliance was being forged: the United Irishmen persuaded Tone, who had been thinking of becoming a farmer near Philadelphia, to sail to France and

> *By the middle of the 18th century, only 7 percent of Irish land was in Catholic hands, and peasants had the status of slaves.*

rally support against Britain. Tone assured the French that their arrival in Ireland would trigger a national uprising, supported by the Irish militia, and on 16 December 1796 a French battle fleet of 43 ships set sail.

It was the weather that came to England's rescue. Severe storms dispersed the fleet, and the few troops who landed at Bantry Bay, on the southwest coast, were greeted rather unenthusiastically by the Irish peasants, who believed that the French really had been sent by the northern Protestants to suppress them further.

In the end, it was the United Irishmen who were suppressed. Pitt, fearing a second French expedition, imposed harsh martial law in Ulster. The army, four-fifths of whom were themselves Catholic Irish peasants, began arresting the organisation's outlawed leaders, identifying them as a result of information partly provided by informers, partly extracted through brutal beatings. Soon Ulster was in the grip of terror and the stage was set for a new group to enter the Irish drama. These were the Orangemen, whose role in Ulster remains central today.

The movement began in 1795 after a clash between Protestant Peep o' Day Boys and Catholic Defenders at the Battle of the Diamond, near Armagh, in which 30 men died. The Protestants, fearing worse was to come, reorganised as the Orange Society, named after their hero, William of Orange, and preyed as lawless bandits on Catholics. In defeating the United Irishmen, the government was glad of their vicious support.

Ireland joins the British Empire

The Great Rebellion of 1798 (see page 39) exhausted what little patience the English had. William Pitt's exasperated response was to propose a full union between Britain and Ireland. The 300-seat Irish parliament in Dublin would be abolished and 100 seats for Irish representatives would be created within the Imperial Parliament in London. Englishman, Irishman, Welshman and Scot would be treated equally.

Opinion in Ireland was split, less on any patriotic principles than on cool appraisals of individual self-interest and economic prospects. But London's mind was made up and, after a period of political wheeler-dealing, a majority of five voting against the union was turned into a majority of 46 voting for it. Ireland's parliament had, in effect, abolished itself.

On 1 January 1801, Britain and Ireland entered, in Pitt's phrase, their 'voluntary association' within the Empire with 'equal laws, reciprocal affection, and inseparable interests'. As with most marriages, the intentions were good. Perhaps the two partners might even live happily ever after.

It was not to be. No one present on that day early in a promising new century could have imagined the terrible suffering that lay ahead.

'Horrors of the Irish Union – Botheration of Poor Pat or A Whisper Across the Channel', a 1798 cartoon.

THE GREAT REBELLION

Disaffection with English rule climaxed in May 1798 in a major rebellion. But by then so many of the United Irishmen's leaders had been arrested that most of the risings throughout the country were too poorly organised to succeed. Also, the native yeomanry reacted by torturing and shooting indiscriminately, often butchering the rebels after they had surrendered.

Within six weeks, it was all over. Perhaps 30,000 had died, giving birth in the process to countless ballads commemorating a small nation's struggle for freedom. The notion of an Irish patriotism independent of England's fortunes was taking root with a vengeance.

Napoleon Bonaparte, pressed by Wolfe Tone not to abandon French support for Ireland, belatedly agreed to another expedition, which set sail that August. But again the French had been misinformed. When one party landed at Killala, Co. Mayo, having been led to expect enthusiastic, disciplined battalions, they found instead supporters whom they disdainfully regarded as rapacious simpletons. In October, Tone himself tried to land in Co. Donegal with a party of 3,000 French, but they were beaten back by a Royal Navy force. Tone was captured and died in prison after an attempted suicide. His martyrdom was assured: several Gaelic football clubs are named in his honour and a 1960s rebel music band called itself the Wolfe Tones.

IRELAND'S FINEST RUINS

Visiting ruins not only unveils the drama of Irish history, it often takes you off the beaten path to unusually beautiful corners of the countryside.

To understand why Ireland has so many churches in ruins, consider its history. Located at the western edge of the known world, Ireland escaped conquest by the Romans, and continued to follow a Celtic religion until the mid-5th century, and the arrival of St Patrick and other missionaries. It was a peaceful conversion, and Celtic customs were absorbed into Christian ritual. The earliest monasteries became important centres of learning. Stone carving was used on High Crosses to tell the Gospel story to an illiterate population, and in architectural decoration.

In contrast, Christianity's subsequent history in Ireland has been turbulent. The monastery at Clonmacnoise, established on its vulnerable Shannon-side location in AD 545, had a typical fate, surviving numerous attacks from warring Irish clans, then Viking raiders, and then Normans, only to be destroyed by the English in 1552.

The Penal Laws

In the 12th century the Anglo-Normans arrived, and intermarried with the Irish chieftains. The Normans endowed Continental monastic orders, including the Cistercians, and built abbeys on an ambitious scale. But these institutions were short-lived. From 1536 onwards, the Reformation led to the suppression of the monasteries, and by 1653 Oliver Cromwell had finished off the job. The infamous Penal Laws that followed prohibited Catholic participation in public life, and most of the ruined churches and abbeys were never rebuilt.

But because of the beauty of the stone carving, their scale – which ranges from ambitious to modest – and their often tranquil locations, the ruins of these buildings are most rewarding to visit.

Influences from both Burgundy and the west of England have been detected in the richly carved Cistercian abbey that is Boyle Abbey, Co. Roscommon. Rounded arches of the Romanesque style were in favour in the late 12th century, but in a later phase of building, pointed Gothic arches were introduced.

These decorative Celtic crosses, some dating from the 7th century, are found all over the country. They combine the traditional cross symbolising the Crucifixion with a circle that is usually held to represent eternity.

The beautiful and remote valley of Glencolumbkille, Co. Donegal, associated with St Columba (Latin) or Colmcille (Irish), runs down to the sea at Glen Bay and contains 15 Early Christian pillars and cross-slabs decorated with cross-motifs and geometric designs. At midnight on 9 June a barefoot pilgrimage around the sites begins.

When the monastery at Clomacnoise, Co. Offaly, was founded by St Ciarán around AD 540, its Shannonside location marked the boundary between the provinces of Leinster and Connacht.

Gallarus Oratory was built between the 7th and 8th centuries and is the best-preserved early Christian church in Ireland.

SKELLIG MICHAEL

The monastery of Skellig Michael, 8 miles (13km) off the southwestern coast, is dramatically situated on a barren rocky island. It is the most remarkable Early Christian site in Ireland, and can be visited by boat between May and September. Dating from around AD 800, the monastic remains are on a

The beehive huts at Skellig Michael.

saddle of rock reached by climbing 600 stone steps. Six beehive huts, in which the monks lived, and two rectangular oratories, where they prayed, were built of dry stone on a cliff edge around a small garden area. They are surprisingly well preserved, given their exposed Atlantic location. Below the huts are the remains of a 12th-century church, and there are also early Christian cross slabs and hermitages. Shortly after AD 1200, the monks transferred to the mainland at Ballinskelligs, partly, it is thought, due to persistent Viking raids. The monks, seeking to emulate the desert fathers in their isolation, survived on a diet of fish, seabirds and their eggs (which they traded with passing seafarers), and vegetables from their garden. The island was a place of pilgrimage for penitents until the 20th century.

A cliff-top site on a narrow promontory makes a stunning location for the ruined 12th-century Ardmore Cathedral, Co. Waterford. Its sturdy Hiberno-Romanesque arches contrast with the slender, conical-roofed Round Tower. St Declan's Oratory and Well nearby date from the 9th century, and are still visited by pilgrims annually on 24 July.

THE MAKING OF A NATION

The union with Britain was short-lived and brought
little happiness to either partner. And the divorce
would involve more than a century of bitter bloodshed.

Like many of his contemporaries, Daniel
O'Connell, a Catholic lawyer from a well-
off Kerry family, had been educated in
France, and the ideals of the French Revolution
had entered his thinking. Although he recognised that none of Ireland's basic problems
had been solved by the union with Britain,
he wanted no revolution in Ireland, not even
a separation from the British Crown. What he
campaigned for, with powerful oratory, was
the right of Catholics to become Members of
Parliament. Sir Robert Peel, Britain's prime
minister, was forced to introduce a Catholic
Emancipation Bill, which was passed.

Once in the House of Commons, O'Connell,
by now 'the uncrowned king of Ireland', began
to rally support for his next cause: a repeal
of the union. When his appeals struck few
chords in parliament, he took his arguments
to his country-men, holding monster rallies
throughout Ireland. One meeting was attended
by 300,000.

The formidable Daniel O'Connell, 'the Liberator'.

Ireland's greatest disaster

At that point, fate intervened in the form of the
Great Famine that began in 1845. In reality, it
wasn't a true famine at all, rather a failure of
the potato crop. At its height, wheat and barley
were being freely shipped to England, together
with tens of thousands of cattle, sheep and pigs.
But such produce was beyond the pockets of
the peasants, whose every penny went towards
paying rent to the series of middlemen – often
as many as seven – who stood between them
and their land's ultimate owner. All they could
afford was the humble potato. When it was
blighted, they starved.

Out of a population of 8 million, 1 million
people died in the Great Hunger and well over

a million set off in squalid emigrant ships for
a new life in America, where they would pass
down to future generations a deep anti-Brit-
ish resentment. Around a third of the land in
Ireland changed hands as estates went bank-
rupt, but the new landlords, who were mostly
Irish (of both religions, now that Catholics
were allowed to buy land), were even harsher
than their predecessors in increasing rents.
O'Connell's talk of non-violent nationalism
seemed quite irrelevant. He died in 1847, aged
71, his dreams shattered.

In 1848, a year which saw nationalist
uprisings in several countries of Europe, an
attempted rising in Kilkenny was easily put
down; it was a bungled fiasco, with little

support from a weakened populace. A few wild plans, like one to kidnap Queen Victoria during her visit to Dublin in 1849, didn't materialise.

The birth of the Fenians

On St Patrick's Day, 17 March 1858, James Stephens, a Kilkenny railway engineer, founded a society that came to be known as the Irish Republican Brotherhood, dedicated to the idea of an independent democratic republic. An American branch was set up, called the Fenians after ancient Gaelic warriors. The

The fight for Home Rule

But it was not terrorism that was to further Ireland's cause most at this time. The two principal engines of change were driven by William Ewart Gladstone, who came to power as Britain's prime minister in 1868, and Charles Stewart Parnell, an English-educated Protestant landowner from County Wicklow.

'My mission,' said Gladstone, 'is to pacify Ireland.' He began in 1869 by removing one chronic grievance. Since the Reformation, the Protestant church had been the established church in Ireland, although it represented only

A destitute family about to be evicted from their dwelling during the Great Famine of 1845.

American Civil War, Stephens noted, had given his supporters their valuable experience of battle. After a skirmish in Canada, Fenian participants were referred to as 'The Irish Republican Army.' It was the IRA's first appearance on the world stage.

Stephens was deposed as leader after his failure to organise an army of liberation from the US, but by 1867 armed and well-drilled bands had been set up throughout Ireland to revolt. Some trains were derailed, marking the arrival in the country of a strategy that would shape Ireland's struggles: guerrilla warfare. An explosion meant to spring other Irishmen from Clerkenwell prison killed 12 Londoners and maimed 30.

ENGLAND AND THE FAMINE

The British government was not unaware of the Great Famine's effects. One MP described a large-scale eviction as 'the chasing away of 700 human beings like crows out of a cornfield'. England's refusal to provide relief is regarded by many today as a horrifying failure of imagination. Even compassionate and otherwise enlightened men lacked the vision to question the prevailing economic orthodoxy, the rigid belief that it would make matters worse to interfere with natural economic forces. The same principle was applied to the industrial working classes in England's factories, but their lot was less desperate.

The one part of Ireland to benefit from the Industrial Revolution was Ulster, where linen and ship-building took off. Ulster Protestants saw their prosperity being threatened by anyone who wanted to weaken the link with England.

a sixth of the population. Gladstone abolished this privileged position. Next, he introduced a land Bill designed to make it less easy for landlords to evict tenants. Sensing new hope, nationalists began to demand once more that Ireland should have its own parliament for Irish affairs, leaving international matters to the Imperial parliament in London. This aspiration was known as Home Rule.

On reaching the House of Commons in 1875, Parnell, son of an Irish father and an American mother, scorned its cosy, club-like conventions and perfected filibustering techniques for blocking parliamentary business: proposing endless amendments, and making long speeches. In one case, he forced an infuriated House into a continuous 41-hour session.

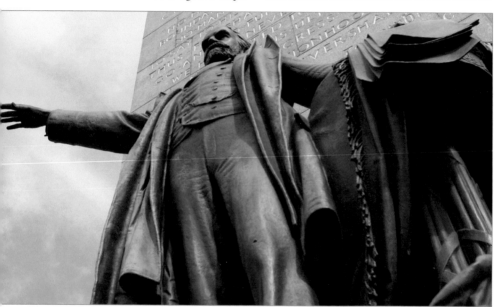

Parnell Monument, O'Connell Street, Dublin.

THE PROS AND CONS OF HOME RULE

Gladstone's 1881 Land Act was regarded as revolutionary. It granted fixity of tenure to tenants who paid their rent; laid down that a tenant should be paid when he vacated a holding for improvements he had made; and decreed that fair rents should be defined not by the landlord but by a Land Court. Progress seemed possible. But then Lord Frederick Cavendish, the new Chief Secretary for Ireland and Gladstone's nephew by marriage, was knifed to death in Dublin. Reform slid down the agenda.

Parnell's next move was to found the Irish National League to campaign uncompromisingly for Home Rule. A general election in 1885 gave him control of 85 of the 103 Irish seats in the House of Commons – and

the balance of power between the Liberals and Conservatives. Home Rule became the main issue in English politics.

The Conservatives argued that Home Rule would still leave the Imperial parliament controlling international affairs, war and peace, even customs and excise. Yet many educated Irishmen, including nationalists, were happy to remain within the British Empire – as long as they could control their domestic affairs. Had Home Rule been granted in 1886, therefore, Ireland might well still be part of the United Kingdom, having 'a distinct but not separate identity' rather like Wales and Scotland. It is one of the big 'ifs' of Irish history.

With Michael Davitt, Parnell set up the National Land League of Ireland. Funds from America flowed in to help the victims of oppression and threats of violence, frequently carried out, gave teeth to the Land League and left it in control of some areas of the country.

Ulster goes on the alert

A million Protestants still lived in Ireland, almost half of them in the northeast area of Ulster, and Home Rule would have severely limited the power of this influential minority. These Ulstermen saw themselves as different, as

Irish language, hitherto regarded as a fast-dying vulgar tongue. W.B. Yeats, the son of a Protestant Irish artist, published collections of folk tales such as *The Celtic Twilight*, conferring a new dignity on the often-ridiculed Irish peasantry. A Gaelic League was set up, declaring itself the archer that would slay the plundering crow of the English mind, its arrow being the Irish language.

In the political arena, however, there were setbacks. Parnell lost political support when the scandal of his long-time affair with Kitty O'Shea, who had borne him three children,

Ulster Unionists bring out the guns in 1912 to demonstrate their resistance to Home Rule.

indeed they were. Their Presbyterian tradition had always been more radical than the loose Protestantism of their southern co-religionists and had given them a formidable self-reliance – some would say stubbornness. Although security of tenure had always been greater in the northeast, the Protestant descendants of the 17th-century Scots settlers felt far from settled; they had retained an ineradicable tribal fear of being dispossessed of their lands by the Catholics, and it was largely their opposition to change that led to the first Home Rule Bill being voted down in 1886.

In southern Ireland, a literary revival was growing, creating a new appreciation of Celtic culture and myths and a new respect for the

erupted in 1889. Parnell died two years later, after being soaked with rain at a political rally in Galway. Gladstone himself retired from the scene in 1893, aged 84, having failed to get his second Home Rule Bill, which had been approved narrowly by the House of Commons, through the Upper Chamber, the House of Lords. It was time for the baton of the Irish cause to pass to a new generation.

The 20th century

As a new century dawned, a Conservative government in England held out no hope of Home Rule. Queen Victoria's visit to Dublin in 1900 and Edward VII's in 1903 were well received, but new forces of nationalism were being assembled by Arthur Griffith, a Dublin printer and journalist, and John McBride, a Mayo-born republican who had fought against the British in the Boer War. Griffith and McBride demanded 'an Irish Republic One and Indivisible.'

Two general elections in Britain in 1910 left the Liberals and Conservatives almost equally split in parliament. Once again the Irish Party, now led by the moderate John Redmond, used its balance of power to press for a new Home Rule Bill. Such a Bill was introduced in 1912 by Prime Minister Herbert Asquith and looked likely to become law in the foreseeable future.

Sir Edward Carson, although born in Dublin, rallies Protestant Ulster against Home Rule.

The Protestants in Ulster began arming themselves. They found as leader a Dublin MP and lawyer, Sir Edward Carson, who had been Solicitor General in a Tory government and who had acted as prosecuting counsel against Oscar Wilde in 1895. What, asked Carson, was the point of Home Rule now that most Irishmen owned their farms, all major grievances had been removed, and even a Catholic university had been set up?

In 1913 recruiting started for a 100,000-strong Ulster Volunteer Force and large consignments of rifles were imported. 'This place is an armed camp,' said Carson. The southerners responded by setting up a counter force, the

Irish National Volunteers, whose badge carried the letters 'FF', for Fianna Fáil, a legendary band of warriors. The problem could be simply stated. The Protestant majority in the northeast wished to remain full British subjects and were prepared to fight Britain to retain that status. The Catholic minority in the area, like the Catholic majority in the rest of the island, sought a more Irish identity. The two attitudes seemed irreconcilable.

Sir Winston Churchill, then a Liberal Minister, was first to voice publicly one possible solution. Of the ancient province of Ulster's nine counties, six – those most heavily settled by Protestants in the early 1600s – might be excluded from Home Rule. Redmond, under pressure to get results, conceded that these Six Counties could *temporarily* be excluded for six years, after which time he hoped the Unionists would see the wisdom of rejoining their fellow Irishmen. From the nationalists' point of view, it was a fatal concession.

The Easter Rising

As England became preoccupied with fighting the Great War (see page 47), a handful of Irishmen were not prepared to shelve their nationalist demands for the duration of hostilities. James Connolly, a labour organiser born into a poor Irish family in Scotland in 1868 and a soldier in the British army at 14, had embraced socialist thinking, setting up an Irish Citizens' Army to defend striking workers against brutal police suppression. Pádraic Pearse, a shy, austere schoolmaster, had developed a mystical belief that bloodshed was needed to cleanse Ireland, in the same way as Jesus Christ, by shedding his blood, had redeemed mankind. Philosophy and physical force came together on the sunny spring holiday morning of Monday, 24 April 1916.

As Pearse, commander of the patriots determined to liberate Ireland, set out to march down Dublin's Sackville Street, his sister pleaded with him to 'Come home, Pat, and leave all this foolishness.' Most Irish people would probably have echoed her sentiments if they'd had an inkling of the ambitions of the small band of unrepresentative middle-class intellectuals behind the Easter Rising. But Pearse proceeded and, with 150 others, armed with a variety of venerable rifles and agricultural implements, took over the city's

General Post Office and solemnly read out, to the reported apathy of bystanders, the proclamation of the new Irish Republic.

Another 800 or so civilian soldiers took over a brewery, a biscuit factory, a lunatic asylum and other key points. Eamon de Valera, a young maths teacher born in America of an Irish mother and a Spanish father, led the occupation of a bakery (see page 51).

Soon Dublin ground to a halt. Alarm and rumours spread. The poor looted stores and children ransacked sweet shops. A British gunboat on the River Liffey began to shell the rebel strongholds. The inevitable end, when it came, was swift. The British set fire to the area around the GPO. By the time Pearse surrendered on the Saturday, 64 rebels, 134 police and soldiers and at least 220 civilians had died. The centre of Dublin lay in ruins. Martial law was imposed and 4,000 jailed. 'So far the feeling of the population in Dublin is against the Sinn Féiners,' one Irish MP wrote to his party leader, Redmond. 'But a reaction might very easily be created.' He then added the prophetic words: 'Do not fail to urge the government not to execute any of the prisoners.'

Dublin's O'Connell Street in ruins after being shelled by British gunboats during the Easter Rising.

THE IMPACT OF THE GREAT WAR

Larger problems than Ireland loomed for Britain in 1914 with the outbreak of World War I. A deal was rapidly done under which politicians in London passed a Home Rule Act, together with an order suspending its implementation for the duration of the war or until such time as some kind of amendment could be added to take account of the concerns of Ulster Unionists.

Ireland was thus bought off, to the extent that a greater proportion of Irishmen – from both the north and the south – volunteered for the British army than any other part of the United Kingdom's population. Irishmen won 17 Victoria Crosses in the first 13 months of the war. Surely, the Irish nationalists reasoned, such courage would eradicate even Ulster Unionist worries about the reliability of their Catholic countrymen.

The reality was different. Sir Edward Carson, now a member of Britain's War Cabinet, saw the Ulster regiments' heavy losses in the war, particularly during the Battle of the Somme in 1916, as a subscription towards permanent membership of a grateful UK.

In Dublin, not everyone was prepared to wait until the war with Germany ended. Many still remembered the old adage that England's misfortune is Ireland's opportunity, and nationalists led by Arthur Griffith began grouping under the broad banner of Sinn Féin (pronounced '*shin fayne*' and meaning, self-reliantly, We Ourselves).

Executions and amnesty

Fatally, Redmond's urgings went unheeded and on 3 May the first three leaders, including Pearse, were shot at dawn. The next day, four more were shot. On 5 May, one more. On 8 May, four more. On 12 May, two more – including Connolly, who, because a bullet during the fighting had fractured his ankle, sat in a chair before the firing squad. Nobody knew how long the executions would go on. It was, someone said later, 'like watching a stream of blood coming from beneath a closed door.'

That Christmas, as a goodwill gesture, David Lloyd George, the 'Welsh wizard' who was now Britain's charismatic prime minister, released 560 Irish internees from prison in England. Among them were Arthur Griffith, Sinn Féin's founder, and a 27-year-old west Cork man, Michael Collins, formerly a clerk in London with the British civil service. Another batch of prisoners given an amnesty at Easter 1917 included Eamon de Valera, the sole surviving Easter Rising commandant. The cast was in place for the climactic act of Ireland's drama.

Children in Dublin wave American flags to celebrate the ending of the Anglo-Irish war in 1921.

HUNGER STRIKES

Sinn Féin candidates stood for parliament at by-elections, and began winning. When jailed supporters had their demands to be recognised as political prisoners rejected, hunger strikes began. When one striker died after being force-fed, General Michael Collins organised a show funeral, massively attended. Arms were stockpiled. Lawlessness spread in rural areas. By the time the Irish Party's leader John Redmond died in March 1918, his hopes of bringing about Ireland's independence peaceably had evaporated. In a strange repetition, the hunger strike was again adopted by prisoners belonging to the IRA in the 1970s and 1980s.

The rise of Sinn Féin

In April 1918, panicked by a setback in the war in France, Britain finally extended conscription to Ireland, throwing in as a sop new Home Rule legislation based on partitioning the island. It was a foolish move. The Catholic Church's hierarchy condemned conscription – which turned out to be unnecessary anyway, as the war was soon to end – and the Irish Party walked out of the Commons. Sinn Féin, having found a rallying cry, won sweeping victories in the post-war general election of December 1918. The new MPs boycotted the Commons, forming their own parliament, Dáil Eireann, in Dublin's Mansion House. As president of their new 'republic', they elected De Valera, still languishing in jail at the time.

Standing behind Sinn Féin were the Volunteers, known in the countryside as the Irish Republican Army, who increasingly saw violence as an effective weapon. They began killing anyone in uniform who stood in their way, then progressed to selective assassinations. Like so many Irish conflicts, this one rapidly took on some of the characteristics of a civil war. The corpses found labelled 'Spy – Killed by IRA' were usually those of Irishmen.

After an attempt was made in broad daylight on the life of Viceroy, the king's representative in Ireland, England, perplexed as ever, suppressed

November 1920, 'Bloody Sunday', Michael Collins had 12 British officers shot dead, mostly in their beds. That afternoon, at a Gaelic football match in Dublin's Croke Park, police shot dead 12 civilians. In the countryside, fearful families took to sleeping in hedgerows to escape the revenge killings. Guerrilla warfare spread, out of control.

A deal is done

In May 1921 Britain tried out a new idea, holding elections for two Irish parliaments, one in the North, one in the South. Sinn Féin swept

On 6 December 1921, in London, Michael Collins signs the controversial treaty setting up the Free State. Arthur Griffith is seated on the left.

Sinn Féin. Undeterred, Sinn Féin did well in the municipal elections held in January 1920.

When some of the boycotted police force resigned, they were replaced by recruits from England, many of them demobilised soldiers hardened to killing on the battlefields of France. Forming motorised squads, they hit back quickly at any trouble. But there were areas into which even they dared not go. In these, policing was taken over by the Volunteers, who arrested petty criminals and enforced licensing laws. The government, with 10,000 police and 50,000 troops, was humiliated. Before long, the police began fighting back, carrying out undisciplined reprisals after every IRA atrocity. On 21

the board in the South and the Unionists dominated the North. In October, a conference was called in London at which Britain and Ireland, faced with the prospect of declaring war on each other, sat down to thrash out a settlement.

The compromises were agonising. But on 5 December 1921, at 2.20am, a deal was done. The island was to be divided. The consequences would be huge, for this was the first fissure, signalling the eventual break-up of the British Empire. To those present, the significance was narrower. Eight centuries of attempts by England's monarchs and ministers to rule their neighbouring island had, with surprising abruptness, come to an end.

DUBLIN AT WAR

Bullets and shellfire ripped the heart out of the city centre between the Easter Rising of 1916 and the end of the Free State's bitter and bloody civil war in August 1923.

Few ordinary Dubliners supported the small band of middle-class intellectuals and their 150 supporters who, armed with a variety of rifles and agricultural implements, took over the city's General Post Office on the spring holiday morning of 24 April 1916 and solemnly read out, to the apathy of bystanders, the proclamation of the new Irish Republic. Many, indeed, saw the action as treacherous: World War I was at a critical point and many Irishmen were serving – and dying – in British regiments in France.

It was only when Britain, having crushed the revolt, began to execute the rebels, a few at a time, that derision for the upstarts turned to sympathy. The way to post-war independence was clear, but the compromise that led to Britain retaining six northeastern counties divided the nation and led to a civil war in the new Free State in 1922. O'Connell Street was in flames again, with 60 dying in the first eight days of fighting. Between 1916 and 1922, three-quarters of the street was demolished, never to regain its former elegance.

Eamon de Valera defended Boland's Mill during the 1916 Rising. His rejection of the treaty with Britain led to civil war.

The 1916 Rising ended when a British gunboat on the Liffey shelled rebel strongholds, burning out the revolutionaries.

This 1922 battle caused a fire at the Four Courts which destroyed historic deeds and documents dating back to the 12th century.

Michael Collins, head of the provisional government, leaves Dublin Castle in January 1922. He would be shot dead 19 months later.

DE VALERA: THE GREAT SURVIVOR

In 1916 Eamon de Valera, a 33-year-old maths teacher, liberated a bakery against the wishes of its workers, who felt that even in a republic people had to eat. Because he had been born in New York, of an Irish mother and a Spanish father, he was the only Easter Rising commandant not to be executed by the British.

Although president of Dáil Eireann in 1921, De Valera sent others to London to negotiate an independence treaty. That left him free to oppose their compromise, setting him against them in the Civil War that followed.

The war ended in 1923 with De Valera's effective surrender and he did not achieve power until he headed the Fianna Fáil government in 1932. The economy stagnated, but he built Fianna Fáil into a formidable populist party and kept Ireland neutral during World War II. He served two terms as Irish president (1959–73) and died in 1975, aged 92.

Constance Markievicz, an Irish Protestant who had married a Polish count, was a 1916 rebel. Later she was the first woman elected to the London parliament.

Church Street after the 1916 Rising. The death toll was 64 rebels, 134 police and soldiers and 220 civilians. Martial law was imposed and 4,000 were arrested.

Suspects are frisked by troops in 1920. Many troops, recently returned from World War I, were not best suited to civilian duties.

LIVING WITH PARTITION

Instead of coming together, the Catholic South and the
Protestant-dominated North ignored each other for 50
years. Then civil strife and terrorism erupted in the North.

To David Lloyd George's dexterous political mind, the fact that the Anglo-Irish Treaty gave everyone *something* they wanted but nobody *everything* they wanted meant it must stand some chance of success. This was the old mistake: the belief that the Irish were really Englishmen with brogues. In reality, the two peoples' expectations were quite different and, after eight centuries during which Irishman had fought Irishman over conflicting national allegiances, the first fruit of independence was true civil war.

The treaty gave the nationalists more than many had expected: an Irish Free State with a dominion status within the British Empire similar to Canada's. This was far greater freedom than Home Rule had ever promised.

The border question

But one dark cloud cast a shadow over the deal. Six counties of Ulster – Antrim, Down, Tyrone, Fermanagh, Armagh and Derry – were retained within the UK, the British having recognised that even a world war had not softened the resolution of the Protestants. Sir Winston Churchill expressed the dilemma graphically: 'As the deluge subsides and the waters fall short, we see the dreary steeples of Fermanagh and Tyrone emerging once again. The integrity of their quarrel is one of the few institutions that's been unaltered in the cataclysm which has swept the world.'

To sell the long-resisted division of Ireland to nationalists, the government added a proviso: a Boundary Commission would decide which Roman Catholic-dominated areas of Northern Ireland would later be incorporated within the 26 counties of the Free State. This promise permitted patriots such as Michael Collins to swallow the bitter pill of partition: after the Catholic

A farewell to Empire as Queen Victoria's statue is removed from outside Ireland's parliament building.

areas of Tyrone, Fermanagh and south Armagh had been removed, they reckoned, what would remain would not leave the new north-eastern state a viable entity.

But Collins's hopes, faint though they were, were not universally held. Ferocious arguments split the infant Free State, laying bare long suppressed personal animosities. On the one side stood the pro-Treaty provisional government led by Arthur Griffith: on the other, the anti-Treaty forces massing behind Eamon de Valera. After a bitter 12-day parliamentary debate, the Treaty was carried by 64 votes to 57.

It was too narrow a margin to ensure peace, especially since the Irish Republican Army, mirroring the split in the country, was marching in opposite directions; about half with Collins, transforming itself into the regular army of the Free State, and the other half refusing to recognise the new government, relying instead on force to win them a free and united Ireland.

By 1922 Dublin's O'Connell Street was in flames again, with 60 dying in eight days. Northern Protestants, looking on, vowed to have nothing to do with any redrawing of borders, declaring: 'What we have, we hold.' Fighting broke out in Northern Ireland, too, with the death toll rising to 264 within six months.

The new Ireland's first prime minister did not live to see the end of the struggle: in August 1922, heavily overworked, Griffith collapsed and died. Collins had a more violent end, being shot dead in an ambush on the Macroom to Bandon road in his native County Cork. He had been expecting just such an outcome: after putting his name to the Anglo-Irish Treaty, he had written to a friend: 'Will anyone be satisfied with the bargain? Will anyone? I tell you this – early this morning I signed my death warrant.'

The Boundary Commission recommended only minor adjustments, and even these were

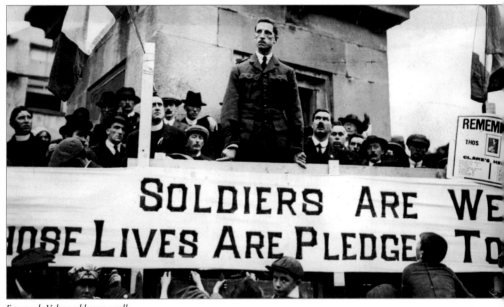

Eamon de Valera addresses a rally.

THE TRAVELLING PEOPLE

There are probably more than 3,000 families of travellers in Ireland, adding up to an estimated 25,000 people. Although they bear some resemblances to the Gypsies of France, Spain and Romania, they are entirely Irish in their ethnic origins – the true Romanies, like the Romans, never reached Ireland.

Many lived in illegal campsites by road sides, on waste ground, or on land cleared for development, and were frequently forced to move on. Until the 1960s, almost all travellers lived in brightly painted horse-drawn caravans or in tents. They fulfilled a useful economic role in a society that was still mainly rural: mending utensils, making baskets and

sieves, peddling knick-knacks, dealing in horses and selling scrap. By the 1990s, traditional caravans had been replaced by motorvans or more spacious modern caravans. Now most councils provide serviced sites, and some travellers have moved into rented housing, in search of better education for their children, and a higher standard of living (travelling people have a far lower life expectancy than settled people). But many take to the road again in summer, making the traditional round of horse fairs, which is where you are most likely to encounter these radically different and often much-maligned (by settled folk) characters.

never implemented. De Valera's view of the border as 'an old fortress of crumbled masonry, held together with the plaster of fiction' had proved false. Permanent partition had arrived.

Fine Gael and Fianna Fáil

The Civil War ended in 1923 with De Valera's effective surrender. But it was to dominate every aspect of political life in the Free State for the next half-century. The country's two main political parties today, Fine Gael (*Tribe of Ireland*) and Fianna Fáil (*Warriors of Ireland*) are direct descendants of the pro- and anti-Treaty forces.

Eamon de Valera's vision for a new Ireland had a strong emphasis on rural values.

In 1927, De Valera entered parliament (the Dáil) at the head of Fianna Fáil. He came to power in the 1932 election, vowing to reinstate the ancient Gaelic language and culture, ushering in a new era of pious respectability, based firmly on Catholic values. The poet W.B. Yeats, a member of the Irish Senate, warned Eamon de Valera of the dangers of alienating northern Protestants by allowing the Catholic Church too much influence in the South. 'If you show that this country, Southern Ireland, is going to be governed by Catholic ideas and by Catholic ideas alone, you will never get the North,' said Yeats. 'You will put a wedge into the midst of this nation.'

In the following three decades, De Valera built Fianna Fáil into a formidable populist political movement, drawing support from small farmers, the urban working class and the newly moneyed. Fine Gael's heartland was among larger farmers and the professional classes. The Labour Party, which pre-dated partition, found it hard to build support: the trade unions, while nominally pro-Labour, often did deals with Fianna Fáil, and the Church's anti-communist propaganda encouraged a fear of the Left.

Endless emigration

'Dev,' as he became affectionately known, pursued a policy of economic nationalism, raising tariff barriers against England, which retaliated. A tax was even imposed on English newspapers. Yet not everyone was thrilled when, for example, Dev announced that Ireland was self-sufficient in shoelaces. Emigration, mainly to England and America, claimed yet another generation of younger sons unable to inherit the family farm and younger daughters unable to find husbands. In the early 1920s, an astonishing 43 percent of Irish-born men and women were living abroad. At the opposite end of the social scale from the farmhands, the once affluent Anglo-Irish – sometimes called the Protestant 'Ascendancy' – fell into decline and their 'Big Houses' at the end of long, tree-lined avenues began to look dilapidated.

Many southerners began to question the wisdom of following their leader's 'Small is Beautiful' signposts. 'It was indeed hard,' said one observer, 'to muster up enthusiasm for the carrageen moss industry, in the possible utilisation of the various parts of the herring's anatomy, down to the tail and the fin, in portable, prefabricated factories themselves made of herring-bone cement along the west coast.'

But what was the alternative? Certainly not to imitate the UK, Dev insisted, and, to emphasise the point, he produced a constitution in 1937 which abolished the oath of allegiance to England's king, claimed sovereignty over all 32 counties of Ireland and underlined the pervasive influence of the Roman Catholic Church.

The new constitution created a curious equilibrium. The bishops in the South and the Orangemen in the North each exercised a sectarian and politically conservative pressure on their respective parliaments.

Although the Unionists would have been happy to remain an integral part of Britain, Lloyd George, emphasising Ulster's 'otherness', had given them their own parliament, Stormont – built on the outskirts of Belfast in the style of Buckingham Palace, only grander. And they had lost no time in making their makeshift state impregnable. London, relieved to be rid of the perennial Irish problem, did nothing to stop them. Nor, fatally, did the Roman Catholics' elected representatives, who boycotted Stormont. The assembly, the Unionists boasted, was 'a Protestant parliament for a Protestant

World War II

While Irish history was repeating itself, European history concocted another world war. The Unionists felt their self-interest had been justified when, as soon as Britain declared war on Germany in 1939, De Valera announced that Southern Ireland would remain neutral. Behind the scenes, Winston Churchill, Britain's new wartime leader, offered De Valera a united Ireland at some point in the future if Ireland were to enter the war and allow the British navy to use its ports.

De Valera said no. After all, to enter the war would leave Ireland – with no navy or air force

A Traveller family in 1970's Ireland.

people? The historic hatreds between the two communities were left unhealed.

If anything, they were deepened. Taking advantage of the nationalists' boycott, the Unionists made sure that the plum jobs and the best housing went to their own supporters. Two distinct communities developed: Protestant dentists pulled Protestant teeth, Catholic plumbers mended Catholic pipes.

An all-Protestant part-time special constabulary (the 'B' Specials) maintained close links with the Orange Order and helped the police keep dissension under control. The IRA, making little headway in Ulster, began a campaign in English cities in 1938, setting off suitcase bombs, but the English declined to over-react.

DE VALERA'S VISION

As the new leader of Fianna Fáil, Eamon de Valera declared: 'No longer shall our children, like our cattle, be brought up for export.' He spelt out his vision for the Free State's future in a famous St Patrick's Day address, in which he described his ideal Ireland as 'a land whose countryside would be bright with cosy homesteads, whose fields and villages would be joyous with the sounds of industry, with the rompings of sturdy children, the contests of athletic youths and the laughter of comely maidens, whose firesides would be forums for the wisdom of serene old age.' A noble aim, but it didn't belong to the 20th century.

– wholly dependent on the protection of its old enemy, England, and its long-term prospects if Germany won the war, which seemed entirely possible, would hardly be enhanced.

Churchill's fears had not been unfounded. The Germans had been planning an invasion of Ireland, 'Operation Green', as a springboard to an assault on Britain. In a handbook designed to brief their battalions, they noted that 'the Irishman supports a community founded upon equality for all, but associates with this an extraordinary personal need for independence which easily leads to indiscipline and pugnacity.'

Northern Ireland became a target. A ferocious night raid on Belfast in April 1941 killed more than 700 people. The Unionists claimed that the neutral South's lack of a blackout helped German bombers pinpoint their targets in the darkened North. Another grudge was chalked up on the blackboard of Irish history.

Over the years even the name of the Free State had been fiercely argued about. Both the English and the Irish seemed to find 'Eire' (Gaelic for 'Ireland') acceptable. But in 1948 a coalition government fixed the name of the country as the Republic of Ireland. Britain declared that, as a

Two armed soldiers inside a road block in Belfast in 1970.

WHY THE NORTH DISTRUSTED THE SOUTH

Although politically free, the 26 counties of the Free State remained economically and culturally stunted. Emigration reached epidemic proportions, triggered by the unattractive nature of life in rural Ireland, and also by the restrictions placed on entertainment. In 1954 a record 1,034 books were banned, and cinemagoers, if they wished to follow the plots of many films, had to cross the border to see the unscissored versions. London's more lurid Sunday newspapers published tamer Irish editions. In *Mother Ireland*, the novelist Edna O'Brien described the constricting parochialism and the awful predictability that led her to flee to London: 'Hour after hour I can think of Ireland, I can imagine without going too far wrong what is happening in any one of the little towns by day or by night... I can almost tell you what any one of my friends might be doing, so steadfast is the rhythm of life there.' Northern Protestants noted not only the southern state's poorer standard of living and also its intrusion into personal freedoms – its outlawing of divorce, for example, and its ban on the importation of contraceptives. Northern Ireland, Britain had pledged when the Republic left the Commonwealth, could remain part of the United Kingdom as long as a majority of its people wished. Since Protestants outnumbered Catholics by two to one in the Six Counties, that might mean forever.

result, Ireland was no longer part of the Commonwealth. At last, Ireland – or at least 26 counties of it – was politically free.

The green consumers

In 1958, under the premiership of Sean Lemass, Ireland decided to rejoin the 20th century. He set out vigorously to create new jobs by opening up the economy to foreign investment, attracting light engineering, pharmaceutical and electronics companies.

The dream of De Valera – now the president, a largely symbolic office – faded fast. Interest in Gaelic language and culture waned and the voice of management consultants was heard in the land. The Irish, embracing consumerism with relish, were becoming more like the English. Even the IRA failed to command much support in its fight for a united Ireland. A campaign of border raids between 1956 and 1962 netted a few arms hauls but then petered out. By 1965, it seemed the most natural thing in the world for Lemass to have a neighbourly meeting with Northern Ireland's premier, Captain Terence O'Neill. But it seemed shockingly unnatural to hardline Unionists. Several Cabinet colleagues and a popular fundamentalist preacher, the Reverend Ian Paisley, reminded him that Lemass's Republic still claimed jurisdiction over the Six Counties.

The upper-class O'Neill was ill equipped to cope with the Pandora's Box that was opened just three years later. It began routinely enough, when a Unionist-controlled council in Caledon, Co. Tyrone, where many Catholic families were badly in need of housing, allocated one of its dwellings to a young, single Protestant girl. Local nationalists, following the example of blacks in the US, first staged a sit-in, then a civil rights march. A second march was planned for October 1968, inside the walled city of Londonderry. This is a symbolic place for Unionists, who still commemorate the breaking of the city's siege in 1689 when Protestant supporters of William of Orange defeated Catholic supporters of James II, thus cementing Protestant supremacy (Nationalists, equally tutored in the city's history, reject its 'English' name in favour of the original Derry).

O'Neill's government, viewing the march not as a civil rights protest but as a nationalist conspiracy, banned it. Two thousand people marched anyway, and were met by the massed forces of the Royal Ulster Constabulary (RUC), complete with two mobile water cannons. TV viewers around the world watched as the RUC took their truncheons to the demonstrators with what looked suspiciously like enthusiasm. Further marches ended in violence and O'Neill, having seen his dreams for a civilised relationship between the two Ire-

> As Britain rebuilt its economic strength in the 1950s, Northern Ireland began to feel the benefit of its welfare state and industrial incentives, while the Republic remained essentially a humdrum peasant economy.

The Rev. Ian Paisley protesting outside St Paul's Cathedral, London, in 1969.

lands consumed by the fires of sectarian hatred, was forced out of office by militant Unionists.

Almost inevitably, the Protestants' annual march through Londonderry in August 1969 sparked off violence. Petrol bombs were hurled, along with broken-up paving stones. The police responded with CS gas. Fighting spread to the Catholic Falls Road and the Protestant Shankill Road in Belfast. The RUC, hopelessly out of its depth, appealed for reinforcements and, on 16 August, a reluctant British government sent troops on to the streets of Derry and Belfast 'in support of the civil power'. What was the choice? Northern Ireland was, after all, part of the United Kingdom. It was meant to be a temporary arrangement.

IRELAND TRANSFORMED

As violence dragged on, the South left the North to its own devices and looked instead to Europe. The North eventually agreed to power-sharing and the Republic's economic boom turned to bust.

At first the British soldiers arriving in what was technically British territory were welcomed as saviours. Catholic housewives, many of whom had been preparing to take refuge in the Republic, plied them with endless cups of tea. Girls smiled sweetly at them. Perhaps, it seemed for a moment, all would be well. But it was already too late for such hopes, for this latest chapter of Ireland's Troubles had caused a fearful resurrection: that of the IRA.

As a fighting force, the Irish Republican Army had virtually ceased to exist in 1962. By the late 1960s the declared aim of the small group of Marxists who constituted the rump of the IRA was to overthrow the conservative establishments in both parts of Ireland, then set up an ill-defined workers' republic. Lacking modern weaponry, they were acutely conscious of their failure to protect Catholic communities against Protestant mobs, a failure brought painfully home by graffiti which interpreted IRA as 'I Ran Away'. The movement split into two groups: the traditionalists ('the Officials') and a new Provisional wing (the 'Provos'). Recruitment to the Provos soared when the British army embarked on late-night arms searches in Catholic areas of Belfast and soon the army, having arrived as mediator, found itself in many areas the enemy.

A mural proclaims loyalties in Derry City.

Violence spreads

The IRA's armed offensive gathered pace, spreading terror by means of snipers' bullets, booby-trapped vehicles and bombs in crowded bars. Protestant vigilante and terrorist groups such as the Ulster Defence Association and the Ulster Volunteer Force began to match violence with violence. The situation worsened dramatically when, on 30 January 1972, shooting broke out at an anti-internment rally in Londonderry. At the end of it, 13 civilians lay dead, shot by paratroopers. The date, Bloody Sunday, became yet another Irish anniversary to be commemorated violently. The following month, as a reprisal, a bomb exploded at Aldershot Barracks in England, killing seven.

Ireland joins Europe

As bombs and bullets ripped Northern Ireland's economy to shreds, the Republic was enjoying unprecedented affluence. After the country's entry into the European Economic Community at the beginning of 1973, financial subsidies descended, as seemingly inexhaustible as Ireland's rain. Former farm labourers, much to their delight, found themselves earning good money assembling electronics components, and one euphoric trade minister dared to describe Ireland as 'the sunbelt of Europe'.

Culturally, too, the climate was brightening. Writers and artists, once forced to emigrate in search of intellectual freedom, were exempted from paying income tax on their royalties. Some well-known names, such as thriller writer Frederick Forsyth, moved to Ireland to take advantage of the concession. One or two more provocative authors found it peculiar that, while one arm of the government was allow-

Economic recession, and the reluctance of industrialists to site factories in Northern Ireland, made unemployment seem as great an evil as terrorism. And in this respect the South was faring little better. As the effects of the 1970s oil crisis became felt, industrial unemployment rose and inflation neared 25 percent. Both governments were chasing the same investors. The North had the bad luck to win the tussle over who should build John de Lorean's gull-wing sports car: the Belfast factory closed after the UK had invested £17 million.

The worst car bombing was in Omagh in 1998 when 29 people were killed.

ing them to live free of income tax, another was banning their books.

London takes control

In the North, the sky was darkening further. Britain abolished the 50-year-old Stormont parliament, imposing direct rule from London, and tried unsuccessfully to persuade Protestant and Catholic leaders to set up a power-sharing executive. As atrocities multiplied, the death toll passed 2,500 and an entire generation reached adulthood without ever having known peace. Even well-tried nationalist tactics were failing to work anymore: a hunger strike in an Ulster prison was ignored by Britain's Prime Minister, Margaret Thatcher, and 10 men starved to death in 1981.

THE TWO TRIBES

Trust between nationalists and Unionists in Northern Ireland had always been elusive because the two cultural traditions had so few points of contact. Protestant children attended state-supported Protestant schools, while Catholic children went to church schools. Catholic children were taught Gaelic games, Protestants played cricket. Catholics learned Irish, Protestants didn't. Integrating the schools would have meant bussing children from one area to another and was difficult to implement because the Catholic Church in particular argued strongly that Catholic children must have a Catholic education.

The Haughey era

At one stage during 1981–82, there were three elections in the Republic within 18 months. A complex system of proportional representation meant that Fianna Fáil minority administrations, now led by the charismatic Charles Haughey (see box), alternated with Fine Gael-Labour coalitions. The last of these coalitions, from late 1982 to 1987, had one major achievement: it succeeded in negotiating, with the British Prime Minister Margaret Thatcher, the Anglo-Irish Agreement. This gave the Irish Government a consultative role in the administration of Northern Ireland, while com-

Charles Haughey and other leaders at the European Summit in Dublin, 1990.

mitting British and Irish law and security forces to work together against terrorism and reaffirming that the Six Counties would remain part of the United Kingdom as long as a majority of their people favoured that option.

It was a Haughey administration that eventually introduced fiscal measures brutal enough to halt the Republic's economic deterioration. Public services were cut and unemployment soared, but the ground was laid for better times in the 1990s. That decade was ushered in by the election as Ireland's president of the left-wing Mary Robinson, a leading lawyer and feminist who stood for liberal and pluralist values. In her seven-year term, she was to transform the presidency from being a

dumping ground for retired politicians to a force for social change.

European Union Funding

The European Union was largely responsible for the economy's upturn. Jobs were created and roads built as billions of pounds poured into the country from the European social fund. A sharp fall in interest rates gave rise to a boom in property development and construction. Cheques from Brussels made up almost half the income of Irish farmers. Psychologically, any lingering inferiority complex towards Britain was eroded as the new wealth reduced the country's economic dependence on trade with its larger neighbour.

Ireland began promoting itself as the Silicon Valley of Europe. Its combination of a youthful, well-educated workforce and generous grants and tax incentives lured more than 300 electronics companies to the Republic. Computer giants such as Dell and Intel began assembling computers and microchips there, while Microsoft established its European operations centre in Dublin.

The buoyant job market eroded the emigration figures, which had reached 30,000 a year in the 1980s – mainly to Britain and the United States. Suddenly many of those who had gone in the 1980s came home, flaunting the experience they'd gained abroad and grabbing many of the new jobs. Refugees from destinations as diverse as Romania and Zaire, learning of Ireland's comparatively liberal immigration laws, arrived in Dublin. Applications for asylum, which had been only 30 to 40 a year at the beginning of the decade, soared to several thousand a year. As unemployment figures among the Irish dropped,

THE HAUGHEY PHENOMENON

Once compared to a Renaissance potentate, Charles Haughey dominated politics in the Republic for two decades. In 1970, when Minister for Finance, he had been acquitted of conspiring illegally to import arms for use in Northern Ireland. As prime minister, he lived flamboyantly beyond his means.

Suspicions grew about his financial probity and in 1992 he was forced from office. Five years later he was charged for having received while in office millions of pounds of undeclared funds from Ben Dunne, a supermarket tycoon. Condemned by *The Irish Times* as a 'symbol of the degeneracy of political culture,' he died in 2006 aged 80.

During the boom years, Dublin-owned companies acquired expensive commercial properties in the UK and USA: it was remarked that skyscrapers built with Irish labour were now owned by the labourers' descendants.

people overcame their resentment of economic migrants from the EU, prepared to do the menial jobs spurned by the newly affluent Irish.

Happily, Europe loved Ireland just as much as Ireland loved Europe – if nothing else because its support acted as a useful counterweight to Britain's often-antagonistic attitude. Being small and remote lent enchantment, too: Ireland could never have got away with offering corporate tax incentives that made a mockery of EU harmonisation if it had been a serious economic competitor to France or Germany.

The Alice in Wonderland nature of Irish politics was highlighted in 1997 by the election of Mary McAleese, a Belfast academic with strong nationalist sympathies, to the presidency. Being a citizen of Northern Ireland, Mrs McAleese could not cast a vote in the Republic's presidential contest, yet she could legally stand as a candidate – and win.

Tourism benefited as Ireland suddenly became a hip tourist destination. For the first time, a £30 million ad campaign, an initiative of a new joint marketing body, Tourism Ireland, promoted both the Republic and Northern Ireland as a joint destination.

Criminal racketeering

But the Emerald Isle hadn't become a Garden of Eden. Dublin in particular was bedevilled by racketeering, much of it centred on the drugs trade. The scale of the problem became apparent in 1996 when gangs gunned down Veronica Guerin, a leading investigative journalist.

In Northern Ireland, a peace agreement had been signed on Good Friday 1998 by all the main political parties, including Sinn Féin, and the Republic changed its constitution to renounce its territorial claim to the North.

But another shocking incident occurred on a Saturday afternoon in August 1998, when a car bomb exploded in Omagh's busy town centre killing 29 innocent people and injuring more than 200. A splinter group called the Real IRA, opposed to the Good Friday Agreement, claimed responsibility. Public reaction to this atrocity helped to

spur on the peace process. Not until 2013 were two men found liable, following a civil action.

The Irish had few qualms about embracing the euro in 2002 (although Northern Ireland, as part of the UK, retained the pound). Suddenly the Irish discovered the joys of cheap credit, made possible by Europe's low interest rates, and embarked on a spending spree. Property prices spiralled, especially in and around Dublin, and in a bid to create affordable homes, the commuter belt expanded to estates built on the outskirts of towns an hour's drive and more from the city.

In 2005 the IRA formally declared that the

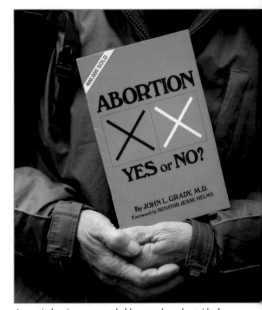

An anti-abortion protestor holds up a placard outside the Marie Stopes clinic, the first private clinic to offer abortions to women in Belfast, in 2012.

Economic growth and foreign investment policy brought real, not fool's, gold to the end of the Irish rainbow. Mercedes and Toyotas sped foreign execs through rural lanes, adding more hazards to Ireland's unpredictable traffic.

armed conflict was over and that they had scrapped their weaponry.

Peace breaks out

Although a low level of violence continued in both of Northern Ireland's communities, everyday life in Belfast seemed relatively normal. Clubbers from Britain and further afield discovered the city's vibrant nightlife, and the growth of low-cost airlines such as Ryanair enabled them to sample it.

Meanwhile, in the North, progress was being made on the political front. Having been stubborn enough to resist all compromises, the Unionists' leader, the Rev. Ian Paisley told his supporters that his essential demands had been met and that he was now ready to join a power-sharing Assembly with his former sworn enemies. Because no parliamentary 'opposition' was built into the system, co-operation was essential. So, as

Bertie Ahern heads for another election win.

first minister, Protestant firebrand Ian Paisley had to get on with his deputy, former IRA man Martin McGuinness, or the Assembly would collapse.

Property bubble bursts

The first rumblings of trouble in the financial sector surfaced soon after the resignation of Bertie Ahern in May 2008. By September, it appeared that the international financial crisis was affecting the Irish economy. However, it eventually emerged that the Irish economy was suffering a home-grown crisis, and was massively under-capitalised.

Irish banking had been operating in an effectively unregulated environment, encouraging speculation by property developers, leading builders into dire trouble, precipitating mass unemployment as workers were laid off, with raised taxes and lower salaries for the workers, leaving few if any buyers for thousands of houses and offices built during the boom. House prices have recovered, especially in the more desirable parts of Dublin and to a lesser extent around the country. Stringent mortgage rules and a lack of new units have led to spiralling rents in Dublin as many people have no choice but to keep renting. Homelessness is now at record levels as a result of the housing crisis.

The Fianna Fáil government decided to bail out the banks, leading to a severely austere regime. In the 2011 election Fianna Fáil suffered a massive defeat, and the centre-right Fine Gael party formed a coalition government with the Labour Party under Taoiseach Enda Kenny. In 2016, the electorate returned a hung parliament with Fine Gael eventually forming a coalition government with the Independents and Enda

THE GREAT DEBATES OVER ABORTION AND DIVORCE

In 1992 the Republic was asked to vote by referendum about abortion. The government's chief legal advisor had sought an injunction to prevent a 14-year-old rape victim going to England to have an abortion. To many, it seemed both hypocritical since an estimated 4,000 Irish women travelled to Britain each year for abortions. But after a vitriolic public debate, the Constitution was amended to defend the right to life of the unborn.

However, the ground shifted on other social issues and in 1997 divorce was legalised in the Irish Republic

As regards abortion, the situation for medical practitioners remained ambiguous, and the issue resurfaced in 2012 when Indian dentist Savita Halappanavar died

during a miscarriage in Galway, in spite of her requests for a termination. In 2014, a pregnant refugee, Ms Y, was denied the right to travel to the UK to seek a termination and was forced to deliver her baby by caesarean section. In 2014, a clinically dead pregnant woman was kept alive against the wishes of her family for several weeks, while the courts attempted to find a legal solution to the situation. The EU insisted that Ireland legislate to clarify the position, and the rift between those putting the foetus's right to life before the mother's led to demonstrations and heated debate. While Abortion in extreme medical emergencies was legalised in July 2013, there is still a big debate over liberalising abortion law.

Kenny remaining as Taoiseach for another term. Fianna Fáil recovered significantly in the 2016 elections and are now back as a political force - at the expense of the Labour Party, which has been decimated.

A popular president

In November 2011 Michael D. Higgins, a former Labour Party TD, took office as President, following a bitterly fought election campaign with seven candidates. Higgins has brought dignity, erudition and warmth to the office, and is (almost – this is Ireland) universally popular.

The Catholic Church suffered a strong decline in public esteem following revelations of its failure to protect children from sexually abusive priests, and to punish the abusers. Its anti-abortion stance, firmly restated following the death of Savita Halappanavar (see page 62), further increased the Church's unpopularity, as did revelations of the injustices perpetrated to unmarried mothers and other marginalised women in the Church-run 'Magdalen Laundries'.

Lack of jobs in the construction industry and lack of opportunities for graduates led to an increase in emigration by young people, many heading for Australia and Canada, unsure for how long. In 2012, 39,500 people between 25 and 44 years old left the country, while some 52,700 immigrants arrived.

Following pressure from the EU, a property tax was introduced in 2013 and water charges in 2014. Banks agreed to negotiate with those owner-occupiers (17 percent and growing) in serious mortgage arrears, and to tackle the problem of negative equity. With pubs and retail outlets closing, 'ghost estates' crumbling, and most people feeling the pinch, morale was only slightly raised by a successful Irish Presidency of the EU in 2013, and words of praise from the Troika for Irish efforts to regain financial stability. The thorniest problem for the government in recent years has been the hugely unpopular Irish Water semi-state: monster rallies were organised around the country by the 'Right to Water' campaign, fuelled by outraged citizens. The water charges have since been deferred by the current coalition government for the foreseeable future.

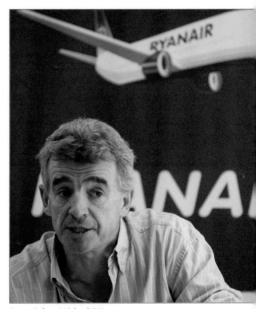

Ryanair boss Michael O'Leary.

THE ENVIRONMENT: IS IRELAND REALLY GREEN?

Ireland's green credentials are somewhat mixed. On the one hand, its per capita emissions of greenhouse gases are surpassed in the EU only by Luxembourg, and emissions from transport have been growing as more cars take to the roads. The widespread use of peat to generate electricity also adds to greenhouse gas production.

On the other hand, renewable energy sources are increasing, with one-tenth of electricity generated from wind, hydro, biomass, landfill gas and biogas. Wind power is the fastest growing sector, with 88 wind farms in 19 counties, including 12 facilities in Northern Ireland, and one scheme at the Arklow Banks, off the east coast.

Although fertiliser use is decreasing, only 0.9 percent of farmland (39,000 hectares) is organically cultivated. The Department of Agriculture has a target of 3 percent. Irish consumers have opened their wallets to embrace the organic idea, dramatically increasing their spending on ecologically raised products.

In 2005 the government introduced refuse charges for domestic waste, transforming the Irish into a nation of recyclers. A tax on polythene carrier bags was introduced in 2002. The 22-cent tariff, collected by retail outlets, goes into an environmental fund. Ireland was also one of the first countries to ban smoking in public places, including bars.

Traditional music is played in many pubs.

MUSIC

Many kinds of music, from classical to rock, are popular in Ireland. Whatever your taste, there are performances to enjoy all over the country.

Irish traditional music is organic, constantly evolving. It has always drawn on many influences and sources, absorbing, retaining and changing them. Over the centuries hornpipes, polkas, barn dances, waltzes and other styles were imported from all over Europe and acquired a distinctly Irish flavour.

There are two basic types of Irish tune – the jig and the reel. The reel is the older and faster form, played in 4/4 time, while jigs have a 6/8 rhythm. Many thousands of different tunes make up the repertoire, which each musician performs in his or her unique style. Some airs and songs or how they are performed are associated with a particular area of the country.

Wherever you travel in Ireland you will encounter traditional music – from buskers performing on the streets to the hundreds of regular sessions (*seisiún* in Irish), running year round all over the island – many with free admission.

Traditional variations

Traditional music falls into two categories – instrumental and song. Instrumental music was originally dance music but gradually evolved and nowadays is also performed for a listening audience, as well as to accompany dancing. Musicians usually perform sets of, for example, two different jigs followed by a reel, which builds up excitement as the music speeds up.

There is also a very strong song tradition – including unaccompanied solo singing known as *séan nós*, usually performed in Irish, as well as accompanied songs in English. *Séan nós* is rooted in the Irish-speaking areas with a distinct style unique to each area. *Séan nós has* influenced other genres due to its high emotional impact. Sinead O'Connor and The Hothouse Flowers both cite séan nós as an influence.

Traditional Irish dancers.

The harp, a national emblem, is the instrument most associated with Ireland but, while still widely played, you should not be surprised if you attend a music session where it does not feature. Other instruments include *uilleann* pipes, fiddle, flute, tin whistle, banjo, button accordion, *bodhrán*, harmonica and the spoons.

Uilleann pipes (pronounced '*ill-un*' or '*ill-yun*' and meaning elbow) are bellows-blown bagpipes, which evolved between the 18th and 19th century to their present form. The player performs seated, with the bag under one arm and the bellows under the other. The bodhrán (pronounced '*bow-raun*') is a hand-held drum made from goatskin, which has become particularly popular since the 1960s. Ordinary spoons, in the hands of a master, produce a great sound, often setting the pace of a piece of music.

Comhaltas Ceoltóiri Éireann, founded in 1951, is the largest body involved in the promotion of Irish traditional music; its activities include concerts, festivals, competitions and summer schools, with workshops and classes in a range of instruments. It is well worth looking at its website: www.comhaltas.ie.

Revival of interest

While traditional music was always popular, it was a predominantly rural phenomenon until the 1960s, when there was a massive revival in interest, at least partly influenced by Irish music composer Sean Ó Riada (1931–1971), and the founding of companies including Claddagh Records by Garech Browne (b. 1939). Today, bands such as Beoga, Danu, Gráda and Téada are introducing the music to a whole new generation.

Music composed in earlier times has been revived and given new arrangements. Works by, for example, Carolan, the 17th/18th-century itinerant blind harper and composer, are enjoyed today.

An uilleann piper.

IRISH DANCING: ALIVE AND KICKING

Irish dancing is enjoying a popularity like never before. Riverdance and, more recently, Lord of the Dance transformed traditional Irish dance forever. These shows continue to tour worldwide, making the principal dancers, Michael Flatley and Jean Butler, into stars.

Until Riverdance, Irish dance was seen by many as stiff ritual associated only with hard-fought competitions or *féis* (pronounced 'fesh'). The Riverdance effect has led to a worldwide boom. The World Irish Dancing Championship (www.worldirishdance.com) attracts some 4,500 competitors and supporters from 32 countries, and has been held in Boston to facilitate the many American participants. Small fortunes are spent on cos-

tumes, wigs and tuition (see www.worldirishdance.com).

Its popularity has a simple explanation: Irish dancing is great fun. Similar to the square dance, the *ceílí* is the best introduction. There are four basic dance forms – the reel, light jig, slip jig and hornpipe – with variations. There are more than 100 different set dances.

The Irish word *ceílí* means a gathering of neighbours in a house to enjoy music, dance and storytelling and, while today they are held in halls or pubs, that welcoming atmosphere survives. Avoid those organised purely for tourists. Cairde Rince Céilí na hÉireann (Friends of Irish Céilí Dancing; www.ceilidancing.com) hold regular set-dancing classes and workshops throughout Ireland.

The remaining members of some groups formed in the 1960s continue to tour today – among them The Chieftains, one of the most influential in building the international appeal of Irish music. The group has collaborated with some of the biggest names in rock and pop, including musical legends Sting and Van Morrison, as well as with symphony orchestras and traditional groups. The Irish folk band The Dubliners retired in 2012, the band's 50th anniversary, following the death of the last original member, Barney McKenna. However, surviving non-original members have formed The Dublin Legends and now tour.

Celtic fusion

Irish music has fused with rock and roll, punk and other genres since the 1970s, when Horslips merged the traditional and rock. Some fusion artists have been very successful both at home and internationally – among them the uncompromising Van Morrison and the wistful Enya.

Van Morrison's songs are often described as Celtic Soul. He was exposed to many musical influences, growing up in Belfast, as his father collected US jazz recordings and his mother was a singer. His work is thoughtful, and combines elements of jazz and R&B with Irish traditions.

Enya was a member of successful Donegal group Clannad with her siblings, but today is the best-selling Irish solo artist. She rarely performs in public and has not toured since 1988. The huge popularity of the Irish band, Kila, fusing music played on traditional Irish instruments with the strong and varied percussive beats of world music, is seen by many as evidence of the growing multicultural nature of Irish society.

Pop

Showbands were an Irish phenomenon in the 1960s and early 1970s. The largest of them were modelled on American big bands. They toured dance halls all over the country, performing covers of American and UK chart hits. They died out with the arrival of television and the closure of most halls, particularly those in rural areas.

That tradition lives on in a different form – with boy bands. The most successful of them internationally was Westlife. It should not surprise anyone to learn that both Westlife and its precursor Boyzone were manufactured and managed by Louis Walsh, who learned his trade on the showband circuit. Like the showbands,

> The Great Music in Irish Houses festival brings chamber music concerts to historic buildings, including the Casino in Marino, Co. Dublin, Kilruddery House, Co. Wicklow and Emo Court, Co. Laois, www.greatmusicinirishhouses.com.

Enjoying the craic in Ireland.

many of the groups' songs were covers of hits by other artists.

The most famous and successful of all Irish musicians on the contemporary scene is rock band U2. Their soaring stadium sound is not obviously influenced by Irish traditions.

Singing

The Irish love singing – and do so at any opportunity – just listen to them at a sporting event or on social occasions. Traditional songs fall into four categories: historic lays, fictional ballads, documentary come-all-ye's (so named as they start with 'Come all ye..') and lyric song in Irish or *sean-nós*. The majority of songs in the Irish language collected in the 19th and

20th centuries are love songs, most composed between 1600 and 1850. After that period, and the disastrous famine, there was a growing dependence on English and that is reflected in the songs – some are bilingual, but most are in English.

Political songs support the Irish against the foreigner or glorify the feats of warrior heroes such as Finn Mac Cual and Brian Ború. Others commemorate a disaster, such as a ship sinking, or are about the heartbreak of emigration. 'Rebel songs,' as they came to be known, with titles including *Kevin Barry* or *Boolavogue*, hark

recordings are still available. That versatility is typical of many Irish traditional musicians – they may even belong to more than one group at a time.

Sinead O'Connor is another hugely talented singer who is massively influenced by traditional music and Celtic mysticism.

Singer songwriter Glen Hansard, who had a supporting role in The Commitments, and the lead role in the musical drama film *Once*, is making a mark, both as a solo artist and with The Frames. Irish-speaker Iarla Ó Lionáird, a producer and performer with the Afro-Celt

Van Morrison.

Ronan O'Snodaigh of Kila.

back to times of British oppression. The band The Wolfe Tones, formed in the early 1960s, continues the tradition of singing rebel songs, and still tours to the UK and the US.

Most young Irish nowadays are unlikely to know the words of traditional songs, although they will be familiar with *The Fields of Athenry* (about deportation), and similar songs, written in recent decades and popular at sports events.

Singers

Christy Moore is a perennially popular solo artist, whose songs reflect contemporary concerns. In the past he was also a member of bands, including Planxty and Moving Hearts, whose

Sound System, a musical group that fuses hip hop and techno with Celtic and West African music, is also the first *sean-nós* singer to break into the mass market.

Damien Dempsey is a Dublin singer-songwriter who is influenced by traditional music but uses his lyrics to critique the social problems in modern Ireland.

Classical music

The main classical performing groups are the National Symphony Orchestra of Ireland and the Ulster Orchestra, based respectively in Dublin and Belfast. Visitors to Ireland are surprised at the low ticket prices for their concerts, excellent value for world-class orchestras. Also look out for performances by students and graduates of colleges of music, particularly when visiting Belfast, Dublin, Cork or Limerick.

This being Ireland, politics naturally gets a look-in. In the hope that music might be the fruit of love, the Cross Border Orchestra of Ireland brings together 130 Protestants and Catholics aged from 12 to 24 from both sides of the border in the hope of breaking down prejudices, www.cboi.ie.

The only Irish classical composer to be known internationally is John Field (1782–1837) who invented the nocturne. His music was brought to new audiences in the 20th century by Irish pianist John O'Conor.

Opera has always been popular, and in the 19th and early 20th centuries attracted huge audiences. Today, Ireland's national opera touring company, the Opera Theatre Company (www.opera.ie) tours all 32 counties, Classically trained singers still lack career opportunities, and often have to go overseas. Some have formed trios such as The Celtic Tenors, The Priests and The Irish Tenors, performing a mixture of classical and traditional songs.

Ulster Orchestra.

WHERE TO FIND THE BEST MUSIC FESTIVALS

The **West Cork Chamber Music Festival** (June–early July), epitomises the specialist music festival: a beautiful location – Bantry House, overlooking Bantry Bay – and an intensive programme of international stars performing highlights from the chamber repertoire, public master classes, and a Young Musicians platform. The day starts at 10am with a Morning Talk and ends with a Late Great Show at 10.30pm, with four concerts in between, and events featuring young musicians. www.westcorkmusic.ie. Opera lovers in evening dress enjoy full-scale performances in late October at the **Wexford Festival Opera** in Ireland's National Opera House. Three operas from the lesser known repertoire

feature every year, alongside a programme of recitals and orchestral concerts. www.wexfordopera.com.

The **Shannon International Music Festival** (January) showcases the Irish Chamber Orchestra and guests – some from the world of jazz – with 11 concerts in five days in Limerick. www.irishchamberorchestra.info.

East Cork Early Music Festival (Autumn) uses historic local landmarks as venues for small ensembles, including Cloyne Cathedral, Ballymaloe House and the Palladian masterpiece, Fota House. www.eastcorkearlymusic.ie.

The **Sligo Baroque Music Festival** (Autumn) takes place in the Model over four days of concerts, workshops and talks. www.sligobaroquefestival.com.

THE IRISH WAY WITH WORDS

Whether in the theatre, the street, in parliament or even the pub, the Irish are renowned for having the true gift of the gab.

Mary Donnegan, a traditional Irish storyteller from Donegal, photographed in 1947.

The Irish love telling stories, and many of them are very good at it – that's one of the reasons Irish writers are so popular all over the world and why an evening in a Dublin pub can be vastly entertaining.

Before the population of the country could express itself on paper, travelling storytellers – *seannachie* (pronounced 'shan-ah-key') – entertained and informed; their stock-in-trade included discursiveness, allusiveness, hyperbole and lots of high spirits. That tradition lives on today in the popularity of Irish stand-up comedians and broadcasters in the UK and abroad.

> *Before the days of mass literacy, professional storytellers called seanachies (pronounced 'shan-ah-keys') travelled from house to house to entertain around the fire. The tradition is sometimes revived in today's pubs.*

Writing in Irish

For centuries the Irish language survived despite invasions by the Vikings and Normans, and the arrival of English and Scottish planters. It was not until the mid-19th century that its use began to decline, to be replaced by English. This was due to the introduction of the National School system in 1831 and the effects of the 1845–49 Great Famine and the mass emigration that followed. The erosion was dramatic: in 1835 there were an estimated 4 million Irish speakers, but by 1891 the number had tumbled to 680,200.

As Ireland established its independence in the 20th century, interest in the native language increased, though its everyday use was confined mainly to the Gaeltacht areas along the western seaboard. Some writers produce work in both languages, slipping easily from one to the other.

Yet how English is spoken and written in Ireland differs greatly from how it is used elsewhere. Here it is less precise and concrete, much more lyrical, often using phrases directly translated from Irish. The almost physical delight in words seems to spring from a sharpened sensitivity to a language that has never been entirely adopted.

The Irish love of language

If you travel on public transport in Ireland, you will see how much its people enjoy reading. If you get to know Irish people, you will be surprised to learn just how many of them write poetry or try their hand at prose. These literary inclinations probably explain why, although successful writers are admired, their fellow countrymen are not over-awed by them.

Public readings of poetry and prose are relaxed, enjoyable occasions where all are welcome. Writing competitions and festivals are hugely popular, many of them offering workshops with experienced writers, which are often over-subscribed. The Arts Councils on both sides of the border encourage writing by giving financial assistance.

Learning about writers

There are lots of places to visit where you can learn more about writers. They include the Irish Writers' Centre and the Dublin Writers' Museum next door to each other on Parnell Square in Dublin (see page 132). In the Munster Literature Centre in Cork, visitors can discover short story writers Frank O'Connor and Seán Ó Faoláin, among others. The Seanchaí - Kerry Literary & Cultural Centre in Listowel, focuses on writers from that area, including the late John B. Keane, whose plays are hugely popular. The Verbal Arts Centre

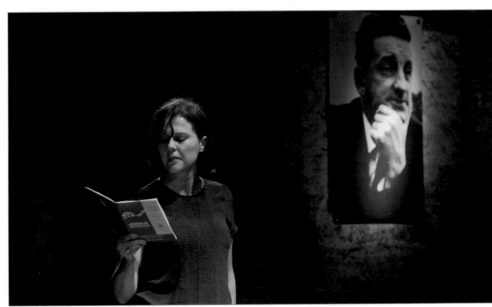

Listowel Writers' Week is an internationally acclaimed literary festival.

IRELAND'S BEST LITERARY FESTIVALS

Dublin Writers Festival is a four-day event featuring 30 of the world's most celebrated poets and fiction writers, coinciding with 16 June, Bloomsday, which commemorates James Joyce's Ulysses. www.dublinwritersfestival.com.

Galway's Cúirt International Festival of Literature is a big event in a small, festival-friendly town, held over six days in late April. Past visitors include Nobel Prize winners J.M. Coetzee, Nadine Gordimer, Derek Walcott and Seamus Heaney. It's a convivial event, with masterclasses, launches, theatre performances, readings and debates. www.cuirt.ie.

Listowel Writers' Week is held in June in a north

Kerry town that prides itself on its literary connections, including the late John B. Keane (The Field). Events include writing competitions. www.writersweek.ie.

West Cork Literary Festival in Bantry has free lunchtime readings from writers, many who also offer afternoon masterclasses. It attracts some big names and an enthusiastic audience who enjoy the informal contact. Many people stay for all six days. www.westcorkmusic.ie/literaryfestival.

Immrama, a mid-June weekend of literary events organised around a travel writing theme, is held in Lismore in west Waterford, the home of travel writer Dervla Murphy. www.lismoreimmrama.com.

in Derry and the Creative Writers' Network, based in Belfast, both organise readings and workshops. Events featuring writers also take place in libraries, bookshops and arts centres all over the country – look out for posters or call in and ask.

It is often difficult to categorise Irish writers, as many work across various genres – poetry, novels, short stories, stage plays and screenplays.

Notable writers of the past

Jonathan Swift, satirist and author of Gulliver's Travels, playwright Richard Brinsley Sheridan

Dublin Writers' Museum.

and poet and dramatist Oscar Wilde are among Ireland's writers whose works continue to be enjoyed all over the world.

John Millington Synge (1871–1909) used his knowledge of Irish to transform theatrical language in works including The Playboy of the Western World (1907), which caused a riot when first performed at the Abbey Theatre for its raw depiction of peasant life.

James Joyce rewrote the rules of prose with *Ulysses* (1922), a portrait of a day in the lives of three Dubliners. Bloomsday (16 June) is an annual celebration of this towering literary achievement. (see page 140).

Contemporary writers

A ruthlessly selective list would include:

Michael Davitt (1950–2005) attended university in Cork, where his lecturers included two Irish language poets – Seán Ó Tuama and Seán Ó Ríordáin. He founded the poetry magazine *Innti* in 1970 and is credited, along with Nuala Ní Dhomhnaill, Liam Ó Muirthile and Gabriel Rosenstock, with much of the continuing interest today in poetry written in Irish.

John McGahern (1934–2006) wrote about a society moving from insular repression in his early work towards self-confidence and freedom in his final novels, Amongst Women (1990) and That They May Face the Rising Sun (2001). His second novel, The Dark (1965), was banned by Ireland's censors. Its content led to dismissal from his teaching job, and the resulting isolation touched his writing.

IRISH WINNERS OF THE NOBEL PRIZE FOR LITERATURE

George Bernard Shaw (1856–1950) spent most of his life in England. He wrote over 50 plays and revolutionised the theatre with dramas about ideas and issues. Works include *Man and Superman, Saint Joan* and *Pygmalion*, which inspired the film *My Fair Lady*.
W.B. Yeats (1865–1939), a hugely influential poet and dramatist, was a founder of the Abbey Theatre in Dublin. His plays are rarely performed today, but he is considered one of the most influential poets of the 20th century. Although patriotic, he hated the bigotry of the nationalist movement, reflected in some of his best-known poems.
Samuel Beckett (1906–89) spent most of his life in

Paris where, during World War II, he worked with the French Resistance. He wrote mostly in French and then translated into English. His best-known play, *Waiting for Godot*, was first produced in 1953.
Seamus Heaney (1939–2013) was born in Co. Derry; his early works combine personal memories with images of Irish heritage and landscape. His collections *North* (1975) and *Field Work* (1979) explore the political situation, while later works, including *Station Island* (1984) and *Seeing Things* (1991) convey an individualistic and meditative mood. As a translator, his work includes *Sweeney Astray* (1983) from a medieval poem in Irish, and the Anglo-Saxon poem *Beowulf* (1999).

Brian Friel (1929–2015) is one of Ireland's most important playwrights. Born in Omagh, Co. Tyrone, some of his writing is influenced by the political situation in Northern Ireland. His most successful play is *Dancing at Lughnasa* (1990), which won three Tony Awards on Broadway. Among his other works are *Philadelphia, Here I Come!* (1964), Lovers (1967), and *Translations* (1980).

Paul Durcan (b. 1944) is a satirical and idiosyncratic poet. He is often compared to the poet and novelist Patrick Kavanagh (1904–67), who also attacked Irish society.

(2007) draws on some of the same characters, and Ghost Light (2010) completes the trilogy.

Martin McDonagh (b. 1970) was born in London to parents from the West of Ireland, where he spent many holidays. His plays are black comedies, written in a language much influenced by Hiberno-English. *The Beauty Queen of Leenane* (1996) won four Tony Awards on Broadway. His debut feature film, the darkly humorous *In Bruges* (2008) was nominated for an Academy Award.

The tradition of short-story writing has been carried on by Edna O'Brien, William

Roddy Doyle.

Claire Keegan.

Roddy Doyle (b. 1958) is best known for his Barrytown trilogy, a highly comic portrayal of contemporary working-class life in Dublin. His debut novel *The Commitments* (1987) was made into a highly successful film. He won the Man Booker Prize in 1993 for *Paddy Clarke Ha Ha Ha*. In *The Dead Republic* (2010) he completes a picaresque trilogy through 20th-century Irish history.

Joseph O'Connor (b. 1963, brother of singer Sinéad) has written seven novels, and is popular on the middlebrow Irish literary scene. He was first known for his witty newspaper articles, and gained international recognition with Star of the Sea (2002), which focused on the Great Famine and emigration. *Redemption Falls*

Trevor and Colm Toibin. A younger generation led by Claire Keegan (b. 1968), Nuala Ní Chonchúir (b. 1972) and Kevin Barry (b. 1969) is making its distinctive voice heard.

Popular fiction

Maeve Binchy (1940-2012), a former journalist with *The Irish Times*, was one of Ireland's best-loved writers both at home and abroad. Her sense of humour always shone through her writing. Among her bestselling books are, *Circle of Friends* (1990) and *Light a Penny Candle* (1982).

Other notable contemporary writers of popular fiction include the often amusing Marian Keyes, Cathy Kelly, Sheila O'Flanagan and romance writer Cecilia Ahern.

ARTS FESTIVALS

The economic boom has not only given Ireland traffic jams and housing estates. The new wealth has also led to a boom in the arts.

The Irish have an international reputation as entertainers. But the visual artists, musicians, dancers and actors who once had to emigrate to find work now have jobs at home in these better economic times. Most Irish towns have a busy multi-purpose arts centre with exhibition spaces and auditorium.

Participating in cultural activities is one of the most popular pastimes for visitors to Ireland, and this has led to an explosion in the number of arts festivals taking place around the country, livening things up for residents as well. The concept of 'the arts' involved is the broadest possible one, with comedy, cabaret, street performers and rock gigs sharing the programme with more conventional theatre, dance, classical music and readings.

Film and theatre

Autumn and winter are the time for film festivals – in Cork, Dublin and Belfast – and theatre festivals. In a country that loves to party, arts festivals are easy-going, unstuffy affairs, with many events held in pubs. The big summertime arts festivals – the Cork Midsummer Festival (June), the Galway International Arts Week (July) and the Kilkenny Arts Festival (August) – co-exist with lively festivals in smaller towns that present ambitious multidisciplinary programmes of theatre, music, cabaret, comedy, street entertainment, children's workshops and visual art. The talent might be mainly local, or you might be surprised by a big international name. While the main events will usually have modest ticket prices, all arts festivals generate free entertainment, and an unforgettable party atmosphere – which also makes them great places to meet people.

Overseas visitors (especially Americans) throng the streets of Dublin on 17 March, many of them taking part in the city's massive St Patrick's Day parade. The St Patrick's Festival provides a full week of carnival, music and street theatre, but its highlight is still the traditional parade through the city centre.

The popular resort of Kinsale, south of Cork city, makes the most of its magnificent harbour during Arts Festival in early July. Concerts in unusual venues are a strong point of the 10-day festival.

Féile na Bealtaine celebrates the arrival of Summer with a music and arts festival in Dingle.

Fireworks at Galway International Arts Festival every July.

GALWAY: FESTIVAL CITY

Galway is the closest Ireland gets to a city that never sleeps: its compact centre and lively pub scene make it an ideal festival venue. Its festival calendar is a challenging test of stamina: late April heralds the Cúirt Literature Festival, five days of readings from Irish and international authors. If you think literary festivals are quiet, polite occasions, Galway will change your mind. July is the year's highlight, with the six-day-long Galway Film Fleadh (over 70 Irish and international features, with master classes, seminars and more) leading up to a 10-day extravaganza, Galway International Arts Week, the biggest such event in Ireland with hundreds of events taking place day and night. Does Galway then take a quiet break and catch its collective breath? Not on your life: it's straight off to the Galway Races Festival, which brings the city and its ring road to a standstill, so that the preferred way to travel to the race course is by helicopter. Some 48,000 revellers attend Ladies' Day. The merry-makers assemble again in late September for the Galway International Oyster Festival. Then, in order to get the younger generation into training, mid-October sees the week-long Báboro, Ireland's first arts festival purely for children.

An "urban Glastonbury", the high-spirited Beatyard transforms the Co. Dublin seaside town of Dun Laoghaire for the last weekend in July. Science, music, games, discussion, sports, arts and design.

Street performers at Dublin's New Year Festival.

Earagail Arts Festival is a bilingual music and arts festival that takes place throughout Co. Donegal every July.

CONTEMPORARY ART

Ireland's ancient tradition of visual art was neglected in the 20th century, but a new generation of painters and sculptors has been making an impact.

Ireland's artistic reputation rests largely on the genius of its writers, but from the late 20th century, the visual arts flourished with Irish artists fetching unusually high prices at auction. Irish Art auctions were held regularly in London, New York and Dublin. Sotheby's Irish Art Sale began in 1995; its 2015 auction made sales of £1,831,375. Early 20th-century artists John Lavery, Roderic O'Conor, Jack B. Yeats, William Orpen and Paul Henry all command high prices. Orpen's *Portrait of Gardenia St George, sold for* £1,985,500 at Sotheby's in 2001 and, is the most expensive Irish painting ever to sell at auction (bar the works of Francis Bacon, whose 1969 Triptych of Lucien Freud fetched $142.2m at Sotheby's New York in 2013). With the economic downturn, prices fell, but have since started to recover. Irish painting, especially landscapes, continue to be sought after by collectors worldwide.

These artists are being joined by the next generation, born pre-1930, including Belfast's Gerard Dillon, Dublin's Patrick Collins, Louis Le Brocquy and Cork-born Patrick Scott. Galleries showing contemporary art are thriving in Dublin and Belfast, and younger artists are encouraged by both the Arts Council in Dublin, and the Arts Council of Northern Ireland. Irish art colleges are over-subscribed, with the University of Ulster at Coleraine having a particularly high reputation for post-graduate work in contemporary art. Irish artists Sean Scully and Felim Egan have gained international reputations as abstract artists.

Ancient inspiration

There has of course always been visual art in Ireland, from the spirals, loops and geometric forms of the Stone Age passage and burial graves at Newgrange and Knowth, to the La Tène period of

Louis Le Brocquy's James Joyce, Study 64 (1977), from the Irish Museum of Modern Art.

Celtic art, which arrived from continental Europe around 500 BC. After the arrival of Christianity, artists and craft workers continued to enjoy the Celtic artists' privileged position in society, producing elaborately bejewelled chalices and shrines, as well as manuscript illumination.

The latter led to some of the greatest achievements of Celtic art in works such as the *Book of Durrow* and the *Book of Kells*, whose intricate ornamentation and seemingly endless inventiveness can still take your breath away.

Stone crosses and ornamental metalwork are the only artefacts to survive successive waves of invasions, civil wars and general upheaval which began with the Vikings in the 9th century and lasted well into the 17th century. While the prosperity of the 18th century produced some of Ireland's greatest architecture, it was influenced more by English and continental traditions than indigenous ones. The Royal

> *Many Irish artists live in scenic areas where property prices are still reasonable, and have revitalised hitherto underpopulated areas: Counties Leitrim, Roscommon, Mayo, Sligo, Clare, Kerry and west Cork in particular.*

Hibernian Academy (RHA) was established in Dublin in 1823, in the tradition of its London counterpart. Many Irish artists emigrated to London, and had a significant impact on English art – for example, James Barry (1741–1806), Daniel Maclise (1806–70), Francis Danby (1793–1861) and sculptors such as John Henry Foley (1818–74) and John Lawlor (1820–1901), who worked on London's Albert Memorial.

The Celtic Revival

The Celtic Revival (c.1880–1930), with its use of the Celtic motifs from illuminated

Barrie Cooke's Megaceros Hibernicus (1983), from the Irish Museum of Modern Art.

CONTEMPORARY ARTISTS TO WATCH OUT FOR

Basil Blackshaw: Northern Ireland artist known for his depiction of horses and dogs, and latterly barns, in sketch-like paintings that capture the essence.

Barrie Cooke: American-born and educated in England, Cooke lived in rural Ireland since the 1950s Recent work depicts water pollution in lakes near his Sligo home.

Dorothy Cross: works mainly in three dimensions, sometimes in video and performance, and famously created a real "ghost ship" in Dublin Bay.

Martin Gale: paints eerie super-realist landscapes that mirror the changes taking place in rural Ireland.

Brian O'Doherty: New York-based Irish-born conceptual artist and critic, formerly known as Patrick Ireland.

Clare Langan: artist and cinematographer whose spectacular video work offers visions of a future in which civilization has been overwhelmed by nature.

Connolly Cleary: a Paris-based couple trained in architecture, producing interactive video art.

Anne Madden: paints on a massive scale, usually abstracts inspired by landscape or mythology.

Vivienne Roche: sculptor working on a large scale, often in welded steel, whose austerely beautiful work uses motifs from Viking and early Christian Ireland.

Sean Scully: New York-based, Dublin-born painter whose cool, almost monotone abstracts originate in his study of the stone walls of the west of Ireland.

manuscripts, metalwork and monastic architecture, was an Irish version of the Arts and Crafts Movement, closely allied to the movement for Irish independence. The Honan Chapel at University College Cork is a prime example of this style.

Impressionism began to influence Irish art around the turn of the century, with the work of Nathaniel Hone, John Butler Yeats, John Lavery, Sarah Purser, Walter Osborne, William Orpen and, most importantly, Roderic O'Conor. Jack B. Yeats (1871–1957), brother of the poet W.B. Yeats, stood head and shoulders above his con-

Alice Maher's Berry Dress (1994), made from rosehips, cotton, paint and sewing pins, part of the collection of the Irish Museum of Modern Art.

temporaries, and led the way in his adoption of Irish subject matter, favouring outdoor scenes of his native Sligo, circuses and horse races.

The best-known artist of the time was Paul Henry (1876-1958) who had studied at Whistler's studio in Paris before settling on Achill Island to paint archetypal images of the west of Ireland landscape, cottages set against monumental hillsides and tumbling grey skies, that were used as posters to advertise travel to Ireland. Events of the Civil War and the establishment of the Irish Free State were captured in a series of historical paintings by Sean Keating (1889–1997), and social realism

became the dominant style, espoused by the academic tradition.

Art ignored

Economic conditions, Ireland's cultural isolation during World War II and the dominant ethos of Catholic conservatism did not add up to a favourable climate for artistic activity in the mid-20th century. Stained-glass artists were among the few to flourish, including the Harry Clarke Studios, whose work can be seen in Dublin City Gallery - The Hugh Lane. It was hard to make a living in a country where art was not taught in most schools, and art colleges did not award degrees. This is the era that has given rise to the belief that Ireland has no visual art tradition.

However, the first public gallery in the British Isles devoted to contemporary art was Dublin City Gallery – The Hugh Lane, established in 1908. Its collection of Irish and European late 19th- and early 20th-century art was an inspiration to many Dublin artists. Inspired by what they had seen, Louis Le Brocquy, Norah McGuinness, Evie Hone, Mainie Jellett and others travelled abroad and experimented with Cubism, Futurism and Dada, returning home to lead the modern movement in Irish painting. In 1943 they founded the Irish Exhibition of Living Art as a *salon de refusés* for those whose work was consistently refused by the annual exhibition of the Royal Hibernian Academy. This evolved into an annual show called The Living Art exhibition, which became a forum for artists whose influences were derived from the international language of visual art: Patrick Scott, Patrick Collins, Gerard Dillon, Nano Reid, Barrie Cooke, Cecil King and Tony O'Malley. Living Art also embraced video and performance art, and persisted into the 1980s.

The Irish Museum of Modern Art (IMMA) opened in 1991, but meanwhile the creation of an improved infrastructure for the arts, the establishment of tax exemption for artists in 1969 and the introduction in 1981 of the island-wide Aosdána scheme did much to improve working conditions for artists. There was an unprecedented growth in venues, subsidised exhibition spaces and commercial galleries during the boom years, both in Dublin, Belfast and the provinces, and a corresponding upsurge in artistic activity. Many artists, such as the Manchester-born Hughie O'Donoghue, returned from long or short stays abroad and set up studios in Ireland, some combining their artistic practice with teaching and lecturing.

International taste

Many of the younger generation of artists – Clare Langan, Linda Quinlan and Amanda Coogan, for example, working respectively in video, installation art and performance – produce work that is indistinguishable from their contemporaries in London, Paris or New York. Others continue to be inspired by landscape, even though their work may use forms belonging to the

international contemporary art scene. Examples include Sarah Walker's coolly modernist wild flower grids, Charles Tyrrell's rigorous abstracts and Gary Coyle's dramatic photographs of Dublin Bay from a swimmer's perspective.

There are many less ambitious contemporary artists who continue to work in the old tradition, producing attractive landscapes and easy-to-live-with genre scenes of Irish life, whose work can also be found in contemporary galleries. With prices starting from around €200 for a landscape by an up-and-coming artist, it could well be worth making an investment.

Void Contemporary Art Space, Derry.

HOW IRELAND REWARDS CREATIVITY

Aosdána, an association of writers and artists, was set up in 1981 by the Taoiseach, Charles J. Haughey (1926–2006), who as Finance Minister in 1969 had introduced a tax exemption for writers and artists. Both initiatives were intended to lure home Irish artists living abroad. Haughey's cultural advisor, the poet Anthony Cronin, inspired by the Celtic respect for the *aes dána* – the men of talent – drew up the plan.

Membership, limited to 250 people, includes most of Ireland's artistic elite: Sean Scully is in, but John Banville opted out. It was intended as recognition of artistic achievement. But to ensure that a new generation did not suffer the poverty of their predecessors, membership

also awards an optional annuity of €17,180 to those earning under €25,000 annually. Thus, enabling members to work full time on creative projects.

The assembly meets once a year to elect new members, and debate resolutions, many concerning its own workings. It was originally limited to writers, composers or visual artists; architects and choreographers are now eligible, but not performing artists. Aosdána receives government funding of €2.7m annually – a fraction of the €72m arts budget. But in a nation famous for 'begrudgery', many consider this amount excessive, and Aosdána remains controversial. www.aosdana.artscouncil.ie.

FOOD

Despite an abundance of fresh ingredients, the Irish have never shown much interest in haute cuisine. Until recently...

Ireland has long been promoted as 'Ireland, The Food Island', an ingenious marketing slogan invented by Bord Bia (The Irish Food Board). Despite the recent cycle of economic boom and bust, Ireland remains an agricultural country that produces far more food than it can eat. Its grass-fed beef and lamb produce superb meat and dairy produce and speciality foods including a completely unique range of farmhouse cheeses that are exported throughout the world. Stand in any fishing port and see how foreign fish merchants covet the fresh seafood caught in the country's clean Atlantic waters.

Ireland is clean, green and fertile – a moist, temperate climate and the benign influence of the Gulf Stream deflect the cold temperatures of Northern Europe. Tourism is equally important, so there is a sophisticated hospitality industry.

> Many country house restaurants use produce from their own farms and gardens, rivers and game shoots. It's part of the fun to inspect the estate or the kitchen garden before dinner and guess what will be on the menu.

Eating out

Ireland is not a low-cost destination. However, if good food is what you seek there is value for money to be had at all levels – if you know where to find it. The best value (as opposed to the cheapest) is offered on 'Early Bird' or 'today's market' dinner menus, fixed price two- or three-course menus, and (the Irish way to experience a meal in leading fine-dining restaurants without blowing your budget) at lunchtime.

Tempting baked goods testify to the increased demand for artisan foods.

The pursuit of individualism is strong in Ireland. This can make it difficult for visitors to tell whether an establishment offers formal/fine dining with set four or five course menus (with a price tag to match), or casual/informal food where you can order as much or as little as you like. You'll come across restaurants, bistros, brasseries, café/bars, wine/café bars, or just plain cafés, pub/restaurants, pubs with bar food, pub carveries and seafood bars. The only sure way to distinguish between the first three is to inspect the prices on the menu, which must, by law, be displayed outside.

Café/bars and wine bars usually offer informal meals where you can order as much or little as you wish; you rarely need to make a reservation. Some cafés are quite expensive, restaurants in all but name; most offer an all-day menu and (sometimes) a lunch menu.

Dining in pubs

Pubs vary even more widely – some have restaurants with full lunch and dinner menus. Others offer 'bar food' – a proper lunch and dinner menu with table service in some cases, and self-service in others. Many pubs advertise a 'carvery' lunch, a self-service meal featuring at least one joint of meat, carved to order, and

restaurants concentrate on weekends and close for a couple of months in mid-winter.

Contemporary Irish cooking

A distinctive style of Irish cooking has emerged over the past 20 years. A new generation of serious chefs take pride in using indigenous foods and, supported by a growing number of artisan food producers making authentic foods using traditional methods, re-explore traditional Irish recipes and dishes. What has emerged is a lighter, modern style, innovative spin on traditional dishes but

Fresh seafood is one of Ireland's specialities.

other pre-cooked options, filling and inexpensive but unlikely to be a culinary highlight. The best option is seafood (oysters, prawns, crab or mussels) at one of the coastal pubs offering freshly landed catch.

Hotels and restaurants

If eating in a hotel restaurant seems a last resort, think again. As a result of intense competition, most four- and five-star Irish hotels place a great emphasis on dining and employ top chefs. Many have two restaurants, one fine-dining and another informal. Most are open daily – useful to know as many Irish restaurants close after Sunday lunch and do not open for dinner on Sunday or Monday nights. In tourist areas some

WHAT IS EURO-TOQUES?

A sign to look out for is Euro-Toques (the European Communion of Chefs; www.euro-toques.ie), a pan-European organisation with 3,500 members. Euro-Toques has more than 200 members in Ireland and has been influential in the creation of unique contemporary Irish cooking. All Euro-Toques support sourcing top-quality, non-GM, local and seasonal food and deliver dishes of flavour and authenticity. They aim to protect the quality, diversity and flavour of regional food and promote indigenous production methods. Their support in buying artisan food products has re-awakened consumer appreciation and helped young artisan food producers.

firmly based on Irish foods and themes. Leading chefs take enormous care to source Irish ingredients, wild or farmed using traditional methods, and support the ever-growing number of artisan food producers.

Irish chefs continue to be trained in the classic tradition. Most go abroad for a few years for experience and bring back culinary influences from their travels and give them an Irish twist; the most ambitious compete to work under influential Irish chefs so the modern approach is not just confined to fine-dining establishments but can be found in many places.

Talented young chefs have the confidence to open their own restaurants not just in Dublin and other cities but in provincial towns, villages and sometimes deep in rural Ireland.

In many fine-dining restaurants modern Irish cooking allows a natural mingling of traditional Irish produce with an innovative approach to the cooking and presentation of long-established Irish dishes. The result is a contemporary Irish cuisine that is 'entirely itself', an idiomatic expression. The good thing is that this approach to cooking is not confined to formal fine-dining restaurants but

Temple Bar Food Market, Dublin.

THE BEST PLACE TO SAMPLE MODERN IRISH CUISINE

Thornton's, Dublin. Base for superstar chef Kevin Thornton. Creative haute cuisine in an elegant venue.

Cliff Townhouse, Dublin, and **The House Restaurant,** Cliff House Hotel, Ardmore, Co. Waterford. Experimental chef Martijn Kajuiter's twin ventures are the most exciting places to eat in Ireland.

The Tannery, Dungarvan, Co. Waterford. Flamboyant owner-chef Paul Flynn applies foodie trends to well-sourced Irish produce in an attractive warehouse space.

Ballymaloe House, Shanagarry, Co. Cork. Ireland's most famous country house hotel pioneered the use of fresh local produce. Book for Sunday buffet lunch.

Gregans Castle, Ballyvaughan, Co. Clare. Discreet, understated Georgian country mansion overlooking Galway Bay with an outstanding chef.

La Fougère, Knockranny House Hotel, Westport, Co. Mayo. Seamus Commons, probably the best chef in Ireland, presides over this spacious, relaxed hotel restaurant with great views.

McNean House and Restaurant, Blacklion, Co. Cavan. Successful TV series and cookbooks have not distracted young Neven Maguire from his main job as chef in his family's business. Worth the detour.

Deanes Restaurant, Belfast. Chef Michael Deane combines sophistication with modernism.

can be on offer in establishments all over the country (see page 83).

Ethnic restaurants

The Irish have multicultural tastes. Thriving ethnic restaurants are plentiful. Immigration during the boom years has increased their numbers and diversity. Once you might have been lucky to find French, Italian, Chinese or Indian restaurants; now you can choose from a far wider range of ethnic restaurants: Nepalese, Japanese, Vietnamese, Indonesian, Belgian, Breton, Polish and Thai, as well as Indian and Chinese offering authentic regional cuisine. A particular trend has been the huge growth in informal restaurant/café/wine bars offering Spanish tapas, or using the tapas principle to showcase Irish artisan foods including farmhouse cheeses, black pudding, smoked chicken and locally produced charcuterie, which has flourished following immigration from Eastern Europe.

Irish country house cooking

Some of the best dining can be experienced in Irish country houses, almost all located in rural areas. At the top end the facilities are on a par with four- or even five-star hotels, with restaurants and dining experiences to match. Most (although not all) at this level offer modern Irish cooking and menus, tend to be open to non-residents and often attract a loyal local following as well as tourists staying in self-catering accommodation. Other smaller country houses do not employ a large team of chefs. In these the cooking style and presentation is simpler, menus shorter, and feature traditional (even regional) dishes that place an emphasis on allowing natural flavours of carefully sourced local and seasonal foods to shine through.

Farm to fork

The Irish place high value on knowing where food comes from – the entire route from farm to fork – and, by and large, they want it to be from an Irish farm. To satisfy consumer demand, the name of a product, its producer or the locality in which it was produced, is often incorporated into a dish's menu description. There are a growing number of artisan producers offering traditional and speciality foods. The demand for organic food has grown too and is used as a selling point in many restaurants.

Féile Bia

'Bia' is the Irish word for food and the word 'Féile' means a festival or celebration. The thrust of this voluntary programme run by Bord Bia (The Irish Food Board) is for restaurants to source fresh, authentic Irish food. Members are required to provide information to customers about how the food they serve is produced and where it comes from; they must source meat, poultry and eggs from approved quality-assurance schemes. There are 1,450 Féile Bia members in Ireland. Some top restaurants are not members as they source their foods from unique, organic producers.

Chef at work at Balloo House.

FARMERS' MARKETS

A visit to a farmers' market is a must. Look out for farmhouse cheeses (each unique to the farm and the cheesemaker), cured, smoked, spiced and air-dried meats, dry-cured bacon, black and white puddings, speciality sausages and pâtés, fish and shellfish, mountain lamb, wild game, home-grown fruit and berries, traditional breads and baking, jams, chutneys and sauces. For information on local markets, go to www.bordbia.ie/aboutfood/farmersmarkets.Country markets – smaller affairs held weekly in nearly 60 locations by a long-established cooperative – specialise in home baking and local produce.

PUBS

The counterfeit Irish pub has conquered the world. But the authentic pubs in Ireland, whose most intoxicating product used to be talk, are struggling to come to terms with a changed society.

Dublin's hostelries – there are about 800 of them – are a mix of the very old and the very new. Some are vast drinking emporiums offering live sport on huge screens and palatable food to more than 1,000 people; others are spit-and-sawdust drinking dens. It's the characterful old-school watering-holes that are worth visiting: O'Donoghue's, The Palace Bar, Mulligan's, the Stag's Head, the International and M.J. O'Neill's – to name but a few.

These classic Dublin bars are peopled with wisecracking philosophers sharing their observations with anyone who'll listen – or buy them a drink. Old wooden bars, with creamy pints of stout, remain untouched by the hand of the modernisers. They have a well-lived-in and well-drunk-in look and feel, decked out in brass and mahogany, with antique mirrors proclaiming the merits of whiskies long since defunct. Some such pubs look much as they did in 1850.

One hundred miles (160km) to the north, Belfast is also richly endowed with pubs. A rash of bars such as the Apartment, Café Vaudeville, 21 Social, and the Cloth Ear are the contemporary, cool venues. But the most-visited remains the iconic Crown Liquor Saloon, owned by the National Trust, with its wood-panelled snugs, gaslights, ornate tiles, woodcarvings and brasswork. Other venerable venues include White's Tavern, the Duke of York, Kelly's Cellars, the Garrick, the Morning Star, Bittles Bar, Madden's or the John Hewitt, named after a local poet.

The drinking culture

A recent European Union survey showed that Ireland has the highest proportion of binge drinkers in any European country. Just over a third of people living in Ireland were reported to consume on average five or more units of

Perfect pints of "the black stuff".

alcohol in a single sitting – more than three times the EU average. And four out of five drinks are consumed in bars rather than at home, compared to only one in three in Germany, confirming the image of the Irish as an incorrigibly gregarious people.

Despite this, economists have long been predicting the downfall of the Irish pub, and many smaller rural pubs have indeed been forced out of business. But the country still supports about 9,000 pubs (7,500 in the Republic; 1,500 in Northern Ireland), and the rural pubs that *have* survived remain the epicentre of small towns where the community still comes together for its social and neighbourhood business. The paint may be peeling in some, but traditionally, they have been places where people meet, not just to drink and hold parties or wakes, but to gossip, talk football, solve the world's political problems, try to pick a winner in the 2.30 Leopardstown race meeting, tell tall tales or simply *céilí* the night away.

These traditions survive. From the regular sessions of the *seanchaí* (storyteller) in the Red House in Lismore, west Waterford, to Osbourne's pub in Clongeall, south Carlow; from O'Loclainn's in Ballyvaughan, Co. Clare, to Kate Lavin's in Boyle, Co. Roscommon; and from Blakes of the Hollow in Enniskillen, Co. Fermanagh, to the pub from Father Ted Vaughan's in Kilfenora, the customs and atmosphere – like the best whiskey – remain undiluted.

Many bars – especially the part-grocery/part-pub ones – are family-owned and can trace their longevity back several generations, although only about 200 pubs have been in one family for at least 100 years. Some commentators have pointed out that if such a lack of stability of ownership were to be found in farming, it would be declared a national scandal. Fortunately the days of the characterful country pubs with a thatched

Out drinking in Ireland.

HOW THE SMOKING BAN MADE AN IMPACT

The sight of smokers huddled up outside the doorways of pubs has become common all over the Republic of Ireland since 2004. (Northern Ireland bars went smoke-free in 2007). Ireland was the world's first nation to introduce a smoking ban in pubs and many predicted ruin for one of the most convivial of meeting places.

There were a few acts of defiance against the ban, but the law, like a decent pint of Guinness, eventually settled down. Pubs in rural Ireland continued to close at the rate of one a day, but the smoking ban did not play a significant part in their demise – the trigger was the same social upheaval that was forcing the closure of village shops and post offices in remote areas.

The drink-driving laws have also hit hard. The traditional tolerance for the jovial drunk eroded as the number of young people killed or injured in early-morning road accidents at the weekends spiralled to alarming numbers. The police took a strong stand by introducing random breath testing of motorists, and some publicans, conscious of the lack of public transport in outlying areas, turned themselves into taxi drivers, transporting customers home in a courtesy minibus. If any one thing symbolises Ireland's embrace of modern European values, this behavioural change may be it.

roof and turf fire have still not disappeared, although many don't open until early evening as there are fewer daytime customers.

Traditional music

Informal traditional music sessions or set dancing have great appeal, though performance times can be erratic and the entertainment may not start before 10pm. Most sessions are held indoors but during a *fleadh cheoil* (music festival) when thousands flock into towns, the performers spill out on to the pavement and music flows down the streets.

Generally, music sessions fall into two categories. Some bars hold set-piece evenings that are turned on like a tap for the tourists; these occur regularly and are premeditated with a practised set list. Others are spontaneous where the players drop in for an unplanned evening and the result is a happy meeting of musical minds. The quality of the playing in both is equally good, but the impromptu session often has the edge because the unexpected may happen.

The informal nature of it means that it's open to all-comers to strut their musical stuff whether playing, singing or dancing.

A music session in Co. Offaly.

SIX BARS WORTH TOASTING

Tigh Neachtain, Cross Street, Galway. A popular city centre bar with old-fashioned painted wooden interior and features. The building dates back to medieval times and the tiny snugs are more than 100 years old. There's an open fire in the back room and music.

Morrissey's, Main Street, Abbeyleix, Co. Laois. Opened as a grocery in 1775 and now solely a pub, it has the air of a venerable institution. It has dark walls, a pot-belly stove and rules forbidding cards, TV and singing.

Shoot the Crows, Market Cross, Grattan Street, Sligo. Opened in 1876, this long, narrow pub has retained its original wooden interior. Good music on Wednesday nights.

P.J. O'Hare's Anchor Bar, Carlingford, Co. Louth. P.J.'s has been in the family for 150 years and is decorated with pub mirrors and curios. On sunny Sunday afternoons the yard becomes a dance area.

Anderson's Thatch Pub, Elphin Road, Carrick-on-Shannon, Co. Leitrim. This inviting roadside pub dates back to 1760. The owner, who plays 11 instruments, holds music sessions on Wednesdays and Saturdays.

Nancy's, Front Street, Ardara, Co. Donegal. This tiny hospitable bar is now in the seventh generation of family ownership. Seafood, especially the chowder, is a speciality. Traditional music is played.

Often these sessions are the ones that will be imprinted in visitors' minds. The memory of the haunting *Nancy Spain*, the well-worn words of *The Wild Rover* or *Whiskey in the Jar* and the intoxicating talk will all remain long after the recollection of a visit to a spanking new interpretative centre has faded to oblivion.

In some parts of the country, old customs live on; search hard and you will find in Cork city a few 'early houses' – pubs that open their doors at 7am to cater for night-shift workers including dockers and bakers, or those in search of 'the cure' (a remedy for the morning-after hangover). On

If the pint isn't good, it is sent straight back. Experts (which is to say anyone who drinks the stuff) embark on long discussions on the pint's quality in different bars throughout the country. The visitor's best criterion is this: if the place is crowded with locals, then the pint is probably good. And you'll know a good pint when you get one. It won't taste like what passes for Guinness in Britain, where the beer is sloshed into the glass by insensitive barmen, or like the Guinness in America, where the long sea journey from Dublin does nothing for the quality. It will taste, in a good pub in Ireland, as smooth as velvet.

Guinness is good for you – purportedly anyway.

a Monday morning around 9am as office workers throughout the city scurry to work, you may be startled to stumble across several bars in the docks area almost as busy as on a Saturday night.

The mystique of Guinness

The respect paid to this national beverage, a strongish dark beer with a creamy white head, is genuine and not something conjured up by a marketing department. Brewed in Dublin since 1759, it is a temperamental drink, needing great care in pouring from the tap to the glass. Constant temperature in the cellars, the distance from cask to tap and the frequency of the flow are all considered important factors in the art known as 'the pulling of a good pint.'

EXPORTING THE IRISH BAR

If America can persuade the world to eat hamburgers, can Ireland persuade it to drink Guinness? More than 1,000 'traditional' Irish pubs, from Durty Nellie's in Amsterdam to Finnegan's in Abu Dhabi, from Shifty O'Shea's in Leicester, England, to O'Kims in Seoul, Korea, are trying to do just that.

Brewers such as Guinness set up companies to export the Irish pub concept. They'll help entrepreneurs anywhere in the world to design their hostelry – you can pick a standard model such as Country Cottage, the Victorian Dublin or the Brewery – and also aid them in locating authentic fittings and recruiting staff.

A SPORTING NATION

Wild, energetic and thrilling, native sports such as hurling and Gaelic football will get the adrenalin pumping on or off the field. Then there's the widespread love of horses and passionate rugby and soccer fans...

Sport enthusiasts will have a field day in Ireland as all the major international sports are played to some extent and only a few, like soccer, athletics and hockey, are affected by the political division of the island. But the most popular sports are the native ones of hurling and Gaelic football. These are fast-paced, thrilling, high-voltage games, amateur in nature and organised around the parish and controlled by a body called the Gaelic Athletic Association (GAA).

The GAA was founded in 1884, in Thurles, County Tipperary by Michael Cusack, a fiery nationalist from the Burren in County Clare, who was immortalised by James Joyce as 'The Citizen' in *Ulysses*. Organised for a purpose that was political as much as sporting, the association's *raison d'être* was to revive the native games, under native control, as a means of strengthening national self-respect at a time when national morale was at low ebb.

At the end of the 19th century, most of those involved with the GAA were farmers, labourers and shopkeepers but by the 20th century the new Roman Catholic middle class fired up by a Celtic Revival joined the movement. In 1918, the GAA was included on a list of organisations banned by the British Government, but despite this Gaelic Games were still played and in the 21st Century they still hold a hallowed position in Irish culture and are intrinsically linked to a sense of independence and identity.

Dublin and Carlow clash at a hurling match.

Hurling

Hurling has been played in Ireland since pre-historic times and some of the country's oldest sagas tell of hurling matches that went on for days. It's the fastest of all field team games and its rules are relatively simple, although watching it for the first time can be a dizzying, bewildering experience as the ball hurtles around at breakneck speed and players bat their hurleys about, narrowly missing teeth and foreheads.

The hurley itself is made from ash and is around 3.5ft (1 metre) long with a paddle at the bottom that measures about 3ins (7.6cm) across at its broadest. The hard ball consists of yarn, tightly wound round a ball of cork and covered with leather, stitched along the outside in a ridge to facilitate handling. The object of the game is to get the ball either between the posts to score one point or under the bar to score a goal (for three points). As a result, scores tot up fast on this game, making for exhilarating viewing.

What makes the game so crazy to watch is that the ball can be propelled along the ground *or* hit in the air, but it can only be taken into the hand if it's been caught in full flight – something that requires considerable skill. The best

> The first mention of football in Ireland can be traced to 1308, when John McCrocan, a spectator at a football game at Newcastle, Co. Dublin, was charged with accidentally stabbing a player named William Bernard.

players can take the ball onto the hurley, from the ground, while running at full speed and carry it, balanced or bouncing, on the broad end before passing or scoring. Tricky? Yes. Exciting to watch? Absolutely. The main traditional hurling areas remain south of a line from Dublin to Galway, with a small pocket in the Glens of Antrim. Cork and Kilkenny are the top hurling counties.

Football, Gaelic-style

Like hurling, Gaelic football is played by teams of 15-a-side. The layout of the pitch

Gaelic football is spectacular, but its rules are subject to constant revision.

GREAT SPORTING MOMENTS

Croke Park in Dublin has been home to the GAA for over 100 years and is the largest stadium in the country with capacity for over 82,300. Steeped in history, the venue lies at the heart of Ireland's troubled history and in 1920 the British Crown fired into the crowd at a Dublin vs Tipperary match and shot dead 11 spectators – and the Tipperary captain – in a raid that became known as 'Bloody Sunday'.

Since those early days, the stadium has remained central to Irish sporting and cultural life. During the boom Croke Park (www.crokepark.ie) was transformed into one of Europe's finest venues, with a museum and stadium tour. Having been exclusively used for Gaelic

Games, 2005 saw a defining moment as the GAA agreed to allow 'Croker' to host 'foreign games' of soccer and international rugby, while their usual stadium of Lansdowne Road prepared for redevelopment.

The most controversial match of all was the 2007 Ireland vs England rugby international: because of Bloody Sunday, many Irish fans objected to the British national anthem being sung in the stadium. On 24 February, with phenomenal media hype, the historic match kicked off with emotions running high. As the Irish anthem was sung, there was barely a dry eye in the house with Irish fans and players feeling the weight of history thick in the air. Ireland won by 43–13.

and methods of scoring are also the same as for hurling. Played with a ball similar to that used in soccer, Gaelic football is something of an invented game so the rules are ultimately imperfect and subject to constant revision. Players can handle the ball, lift it off the ground with the foot, run with it while passing it between hand and foot, kick it, or fist it, or play it with the feet on the ground as in soccer. Its main flaw is that there is no clear method of dispossessing a player in possession. But it's a spectacular game and attracts huge crowds.

Breeding greyhounds is a minor industry.

Australian Rules, although played with an oval ball on an oval pitch, has features similar to those of Gaelic football. It's thought that Irish emigrants had a hand in influencing long kicking and the great leaps in the air to catch the ball. In an attempt to gain an international dimension for a game played only in Ireland (with the exception of Irish emigrants in the USA and Britain) the GAA has run tours to and from Australia, with games played under compromise rules. The fact that the Australian players are all professionals have so far given the contests more bite than was anticipated. Pros don't relish being beaten by amateurs.

The high point of the GAA year is in September with the All-Ireland hurling and football Finals in Dublin's Croke Park, which now incorporates a museum devoted to Irish sports. Tickets for the Finals do not go on sale to the general public and are distributed for purchase only through clubs and county boards.

Hares and horses

Greyhound racing (on tracks) and coursing in enclosed fields with live hares are popular sports in Ireland. The fact that races are over in a matter of seconds is no deterrent to the small army of punters who attend. Coursing is a winter sport, which has come under fire from animal-rights campaigners because of cruelty to hares. Two dogs are released to chase a hare. Points are scored by deflecting the hare from its course, or by killing it before it gets to the escape exit. Protests have resulted in greyhounds being muzzled by law.

Sports in all its glory

Casual perusal of the sports pages of any Irish daily newspaper will show that an extraordinary range of sports is covered, and a surprising number of people excel in a variety of sports at the highest level. To mention just a few: Sean Kelly dominated the world of cycling throughout the 1980s, and in 1987 Stephen Roche won the sport's ultimate prize, the gruelling Tour de France. In professional boxing, world titles were held by Barry McGuigan, Steve Collins, Michael Carruth and Dave McAuley. Alex Higgins, Ken O'Doherty and Dennis Taylor all claimed the world championship at snooker. To that list can be added two players with the most international appearances: Mike

---

THE SPLIT IN SOCCER

Soccer is split by the internal political border. The island fields two international sides: Ireland, as the Northern Ireland team is designated, and the Republic of Ireland. Despite limited resources, Northern Ireland qualified for the World Cup in 1982 and 1986, while the Republic stood out in the 1988 European Championships finals and in the 1990 and 1994 World Cup. Both teams qualified for the UEFA Euro 2016 tournament in France. Because Ireland's domestic football leagues are small, many top Irish footballers make names for themselves in UK leagues.

Gibson, in rugby football, and Pat Jennings, as a soccer goalkeeper. In 1998 Sonia O'Sullivan crowned an already illustrious career in athletics by winning both the 5,000-metre and 10,000-metre European championship titles, and Catherina McKiernan won four silver medals in the World Cross Country Championships. Top golfers on the international circuit include Darren Clarke, Dubliner Padraig Harrington, who won the Open in 2007 and 2008, also winning the PGA in 2008, and Northern Ireland's Rory McIlroy, who turned pro in 2007 on reaching the age of 16. In 2010

McIlroy had his first PGA tour triumph, winning the Quail Hollow Championship days before his 21st birthday.

In international rugby Ireland fields a team drawn from Northern Ireland and the Republic. Rugby is the one international sport (except for professional boxing) that unites all political elements on the island, at least temporarily. In July 2010 the newly built Aviva Stadium in Dublin's Lansdowne Road, home of both rugby and soccer internationals, with a seated capacity of 50,000, hosted its first rugby match.

The unusual sport of road bowling.

ROAD BOWLING

Road bowling is a strange game, played only in South Armagh, Cork and parts of Waterford and Limerick. The game is very simple: two players throw or bowl a heavy iron ball along an ordinary public road, and the winner is the one who covers a set distance with fewer throws. The bowl, or 'bullet', can be 28, 21 or 16oz (between 800 and 450 grams, and is believed to be of military origin: the original 'bowl' was probably a cannon ball. One of the skills of the game is the negotiation of a bend in the road, either by lofting the bowl over the corner or by curving the throw. If the bowl leaves the road, the player is penalised.

While it might not be the most organised of sports, road bowling attracts major betting activity and large sums of money change hands when noted players meet. Not only are bets laid on the result of the contest, but side-bets are also laid on individual shots.

Road bowling is illegal as sections of public roads are barred to traffic during the contest, but volunteers keep a careful watch and marshal passing traffic through safely, in a generally good-humoured operation. Prosecutions are rare, and would be very unpopular in the course of a true 'sport of the people'.

GOLF

Ireland may lack the sun-soaked allure of Bermuda or the cachet of the Caribbean, but it is one of the most exciting golfing destinations in the world right now. It's crammed with jaw-droppingly beautiful, impressively designed and technically challenging courses.

Always a popular golfing spot for players in the know, Ireland hit the world stage in a big way in 2006 with the hosting of the Ryder Cup at the sleek and luxurious K Club golf resort in County Kildare. Major international Irish names, such as Padraig Harrington, Darren Clarke, Graeme McDowell and Rory McIlroy have highlighted the skill of Irish golfers at international competitions. The Irish Open is part of the European tour and attracts record crowds. In 2016, Dun Laoghaire Golf Club hosted the Curtis Cup for women amateur golfers.

Rory McIlroy.

A variety of courses

Golfers are spoilt for choice. There's the drama of Doonbeg in County Clare, the elegance of Druid's Glen in County Wicklow, and the untamed magnificence of links courses, such as the Old Head of Kinsale in County Cork or the magnificent lake and mountain scenery of the Killarney Golf and Fishing Club, host of the 2010 Irish Open. Dotted throughout the land and outside all the major cities are internationally recognised courses, as well as smaller lesser-known spots that can be equally delightful to play on, depending on what you're looking for.

Top clubs and hidden gems

Among the big hitters are Lahinch in County Clare; Ballybunion and Waterville in County Kerry; and the Royal County Down. If you're looking for a quieter course, then try a hidden gem like Enniscrone in County Sligo; Ballyliffin in County Donegal; Kenmare in County Kerry and Killerig in County Carlow.

There are also an impressive number of luxurious golf resorts where you can complement a round of golf with some fine dining, spa and leisure facilities, along with deluxe accommodation. Mount Juliet in County Kilkenny boasts a Jack Nicklaus-designed course and is famed for its 1,500 acres of lush, rolling landscape and exquisite Georgian house. Carton House, County Kildare, host of the Irish Open in 2013, is an opulent castle hotel in a beautiful location, or if you fancy living it up like one of the landed gentry, Dromoland Castle has sumptuous rooms and fine food and wine.

The older the better

Unsurprisingly for a country with over 440 courses, the Irish take golf seriously. The country's golf pedigree dates back to the late

19th century and clubs, courses and even clubhouses battle it out for the title of "oldest". The Curragh Golf Club in County Kildare is reputed to have the oldest course in Ireland dating back to 1852; the oldest club, The Royal Belfast Golf Club was founded in 1881 and the Ardglass Golf Club in County Down has the oldest clubhouse – parts of which date back to the 14th century.

Traditional roots

While golf has attracted a new generation of hip, young swingers in the UK and the US, in

delayed behind wayward cattle along some rural backroads.

In terms of cost, green fees vary – the Arnold Palmer-designed Ryder Cup course at the K Club, charges €240 for a non-resident from May to September – but if you're looking for a bargain there are lots of smaller clubs that will only set you back around €30 or so.

Remember to check with the specific club regarding rules as some can be somewhat picky about dress codes, and nearly all clubs require advance booking for play, particularly during the busy summer months.

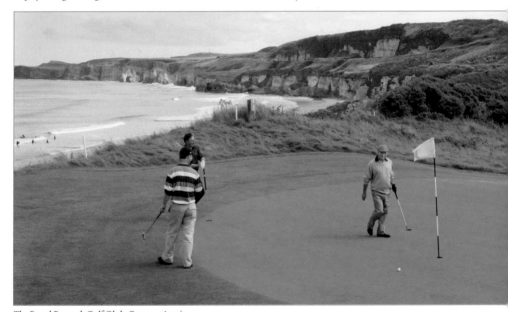

The Royal Portrush Golf Club, Country Antrim.

Ireland the game is still rooted in tradition. There may not be as many Pringle sweaters on the courses as there used to be, but clubs like Portmarnock Golf Club in Dublin are stalwarts of the old-school and bastions of male privilege. This beautifully situated links, nestled into the curve of coastline formed by Howth Peninsula, refuses to relax its age-old rule that excludes women from becoming full members, although visitors of both sexes are warmly welcomed on the course as long as you have a certified handicap.

Ireland's small size means that it's easy to take in a few clubs in a short space of time. But give yourself plenty of time to meet your tee-off booking, too, as you can be seriously

IRELAND'S BEST COURSES

The K Club, Co. Kildare. Two parkland courses. The choice of plutocrats.

Portmarnock, Dublin. On a peninsula north of Dublin; holding out against women members.

Ballybunion, Co. Kerry. Tiger Woods warms up on the Old Course for a European tour.

Killarney Golf and Fishing Club. Three courses amid stunning lake and mountain scenery.

Lahinch, Co. Clare. Challenging links course on the Atlantic coast, famed for massive bunkers.

Royal County Down. Nr Mourne Mountains. Tough.

Royal Portrush. Co. Antrim. The only Irish club to have hosted a British Open. Coastal location.

ANGLING

Unsurprisingly for a country that's surrounded by sea, that enjoys an abundance of lakes and has a whopping 8,500 miles of fish-rich rivers, Ireland is one of Europe's most popular angling destinations.

Ireland's mix of year-round rain, reasonably mild winters and gentle summers results in a profusion of cold and warm water species, so there's a really broad range of experiences on offer including salmon fishing, coarse fishing, pike fishing, sea fishing and trout fly-fishing right across the island.

While it's undeniably possible that you might be lucky enough to reel in a Mediterranean bass for your supper, you're probably more likely to have success with one of Ireland's native fish. Coarse fishing in Ireland isn't enormously popular with locals so the country's lightly fished freshwaters are teaming with species like pike, bream, tench, roach, eel and rudd. Admittedly, you're unlikely to be rustling up a gourmet dinner with a freshly taken rudd, but it's all about the experience, and coarse fishing in Ireland is contemplative and tranquil thanks to the haunting beauty of the magnificent landscapes.

From the big rivers like the vast River Shannon, which dominates the midlands, to the small - crystal-clear waters of Ireland's loughs such as County Roscommon's Lough Gara, Ireland offers a diversity that few other countries can compete with, and coarse fishing is a sport that thrills regardless of your level or experience. Or you could always opt for a showdown with a pink-fleshed salmon, trout or sea trout, which hold an honoured place in Irish culture and folklore.

Angling in the south of Co. Dublin.

The reel regulations

You'll need a licence, though, which you can pick up from fishing tackle shops and fishery offices. And, as the majority of waters are either privately owned or owned by the state, you'll also need a fishing permit. There are strict bylaws and conservation measures governing coarse and salmon fishing, including bag limits, mandatory catch and release and gill tags. It's best to contact the relevant Regional Fisheries Board (for contact details for each region, check with the Central Fisheries Board; tel: 1890 347424; www.fishinginireland.info) close to the time of travel as these regulations change.

On the seashore

Sea fishing in Ireland is a real thrill, with more than 4,000 miles (6,400km) of coastline covering landscapes that range from towering sea cliffs that plummet into the crashing Atlantic Ocean along the west and northwest coast, to the gentler waters of the sunny southeast. There are over 80 species in the waters and the warming influence of the North Atlantic Drift means that you can take fish from spring to autumn, which would usually be found only in the summer months elsewhere. Whether you want to boat fish languidly on a warm August afternoon, wreck fish for conger,

> Pike fishing is a huge draw for competitive anglers – the largest line-caught pike in a lough is 39lbs 3oz (17.7kg) and a whopping 42lbs (19kg) in a river, but don't expect to hook one that size; most average 20lbs (9kg).

magnificence and a physical vitality that never fails to impress, and these rocky coastal shores provide the angler with one of the most picturesque fishing locations in the world. In terms of fish, you'll find species of wrasse and pollack ready for the taking. But arguably the most Irish of angling experiences has to be a battle with the enormous native pike. The quality of the clear, clean waters is attributed to the large numbers of pike in Ireland, and the fisheries of the Shannon, Lough Allen, Lough Derg, River Suck and River Inny are prolific with these legendary creatures, which average around

Fishing in Co. Galway.

ling, pollack or coalfish, or take the sociable approach with a big-fun bout of deep-sea fishing on a chartered boat, you're guaranteed an exciting experience. Best of all, after a day bobbing around in sea spray, a night in the pub dissecting the day's catch over a pint of Guinness is a particular treat.

For many anglers, Ireland is a dream location for shore fishing and nothing beats the pure adrenalin-rush of battling with big surf on the west coast during one of the area's legendary storms. This isn't for the faint-hearted, though.

There are few parts of Ireland that can beat the wild untamed beauty of the Beara, Iveragh and Dingle peninsulas in the southwest. It's a beguiling part of the country, with a raw

20lbs (9kg). The chance of reeling in a vast fish fires up anglers from across the world who are drawn to Ireland because of the unspoiled habitat that enables the fish to breed and swell to such an impressive size.

Conservation efforts

It's important to remember conservation issues, and this is evident in the ever-changing bylaws. In sea fishing, most cartilaginous fish are tagged and returned alive, and freshwater anglers are encouraged to limit the number of wild fish taken. The aforementioned Central Fisheries Board can supply current details. The CFB also offers a free download of *Irish Sport Fishes – A guide to their identification*, and more besides.

WALKING IN IRELAND

'The men of Ireland are mortal and temporal, but her hills are eternal,' wrote George Bernard Shaw. As well as nurturing a rich store of mythology and folklore, the Irish hills offer spectacular opportunities for walkers.

From the top of Slieve-na-Calliagh (hill of the witch) in County Meath, it's possible, on a clear day, to look down across 18 Irish counties. No great effort is needed to reach the summit as it's only 911ft (275 metres), and you can drive to a small car park 10 minutes' walk from the top. If the spirit moves you, and you have the key, you can enter a cross-shaped chamber covered with a mound of stones. Inside, the stones are riotously decorated with ancient rock art carvings and radial line patterns including zigzags and spirals that, it is believed, mark the expected variations of the sunbeam with the drifting of the equinoctial rising sun.

Although not huge in European or world terms, the mountains of Ireland have a seductive and, in the case of Slieve-na-Calliagh, enigmatic quality. For walkers, the countryside offers a spectacular range of opportunities. From the high peaks of Cork and Kerry to the Glens of Antrim, and from the Donegal highlands to the small hills or drumlins (low rounded hills) of the midlands, the range of walking possibilities is enormous.

There are few mountains that need more than half a day to scale, but walking an entire range will take two days or more to complete. Most peaks have their own qualities of visual drama. Many, including the Twelve Bens in Connemara, the Mourne Mountains in County Down, or Ireland's most climbed holy mountain, Croagh Patrick, have a distinctive triangular symmetry. Brandon in Kilkenny and the quartzite cone of Errigal in Donegal have an implacable presence, yet are intimate and inviting, their significance to the people living around their foothills out of all proportion to their height. Others are

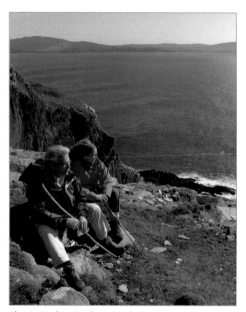

Sheep's Head Peninsula, Co. Cork.

more subtle and don't always emphasise their glories.

Organised walks

Walking in Ireland has grown rapidly as an activity; it is big business and well organised. There are more than 30 national waymarked walking trails and over 100 walking clubs.

The clubs are all affiliated to Mountaineering Ireland, the representative body for hill walkers and climbers in Ireland north and south. The waymarked ways offer 1,860 miles (3,000km) of marked walking routes and one of their most appealing aspects is that they are suitable for walkers of all ages and abilities. The network ranges from towpath strolls and walks along scenic coastal stretches, to circuits of the high mountainous peninsulas. You can take your pick from one of the shortest, the Cavan Way at 16 miles (26km), to the Kerry

An average of two people a year die on the MacGillycuddy's Reeks near Killarney. A mobile phone is useful in an emergency but network coverage is often poor. Check the weather forecast, dress appropriately and avoid walking alone.

Way stretching to 133 miles (214km). These trails rarely rise above 3,000ft (900 metres). While there are a few rugged stretches over open mountain passes, the routes mainly follow disused roads, grassy trails or forest tracks. They are signposted with yellow arrows and a walking man to guide you through the countryside and over stiles and bridges.

Tougher hikes

For those wanting a greater challenge, there are much tougher day-long annual hikes across some of the bigger ranges organised by

Killarney National Park is a hiker's paradise.

WHEN A WALK BECOMES A FESTIVAL

Practically every area that contains some high ground organises outings to the hills lasting a weekend (or longer) as part of structured walking festivals. Many of these take in features of the countryside led by local guides knowledgeable about heritage sites, the archaeology and geology of the area as well as the wild flowers and birdlife to be seen. There is also a social side to the festivals with evening entertainment in the pubs.

There are more than 30 walking festivals in Ireland. These include the Ballyhoura International Walking Festival on the borders of Cork, Tipperary and Limerick, the Castlebar International 4 Days' Walks, the Sperrins and Killeter Walking Festival and the North Leitrim

Glens Walking Festival. The Wee Binnians, which labels itself 'the social group that walks', holds a popular annual festival in the Mourne Mountains.

The Slieve Blooms, in the centre of Ireland, offer Eco Walks as part of their biannual weekends. This lesser-known range covers an astonishing 60,000 acres (24,000 hectares) spread across Laois and Offaly. The writer Hubert Butler once described the Slieve Blooms as 'a low, demure-looking range of hills, very suitable for middle-aged, unadventurous mountaineers with children and picnic-baskets.'

For more information on walking festivals see www. discoverireland.ie.

mountaineering clubs. The Maumturks Walk in Connemara each spring covers 15 miles (24km), while the Glover Highlander in Donegal is held in early September. Most clubs have programmes of walks throughout the year and welcome visitors.

The mist can come down quickly in mountainous regions and it's easy for the walker to go astray, so check the weather forecast before setting out. The old red sandstone Mountains of Kerry are the most dangerous in Ireland and can be treacherous, as the mist can descend with no warning, severely limiting visibility.

At 3,414ft (1,039 metres), Carrauntoohil is the country's highest mountain and attracts thousands of walkers annually.

It's essential to have proper gear: walking boots with ankle support, rainwear, warm clothes, gloves and hat, maps, compass and guidebook and sufficient snacks such as chocolate or fruit, as well as a warm or hydrating drink.

Planning an advance itinerary and working out a route using the Ordnance Survey (OS) maps is the safest way. You should also leave word with someone where you are going and your approximate return time. The OS maps

Waymarker on the Ring of Kerry.

USEFUL WEBSITES

For details of routes on waymarked walking trails, loop walks, trails in forest parks, national parks and city or town walks (known as *Sli na Slainte*) as well as information on walking festivals go to www.irishtrails.ie.

Seven pilgrim paths in Ireland follow medieval pilgrimage routes. Details: www.heritagecouncil.ie.

The Mountaineering Council of Ireland has a helpful website: www.mountaineering.ie.

To learn more about looped walks, forest and nature walks, festivals and events and accommodation for walkers have a look at www.discover ireland.ie.

in the Discovery Series, drawn up to 1:50,000 scale, will help you find ancient monuments, holy wells and castles as well as landmarks in towns and villages. You will also find on them scores of names tucked away into the crevices and foothills such as Crotty's Rock, the Colleen Bawn Cottage, and, at the summit of Slieve Gullion in south Armagh, Calliagh Berra's Lake. According to legend, any man who swims in the lake comes out visibly aged.

Magnificent scenery opens up in many mountainous areas such as Mayo's Doolough Pass, the Spelga Pass in south Down and the bleak but beautiful Gap of Dunloe in Kerry. But be careful as you drive on these remote roads as a PhD in these parts refers to "Pot-hole Dodging".

Ireland's Top 10 Walks

From The Brandy Pad and The Dingle Way to coastal walks and a climb up Diamond Hill, there are hikes to suit everyone in the Emerald Isle.

A favourite walk is **Errigal Mountain** (Co. Donegal). The most direct route starts from Dunlewy at the car park on the main R521. After crossing heathery slopes, you will reach firmer footing and it's relatively easy to pick your way to the top through rocks and over loose stones for a view of a large area of northwest Ireland.

The Brandy Pad (Co. Down). This route follows an old smugglers' path across the northern section of the Mourne Mountains. The whole walk, which is way-marked throughout and marked on maps, is 7 miles (11km). It's not overly strenuous and the reward is spectacular views across the highest range in Ulster.

The Dingle Way (Co. Kerry). For a taste of dramatic scenery you could walk all, or part, of the 110-mile (180km) Dingle Way on the Dingle peninsula. The walk begins in Tralee, leads west to Camp on the northern side, then loops round the peninsula, taking in the imposing Brandon Mountain, and dropping down to Clogher Head before turning back along the southern stretch of the peninsula.

Croagh Patrick (Co. Mayo). On the last Sunday in July you'll have trouble creating elbowroom for yourself amongst 30,000 pilgrims on their annual hike to the summit. A well-trodden path takes you to the chapel at the summit of this conical, aloof peak, from which you can view the islands beneath you in Clew Bay.

Burren Coastal Walk (Co. Clare). Along the stunning coastline from Black Head down to Doolin, you will cross a variety of terrain that includes limestone pavement, beaches, grass and sand dunes all offering pleasant walking among grey walls, stones and rocks. You will come across seabirds and rare arctic–alpine plants that flower in the spring and early summer. The five-hour walk also takes you across Fanore beach, a European Special Area of Conservation.

Diamond Hill (Co. Galway). The path to the top of Diamond Hill starts from the Connemara National Park visitor centre. The 5-mile (8km) route follows the Sruffaunboy Nature Trail before branching off towards the cone of Diamond Hill. From the cairn on the summit ridge at 1,460ft (442 metres) the breathtaking view embraces islands, bays, beaches, loughs and mountains.

Sawel (Co. Derry). The large expanse of the Sperrin Mountains are in a sparsely populated region of north Tyrone. The walking covers bog, heather and moorland and will take you through quiet valleys and encounters with sheep and birds.

The Grand Canal Way (Co. Dublin and Midlands). This flat canalside walk leads westwards from the outskirts of Dublin through the central plains to the village of Shannon Harbour, covering a distance of 80 miles (130km). The walk offers a variety of wildlife, canal features and pretty villages to stop in for

The Mourne Mountains in Co. Down were the inspiration for C.S. Lewis's Chronicles of Narnia.

refuelling. You can pause to explore Ireland's finest monastic settlement at Clonmacnoise.

The Slieve Bloom Way (Cos. Laois & Offaly). This 43-mile (70km) route covers a wide circuit of an isolated range of mountains in central Ireland and takes two days. It provides panoramic views from the paths and tracks through the bog land; the ascents of the hills are not too strenuous.

Carrauntoohil (Co. Kerry). The most popular route to the top of Ireland's highest mountain is via the Devil's Ladder, although it can be dangerous in wet weather. Walkers have to scramble through a wide gully with loose boulders that can easily dislodge. The return time is a minimum of five hours, so this one is for more experienced walkers.

IRELAND'S ARCHITECTURE

Ireland has a long and turbulent history, and its buildings reflect a catalogue of conquest, and also its roots as an agrarian economy with extremes of wealth and poverty.

"Never accept a commission in Ireland," a 19th-century English architect warned his colleagues. His fear was that only the most rugged buildings could withstand the Atlantic winds and rain. In the 20th century, two greater threats emerged: bitter warfare which would see great Anglo-Irish manors burnt to the ground, and the rapacity of 1960s property developers which would devastate Dublin's Georgian heritage.

Ireland's buildings reflect a history of conquest. From the 12th century, Anglo-Norman fortresses were built to intimidate. But Ireland proved hard to subjugate and fortified tower houses continued to be built until the end of the 17th century. In the 18th century, the British imported Palladian and Georgian styles, and neoclassical influences spread to humble farmhouses. But the crude thatched cottage didn't die: it evolved into the crude bungalows that disfigure the countryside today.

Leamaneagh Castle is a striking ruin of an extended tower house, dating from 1480 and attached to a 17th-century four-storey mansion. It can be found in the Burren area of Co. Clare, on route R476 from Kilfenora through Killinaboy.

Bantry House in Co. Cork is about as far as you can get from the cliché image of an Irish cottage, and hints at the lifestyle enjoyed by the Anglo-Irish aristocracy. When the 2nd Earl of Bantry inherited this Georgian house in 1845, he began turning it into a repository for the art and antiques he collected on his world travels. An amateur architect, he had a theatrical sense of design. Parallels with the Capitol Building in Washington DC reinforce the claims of Charles Frederick Anderson, who emigrated to the US and said he had a hand in both. Its collection of carpets, tapestries and furniture is open to the public, and it offers one of the best views over Bantry Bay.

Dublin became a showpiece city in the 18th century, with areas such as Fitzwilliam Square (pictured) conveying an elegant simplicity that implied social status. It was clearly a European capital. By contrast, Belfast was an industrial city, whose rapid growth in the 19th century produced a few grand civic edifices but mainly utilitarian Victorian buildings.

Avondale House, a Georgian building in Co. Wicklow, was the birthplace of the politician Charles Stewart Parnell (1846–91). Now a museum, it is surrounded by a forest park.

THE FIGHT FOR OLD DUBLIN

Dublin in the 18th century was one of the ornaments of Europe, its Georgian buildings expressing a distinctive graciousness, the wide streetscapes framing distant mountain views, some of which can still be seen today.

Much of that heritage was destroyed in the unregulated property speculation of the 1960s. Whole streets were razed and replaced by often-unsympathetic office blocks. Classic Georgian terraces vanished. Protests peaked in the late 1970s after an important Viking site at Wood Quay was obliterated to build offices for city officials.

The more recent record has been better. Plans for a huge bus depot in the Temple Bar area south of the River Liffey were shelved in the late 1980s when the city authorities realised that the small shops, galleries and restaurants on the narrow cobbled streets of Temple Bar had turned the area into a prime tourist attraction. So instead of bulldozing the area, it was partly redeveloped, and is now home to the Irish Film Centre, The Ark (a children's cultural centre), Meeting House Square (an outdoor venue), galleries and artists' studios.

Kilruddery House in Bray, Co. Wicklow, is an example of a grand country house within easy reach of Dublin. Built in the 17th century, it was later remodelled along neo-Elizabethan lines. A conservatory was added in 1852, its walls being masonry instead of glass because it was meant to house not only plants but also the statues collected by its owner, Lord Meath.

The classic image of Dublin is of its elegant Georgian doorways. But comparatively few have survived: unchecked developers bulldozed many to create modern office blocks, and public support for preserving Ireland's architectural heritage was sometimes interpreted as nostalgia for the former colonial ruler.

Georgian door knocker in Dublin.

Accommodation Office →

Titanic Belfast.

Thatched cottage and garden,
Adare, Co. Clare.

INTRODUCTION

A detailed guide to the entire island and all its
delights, with principal sites clearly cross-referenced
by number to the accompanying maps.

Ring of Kerry.

What other city but Dublin, capital of the Republic of Ireland, could boast a General Post Office as a national shrine? Where else but Belfast, capital of Northern Ireland, could have transformed itself in so short a time from car-bomb chaos to a popular short-break destination? The stimulating thing about Ireland is that, having provoked so many preconceptions, it constantly surprises.

Open-minded visitors, bringing raincoats and sturdy walking boots but leaving their preconceptions at home, will discover a beguiling cocktail of hidden loughs and ancient towns, burial chambers and strange stone crosses, round towers and ruined castles, holy wells and high waterfalls. Racehorses are the local heroes and the villain is anyone too hurried to bid the time of day to a neighbour or passers-by.

Kerry beckons with opulent valleys, nurturing wild fuchsia and scented orchids; Killarney, with jaunting cars and leprechaun lore designed to charm the euros from tourists' pockets; Dublin, increasingly anglicised, Americanised and hamburgerised, yet still the least lonely of cities; rivers teeming with salmon like Galway's Corrib and the Blackwater that runs through Armagh and Tyrone and Fermanagh's resplendent lakeland, where boats are still gloriously few and far between. It is a small country but, like a good vintage wine, should be savoured slowly. Sometimes

Blarney Castle.

it has to be. A signpost may present you with three ways of getting to a destination or it may show none. Ask for directions and you'll probably be assured 'it's just around the corner' – in Ireland, no one will want to distress you by telling you it's really 40 miles along a narrow, twisting road and you're, well, way off track.

The tensions of the modern world have not bypassed Ireland but many big-city dwellers will find an overall slower pace of life here. And while the economic downturn has left a legacy of unfinished buildings and a shell-shocked national psyche, a remarkable capacity for enjoyment prevails, one that most visitors find wildly infectious.

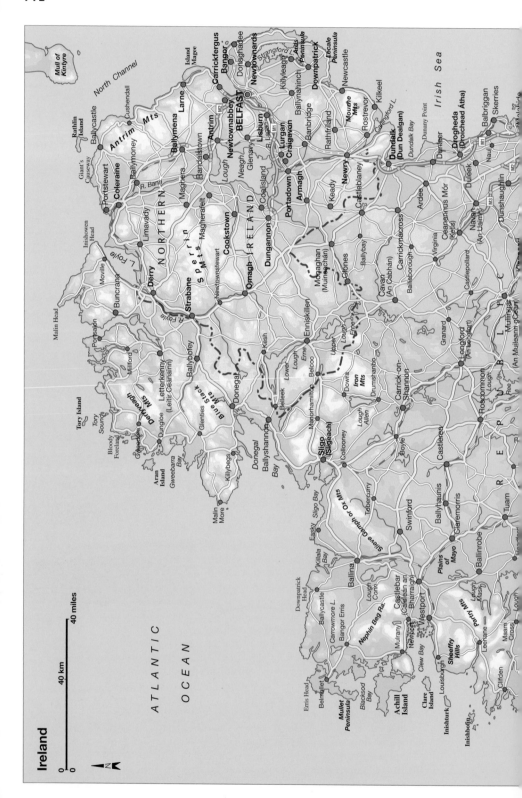

Ireland

ATLANTIC OCEAN

Irish Sea

North Channel

NORTHERN IRELAND

REPUBLIC

40 km
40 miles

Mull of Kintyre

Rathlin Island
Ballycastle
Cushendall
Giant's Causeway
Portstewart
Coleraine
Antrim Mts
Ballymoney
Ballymena
Larne
Island Magee
Carrickfergus
Bangor
Donaghadee
Newtownards
Ards Peninsula
Strangford L.
BELFAST
Newtownabbey
Antrim
Lisburn
Lurgan
Craigavon
Killyleagh
Ballynahinch
Downpatrick
Lecale Peninsula
Newcastle
Mourne Mts
Rostrevor
Kilkeel
Banbridge
Rathfriland
Carlingford L.
Dunany Point
Dundalk (Dún Dealgan)
Dundalk Bay
Drogheda (Droichead Átha)
Balbriggan
Skerries
Malahide
Naul
Duleek
Dunshaughlin
Navan (An Uaimh)
Ceanannus Mór (Kells)
Castlepollard
Granard
Longford (An Longfort)
Mullingar (An Muileann gCearr)
Roscommon
Castlerea
Castlebar (Caisleán an Bharraigh)
Tuam
Claremorris
Ballinrobe
Ballyhaunis
Swinford
Ballina
Plains of Mayo
Nephin Beg Ra.
Bangor Erris
Belmullet
Mullet Peninsula
Erris Head
Blacksod Bay
Achill Island
Clare Island
Clew Bay
Murrisk
Westport
Newport
Sheeffry Hills
Partry Mts
Louisburgh
Leenane
Maam Cross
Inishturk
Inishbofin
Clifden
Tory Island
Tory Sound
Gweedore
Bloody Foreland
Dunglow
Aran Island
Gweebarra Bay
Killybegs
Malin More
Donegal
Ballyshannon
Donegal Bay
Bundoran
Kesh
Belleek
Manorhamilton
Sligo (Sligeach)
Collooney
Ballymote
Curry Mts
Tubbercurry
Slieve Gamph or Ox Mts
Killala Bay
Killala
Downpatrick Head
Carrowmore L.
Lough Conn
Lough Cullin
Lough Mask
Lough Corrib
Malin Head
Inishowen Head
Moville
Buncrana
Portsalon
Milford
Letterkenny (Leitir Ceanainn)
Ballybofey
Derryveagh Mts
Bluestack Mts
Glenties
Errigal
R. Foyle
L. Foyle
Derry
Limavady
Strabane
Newtownstewart
Omagh
Cookstown
Magherafelt
Maghera
Sperrin Mts
Dungannon
Coalisland
Portadown
Armagh
Keady
Castleblaney
Monaghan (Muineachán)
Newry
Clones
Ballybay
Cavan (An Cabhán)
Ballyjamesduff
Belturbet
Virginia
Enniskillen
Upper Lough Erne
Lower Lough Erne
Iron Mts
Dowra
Lough Allen
Drumshanbo
Carrick-on-Shannon
Boyle
Carrickmacross
Ardee
Bandalstown
Lough Neagh
Portaferry
Ballyconnell
R. Bann
Lough Gowna
Lough Ree

Loughs
R. Foyle
Glenavy
Moneymore

Dublin

0 ——————— 250 m
0 ——————— 250 yds

Tram Line and Station

St Brendan's Hospital

St Brendan's Hospital

Well

Font

Western Wa

Dominic

King's Inns

North

Halston St

Beresford

Greek St

Chancery

Chancery Pl

Street

Inns Quay

Four Courts **36**

The Chimney

May Lane

Mary's

35
St Michan

Old Jameson Distillery

Four Courts

Smithfield

St Paul

Hammond Lane

Arran Quay

River Liffey

Usher's Quay

Merchants Quay

Winetavern

Franciscan Church

Brazen Head

Dublinia & The Viking World **22** C

Cook Street

23
St Audoen

An Taisce (Tailors' Hall)

High St

Back Lane

Iveagh Market

St Nicholas of Myra

Nicholas St

Bu

St P Ca

Dept of Defence

Dublin Criminal Courts Complex

Phoenix Park **39**

Parkgate Street

Arbour

Place

Incorporated Law Society

Hendrick Street

Benburb

Museum

40
National Museum of Decorative Arts & History (Collins Barracks)

Street

Blackhall

Ellis Quay

Wolfe Tone Quay

Victoria Quay

Smithfield

Queen Street

King

Street

Bow Street

Church Street

St John's Road West

Heuston Station

Heuston

St John's Road West

Island Street

Usher's Island

Bonham Street

Usher

Street

St Augustine Street

St John's Well

Bridge Street

Commarket

Francis

Irish Museum of Modern Art

Military Road

LUAS Tram (Red Line) Steevens' Lane

St Patrick's Hospital

Guinness Brewery (St James's Gate Brewery)

Watling Street

St Patrick's Tower

Bridgefoot

Oliver Bond Street

St Augustine and St John

Kilmainham Gaol

37

38

Bow Lane West

James's

James's

St Lwr

Basin

Echlin St

St James's

Crane St

Rainsford

Street

St Catherine

National College of Art and Design

Hanbury Lane

Thomas Court

Meath Street

Swift's Alley

John Dillon St

Convent

St James's Hospital

Fatima

Basin Street Upper

24
Guinness Storehouse

Bond St

Newport St

Robert

Bellevue

Lane

Earl St South

Meath Place

Summer St South

Carman's Hall

Dean St

Rialto

Rialto Street

St James's Walk

Our Lady's Rd

Lourdes

Rosary Rd

Pimlico

Marrowbone

John Street South

Ardee St

The Coombe

Newmarket

Ward's Hill

New Row South

Fumbally Lane

Malpas St

Lon

South

Circular

Ave

Street

Dolphin's Barn St

Cork

Cameron St

Brown Street South

St Thomas Rd

Chamber St

Mill Street

Clarence Mangan

O'Curry Road

Donore Avenue

Susan Terrace

Donore Rd

Blackpitts

Road

Clanbrassil Street Lower

Daniel St

Verno

Lombard

DOLPHIN'S BARN

Road

Coombe Hospital

O'Donovan Road

DUBLIN

It's a small capital and not an especially pretty one – but the wit and warmth of its citizens and their hospitality to visitors have made it one of Europe's most popular destinations.

Main Attractions

Trinity College
St Stephen's Green
National Museum
Temple Bar
Ha'Penny Bridge
Dublin Castle
Guinness Storehouse
Custom House
O'Connell Street
Phoenix Park

With its vibrant mix of traditional pubs, hip bars, elegant Georgian architecture, cool shops and a colourful cultural scene to rival any European capital, Dublin bubbles with an infectious energy. The city has recovered remarkably quickly from the economic downturn, making the best of an ambitious but incomplete docklands renewal project and the many empty office blocks left in the wake of the boom. Dublin is a lively place to be, from the café-packed side streets around Grafton Street to the African and Asian stores that rub shoulders with traditional street traders on Moore Street. Culturally, the city is famous for its theatre, literature, art and music, which is no surprise considering that some of Europe's most prestigious writers and musicians including James Joyce, W.B. Yeats, Brendan Behan, and, of course, U2 have all called Dublin home.

Dublin's appeal

As a city, Dublin means different things to different people. For some it's an inspirational centre of historical treasures from ancient Viking areas to the grand Georgian town houses of the 18th century that give the city a grace and beauty. For others, it is a city of talkers, its pubs overflowing with Guinness and an inimitable atmosphere. Some fall in love with the quiet, sophisticated urban parks of Merrion Square and the Iveagh Gardens, while others gorge on the city's collection of chic boutiques, lively street markets, big-name chain stores and the luxurious Brown Thomas department store.

The first thing that strikes nearly all visitors is Dublin's superb natural setting. This vivacious spot sits on a wide plain bisected by the River Liffey, overlooked by hills and headlands and facing a broad sweeping bay. It is still possible to see the Dublin Mountains from the city centre. By contrast, the

Liffey Boardwalk, just the spot for a stroll.

Discover Dublin by glass-roofed boat on the Spirit of Docklands. In the background is the Jeanie Johnston, a replica famine ship and museum.

city itself is a mishmash of gloriously beautiful architecture old and new, dilapidated, almost derelict buildings and tacky neon and plastic signage. But Dublin can still sparkle when it tries.

A divided city

Dublin is divided by the River Liffey, which flows through its centre and also by the social differences, which the river delineates. In the early 18th century, the rich moved north across the river from the old medieval city with its teeming slums to fine new terraces and squares, such as Henrietta Street and Mountjoy Square. But within decades they doubled back again to establish fashionable residences on the south side on Merrion Square and Fitzwilliam Square, continuing in Victorian times through the suburbs of Ballsbridge and out along the coast to the attractive towns of Dun Laoghaire and Dalkey.

There are still middle-class enclaves on the northside, but by and large southsiders are better off, better dressed and (to their own ears) better spoken. Like any snobbery, of course, the north-south chauvinism works both ways, and just as many southsiders 'wouldn't be seen dead on the northside', northsiders are inclined to judge the southside as a wasteland of snobbery and pretension. Old prejudices are confirmed in recent developments: south of the river is the exquisite 2,100 seat Daniel Libeskind-designed Grand Canal theatre for opera and West End musicals (2010), while north of the river is the 14,000-seat 3 Arena (2008) custom-designed for stadium rock.

Bank of Ireland and around

A good place to begin a walking tour is O'Connell Bridge. Retreat from the breadth and bustle of O'Connell Street and instead walk down Westmoreland Street into College Green, which contains two of Dublin's most impressive and historic buildings: the **Bank of Ireland** ❶ and **Trinity College**. The bank, with its curving, columnar, windowless facade, was built in 1729 to house the Irish Parliament. The colonnaded front was added in 1785 by James Gandon. Following the abolition of the Irish

---

PARADOXES OF DUBLIN'S HISTORY

Dublin began by the banks of the Liffey, where Celtic settlements and churches existed at least from early Christian times, near a causeway crossing from which the city's Gaelic name, Baile Atha Cliath, 'The Town of the Hurdle Ford', is derived. But towns as such did not figure in the old Celtic way of things, and it is generally accepted that Dublin was founded in the 9th century not by the Irish, but by the Vikings, who were plundering and colonising all the coasts of Northern Europe.

Dublin was soon a lucrative base for both raiding and trading and the Danes hung on to it – despite persistent attacks by local chieftains and a great defeat at the Battle of Clontarf in 1014 – gradually intermarrying with the Irish and adopting Christianity. The Viking community began to turn into Gaels, and started to build places of worship for their new religion included the forerunner of the medieval Christ Church Cathedral, and St Michan's Church on the north bank of the Liffey. The Anglo-Normans arrived in the 12th century, and captured Dublin in 1170, ejecting the Vikings, who settled on the north bank of the Liffey. By the 14th century the Vikings had been completely assimilated into Irish and Anglo-Norman society. But, until Elizabethan times, direct English rule was restricted to a ribbon of land on the east coast known as 'the Pale', running roughly from Dundalk to the north to just south of Dublin.

The colonisation by landlords from Britain in the 17th and 18th centuries created Dublin's Golden Age, when many great buildings were erected, including the elegant Georgian squares of tall domestic dwellings, so characteristic of the city, and the city's social life was as fashionable as any in Europe.

Legislative independence was granted under the English Crown in 1782, but the Irish parliament in College Green was short-lived. After the rebellion of the United Irishmen in 1798, Britain brought Ireland under direct control again and began a long period of decline in Dublin.

The city was at the heart of the ferment that led to the Rising of 1916, the subsequent War of Independence and the establishment of the Free State in 1921. The next 40 years were a time of economic struggle in a puritan atmosphere that was often culturally and socially stifling.

parliament, it became a Bank in 1809. Visitors can view the impressive, former House of Lords with tapestries of the Battle of the Boyne (tel: 01-661 5933; Mon–Fri, 10am–4pm; free).

Just beside the Bank of Ireland on Foster Place is the newly revamped **National Wax Museum** (year round, daily, 10am–7pm; adult €14, child €9; www.waxmuseumplus.ie) with tons of history exhibits and a chamber of horrors. 10% discount for purchasing online. Cross the road and turn right to the hi-tech **Visit Dublin** tourist office (25 Suffolk Street; year round Mon–Sat 9.30am–5.30pm, Sun 10.30am–3pm; tel: 1850 230 330; www.visitdublin.com), for maps, free, independent advice, booking for accommodation and events, as well the **Dublin Pass** (adult €49, child €29; www.dublinpass.com) for free entry to over 25 top attractions.

Trinity College

Trinity College ❷, whose sober facade is topped by a surprisingly bright blue clock, was founded in 1592 by Elizabeth I on the site of a confiscated monastery, but the frontage was built between 1755 and 1759. The porch inside the main gate leads to a spacious, cobbled quadrangle, on the right of which is the Examination Hall (1779–91), which contains a gilt oak chandelier from the old parliament and an organ said to have been taken from a Spanish ship at Vigo in 1702. On the left is the Chapel (1792) and beyond it the Dining Hall (1743). The 100ft (30-metre) campanile, which dominates the quadrangle was designed by Sir Charles Lanyon and erected in 1853 on a spot supposed to mark the centre of the medieval monastery church.

To the right of the second quadrangle is the **Old Library** (1712–32), where *the Book of Kells is housed*. This magnificently ornate 9th-century manuscript copy of the gospels in Latin is put into context by an exhibition 'Turning Darkness into Light' and should not be missed. Purchase tickets online to bypass the queues (tel: 01-896 2320; www.tcd.ie/visitors/book-of-kells; year round Mon–Sat 9.30am–5pm, Oct–Apr Sun noon–4.30pm; May–Sept Sun 9.30am–4.30pm; adult €14, child €12). It is the greatest

Trinity College.

The Long Room library at Trinity College.

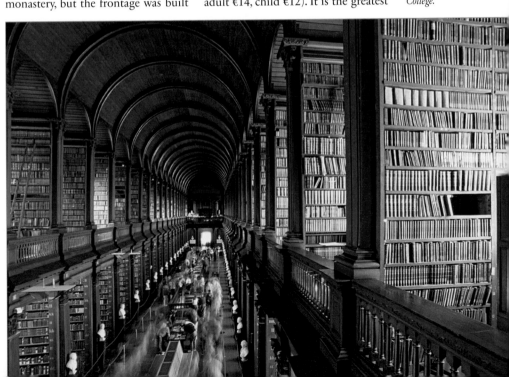

Trinity College

Set up exclusively for the Protestant Ascendancy class, Trinity College nourished many of Ireland's greatest writers, scientists and politicians.

Founded in 1591, Trinity covers 16 hectares (40 acres) in the centre of the city on land reclaimed from the Liffey estuary. It doesn't quite have the grandeur of the nearby Bank of Ireland and was described by James Joyce in *A Portrait of the Artist as a Young Man* as being 'set heavily in the city's ignorance like a dull stone set in a cumbrous ring.'

Trinity remained an exclusively Protestant university for most of its history, having been set up by Queen Elizabeth I to 'civilise' the Irish and keep them from the influences of 'Popery'. The college has lost some, if not all, of its air of Ascendancy since the restriction on Catholic students was lifted in 1873. However, it is only relatively recently - since 1970 in fact - that Catholics began attending the college in greater numbers when the Catholic Church lifted its ban on Catholics attending Trinity without prior special dispensation.

A figure from the 9th-century Book of Kells.

In academic circles, Oxford, Cambridge and Trinity were often mentioned in the same breath, and many English students who failed to make the first two ended up at 'Trinners'. Women students were admitted in 1903, earlier than in most British universities. Famous alumni include literary figures such as Oscar Wilde, Samuel Beckett, Thomas Moore, Sheridan Le Fanu, John Millington Synge, Oliver St John Gogarty and Bram Stoker. Politicians, rebels and statesmen, among them the likes of Edward Carson, Douglas Hyde (Ireland's first president), Henry Grattan, Wolfe Tone and Robert Emmet also made their mark.

Distinguished alumni

Most of Trinity's buildings date from the 18th century. The entrance is flanked by statues of two of Trinity's many famous alumni, the historian and statesman Edmund Burke (1729–97) and the writer Oliver Goldsmith (1728–74).

The Berkeley Library, built in 1967, is named after Bishop George Berkeley, an 18th-century philosopher who came to study at Trinity in 1700 at the age of 15 and later served for a time as the college librarian. Regarded by some as the precursor of Einstein and the father of higher education in America, Berkeley, who was born in Kilkenny, was also a distinguished scientist, economist, psychologist and writer.

artefact of the flowering of Irish culture between the 7th and 9th centuries, the era when Ireland was famed as 'the land of saints and scholars' and Irish monks re-Christianised Europe after the Dark Ages. Also in the library are the *Book of Durrow* (7th century), the *Book of Dimma* (8th century) and the *Book of Armagh* (*c.*807). Upstairs is the breathtaking Long Room, nearly 210ft (64 metres) in length and containing 200,000 of the college's oldest books. Temporary exhibitions highlight the library's fine collection.

Grafton Street

Leaving Trinity by the main gate and turning left, you face the mouth of **Grafton Street,** the southside's principal shopping thoroughfare, a pedestrianised street teeming with people and buskers. A bronze statue at the junction with Suffolk Street depicts Molly Malone who, in the famous song *In Dublin's Fair City,* 'wheeled her wheelbarrow through streets broad and narrow'. With typical Dublin wit, the statue was dubbed 'the tart with the cart'. Worth a visit for its luxurious

atmosphere is the **Brown Thomas** department store, a shopping haven at the start of Grafton Street. Top international brands include Louis Vuitton, Chanel, Hermès, Prada and Tiffany & Co. Remember to avail of tax-free shopping, if you are normally resident outside of the EU. The third floor restaurant is an excellent spot for a little people-watching over a cup of coffee or a glass of wine.

Johnston's Court, a narrow alley off Grafton Street to the right, leads to the rear entrance of the **Powerscourt Centre** ❸, three storeys of stylish shops, antique galleries, a theatre and cafés under the roof of the former Powerscourt Townhouse, built in 1771–74 for Viscount Powerscourt.

St Stephen's Green

On returning to Grafton Street, a right turn and a short walk takes you to the corner of **St Stephen's Green** ❹, a large square with a delightful park bordered by some fine houses, and a landmark glass-domed shopping centre. The gardens, laid out as a public park in 1880, are a relaxing

Molly Malone wheels her wheelbarrow on Grafton Street.

St Stephen's Green.

TIP

Dublinbikes (Tel: 1850 777070; www.dublinbikes. ie) is a hugely-popular bike-sharing scheme with 101 stations throughout the city centre. A three-day ticket costs €5, while an annual ticket is good value at €20 with the first half-hour free and a small fee per hour thereafter. Stations are open year round 5.00–00.30am but bikes can be returned 24 hours a day.

refuge from the traffic, contain several interesting sculptures and are crammed in summer with picnickers and sunbathers. The **Little Museum** of Dublin (15 St Stephen's Green; tel: 01-661 1000; www.littlemuseum.ie; daily 9.30am–5pm, Thu until 8pm; free) on your left arriving from Grafton Street, occupies three storeys of a Georgian house. Owned by Dublin City Council, this museum allows the people to tell the story of their city and offers a fascinating insight into the everyday life of Dubliners over the years. Artefacts on display were donated by ordinary people and range from a signed U2 album to a facsimile of James Joyce's death mask. The curators' tours are rich in Dublin wit and high-grade gossip. The basement café, Hatch & Sons Irish Kitchen, serves traditional Irish fare.

On the green's south side are two elegant Georgian houses: **Newman House**, numbers 85 and 86 (tel: 01-716 7422; June–Aug Tue–Fri, public guided tours at 2pm, 3pm and 4pm) once the seat of the Catholic University of Ireland at which James Joyce,

Flann O'Brien (Brian O'Nolan) and Gerard Manley Hopkins worked or studied. It has fine interior plasterwork. **Iveagh House,** numbers 80 and 81, which was built for the Bishop of Cork, once housed the Guinness family, and is now part of the Department of Foreign Affairs. The **University Church** (www.universitychurch.ie) next door was built in 1856 in a colourful neo-Byzantine style.

On the north side of the green is the **Shelbourne Hotel ❺**. Built in 1824, the hotel has been an intrinsic part of Dublin's social and cultural life for over 180 years. It's now a grand, elegant and exceptionally sumptuous spot, which attracts well-heeled Dubliners to its bars and restaurants. In Earlsfort Terrace, which branches from the southeastern corner of the green, is the **National Concert Hall** (www.nch.ie). The building, beautifully renovated, has first-rate acoustics.

Official Dublin

Back on the north side of St Stephen's Green, Kildare Street leads past the left-hand side of the Shelbourne Hotel

Leinster House.

and a block of modern state buildings to **Leinster House** , built as a town house for the Duke of Leinster in 1746 and now home of Dáil Eireann (Irish parliament). It is flanked by two, nearly symmetrical, edifices with columnar entrance rotundas. These are the National Library and National Museum, both built in 1890.

Apart from more than 500,000 books, the **National Library** (tel: 01-603 0200; www.nli.ie; exhibition area Mon–Wed 9.30am–7.45pm, Thu–Sat 9.30am–4.45pm, Sun 1–4.45pm; free) has an extensive collection of old newspapers and periodicals and a gallery housing temporary exhibitions of its collection. There is also a genealogy advisory service. The enormous reading room in its rotunda is worth a look.

The **National Museum** (tel: 01-677 7828; www.museum.ie; Tue–Sat 10am–5pm, Sun 2–5pm; free) has exhibits ranging from prehistory through the early Christian period and the Vikings to the Independence struggle. Exhibits include such treasures as the Ardagh Chalice and the Tara Brooch, plus fine prehistoric gold artefacts.

Directly opposite Leinster House is Molesworth Street, and a few yards along it is **Buswell's Hotel**, a popular haunt among politicians and political journalists. At its far end, the street meets Dawson Street, location of Hodges Figgis, Dublin's oldest and best bookshop, which was even mentioned in Ulysses by James Joyce.

Turning left at the corner you find **St Ann's Church** (1720), a venue for concerts as well as religious services in the Anglican tradition. A few metres up the street is the **Mansion House** the residence since 1715 of the Lord Mayors of Dublin. A Queen Anne-style house, dating from 1705, it was decorated with stucco and cast iron in Victorian times.

Merrion Square

At the other end of Dawson Street (towards Trinity College), you can turn right along Nassau Street which quickly becomes Clare Street, past the Kilkenny shop and the entrance to the Millennium Wing

A memorial to Oscar Wilde on Merrion Square.

Classic Georgian door knocker and doorway on Merrion Square.

The Natural History Museum.

of the National Gallery into **Merrion Square** ⑩, one of Dublin's finest parks. Laid out in 1762, it has had many distinguished inhabitants; Sir William and Lady 'Speranza' Wilde, surgeon and poetess, and parents of Oscar, lived at No. 1; Daniel O'Connell lived at No. 58; W.B. Yeats, who was born in the seaside suburb of Sandymount but grew up mainly in London, lived at No. 52 and later at No. 83; Sheridan Le Fanu, author of the seminal vampire story *Carmilla*, lived at No. 70. The Duke of Wellington, victor over Napoleon at the Battle of Waterloo, was born at No. 24 Merrion Street Upper, which runs off the southwest corner of the square towards Merrion Row and St Stephen's Green. The lush gardens make up a beautiful public park with a playground, inspired by the children's story *The Selfish Giant* by Oscar Wilde. Artists set up stall on weekends hanging their paintings on the wrought-iron railings.

The main entrance to the **National Gallery of Ireland** ⑪ (tel: 01-661 5133; www.nationalgallery.ie; Mon–Sat 9.30am–5.30pm, Thu until 8.30pm, Sun noon–5.30pm; free, charge for exhibitions; tours at weekends; free) is on Merrion Square West. Apart from a range of Irish work, the gallery has some Dutch masters and fine examples of the 17th-century French, Italian and Spanish schools. The Yeats Collection is a tribute to the artistic achievements of the Yeats family, especially Jack B. Yeats. The Millennium Wing houses temporary exhibitions, the gallery shop and the excellent, self-service Gallery Restaurant.

Leaving the gallery and turning right up Merrion Street Upper past the lawns of Leinster House, there is a fine view to your left along the southside of Merrion Square towards the distant cupola of **St Stephen**'s Church (1825), known locally as the "Pepper Canister Church" and a popular venue for concerts.

Passing the **Natural History Museum** (tel: 01-677 7444; www.museum.ie; Tue–Sat 10am–5pm, Sun 2–5pm; free), on your right you reach the imposing gates of **Government Buildings**, which house the office of the Taoiseach (prime minister) and the Cabinet room. Tours are available on Saturdays from 10.30am–1.30pm; tickets (free) are available that morning from the National Gallery.

A left turn at the next intersection along Baggot Street, then a right up Pembroke Street leads to **Fitzwilliam Square** ⑫, the city's smallest, latest (1825) and best-preserved Georgian square. Jack B. Yeats lived at number 18, on the corner of Fitzwilliam Street, the longest Georgian street in Dublin. In an infamous piece of state vandalism, 26 houses on its eastern side were demolished in 1965 to make way for a new Electricity Supply Board headquarters. Perhaps out of shame, the ESB helped restore **Number 29,** (tel: 01-702 6165; www.esb.ie/numbertwentynine; Tue–Sat 10am–5pm, Sun noon–5pm) on Fitzwilliam Street Lower. This Georgian House Museum offers an elegant recreation of a middle-class house of the late 1700s.

Wander back now to Trinity College, a good starting point to begin exploring the oldest part of the city.

Temple Bar

With your back to the facade of Trinity and the Bank of Ireland on your right, walk along Dame Street, passing on your right the imposing, layered structure of the modern Central Bank. The network of small streets between the Central Bank and the river quays, known as **Temple Bar ⑬**, is Dublin's 'Left Bank'. Temple Bar gained an unsavoury reputation some years ago for bawdy hen and stag parties. However the area has regained its cultural credentials in recent years with efforts made to curtail the rowdier elements.

Temple Bar is a browser's paradise of cobbled streets, jam-packed with art galleries, second-hand bookshops, vintage clothes shops, designer consignment shops, record stores, pubs, clubs, cultural centres, restaurants and everything in between. Temple Bar Square is lively and buzzy with traditional

music blaring out from the pubs. Meeting House Square is a cultural hub, with its Saturday farmers' market and outdoor cinema events.

North of Temple Bar Square, Merchant's Arch – a favourite spot for buskers – leads to the river quay and the **Ha'penny Bridge ⑭** (1816) – so-called because of the toll once charged for crossing it. This cast-iron pedestrian walkway across the Liffey has become one of the best-known symbols of the city. It is a convenient link to the Henry Street-Jervis Street shopping area across the river.

The route from Temple Bar Square to Meeting House Square goes through **Curved Street,** which houses the Irish Rock 'N' Roll Museum Experience (year round; daily; 10am–5.30pm; http://irishrocknrollmuseum. com; adult €16, child €12). Entrance includes a behind the scenes visit to the **Button Factory** rock venue and the **Temple Lane Studios** recording studios. The **Gallery of Photography** on Meeting House Square shows both Irish and international work and has an interesting range of postcards and

Pub entertainment in Temple Bar.

The quirky Temple Bar area.

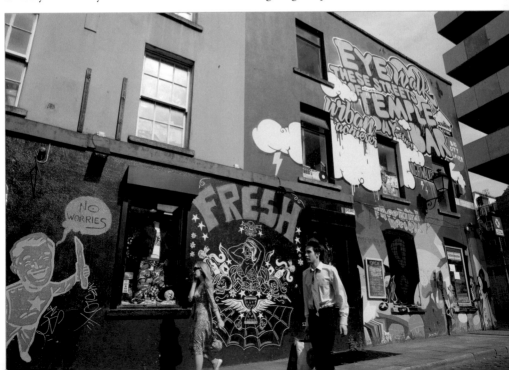

Grafton Street.

books (tel: 01-671 4654; www.gallery
ofphotography.ie; Tue–Sat 11am–6pm,
Sun 1–6pm; free).

On Eustace Street, in a former Presbyterian Meeting House is the **Ark,**
a cultural centre for children (www.
ark.ie) with workshops, camps, film
screenings and more. Opposite is the
Irish Film Institute – an arthouse
cinema with a bookshop, café and bar
(www.ifi.ie).

Continuing along Essex Street East,
you pass the rear of **The Clarence**
(www.theclarence.ie), which fronts onto
the river quay. The hotel's current
owners include members of the U2
rock band, and its art-deco Octagon
Bar is a fashionable meeting place.

Ancient Dublin

Venture across Parliament Street and
down Essex Street to the west of Temple Bar and you'll find a place more
like the original incarnation. Here
there's a good collection of cutting
edge interiors shops, retro treasure
troves and small boutiques, as well as
the stylish Cow's Lane Designer Mart
market, on Saturdays.

Essex Street ends at its junction with
Fishamble Street, the medieval 'fish
shambles,' or market, whose existence
can be traced back to 1467 and which
winds upwards from the quay alongside the Civic Offices.

Back on Dame Street, opposite City
Hall, you see on your right the ornate
Victorian doorway of the **Olympia
Theatre ⓖ** (tel: 01-679 3323). Despite
its modest frontage, the Olympia has
capacity for up to 1,600 concert-goers;
its programme mixes plays, musicals
and rock concerts.

City Hall

Dublin's medieval city once occupied
the area between City Hall and Bridge
Street, bordered by the riverbank to
the north and defensive walls, which
stretched as far as Bride Street in the
south. **City Hall ⓰** (tel: 01-222 2204;
www.dublincity.ie/dublincityhall; Mon–Sat
10am–5.15pm; free) was designed in
1769 as the Royal Exchange by the
London architect Thomas Cooley and
taken over by the Corporation of
Dublin in 1852. The entrance rotunda
has a splendid illuminated dome. The

exhibition The Story of the Capital is housed in the restored vaults of City Hall, and tells the story of Dublin through the ages.

Dublin Castle

Dublin Castle ⑰ (tel: 01-645 8813; www.dublincastle.ie; Mon–Sat 9.45am–4.45pm, Sun noon–4.45pm; by guided tour only), just behind City Hall, was built between 1208 and 1220 on the site of an earlier Danish fortress and was the symbol of English rule in Ireland for almost eight centuries. The building as it now stands is mainly 18th-century; the largest visible remain of the Norman structure is the Record Tower, in the lower Castle Yard, which contains the **Garda (Police) Museum**. When Ireland holds the Presidency of the EU, and on other state occasions, the Castle is closed to the public.

The most impressive parts of the castle are the **State Apartments** (by guided tour only) – St Patrick's Hall, 82ft (25 metres) long and 40ft (12 metres) wide, with a high panelled and decorated ceiling, and handmade

Donegal carpets is probably the grandest room in Ireland. Since 1938 it has been the scene of the inauguration of Irish presidents. The Gothic-style Church of the Most Holy Trinity was built as the Chapel Royal between 1807 and 1814 to a design by Francis Johnston; the exterior is decorated with more than 90 carved heads of English monarchs and other historical figures.

To the castle's rear, the Clock Tower building has been extended to accommodate the award-winning **Chester Beatty Library** ⑱ (tel: 01-407 0750; www.cbl.ie; Oct–Apr Tue–Fri 10am–5pm, Mar–Oct Mon–Fri 10am–5pm, Sat 11am–5pm all year, Sun 1–5pm all year; free). The library has a fine collection of Chinese, Japanese, Persian, Indian and Middle Eastern manuscripts, paintings and ornaments. Audio-visual programmes provide background. It also houses the first-class **Silk Road Café** offering a taste of the Middle East.

Leaving the castle, head a short way down Dame Street towards Trinity College and turn right up busy South

Dublin Castle.

One of Temple Bar's more extravagantly decorated pubs.

THE MESSIAH'S BIRTH

Dublin's otherwise unprepossessing Fishamble Street is celebrated as the venue of the first performance of Handel's *Messiah*, conducted by the composer in 1742 in the Charitable Music Society's Hall, long since demolished. Because the hall was cramped and the attendance large, ladies were asked not to wear hooped petticoats and gentlemen not to wear their swords. *Messiah* was an instant success in Dublin, though London audiences remained cool towards it for several years. A hotel, named after the composer, stands beside the original site; the *Messiah's* birth is celebrated at this spot by a statue of the composer (in the nude), and at noon every 13 April by members of Our Lady's Choral Society (fully clothed), who sing a selection of choruses.

FACT

Sir Alfred Chester Beatty was born in New York in 1875 and became a successful mining engineer in Colorado. Having collected minerals and Chinese snuff bottles as a child, he became interested in Japanese and Chinese paintings. His knighthood was a reward for his help in supplying raw materials to the Allies in World War II. He moved to Ireland in 1950 and built a library to house his art collection.

Great George's Street; on the left side is a Victorian shopping arcade worth a quick look.

Continue from Aungier Street into Wexford Street, turn right, and cross New Bride Street into Kevin Street Upper, where you find **Marsh's Library** ⑲ (tel: 01-454 3511; www.marshlibrary.ie; Mon and Wed–Fri 9.30am–5pm, Sat 10am–5pm, adult €3; free for children), the oldest public library in Ireland and named after its founder, Archbishop Narcissus Marsh (1638–1713). The library, with its original oak bookcases, will be enjoyed by book lovers. Among its 25,000 interesting items is Jonathan Swift's copy of *Clarendon's History of the Great Rebellion*, with Swift's pencilled notes. Readers wishing to peruse valuable books were locked into elegant cages, which can still be seen.

The Liberties

The next junction marks the beginning of the **Liberties,** an area so named because it lay outside the jurisdiction of medieval Dublin.

One of the city's most characterful working-class areas, it also had some of the worst 19th-century slum tenements. Turn right along Patrick Street to **St Patrick's Cathedral** ⑳ (tel: 01-453 9472; www.stpatrickscathedral.ie; Mon–Fri 9.30am–5pm, Mar–Oct Sat 9am–6pm, Sun 9–10.30, 12.30-2.30pm 4.30–6pm, Nov–Feb Sat 9am–5pm, Sun 9–10.30, 12.30–2.30pm). Dedicated in 1192, St Patrick's has been restored many times and, like Dublin's other cathedral, Christ Church, has belonged to the Church of Ireland since the Reformation. Jonathan Swift, Dean from 1713 to 1745, is buried in it, near his beloved 'Stella', Esther Johnson. A simple brass plate in the floor marks his grave.

Continue north to **Christ Church Cathedral** ㉑ (tel: 01-677 8099; www.christchurchdublin.ie; daily 9am–6pm in summer, Fri 9.45am–5 or 6pm in winter; closed Sun am for services). This prominent cathedral was founded by Sitric, the Danish King of Dublin, about 1040, and greatly expanded from 1172 onwards under the aegis of Strongbow and St Laurence O'Toole. The central tower was built about 1600 after storm and fire damage to the original steeples. Lambert Simnel, 10-year-old pretender to the English throne, was crowned here by his supporters in 1487. The structure was greatly rebuilt in Gothic revival style in the 1870s. Two of the cathedral's many tombs are said to be those of Strongbow and his son, whom, according to legend, he executed for cowardice in battle.

Linked to the cathedral by a covered bridge is **Dublinia** ㉒ (tel: 01-679 4611; www.dublinia.ie; daily Mar–Sept 10am–6.30pm with last entry at 5.30pm; daily Oct–Feb 10am–5.30pm with last entry at 4.30pm) an exhibition, run by the non-profit Medieval Trust. State-of-the-art interactives and reconstructions give an insight into the

The Chester Beatty Library.

medieval world of Dublin. There is also an archaeological lab and excavation site, and an exhibition of what life was like aboard a Viking warship. From the top of the 200ft (60-metre) St Michael's Tower, you can enjoy a panoramic view over the city.

St Audoen's Church

High Street, which runs off the west side of Christchurch Place, was the backbone of medieval Dublin. Part of the old city wall and the only surviving city gate has been uncovered near the partially ruined **St Audoen's Church** ㉓ (tel: 01-677 0088; Apr–Oct daily 9.45am– 5.30pm; free). It was named by the Normans after St Ouen of Rouen. Its aisle contains a font dating from 1194; the tower is 12th-century and three of its bells were cast in the early 15th century, making them the country's oldest.

On the other side of High Street, in Back Lane, is **Tailors' Hall,** the only surviving guildhall in Dublin, and now the offices of An Taisce, which works to preserve the country's natural and architectural heritage.

The Guinness tour

One part of the national heritage which seems well able to look after itself is enshrined half-a-mile (1km) to the west along Thomas Street: **Guinness's Brewery,** the biggest in Europe, churning out 2.5 million pints of its celebrated black stout every day. The brewery doesn't admit visitors, but the **Guinness Storehouse** ㉔ (tel: 01-408 4800; www.guinness-store house.com; daily 9.30am–5pm, July– Aug until 7pm; discounts on tickets available online) lets you explore – through sight, touch, taste and smell – the making and history of the world's most famous stout. The building also houses gallery and exhibition areas, events venues, an archives room and the **Gravity Bar,** the highest bar in Dublin with an incredible panoramic view of the city. The admission ticket entitles you to a complimentary pint in the rooftop bar – probably the best-tasting Guinness to be had anywhere, since it hasn't had to travel.

North of the Liffey

O'Connell Bridge is once more your starting-point to explore Dublin's northern half, but before acquainting yourself with the main features of O'Connell Street, stay a little longer on the southside, walking east along Burgh Quay and under the railway bridge for a view across the river to the **Custom House** ㉕, one of the masterpieces of James Gandon, the greatest architect of 18th-century Dublin. Although English, Gandon looked to the Continent for architectural models and it is easier to imagine the Custom House transposed to the banks of the Seine than to the Thames.

Finished in 1791, the building was extensively damaged in a fire started by Republicans to mark the Sinn Féin election victory in 1921 and has been largely rebuilt. The central copper dome, 120ft (38 metres) high, is

Stained-glass window, Christ Church Cathedral.

Christ Church Cathedral.

The toucan, Guinness's long time logo.

A free pint at the end of the Guinness Storehouse tour.

topped by a statue of commerce by Edward Smyth. The keystones over the arched doorways flanking the Doric portico represent the Atlantic Ocean and 13 principal rivers of Ireland.

Gandon later designed Carlisle Bridge (widened and rebuilt in 1880 and renamed O'Connell Bridge), the Four Courts, the eastern portico of Parliament House (Bank of Ireland) and the King's Inns.

The gleaming building just downstream of the Custom House is the Irish Financial Services Centre (known as the IFSC). This is the gateway to Dublin's docklands development, a legacy of the optimistic boom years, spreading east from here on both sides of the Liffey. Those with an interest in contemporary architecture can follow a signposted walking trail.

The Abbey Theatre

From the Custom House on the north bank of the Liffey, walk towards O'Connell Bridge and turn into Marlborough Street, where you find the **Abbey Theatre** ㉖ home of Ireland's national theatre (www.

abbeytheatre.ie). The present building was erected in 1966 to replace a predecessor, which was destroyed by fire.

The Abbey, founded in 1904 by W.B. Yeats, Lady Gregory and their collaborators, played a vital role in the cultural renaissance of the time and earned a world reputation through the great works of John Millington Synge and Sean O'Casey and for its players' naturalistic acting style. Performances were often turbulent: the most celebrated uproar was caused at a performance of Synge's *The Playboy of the Western World* by the use of the word 'shift' (petticoat). Downstairs in the Abbey its sister theatre, the **Peacock**, is used to showcase more experimental work.

O'Connell Street

O'Connell Street ㉗ is still not the Champs Elysées that Dubliners believe it resembles in scale, despite efforts to upgrade this once-elegant street and generally give it a facelift. Broad and impressive, the street was planned (as Sackville Street) in the mid-1700s by the first Viscount Mountjoy, Luke Gardiner, who widened the existing narrow roadway, and planted trees on a central mall.

Reaching to the sky is the **Spire of Dublin**, an aspirational and strangely beautiful 390ft (120-metre) stainless steel pillar, officially entitled the Monument of Light, which has stood at the midpoint of O'Connell Street since 2003. It was chosen to replace Nelson's Column, erected in 1815 to mark Nelson's victory over Napoleon, and blown up by republicans in 1966.

Centrepiece of the street is the imposing Ionic portico of the **General Post Office** ㉘ (1815), headquarters of the 1916 Rising and the place where the rebels proclaimed the republic in ringing terms, to the initial bemusement of Dubliners – a reaction, in Yeats's words, 'changed utterly' by the subsequent execution, one by one, of 15 captured leaders. The GPO's pillars are still pockmarked by bullets; although the building survived the fighting, much of the street was wrecked by British

artillery and it suffered further in 1922 during the Civil War.

O'Connell Street suffered from incongruous developments in the late 20th century, with plastic and neon signs and derelict sites disfiguring Dublin's main thoroughfare. Things haven't changed much between the closure of Cleary's Department Store and increasing numbers of heroin addicts using methadone clinics in the vicinity.

Moore Street market

Off O'Connell Street, just past the GPO, Henry Street is the northside's main shopping street. Its tributary to the north, **Moore Street,** is filled with fruit and vegetable stalls staffed by colourful and vociferous women. It is packed with a hive of ethnic food outlets and hair and beauty stores to cater for Dublin's burgeoning immigrant population. It's well worth visiting for a dose of down-to-earth Dublin, as well as Ireland's new multiculturalism, and there are some great no-frills Chinese restaurants hidden beneath Mandarin-scripted signs.

TIP

When touring Dublin, cross the Liffey river over Santiago Calatrava's stunning Samuel Beckett bridge (2010), to the south side to find Grand Canal Square, a futuristic piazza where the offices of Facebook and Google are located. The exuberant Bord Gais Energy Theatre (capacity 2,100) was designed by the renowned architect Daniel Libeskind. Lively cafés and restaurants and outdoor seating areas abound. This part of the regenerated dockland district is the biggest success story so far.

The stainless-steel spire on O'Connell Street.

KEY TO THE STATUES

The statues lining the centre of Dublin's O'Connell Street are (from the bridge end): Daniel O'Connell (1775–1847), a great leader of constitutional nationalism; William Smith O'Brien (1803–64), leader of the Young Ireland Party; Sir John Gay (1816–75), proprietor of the *Freeman's Journal* (published 1763–1924) and organiser of the city's water supply; James Larkin (1876–1947), a famous trade union leader and co-founder of the Irish Labour Party; Father Theobald Mathew (1790–1856), the 'Apostle of Temperance'; and Charles Stewart Parnell (1846–91), inspiration of the Home Rule movement and a tragic victim of intolerance whose career was ruined by the outcry over his union with Kitty O'Shea, who happened to be married to another Irish politician.

Fresh flowers at Moore Street market.

The Custom House.

On the opposite side of O'Connell Street, walk down Earl Street and turn left into Marlborough Street to visit **St Mary's Pro-Cathedral** ㉙ (1816–25), the city's main Catholic Church. John Henry Newman first publicly professed Catholicism here in 1851. The area was once a notorious red-light district, known as 'Monto' (James Joyce's 'Nighttown').

At the north end of O'Connell Street is the late 18th-century **Rotunda Room,** occupied by a cinema, a music venue and more recently by an exhibition centre. The **Rotunda Hospital** to the left (Europe's first maternity hospital) was financed by concerts in the Rooms. Built in conjunction with the hospital, the **Gate Theatre** at the bottom of Parnell Square East was founded in 1928 by Micheál MacLiammóir and Hilton Edwards; the teenage Orson Welles made his first professional appearance here (www.gate-theatre.ie).

A few yards on past the Gate, the **Garden of Remembrance** (1966) commemorates Ireland's martyrs. The sculpture by Oisin Kelly, beyond the central lake, is based on the myth of the Children of Lir, who were turned into swans.

Modern art

On the north side of Parnell Square is the **Dublin City Gallery The Hugh Lane** ㉚ (tel: 01-222 5550; www.hughlane.ie; Tue–Thu 9.45am–6pm, Fri 9.45am–5pm, Sat 10am–5pm, Sun 11am–5pm; free). Its nucleus is formed by the mainly Impressionist collection of Sir Hugh Lane, who died when the liner *Lusitania* was torpedoed in 1915. As a result of a wrangle over his will, the collection was split, each half being alternated every five years between Dublin and London's Tate Gallery. The gallery employed a team of archaeologists to painstakingly dismantle the London studio of Dublin-born artist Francis Bacon and faithfully reconstruct it here.

At 18–19 Parnell Square North, the **Dublin Writers Museum** ㉛ (tel: 01-872 2077; www.writersmuseum.com; Mon–Sat 9.45am–4.45pm, Sun 11am–4.30pm) displays photographs,

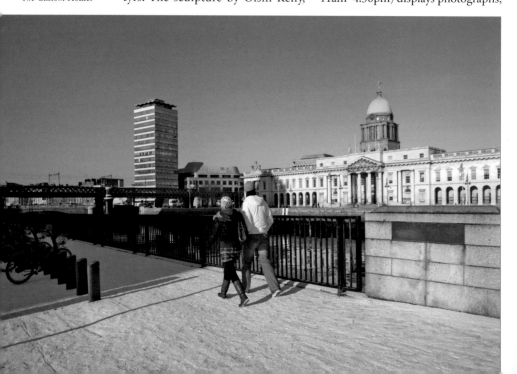

paintings, busts, letters, manuscripts, first editions and other memorabilia relating to celebrated deceased writers such as Swift, Shaw, Yeats, O'Casey, Joyce, Beckett and Behan. The first-floor Gallery of Writers is splendidly decorated. The designation of Dublin as the world's fourth Unesco City of Literature in 2010 gave a great boost to an already vibrant literary scene. In the month of April One City One Book aims to get all Dubliners reading the same book. Visit www.dublincityofliterature.ie for details of free literary events for adults and children.

Parnell Street was always a bit of a rough-and-tumble type of spot with some seriously dodgy pubs, but Dublin's growing Asian community has transformed the street into Dublin's official Chinatown. Chinese New Year is celebrated annually. If you are looking for cheap and authentic Asian cuisine, this is the place to go.

At Parnell Square East, turn left and then right into Great Denmark Street. On the left is **Belvedere College** ㉜, a fine 18th-century mansion, which has been a Jesuit secondary school for boys since 1841.

James Joyce Centre

Turn into North Great George's Street, where many grand Georgian houses have been saved from decades of decrepitude. At number 35 is the **James Joyce Centre** ㉝ (tel: 01-878 8547; www.jamesjoyce.ie; Oct–Mar Tue–Sat 10am–5pm, Sun noon–5pm; Apr–Sep Mon–Sat 10am–5pm, Sun noon–5pm; tours must be pre-booked), located in a beautifully restored late 18th-century townhouse, which features in *Ulysses* as the venue for dancing classes. The centre's most interesting exhibit is a set of biographies of real Dublin people fictionalised in Joyce's masterpiece. There are photographs and storyboards about Joyce's family and the many homes

they inhabited. And, in a suitably Joycean collision of fact and fiction, you can view the front door of No. 7 Eccles Street, home of Leopold Bloom and his wife Molly, the central characters of *Ulysses* (the house itself was demolished). The centre's interior has splendid stucco ceilings.

Returning past The Hugh Lane Gallery to Parnell Square West, turn right, then left into Bolton bearing left into Capel Street. To the left in Mary Street is **St Mary's Church** ㉞, built from 1697 by Thomas Burgh, architect of Trinity College library. Here, in 1747, John Wesley preached his first sermon in Ireland. Theobald Wolfe Tone (1763–98), founder of the United Irishmen and father of Irish republicanism, was born nearby in a street now named after him.

St Michan's

To the other side of Capel Street, Mary Street leads via Mary's Lane to Church Street, where you find **St Michan's Church** ㉟, (Mon–Fri

Where writers are remembered.

The General Post Office (GPO), central to the 1916 Rising.

FACT

After a bloody past, Dublin's Kilmainham Gaol became a popular film location. Interior scenes for the prison in which Noël Coward planned his heist in *The Italian Job* (1969) were shot here. So were scenes from *In the Name of the Father* (1993), *Michael Collins* (1996) and *The Wind that Shakes the Barley* (2006). Execution scenes for the TV series *The Tudors* (2007) were also filmed here.

The Four Courts.

10am–12.45pm, 2–4.45pm, Sat 10am–12.45pm;) founded in 1095 as a Viking parish church. The present structure dates from the late 1600s, but it was much restored in 1821 and again after the Civil War. Handel is said to have played on its organ.

In the vaults are 17th-century mummified bodies, preserved because the limestone walls absorb moisture from the air.

Leaving the church, turn down May Lane and left into Bow Street which will bring you to the **Old Jameson Distillery** (www.jamesonwhiskey.com; Mon–Sat 9am–6pm, Sun 10am–6pm; guided tours; adult €16, child €8), a museum is sited in the old warehouse of the 1791 whiskey factory.

The Four Courts

Return to the quays and turn left to end this section of the tour as you began it: with a look at a Gandon masterpiece. The **Four Courts** ❸❻ (visitors can witness most court proceedings, Mon–Fri 10am–1pm, 2–4pm; free) was built between 1786 and 1802. The dominant lantern-dome is fronted by a six-columned Corinthian portico surmounted by the statues of Moses, Justice and Mercy, and flanked by two wings enclosing courtyards.

In 1922, after the building was barricaded by anti-Treaty republicans, troops of Michael Collins's new government shelled it from across the river. In the ensuing fire, the Record Office was burnt, destroying priceless documents. Restoration was completed in 1932.

West Dublin

Board the westbound Red Line of LUAS at the rear of the Four Courts. After three quick stops, you'll be at Heuston Station.

From here it is only a five-minute walk west along St John's Road before turning north onto Military Road and the entrance to **Kilmainham Royal Hospital**, founded by Charles II (1680–84) 'for the reception and entertainment of antient (sic) maimed, and infirm officers and soldiers.' It's a beautiful French-style building with exquisite grounds and now houses the **Irish Museum of Modern Art** ③⑦ (tel: 01-612 9900; www.imma.ie; Tue–Fri 11.30am–5.30pm, Sat 10am–5.30pm, Sun noon–5.30pm; free, charge for special exhibitions), which combines Irish and international 20th-century art with various educational and community programmes. There's a nice café here and beautiful formal gardens that are a pleasure in summer.

Kilmainham Gaol

Exit the museum the way you came in, a right turn onto Military Road and a right again onto Bow Bridge brings you to the South Circular Road and **Kilmainham Gaol** ③⑧ (tel: 01-453 5984; May–Sept daily 8.45am–7pm, Oct–Apr daily 9.30am–5.30pm), which has been intimately connected with Ireland's struggle for independence from its construction in the 1790s until it ceased to be a prison in the 1920s. Visitors are invited to browse in the museum, which explores 19th-century notions of crime, punishment and reform through a series of well-captioned displays. The upstairs section is devoted to the nationalist figures, some famous, some more obscure, who were imprisoned here, many awaiting execution.

Upstairs visitors can see the '1916 corridor', containing the cells that housed the captured leaders of the Rising, and the stone-breakers' yard where 14 of them were shot between 3 and 12 May of that year. It is well worth a visit.

If you prefer a walk in the park to time in jail, turn left on Bow Lane from Military Road and left again on **Steeven's Lane**. Head past Heuston Station and cross the river to visit **Phoenix Park** ③⑨ whose southern boundary extends west on the Liffey's north bank for about 3 miles (5km). At 1,760 acres (712 hectares), it is over five times as large as London's Hyde Park. Its name is a corruption of the Gaelic *fionn uisce* (clear water). You can rent a bike by the hour at the gatehouse of the Parkgate entrance, the best way to explore the huge open spaces of Dublin's Phoenix Park

This life-size statue of James Joyce stands on North Earl Street, off O'Connell Street.

Kilmainham Gaol.

Sailing boats in Dun Laoghaire harbour.

Showing the Irish at war at the National Museum of Decorative Arts and History.

(tel: 087-3799946; http://phoenixparkbikes.com).

Among its features, all signposted, are: the Wellington Monument, an obelisk 197ft (60 metres) high, erected after Waterloo; **Dublin Zoo** (www.dublinzoo.ie), the third oldest public zoo in the world (1830), well known for the breeding of lions (it supplied the MGM announcer); the President's residence, **Aras an Uachtaráin**, formerly the Viceregal Lodge (1751–54); the US Ambassador's residence; and Farmleigh House and Estate (www.farmleigh.ie), once the home of the Guinness family and now in state ownership hosting cultural events and foreign dignitaires.

On the way back to the city, on the north side of the quays, is the former Collins Barracks, now the **National Museum of Decorative Arts and History** ⓙ with displays of Irish silver, glass, furniture, Japanese art and a permanent exhibition on the Irish furniture designer and architect Eileen Gray (tel: 01-6777 7444; www.museum.ie; Tue–Sat 10am–5pm, Sun 2–5pm; free).

Southside suburbs

Most places mentioned in this section of the book are served by various buses departing from Eden Quay, beside O'Connell Bridge, and by the DART suburban trains.

Travelling out through Merrion Square North, along Northumberland Road past the squat, circular block of the **American Embassy** (1964), you reach the prestigious suburb of **Ballsbridge** ⓚ named after the bridge over the River Dodder. The large greystone buildings to the right on Merrion Road, just past the bridge, are the headquarters of the Royal Dublin Society (the RDS, www.rds.ie), the sponsor of improvements in agriculture and stockbreeding and the venue for the Dublin Horse Show (in August). The RDS's Simmonscourt Extension is used for exhibitions and concerts.

The main road south soon skirts the coast, affording fine views of the bay, and passes through **Blackrock** ⓛ, where Eamon de Valera studied and later taught at the prestigious boys' secondary school, Blackrock College.

Dun Laoghaire

A couple of miles further on is the town and port of **Dun Laoghaire** ⓜ (pronounced 'dunleery'). The harbour, with its long, granite pier, was built between 1817 and 1859 and is exceptionally popular with walkers throughout the year. The pier is particularly beautiful on a summer's day when the sea twinkles and the views of craggy Howth are especially clear.

The next promontory, within easy walking distance, is that of **Sandycove**, with its Martello Tower where Joyce lived for a short time in 1904. He used it as the setting for the opening scene of *Ulysses* and it is now the **James Joyce Museum** ⓝ (tel: 01-280 9265; daily, 10am–6pm, until 5pm in winter; free). **The Forty Foot** bathing place beside it was traditionally a place for gentlemen to swim in the nude, but these days both male and female swimmers of all ages come to plunge into the very cold waters throughout the year – clothing is optional.

Dalkey

Just a 20-minute walk from Sandycove is the affluent and charming village of **Dalkey** ㊺. Dalkey is something of a celebrity hotspot, with lively pub and café scene. Bono, The Edge, Enya, Van Morrison, Neil Jordan are among its residents, as was the late Maeve Binchy. **Dalkey Castle** (tel: 01-285 8366; www.dalkeycastle.com; Mon, Wed–Fri 10am–5.30pm; Sat, Sun 11am–5.30pm), a medieval tower house, has been restored and houses a heritage centre. Its battlements give excellent views of the surrounding land and seascape.

From nearby **Coliemore Harbour** there are summer boat trips (http://kentheferryman.com; daily 10am–6pm) to **Dalkey Island**, a stone's throw offshore; it contains another Martello tower and the ruins of a Benedictine church. The island is a bird sanctuary and the waters are rich with seals.

You can enter **Killiney Hill Park** from Vico Road, which continues along the coast. At the summit of the park there are splendid views of the broad sweep of Killiney Bay (often likened to the Bay of Naples), Bray Head (the humpbacked promontory at its far side) and the two Sugar Loaf Mountains. DART travellers can continue on to **Bray** ㊻ as a seaside resort it has seen better days, but the seascapes en route are impressive and Bray Head offers bracing walks and fine views to the south.

Northern suburbs

The attractions of the northside are more diffuse. But it's worth visiting **Glasnevin** ㊼ (buses 13 and 19 from O'Connell Street) to see the beautifully arranged **Botanic Gardens** (tel: 01-804 0300; www.botanicgardens.ie; Mar–Sep Mon–Fri 9am–5pm, Sat–Sun 10am–6pm; Oct–Feb Mon–Fri 9am–4.30pm, Sat–Sun 10am–4.30pm; free). Only 3 miles (5km) north of O'Connell Street, the gardens make a tranquil contrast to urban sightseeing. The magnificent

The former Collins Barracks has been transformed into an outpost of the National Museum.

Glasnevin Cemetery.

*Glasnevin Museum
entrance.*

Victorian curvilinear glasshouses have been fully restored.

Glasnevin Museum and Cemetery Tour (tel: 01-882 6559; www.glasnevinmuseum.ie; daily Mon–Fri 9am–6pm; shop, café), the Republic's national burying ground, is a popular outing. It contains the remains of Daniel O'Connell, Eamon de Valera, Michael Collins, Brendan Behan and many others. The striking museum (2011) traces the history of Ireland through the lives of the 1.5 million people buried at Glasnevin. The family-friendly tours (included in admission charge) are renowned for the wit and personality of the guides.

Casino Marino

The coastal route northeast by the Custom House leads to the Casino Marino (tel: 01-833 1618; www.heritage ireland.ie; mid-Mar–May & Oct, daily 10am–5pm, Jun–Sep, daily 10am–6pm) a small Palladian building, that is a gem of its kind, with several unusual features: the roof urns are actually chimneys and the columns are hollow, serving as drains. It was originally part of the seaside estate of Lord Charlemont, whose town house is now the **Dublin City Gallery The Hugh Lane**.

Beyond Clontarf the coast road passes the **North Bull Island**, a huge sandbank growing from the North Wall of Dublin Port and containing two golf courses: St Anne's (www.stanneslinksgolf.com) and the famous Royal Dublin (www.theroyaldublingolfclub.com). It is also an important sanctuary for winter migrant birds.

Howth

Carrying on via the isthmus at the suburb of Sutton you reach **Howth Head** (also accessible by DART and bus), whose rugged brow overlooks the northern entrance to Dublin Bay. You can go directly to the village of **Howth** ❹ or start instead at The Summit and walk to the village around the nose of the promontory by a splendidly scenic cliff path, which descends steeply to the fishing harbour. The novelist H.G. Wells called the view from the head 'one of the most beautiful in the world.' The offshore island of **Ireland's Eye** was the site of a 6th-century monastery and is now a bird sanctuary. Howth, along with Malahide, is the most fashionable place to live on the northside, and it is easy to see why. The gardens at nearby **Howth Castle** (http://howthcastle.com; by appointment only) are beautiful, especially if you like rhododendrons.

Five miles (8km) north of Howth lies **Portmarnock** ❹, which has fine beaches and a championship golf course (www.portmarnockgolfclub.ie). At **Malahide** ❺ a pleasant resort and suburban town 7 miles (11km) north of Howth, is **Malahide Castle** (tel: 01-890 5000; www.malahidecastleandgardens.ie; daily 9.30am–5.30pm), inhabited by the Talbot family from 1185 for nearly 800 years, the castle, now publicly owned, is fully furnished with displays on the family's history. The 22 acres (9 hectares) of ornamental gardens contain over 5000 species, fully labelled. There is also a playground, pitch and putt and an Avoca café.

TIP

Kayak with the seals of Dalkey Harbour with Kayaking.ie (tel: 086-168 4755; www.kayaking.ie) Enjoy the scenery of Dublin Bay with views back to the Dublin mountains. All equipment is provided and all ages and ability levels are welcome.

Malahide Castle.

BLOOMSDAY

James Joyce's *Ulysses* takes place on a single day in 1904. Each year on that day, 16 June, the novel's events are re-enacted.

Polls of literary critics have deemed *Ulysses* the greatest novel of the 20th century, although even in Dublin it is probably more honoured than read. Thematically based on Homer's *Odyssey*, it documents a 24-hour period in the lives of an Irish Jew, Leopold Bloom, and a budding writer, Stephen Dedalus, as they move around Dublin; the story reaches its climax when they meet.

The novel was published in 1922 in Paris by Sylvia Beach's Shakespeare & Company bookshop. It was banned in Britain and America – though never, curiously, in Ireland, though it was difficult to obtain there. The first Bloomsday celebrations took place in Dublin on 16 June 1954, the 50th anniversary of the events depicted in the novel. Initially they were designed to appeal mainly to academics, but after Joyce's centenary in 1982, they became increasingly popular so that now they are rivalled only by St Patrick's Day. People who boast that have never opened a copy of Ulysses, happily dress up as Joycean characters and breakfast on kidneys to mark the occasion.

Street performers strike a pose during Bloomsday celebrations in Central Dublin.

Gorgonzola sandwich

Participants, wearing what approximates to 1904 garb, trace the paths of the book's characters. After a Bloomsday breakfast in Sandycove, they can listen to readings delivered by costumed actors, lunch on gorgonzola sandwiches and burgundy in Davy Byrne's pub, walk through the northside, taking in Hardwicke Street, Eccles Street, Gardiner Street and Mountjoy Square, enjoy more readings at the Joyce Centre, and then discuss the book's finer points over a few pints of Guinness.

An actor recites his lines. The 250,000 words of Ulysses, packed with puns, parodies and allusions, formed some of the 20th century's most experimental prose and is quite the feat to complete reading.

Ulysses mentions so many bars that Bloomsday can easily turn into a pub crawl. A prominent venue is Davy Byrne's "moral pub" where Leopold Bloom enjoyed a lunchtime gorgonzola sandwich and a glass of burgundy.

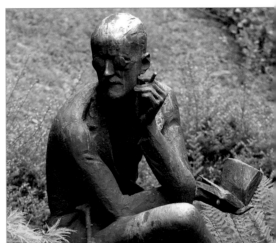

Sculpture of Joyce beside his grave at Fluntern Cemetery in Zurich.

JAMES JOYCE (1882–1941)

One of 10 children, James Augustine Aloysius Joyce was born at Rathgar, Dublin. He graduated from University College in 1902 with a degree in modern languages.

In 1904, while living briefly in the Martello Tower at Sandycove, he met Nora Barnacle, a simple country girl, and they moved abroad, living mainly in Trieste and Paris; they had a son, Giorgio (who later became an alcoholic), and a daughter, Lucia (who became mentally ill), but did not marry until 1931. Joyce's eye troubles began in 1907, leaving him almost blind in later life.

Joyce remained an exile for the rest of his life. In Paris he mixed with writers such as Ezra Pound, Scott Fitzgerald, T.S. Eliot and Ernest Hemingway. As a young man, the playwright Samuel Beckett acted as his secretary. When war drove Joyce out in 1940, he moved to Zurich, where he died a year later. Nora remained in Zurich, where she died in 1951.

Joyce said of Ulysses: There are enough enigmas 'to keep the professors busy for centuries arguing over what I meant, and that's the only way of securing your immortality.'

Celebrating Bloomsday with a pint of the black stuff and a well-loved copy of Ulysses.

Joyce was critical of the debilitating effects the priesthood had on Irish life. At one point he has the hero of Ulysses – Leopold Bloom, a Jew – praise psychological devices such as Confession.

Joyce once boasted that, if Dublin were to be destroyed, it would be possible to reconstruct it from the pages of Ulysses.

EXCURSIONS FROM DUBLIN

To the south lie the Wicklow Mountains, to the north the remarkable historical burial chambers of Newgrange and to the west some of the world's best racehorse country.

Wicklow (www.visitwicklow.ie) is known as 'the garden of Ireland', and while there are scenic spots galore (including some glorious gardens), the county also possesses a savage beauty that equals that of the west of the island. The Wicklow Mountains (www.wicklow mountainsnationalpark.ie), are a rugged mass of granite running from Dublin, through Wicklow and down into Wexford. Blanket bogs clothe the upper slopes, while peaty streams cascade swiftly downhill into deep lakes. The mountains run an impassable wedge through parts of the county, making it difficult to cover the whole area in one day – unless you drive at a non-stop clip.

West Wicklow

West Wicklow can be reached via the M50 and the N81. At **Blessington**, 19 miles (30km) from Dublin, the valley of the River Liffey was flooded in 1940, submerging 74 farmhouses and cottages to create a reservoir; a scenic drive skirts the perimeter. Less than 2 miles (3.2km) south is the grand, 18th-century, Palladian house, **Russborough ❶**. The house has an important collection of furnishings and paintings, including works by Goya, Gainsborough and Rubens. For family fun, there is a huge maze, a fairy trail and a playground (tel: 045-865 239;

Mar–Dec daily 10am–6pm; guided tours, charge).

Follow the N81 to **Hollywood ❷**, no relation to its Californian namesake, but coincidentally, a location for the films *Dancing at Lughnasa* (1998) and *Michael Collins* (1996). From here, a 15-mile (25km) drive on the R756 brings you across the bleakly beautiful Wicklow Gap to **Laragh** where, in summer, teas are served in the grassy village triangle.

A mile before Laragh is the turn to one of the most visited sites in the

Main Attractions

Blessington
Glendalough
Avoca
Powerscourt House
Hill of Tara
Slane
Newgrange
Cooley Peninsula
Celbridge
Kildare

Powerscourt Waterfall.

Excursions from Dublin

east of Ireland, **Glendalough**. Here, in the steep-sided valley between two lakes, St Kevin founded a monastic settlement in the 6th century. The ruins – a 110ft (33-metre) round tower and sacred structures – date from the 11th and 12th centuries (tel: 0404-45325; www.glendalough.ie; daily 9.30am–5pm Mar–Oct, Nov–Feb until 6pm; guided tours; ruins free, visitor centre charge).

Several roads meet in Laragh: take the R755 to the northeast, and after 6 miles (9km) you arrive in **Roundwood** ❸, purportedly the highest village in Ireland, 781ft (238 metres) above sea level. If you take the R155, to the northwest, you come to the gorgeous **Glenmacnass Waterfall**, 6 miles (9km) away.

Avondale

If you continue south from Laragh, the R755 leads through the gently wooded Vale of Clara to **Rathdrum**, 7 miles (11km) away. **Avondale House and Forest Park** ❹ (tel: 0404-46111; Easter & Apr 14th–Oct 31st, Thu–Sun & Bank Holidays, 11am–5pm; last admission 4.15pm), the Georgian home of the great Irish politician, Charles Stewart Parnell (1846–91), is now a museum devoted to his memory and is surrounded by hundreds of acres of forest park.

The picturesque village of **Avoca** ❺ with its multicoloured houses and working weaving mill is another couple of miles south. Also at this end of the county is **Brittas Bay** (off the N11 at 'Jack White's Inn'), with its sandy dunes, beloved of Irish holidaymakers.

Off the N11 at **Ashford**, are the world-renowned **Mount Usher Gardens** ❻, (www.mountushergardens.ie; Avoca Café open all year, gardens Mar–Oct, daily,10am–6pm;), voted the best garden to visit in Ireland by *Gardener's World Magazine*. Walk along the **Devil's Glen**, a mile or two northwest on the R764 and R765, through woodland to the Devil's

Glen waterfall. Birdwatchers should head for the coast (off the R761) between Newcastle and Kilcoole, where migrants often stop to feed.

Powerscourt

The village of **Enniskerry**, sign-posted off the N11 near Bray, has a lovely cut-stone clock tower at its centre. **Powerscourt House and Gardens ❼** (tel: 01-204 6000; www. powerscourt.ie; daily 9.30am–5.30pm, dusk in winter) are about a mile to the south. The 18th-century stately home, gutted by fire in 1974, and restored in the mid-1990s, now houses upmarket shops, a garden centre and an Avoca restaurant. The grounds on one side are dominated by a golf course, but on the other, the heroic Italianate landscape designed by Daniel Robertson in the mid-19th century survives. Robertson, a martyr to gout and the sherry bottle, was said to have conducted operations from a wheelbarrow.

Powerscourt Waterfall, which has a separate entrance gate, is the highest waterfall in Ireland (398ft/121 metres).

Excursions North

The countryside north of Co. Dublin is impressively larded with antiquities, and offers up well-preserved pre-Christian monuments, monastic sites and heritage towns. Some of the attractions, such as the megalithic passage graves in the Boyne Valley, can easily consume the best part of the day.

Co. Meath, which wraps around the northwest shoulder of Dublin, was the terrain of the pagan High Kings of Ireland and is known as the Royal County (www.meathtourism.ie). The ancient seat of the rulers was the **Hill of Tara ❽**, 28 miles (44km) from Dublin, off the M3, 7 miles (11km) beyond the village of Dunshaughlin. The limestone ridge commands fittingly regal views over the central plain of Ireland, smokily framed by distant mountain ranges. Ring forts, ruins and a standing stone mark the place that was the island's spiritual and cultural capital for millennia (tel: 046-902 5903; http://hilloftara.org; access all year; guided tours, May–Sept, daily, 10am–6pm).

One of many statues dotting Powerscourt's Italianate grounds.

Powerscourt House.

Trim Castle.

The town of **Trim** , 13 miles (21km) to the west, has Ireland's largest Anglo-Norman castle, **Trim Castle**, started by Hugh de Lacy in 1173 and used in the filming of Mel Gibson's *Braveheart* in 1994. The restored keep may be visited by guided tour (tel: 046-943 8619; Nov–Jan, Sat–Sun, 9am–4pm, Feb–Mar 16th, Sat–Sun 9.30am–4.30pm, Mar 17th–Sep 30th, daily 10am–5pm). Trim is well furnished with other historic structures, which are strung along the heritage trail that winds through the town and along the River Boyne. In fine weather, the river banks are the perfect place to picnic.

Navan

The Boyne drive takes you to the market town of **Navan** , 9 miles (15km) away, with its fine Solstice Arts Centre (www.solsticeartscentre.com). Famous natives of the palindromic town include actor Pierce Brosnan, comedians Tommy Tiernan and Dylan Moran, and Francis Beaufort, who created the Beaufort wind force scale in 1805.

Standing stone at the Hill of Tara.

From Navan, a 7-mile (12km) drive on the N51 takes you to **Slane** , a beautiful 18th-century estate village above the River Boyne, and bedevilled by traffic travelling between Ireland's northwest and Dublin (it is 30 miles/50km from the capital on the N2).

The central crossroads contains a quartet of identical, three-storey, limestone Georgian houses, gazing implacably at each other across the square. The Gothic revival **Slane Castle** is the home of Lord Henry Conyngham, Earl of Mount Charles, and is a venue for monster rock concerts. Access to the castle is by tour only, with groups of 10 required to book in advance (tel: 041-988 4400; www.slanecastle.ie; May–Aug, Sun–Thu, noon–5pm).

Less than a mile north of the village is the windswept **Hill of Slane** where in 433, St Patrick lit a Paschal fire to celebrate the arrival of Christianity in Ireland, much to the annoyance of the pagan high king, Laoghaire – who had decreed that no flames should be visible from Tara during the festival of Feis Temro. The hill, which is open all year, contains the ruins of a 16th-century Franciscan friary, and has good views of the surrounding countryside.

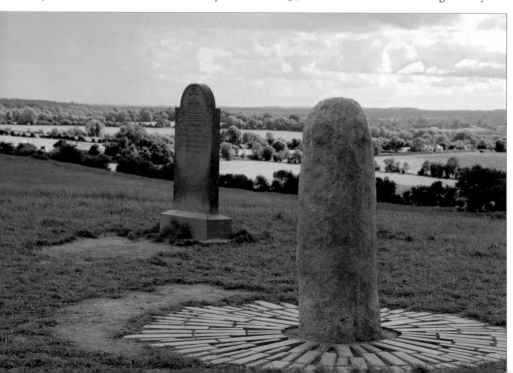

Newgrange

One of Europe's most important prehistoric clusters is just a few miles southeast of Slane: the neolithic burial mounds (a Unesco World Heritage site) at Newgrange, Knowth and Dowth.

Access to Newgrange and Knowth is solely by tour from the **Brú na Bóinne Visitor Centre** ⑫ near Donore (tel: 041-988 0300; www.heritageireland.ie; daily, June–mid-Sept 9am–7pm, May 9am–6.30pm, mid-Sept–end Sept 9am–6.30pm, Oct 9.30am–5.30pm, Nov–Jan 9.30am–5pm, Feb–Apr 9.30am–5.30pm).

Dowth may be visited separately (signposted off the N51) and viewed from the outside. Its shaggy, unrestored mound makes a contrast to the renovated structures of Newgrange and Knowth. Newgrange is the only one of the monuments where access is allowed to the interior passage and chamber – the latter is aligned so that the rising sun sends in a shaft of light at the winter solstice (entry to the chamber for that occasion is by lottery). Built around 3200 BC, Newgrange is several hundred years older than the Pyramids, and 1,000 years more ancient than Stonehenge. The sites are busy in summer, and entry cannot be guaranteed. Go early in the day, and allow at least three hours.

About 5 miles (8km) north, in Louth, Ireland's smallest county (www.louthholidays.com), stand the ruins of **Mellifont Abbey** ⑬ on the banks of the Mattock River. The first Cistercian abbey on the island, its earliest parts date from the 12th century. In 1690, the buildings were the headquarters of King William of Orange, who defeated James II at the Battle of the Boyne.

Not far from Mellifont is a modern monument that can be seen for miles, the **Boyne Suspension Bridge** at Drogheda. Completed in 2003, it has a main span of 555ft (170 metres) and a 310ft (95-metre) -high concrete pylon, from which 28 shimmering cables fan out like the work of a giant spider.

The busy town of **Drogheda** ⑭ is surrounded by rather utilitarian factories and retail outlets, but its core dates from Norman times, when it marked the northern boundary of the Pale. In 1649 the town was besieged and stormed by Oliver Cromwell and thousands of its citizens were killed, or transported to the Caribbean for slavery.

The **Millmount Museum** (tel: 041-983 3097; www.millmount.net) is a fortified complex on a giant mound that includes a 19th-century Martello tower. The exhibits explore the town's industrial past. At **St Peter's Church** (www.saintoliverplunkett.com), in the town centre, a shrine protects the embalmed head of St Oliver Plunkett (1629–81), the Archbishop of Armagh. He was the last Catholic martyr to die in England – hanged, drawn and quartered. The 13th-century **St Laurence's Gate** is an exquisite remnant of the city's medieval walls.

A mile and a half (2km) west of Drogheda (off the Baltray Road) is **Beaulieu House** (tel: 041-983 8557; www.beaulieuhouse.ie; Jun & Sept,

Hill of Slane.

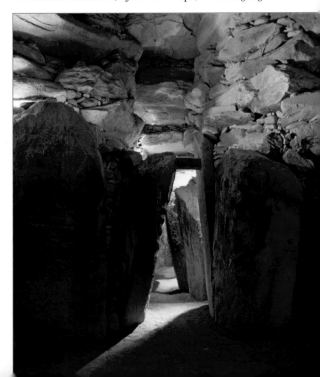

An interior passage at Newgrange.

TIP

For a mini-trip to explore the lesser-known places around Dublin, drive to the Fingal area on the M1 north out of Dublin to the town of Swords, which has a fine castle. Just a little further north, on the R127, is the seaside town of Rush with the impressive Kenure House, a venue used for many film sets. North along the coast road are the attractive towns of Skerries and Balbriggan, and the famous Ardgillan Castle.

The Barbican in Drogheda, also known as St Lawrence's Gate, was built in the 13th century as a gateway through the town walls.

Mon–Fri, 11am–5pm, Jul & Aug, daily, 11am–5pm, guided tour), constructed in the 1660s in the Dutch style. The walled garden dates from the early 18th century. Half a dozen racing and rally cars from the 1960s and 1970s are on display in the car museum.

Six miles (10km) east of Drogheda, via the R150, is the seaside resort of **Bettystown**, where the intricate Tara Brooch (now housed in the National Museum of Ireland), was found in 1850. A couple of miles further south is **Laytown**, where an annual horse racing event takes place on the strand in early September.

Drogheda is just 30 miles (50km) from Dublin on the M1 motorway that moves quickly up to Belfast. **Dundalk** ⓯, 23 miles (37km) beyond Drogheda, is the last town before the border.

To the east is the scenic **Cooley Peninsula** (www.carlingford.ie), the mythical stomping ground of the brown bull of Cooley (Donn Cúailnge), who was the object of legendary Queen Medb's cattle raid, The Táin. Dundalk Bay (on the south side

of the peninsula) and Carlingford Lough (on the north) are both Special Protection Areas for wildlife, and are popular with birdwatchers.

The village of **Carlingford** ⓰ is an absolutely charming place where several stone-built medieval buildings nestle between the whitewashed houses on the narrow streets.

Excursions West

Kildare (www.visitkildare.ie), once known for its stud farms and lush green pastures, has gradually taken on the additional role of a dormitory county for Dublin and it has many commuter apartment and housing developments. Yet the county still holds many attractions, including some of the best horses in the world, grand houses and demesnes, and a peaceful network of canals and towpaths that are popular with walkers.

Castletown House ⓱ (tel: 01-628 8252; www.castletownhouse.ie; daily mid–Mar–Oct; Thu–Sun Nov–Dec) in **Celbridge** is 14 miles (22km) from Dublin, via the M4, taking the R449 Celbridge exit. Ireland's largest

THE M50

Dublin's ring road carries a massive volume of traffic, and often not very effectively. It was designed to cater for a maximum 45,000 vehicles per day, but now carries closer to 100,000. It was under construction or in the throes of upgrading for over 20 years. Its most famous junction, the Red Cow Roundabout (where it meets the N7), features almost daily on traffic news bulletins due to traffic tailbacks. Visitors may decide to give it a wide berth as the toll booths have been removed and you have to pay online or ring a dedicated phone line before 8pm the following day or face a fine. You cannot pre-pay. Rental cars are usually covered already. Morning rush hour is between 7.30–10am; the afternoon rush starting 4 or 4.30pm, the road remaining busy until 6.30pm or later. (www.m50.ie).

Palladian country house, it was built for the speaker of the Irish House of Commons, William Conolly in 1722.

Four miles (7km) to the southwest is **Straffan** with its Steam Museum (tel: 01-628 8412; www.steam-museum. com May & Sep Sat–Sun; Jun–Aug Fri–Sun) and pretty 18th-century walled garden at Lodge Park.

Head back north for 5 miles (8km) on the R403 and R406, and you come to the 18th-century university town of **Maynooth**, along the Royal Canal.

A few miles northwest (on the R148, R158 and R125) is **Larchill Arcadian Garden** ⑱, beyond **Kilcock** (tel: 01-628 7354; www.larchhill.ie; daily 10am–2pm May; Mon–Fri 10am–2pm Jun; charge). The restored ornamental landscape is a fine example of an 18th-century *ferme ornée*, with rare breeds and a large lake.

Head back to Kilcock, and take the R407 to the rapidly expanding village of **Clane**. From there the R403 passes through **Prosperous**, one of the first towns where the United Irishmen rose in the 1798 rebellion. The road continues to **Allenwood**, from where the R414 travels through the Bog of Allen to the **Irish Peatland Conservation Council's Nature Centre** (tel: 045-860 133; www.ipcc. ie; Mon–Fri, 9am–5pm, except bank holidays) at Lullymore, about 3 miles (5km) before **Rathangan**. Here you may learn about bogs and peat, take guided walks and examine dozens of species of carnivorous plants from around the world.

Kildare

From Rathangan it is 7 miles (11km) southeast to the town of **Kildare** ⑲ on the edge of the Curragh, the central plain of Ireland, which lies like a flat green blanket on the landscape. A mile outside the town, at Tully, is the famous **Irish National Stud**, with its Japanese Gardens and St Fiachra's Garden (see page 163).

Just over 7 miles (12km) to the east on the M7 and the R445 is **Newbridge**, home of Newbridge Silverware (www.newbridgesilverware.com). From here, it is a 30-mile (50km) drive to Dublin via the R445, the N7, and the M50 (see page 148).

Castletown House.

HORSE CULTURE

Whether they're breeding them, racing them, exporting them or betting on them, the Irish have an extraordinary affinity with horses.

In 1809 *The History and Delineation of the Horse* recorded that 'the Irish are the highest and the steadiest leapers in the world.' They still are.

The pre-eminence of Irish-bred steeplechasers and hurdlers on the racecourses of Britain has been remarkable, and, given the legions of horses exported annually to trainers in England, it's even more remarkable that the greatest steeplechasers of the modern era were trained in Ireland. Perhaps the greatest of all was Arkle, who won the Cheltenham Gold Cup three years in succession in the 1960s. Had Arkle entered a referendum for the Irish presidency, the world might well have had its first equine statesman since Caligula.

The Irish prefer the reckless and often threadbare thrills of steeplechasing to its rich relation, racing 'on the flat'. Whereas top-class flat-racing throughout the world is dominated by the commercial requirements of the multi-million dollar bloodstock industry, this aspect is absent from racing 'over the sticks' because nearly all jumpers are geldings.

Europe's only official race to be held on a beach takes place in July/August (depending on tides) at Laytown, an east-coast resort.

Many Irish people have a natural ability to understand and handle horses, which can still be seen in many small towns.

Ireland's prosperous bloodstock industry owes much to a 1969 government ruling that fees for the services of thoroughbred stallions would be exempt from tax.

Policemen on horseback.

HORSES THROUGH HISTORY

Until the 1990s the Garda Síochána was one of the major police forces that didn't have mounted police, but today a handful of Irish Draught Horses (a native breed, known for its versatility and good temperament) patrol the streets of Dublin.

Although horses have played a vital role in Ireland's economy over the centuries, it was the racing scene that inspired excitement. The Red Branch Knights of pre-Christian Ireland raced each other on horses, and horse racing was an essential part of public fairs in the early centuries AD.

In Co. Cork in the year 1752, a Mr Edmund Blake and a Mr O'Callaghan raced each other on horseback across the countryside from Buttevant Church to the spire of St Leger Church 4.5 miles (7km) away, jumping hedges, walls and ditches on the way. As a result, a new word, 'steeplechasing', entered the English language, and a new sport was created.

Steeplechasing was soon all the rage. Races were run, like the original, across open country from one point to another with the precise course left largely to the discretion of the riders. The tradition continues in its purest form during Point to Point races, informal meetings in which horses race around a track that has no railings.

Equine symbolism is frequently found in Ireland, as in this beast guarding the gates to the Powerscourt estate in Co. Wicklow.

Bookmakers in Ireland have been slow to embrace online betting. Cynics claimed that's because the profit margins aren't so good.

The Curragh is the fashionable setting for all the Irish classic races: the 2,000 and 1,000 Guineas, the Derby, the Oaks and the St Leger. Prize money at the Derby now exceeds €1.5 million.

THE SOUTHEAST

In the sunny southeast you can find opera and national parks, pretty beaches, horse racing, medieval towns and ancient historical sites.

Main Attractions

Irish National Heritage Park
Dungarvan
Lismore Castle
Ardmore
Ballymaloe
Kildare
Kilkenny
Jerpoint Abbey
Rock of Cashel

The 'sunny Southeast', as it is popularly known, has one obvious advantage over the rest of Ireland: good weather. With almost double the annual sunshine quota for other regions, it has long been favoured as a holiday destination by the Irish themselves, and many Dubliners have holiday homes there. In high summer, therefore, traffic is heavy.

The region bears a distinct geographical contrast to the rest of the country with undulating flat plains intersected by meandering river valleys producing some of the most fertile agricultural land in Tipperary, Kilkenny and Carlow. Unlike the rugged South and West, the Southeast has a relatively gentle coastal aspect of long sandy beaches, rocky bays and low cliffs along the Wicklow, Wexford and Waterford shorelines.

This chapter suggests two different routes – one coastal and one inland – for exploring.

Option 1: Dublin to Cork via the coast

The first tour travels from Dublin to Cork, through Wexford, Waterford, Dungarvan and Youghal. This route takes 4.5 hours – two hours longer than the main M7/M8 route, but it is far more scenic, with frequent sea views. Take a full day for the drive, or plan one or two overnight stops.

Leave Dublin on the N11 Bray road, and follow this to **Arlow ❶**. This is a small but lively fishing port and seaside resort on the estuary of the River Avoca known for boat building, and now a thriving commuter town with a population of 13,000. Sir Francis Chichester's yacht *Gypsy Moth III*, in which he won the transatlantic single-handed yacht race, was built at Tyrell's boatyard, as was the Irish Navy's late and much-lamented sail training vessel, the brigantine *Asgard II*, which sank in the Bay of Biscay in 2008. The

Courtown Harbour, Co Wexford.

Arklow Maritime Museum (Bridgewater Centre, North Quay; tel: 086 446 0784; Tue–Sat; free) contains a comprehensive display of artefacts and memorabilia tracing the maritime history of Arklow through the centuries. Its eclectic collection includes World War II mines and salvaged items from the wreck of the *Lusitania*, sunk by a German submarine in 1915.

Leave the M11 at interchange 23 for to R 472 to **Courtown** a pleasant alternative route to Wexford passing the first of several long sandy beaches.

The R742 leads to **Curracloe Strand**, 7 miles (11km) northeast of Wexford Harbour. The totally unspoilt strand is backed by dunes, and stretches for 6 miles (10km). It 'stood in' for the Normandy beaches when Steven Spielberg filmed *Saving Private Ryan* (1998). In winter it is home to numerous Canada geese. Information on the region's birds can be found at the **Wexford Wildfowl Reserve** (tel: 076-100 2660; www.wexfordwildfowlreserve.ie; free), which is signposted off the R741 just outside Wexford at the quaintly named North Slob, an area of mud flats at the mouth of the River Slaney. The harbour is partly silted up, and its mud flats attract a variety of ducks, geese and swans.

The Southeast

Wexford

Wexford ❷ is a small, easy-to-explore town consisting of a series of quays parallel to the water, with a compact network of smaller streets parallel to the quays. Crescent Quay is decorated with a large statue on a plinth of locally born Commodore John Barry (1745–1803; see page 154). Walking tours leave from the nearby **Tourist Information Office** (The Quay Front; tel: 053-912 3111; daily 11am) visiting the remaining sections of the Norman town walls and the 13th-century Franciscan Friary.

Wexford, which has an interesting selection of small, old-fashioned shops and pubs, is at its best in October during the two-week run of the **Wexford Festival Opera** (tel: 053-912 2144; www.wexfordopera.com). Three full-length operas are performed at the fabulous **Wexford Opera House** with an international cast of up-and-coming stars. The tradition is to choose little-known works, with consistently interesting results. A series of fringe events guarantees musical entertainment from 11am to midnight.

The **Irish National Heritage Park** (tel: 053-912 0733; www.inhp.com; daily, May–Aug 9.30am–6.30pm, Sept–Apr 9.30am–5.30pm) at Ferrycarrig, 3 miles (5km) northwest of Wexford on the N11 Enniscorthy road, is an open-air museum on the banks of the River Slaney. A couple of hours among its life-size replicas of typical dwelling places will make you an expert on Irish history and architecture, from Stone Age man in 6000 BC, up to the 12th-century Norman settlements.

The 35-acre (14-hectare) museum includes a prehistoric homestead, a *crannóg* (lake dwelling), an early Christian fortified farm, a Christian monastery and a Norman castle. All the exhibits have guides dressed in the styles of the various periods.

Follow the N25 for 3 miles (5km) in the Rosslare direction to visit **Johnstown Castle Gardens** (tel: 053-918 4671; gardens open daily all year). The castle is a grandiose grey stone Gothic building dating from the mid-19th century. Only the entrance hall is open to the public but the attractively landscaped gardens can be visited. Built for

Celtic cross at the Irish National Heritage Park.

The harbour at Wexford.

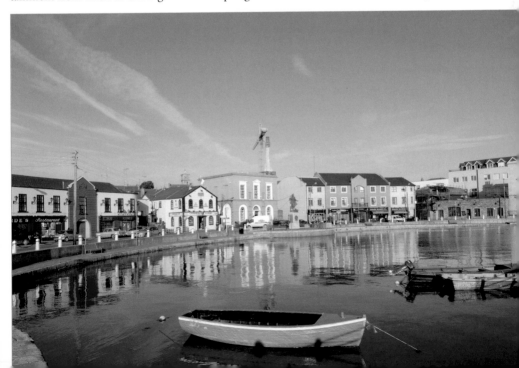

the Morgan family around 1810, the estate contains splendid plantings of Japanese cedars and Lawson cypresses, lakes, ornamental gardens, nature trails and a walled garden.

The **Irish Agricultural Museum** (www.irishagrimuseum.ie; Mar–Oct Mon–Fri 9am–5pm, Sat–Sun 11–5pm, Nov–Feb Mon–Fri 9am–4pm Sat–Sun 11–4pm) is in the stables. It has extensive displays of artefacts from Ireland's rural past, and a collection of Irish country furniture.

The scenic route to Waterford

The N25 travels to Waterford via New Ross, but we suggest this scenic alternative: take the N25 towards Rosslare and turn off at Piercetown for **Kilmore Quay ❸**. This quaint little fishing village of thatched, whitewashed cottages and friendly pubs is built between the dunes and a stone harbour wall, and looks out to the uninhabited **Saltee Islands**, one of Ireland's most important bird sanctuaries. In late spring to early summer, three million birds from 47 species

The Irish National Heritage Park.

stop here, and can be observed from local boats.

In mid-summer, the sea bird colonies on Gannet headland make for a memorable, and noisy, sight with vast numbers of guillemots, fulmars and razorbills packing the cliff faces. Towards dusk, the sight of the puffins congregating in small groups near their nestling sites adds to the spectacle.

Heading west, the R736/R733 will take you to the **Hook Head Peninsula,** which forms the eastern side of Waterford harbour. At its extremity is the **Hook Lighthouse Visitor Centre** (tel. 051 397 055; www.hookheritage.ie; daily year round, tours June–Aug). The original lighthouse tower was built by the Normans, 800 years ago, and can be visited on a guided tour. It is said to be the oldest operational lighthouse in the world there are spectacular views from the balcony. On the east side of Waterford Harbour is **Ballyhack**, a picture-book pretty waterside village dominated by **Ballyhack Castle** (tel: 051-389 468; mid-May–Aug, Sat–Wed; free), a 16th-century tower house. The castle is thought to have been built around 1450 by the Knights Hospitallers of St John, one of the two military orders founded in the 12th century at the time of the Crusades. A short car ferry hop (www.passageferry.ie) across the estuary from Ballyhack to Passage East provides a short-cut to Waterford City.

Continue north on the R733 for 3 miles (5km) to **Dunbrody Abbey** (tel: 051-388 603; www.dunbrodyabbey.com), an impressive ruined Cistercian abbey dating from 1175.

The farmhouse near Dunganstown from which US President John F. Kennedy's grandfather emigrated to Boston is now the **Kennedy Homestead** (tel: 051-388 264; www.kennedy homestead.ie; daily 9.30am–5.30pm). Displays for visitors (audio visual and photographic) are in the original farmyard, and include coverage of President John F. Kennedy's visit in 1963. The smallholding is still farmed by Kennedy descendants, and it is a touching experience to witness the humble origins of the great Irish-American dynasty.

Waterford

Waterford ❹, a city of 49,000 people, has a proud past as an important European port, but nowadays its wide, stone quays are mainly used for car parking. Its heyday was in the 18th century, when the famous glass-manufacturing industry was established.

The Tourist Office is on Parade Quay (tel: 051-875 823; Mon–Sat 9am–5.15pm). There is ample parking on the town's quays, and at the eastern extremity is the distinctive circular 'pepper pot' landmark, **Reginald's Tower** (The Mall, tel: 051-849 501; www.waterfordtreasures.ie), a massive, 12th-century cylindrical tower built by the Normans on a former Viking site. It is said that when the Norman Strongbow married the daughter of Dermot McMurrough, thus peacefully uniting the Norman invaders and the native Irish, the wedding took place here. It has subsequently been used as a mint, a prison and a military store. Today it houses The Viking Exhibition, original artefacts including 12th-century Viking

THE SOUTHEAST: GATEWAY FOR INVADERS

Given its close proximity to mainland Europe and Britain, the Southeast region carried the lion's share of invasions dating back to early monastic civilisation. The Vikings, who raided here regularly, were the scourge of early Christian settlements at Ardmore, Lismore, Kilkenny and Cashel. St Declan, for example, who founded a monastery at Ardmore in 416, was preaching the Christian message long before the arrival of St Patrick, Ireland's patron saint.

The beautiful illuminated manuscripts and precious metal implements fashioned by monks during this golden age of learning were prized booty sought by the Vikings. Irish round towers, tall, narrow stone buildings with a conical cap, and only one entrance high above the ground, were originally built at Irish monasteries with a dual purpose: as lookouts, and to provide a safe hiding place for Christian treasures in the event of a Viking raid. The Vikings persisted in their raids, and attracted some reckon by the relatively mild climate, and fertile land, went on to found the cities of Waterford and Wexford sometime in the 9th century.

The Anglo-Normans led by the aptly named Strongbow arrived in 1169, ironically at the invitation of the then King of Leinster, Diarmuid, as part of a political alliance that would change the course of Irish history by allowing England a firm foothold for Henry II and his successors. At the behest of Henry VIII, Oliver Cromwell's bloody campaigns of 1650 destroyed many of the region's churches and monasteries. From the Middle Ages through to the 18th century, English influence in the Southeast was stronger than elsewhere in Ireland with many of the great estates of Russborough House, Kilkenny Castle, the Fitzgerald clan's headquarters Waterford Castle, and Johnstown Castle withstanding the political turbulence.

The most emotional touchstone of history in the region remains the 1798 Rebellion, when over 20,000 rebels wielding only pitchforks and clubs died in a hail of cannon and rifle fire at Vinegar Hill in Wexford. While the ill-fated attempt at forming a United Ireland inspired by the French Revolution of 1789 ultimately failed, it did ignite the fuse of liberty that would eventually succeed 100 years later.

jewellery, excavated during the recent rebuilding of Waterford's shopping district nearby. Georgian Waterford starts behind Reginald's Tower, on **The Mall. City Hall** (office hours; free) is a neo-classical building dating from 1788, which contains some good examples of early Waterford crystal, including a huge chandelier. The same building contains the **Theatre Royal** (www.theatreroyal.ie), which has been tastefully restored, and is one of Ireland's few remaining 19th-century theatre interiors with three tiers of horseshoe-shaped balconies. Just beyond it is the **Bishop's Palace** (The Mall, tel: 051 304500; www.waterfordtreasures.ie; free) originally an imposing town house. It now displays the **Waterford Treasures**, a collection of objects dating from 1700 to the present day. It illustrates Waterford's mid-18th-century heyday, and includes silverware, cut glass, and the sword of Thomas Francis Meagher, Irish patriot and hero of the American Civil War.

Behind the palace is **Christ Church Cathedral,** which replaced an older church in 1773. Designed by local architect John Roberts (1712–96), it is the only neoclassical Georgian cathedral in Ireland with trademark white stucco trim designs of florets and laurels and huge Corinthian columns. From here you can follow the crowds (heading left, that is, upriver) to explore Waterford's largely pedestrianised shopping centre.

The ruins of French Church on Greyfriar's Street to the right of the cathedral date back to an original 13th century Franciscan abbey. In 1695, it was given to a group of Huguenot refugees – hence the 'French' prefix. A splendid east window is all that now remains intact.

Opposite the City Hall, **The Waterford Crystal Experience** (The Mall; tel: 051-317 000; www.waterfordvisitorcentre.com) celebrates the city's long tradition of glassmaking, which dates back to 1783. The dramatic 50-minute tour features glass-blowing, before which the glass is heated to high temperatures in a blazing furnace, and cutting and engraving carried out by skilled master craftsmen.

Waterford.

The main N25 takes a fast inland route to Dungarvan. If you have time, take the coastal route leaving Waterford on the R684 for **Dunmore East.** This pretty cliff-side fishing village and holiday resort of thatched cottages is on the open sea at the head of Waterford Harbour.

Tramore is a total contrast, with a long, flat sandy beach, a fun fair, caravan parks and other facilities aimed at the budget holiday market. The coast road continues through a series of villages with good beaches – **Annestown, Bunmahon** and **Clonea.** Known as Waterford's Copper Coast, the region was designated European Geopark status by Unesco in 2004 in recognition of its volcanic geology and its 19th-century copper mining heritage. Find out more at the Geopark Information Point (Bunmahon; tel: 051-292 828; www.coppercoastgeopark.com). Elsewhere in the sandstone cliffs secluded coves can be reached on foot. **Dungarvan ❺**, situated on Dungarvan Harbour and backed by wooded hills, is the county town of Waterford. It has some lively waterside pubs, and is increasingly popular as a centre for activity holidays.

If you're headed for Cork, skip to Ardmore below. Those heading for Killarney, or with time for a scenic detour into the Blackwater Valley, should pick up the N72 Cappoquin road outside Dungarvan.

Vee Gap: the scenic route to Lismore Castle

Cappoquin ❻ is a quiet village nicely situated on a wooded hillside on the River Blackwater, a beautiful salmon and trout river. About 3 miles (5km) north of the village is **Mount Melleray** (tel: 058-54404; www.mount mellerayabbey.org; free), a Cistercian (Trappist) abbey dating from the mid-19th century that welcomes visitors in search of solitude. The Vee Gap route is signposted form here, going north on the R669 into the Knockmealdown Mountains. There are a number of waymarked walking trails and places to stop on the side of the road. The Vee Gap is at the summit, from which you can see the Galtee Mountains in the northwest, and in good visibility the

The small fishing village of Dungarvan.

Celebrating Waterford's glass-making tradition.

The Clock Tower in Youghal.

Lismore Castle.

Rock of Cashel due north, rising out of the Tipperary Plain. Turn back here, and take the R668 to Lismore.

Lismore N, a pretty wooded village of 900 inhabitants approached over a stone bridge, was an important monastic centre from the 7th to the 12th centuries, which is why the village has a cathedral. **St Carthage's** (1633) has some interesting effigies. More information on the village's past can be found at the **Lismore Heritage Centre** (tel: 058-54975; charge) opposite the castle car park. The village is dominated by the grey stone turrets of **Lismore Castle** (tel: 058-54424; www.lismorecastle.com; gardens and art gallery: 17 Mar–mid-Oct, 10.30am–5.30pm). Built on a rock overhanging the river in the mid-18th century, the castle is a dramatic and imposing building. It is used as a summer residence by the Duke of Devonshire, and is not open to the public. The gardens include an 800-year-old yew walk. The Castle's west wing features a contemporary art gallery, and the gardens have a fine selection of contemporary sculpture by leading artists.

The structure, often described as the most spectacular castle in Ireland, dates back to 1753 and is situated in a panoramic position overlooking the Blackwater Valley with views over rolling, wooded hills to the Knockmealdown Mountains beyond. Private groups of up to 23 guests can rent the castle when the Duke is not in residence, and they are looked after by his personal staff.

Ardmore

If you are heading for Killarney, follow the Blackwater valley on the N72 from Lismore to Fermoy to Mallow, and on to Killarney, about a two-hour drive.

Beyond Dungarvan the main tour joins the N25, which climbs the **Drum Hills** giving good views back across Dungarvan harbour. **Ardmore** involves a 5-mile (8km) detour, but is worth the effort. St Declan established a monastery here in the 5th century (freely accessible). Today the remains of a medieval cathedral and round tower stand on a cliff top with stunning views over Ardmore Bay. The 12th-century cathedral with its sturdy, rounded arches is a prime example of the Hiberno-Romanesque style, while the slender round tower with its conical roof is an elegant contrast. There are also interesting stone carvings. The tiny village is at the bottom of the cliff, and is a pleasant place with good sandy beaches.

Youghal N (pronounced 'yawl'), famous for its long sandy beaches and historic town centre, found fame in 1956 when John Huston filmed the New Bedford scenes of *Moby Dick* here. Photos of Gregory Peck and other cast members on location can be seen in Paddy Linehan's Bar on the quay. Also on the waterfront, the quayside **Youghal Tourist Office** houses a heritage centre, and is the starting point for walking tours of the town's historic centre (Market Square; tel: 024-20170; www.youghal.ie). The Clock Tower is a distinctive landmark built in 1776 as a jail that straddles the road in the town centre. The steps beside it lead to a street with excellent harbour views, and to the 13th-century St Mary's Collegiate Church. Sir Walter Raleigh (*c*.1552–1618) lived next door, where he smoked the first tobacco and planted the first the potato plant in Ireland – a claim disputed by several other places. The famous sandy beaches which have made Youghal a favourite holiday destination for generations of Cork people (though nowadays beach lovers tend to live in Youghal and commute to work in the city) are outside the town on the Cork side, and extend for 3 miles (5km).

Quaker connections

Turn left off the N25 in Castlemartyr for **Shanagarry ❾**, a tidy village built of grey stone with many Quaker connections. The famous hotel, **Ballymaloe House** is to the east of the village. **Ballymaloe Cookery School, Farm Shop and Gardens** have a geometric potager (kitchen garden), a formal fruit garden and a shell

house. **Shanagarry Design Centre** (tel: 021-464 5838) beside the parish church, is a large craft shop with a good café, run by the Kilkenny Shop, stocking ceramics by artists including Stephen Pearce. **Shanagarry House** where William Penn, the founder of Pennsylvania, grew up, is opposite the Design Centre.

Ballycotton, 3 miles (5km) beyond Shanagarry is a fishing village built on a cliff top overlooking a small island and lighthouse. There are good cliff walks, and numerous nesting sea birds can be seen in early summer. The brightly coloured fishing fleet supplies much of Cork city's fish.

Midleton ❿, a pleasant market town, is the home of Ireland's largest distillery. A new distilling complex was built in 1966, and the **Old Midleton Distillery** (tel: 021-461 3594; www.jamesonwhiskey.com; daily 10am–6pm) now houses an audio-visual display and an optional guided tour that explains the distilling process of Irish whiskey. You can sample a drop of the famous product in a traditional Irish pub. Admirers of industrial

Don't miss out on home-baked treats.

Darina Allen teaches a class at the Ballymaloe Cookery School.

Jameson whiskey being distilled in Midleton.

The Dubai Duty Free Irish Derby Festival takes place at the Curragh Racecourse.

architecture will enjoy the carefully restored 11-acre (4.5-hectare) 18th-century site. Most of the buildings are of cut stone, and the original waterwheel still functions. The N25 continues for 15 miles (24km) into Cork city.

Option 2: Kildare to Cashel via Kilkenny

This alternative, inland route from Dublin to Cork takes in some of the Southeast's most interesting historical sites. Kildare, with its Japanese Gardens and National Stud, has a Cathedral and a 12th-century Round Tower associated with St Brigid. The historic medieval town of black marble, Kilkenny, lies 23 miles (37km) south of Kildare, and the magnificently restored castle is a must-see.

You can linger in the Kilkenny area exploring the pretty riverside villages of the Nore and the Barrow, or continue to Clonmel, a compact market town on the River Suir, and head into the Nire Valley for a taste of unspoilt hill and bog land. Both options lead to Tipperary, and the spectacular ecclesiastical ruins on the Rock of Cashel.

At Cahir, there is a massive castle to visit, and quiet woodland walks through the relatively unfrequented Glen of Aherlow.

Leave Dublin on the main N7 Limerick motorway, taking the Kildare exit. The road cuts through **The Curragh ⓫** a broad plain of 6,000 acres (2,400 hectares). The **Curragh Racecourse** is the heart of the Irish racing world, and the Irish Derby is held here every June. If you are lucky, you might see a string of race horses galloping by. Otherwise, the plain is used for exercises by the Irish Army which has a large camp here.

St Brigid founded a religious settlement in **Kildare ⓬** in the 5th century. The present Cathedral dates partly from the late 17th century and partly from the 19th century. The 108ft (33-metre) **Round Tower** beside the cathedral belongs to a 12th-century monastery. If you're feeling lively, you can climb to the top for excellent views of the surrounding countryside.

SELLING THE AULD SOD

When the Irish emigrated to America, it's said, they brought their churches, schools and music, but the only thing they couldn't bring was the soil. That omission was rectified in 2006 when the Auld Sod Export Company began selling 12oz (340 grams) plastic bags of 'Official Irish Dirt' from a field in the village of Cahir, County Tipperary, to a warehouse in Speonk, New York. At US$5 a bag (including a packet of shamrock seeds) it wasn't exactly dirt cheap, but the company piled up $2 million of sales in its first four months.

Auld Sod advised the 40 million Americans who admit to Irish ancestry that they could use the soil to grow an Irish rose for their sweetheart or scatter it over the casket or grave of the dearly departed (http://auldsod.software-development.ie).

The National Stud

Nowadays Kildare is a prosperous town, closely associated with the horse racing business, with dozens of small studs in the area. Admission to the most prestigious of them all, the **National Stud**, where top-class breeding stallions are stabled, and **the Irish Horse** Museum (tel: 045-521 617; www.irish-national-stud.ie; Feb–Nov, daily, 9am–5pm) also allows you to visit the rather strange **Japanese Gardens**, laid out between 1906 and 1910 by Japanese landscape artist Tassa Eida and his son Minoru, which have been carefully preserved as one of the country's horticultural gems. The significance of the gardens is not only artistic and horticultural but also religious, philosophical and historical.

Also in the National Stud grounds is **St Fiachra's Garden**, created to celebrate the millennium with 4 acres (1.6 hectares) of woodland and lakeside walks.

Medieval Kilkenny

Kilkenny ⓭ was founded as a monastic settlement by St Canice in the 6th century. In 1641 a Catholic parliament, the Confederation of Kilkenny, tried to organise resistance to the persecution of Catholics. Cromwell's destructive 1650 campaign put a brutal end to such aspirations. While **Kilkenny** likes to promote itself as 'Ireland's medieval capital', its rich heritage is not immediately obvious. Start at the Tourist Information Office in **Shee Alms House,** Rose Inn Street (tel: 056-775 1500; www.kilkennytourism.ie; free) where you can equip yourself with free maps. This charming stone house with mullioned windows was built in the mid-17th century as a hospital for the poor. Frequent walking tours leave from here daily.

The sites of medieval Kilkenny start with St Canice's Cathedral at one extreme and end with the Castle at the other. Between them is a **Tholsel** (town hall) dating from 1761, the ruins of a 13th-century friary, the **Black Abbey**, and **Rothe House**, a 16th-century merchant's town house.

Built by John Rothe around 1594, it is a fine example of a merchant's house of the Tudor period. Owned by

The Japanese Gardens at the Irish National Stud, Co. Kildare.

Ceramics at Kilkenny Design Centre.

the Kilkenny Archaeological Society, it contains a collection of Bronze Age artefacts, period costumes and Ogham stones. Rothe House also has a genealogical centre for tracing ancestors (www.rothehouse.com).

Kilkenny Castle (tel: 056-770 4100; daily; guided tours only; charge, access to castle grounds and art gallery free) has been sumptuously restored. The grey stone, turreted landmark towers over the River Barrow, which serves as its moat. The original castle was built by the Butler family and dates from 1659. It has since been rebuilt several times.

The ornate Georgian stable yard of the castle across the main road is occupied by the Kilkenny Design Centre, which has a big display of local and national crafts and several workshops.

While walking along Kilkenny's main street to reach St Canice's Cathedral note the narrow covered passageways on either side of the road that lead to cobbled alleyways lined by small houses, many with attractive floral displays. Known as 'slips', these are a particular feature

Kilkenny Castle.

of Kilkenny, and a reminder of its medieval past.

St Canice's Cathedral, dating from the 13th century, is built in the Early English style. The Gothic interior is remarkable for its wealth of medieval monuments and life-size effigies, many carved from a locally quarried black marble. Amidst the many Norman memorials, be sure to view the female effigy in the south aisle wearing a Kinsale cloak, and St Ciaran's Chair, in the north transept, made of black marble with designs from the 13th century.

The 6th-century **Round Tower** in the Cathedral grounds is the only remnant of St Canice's monastery. You can climb its 167 steps, and enjoy an astounding view. In rainy weather it is closed to visitors for safety reasons.

Kytler's Inn on Kieran Street (tel: 056-772 1064; www.kytelersinn.com) dates back to 1324 when Dame Alice Kytler, 'the sorceress of Kilkenny', was accused of poisoning her four husbands, and of being a witch and brothel keeper. (She fled to England and stayed there.) The restaurant retains a medieval air with exposed beams and 14th-century stonework.

Riverside villages

If you have time for a day-long drive around the Kilkenny area, explore one of the pretty villages on the rivers **Nore** and **Barrow**. The rivers meander through rich countryside with gently sloping wooded hills dotted with old villages of grey stone buildings, until they meet in New Ross and flow into the sea at Waterford.

Leave Kilkenny on the R700 south for **Bennettsbridge** ⓮. Some of Kilkenny's best craft makers live and work in this old-world village, which straddles the River Nore, and have created their own craft trail (www.madeinkilkenny.ie). You can visit **Nicholas Mosse Pottery** (tel: 056-772 7505; http://nicholasmosse.com), for lovely pottery, museum and excellent café. Candle makers Moth to a Flame (tel: 056-772 7826; www.mothtoaflame.ie) is also worth a look.

Thomastown is a small market village (pop. 2,273) with a couple of delightful pubs, award-winning Blackberry Café (open Monday to Saturday from 9:30am to 5:30pm; from 10:00 Saturdays; www.theblackberrycafe.ie) – great for breakfast, lunch and afternoon tea and restaurant Café Sol (056-775 4945). It is also home to the well-respected **Grennan Mill Craft School** (http://grennanmillcraftschool.com). In the 13th century the town was walled and fortified and the 18th-century stone-arched bridge over the Nore indicates its former importance.

Cross the bridge for a short (1.5 miles/3km) detour to **Jerpoint Abbey** (tel: 056-772 4623; http://jerpointpark.com), one of the most attractive monastic sites in Ireland. The ruined Cistercian monastery is 12th-century. The church, with its Romanesque details, dates from this period. In the transept chapels the visitor can see 13th- to 16th-century tomb sculpture. The tower and cloister date from the 15th century. Another Kilkenny

artisanal favourite is **Jerpoint Glass** (tel: 056-772 4350; www.jerpointglass.com; free), where you can watch heavy, uncut glass being shaped by hand into modern designs. It is just two miles up from the abbey, take the right turn off the main road signposted for the **Mount Juliet estate** and it's just after the Mount Juliet entrance on your left.

Return to Thomastown and cross the Nore again to reach **Inistioge**. The village is on a bend of the river and has a picturesque tree-lined square beside a 10-arched stone bridge. Its narrow, sloping streets of small stone houses, village pubs, cute café, and antique store make it a popular location for filming period movies such as *Circle of Friends (1995)*, based on a novel by Maeve Binchy which starred Colin Firth and Minnie Driver. **Woodstock Gardens and Arboretum** (tel: 087-854 9785; www.woodstock.ie) which was laid out in the 19th century with interesting trees and shrubs from the Far East, is open to the public and has tea rooms in a cast-iron conservatory, but the house itself was burnt down in 1922.

Leisure boating at Graiguenamanagh.

The Butterslip, Kilkenny.

Seven miles (11km) south of Inistioge, turn left off the N700 to The **Rower**. This little village marks the start of an especially scenic stretch of road, with views over the River Barrow on the right-hand side, and the Blackstairs Mountains beyond the river.

Graiguenamanagh (The Hamlet of the Monks) **⑮** was an important commercial centre in the 19th century, when the River Barrow was used to transport coal and grain. Nowadays herons fish along its weir, and one of its stone-built warehouses is now a stylish waterside B&B and restaurant.

There is a genuinely nostalgic stretch of old-fashioned pubs on the hill to the west of the bridge, in whose dark interiors you can buy groceries as well as pints. At the top of this hill on the right is **Duiske Abbey** (tel: 059 972 4238), a Cistercian Abbey founded in 1204. The exterior is pebble-dashed and does not look very promising. However, the main nave of the abbey was adapted in 1983 to serve as the parish church. Its combination of modern and ancient features is much praised by some, and lamented by others. Whatever your opinion, it is certainly worth a look at its light-filled interior. Look out for the Knight of Duiske, an effigy in chain mail, the hammer-beam roof in Irish oak and the magnificent Romanesque processional door in the south transept.

Both the R705 from Graiguenamanagh and the R700 Thomastown–Inistioge road lead to **New Ross** **⑯** where the River Nore and the Barrow form a long estuary before reaching the sea. The town, which is in County Wexford, was built on a steep hill overlooking the River Barrow at a strategically important river crossing. On the river bank you will see the tall masts of the **Dunbrody Famine Ship** (tel: 051-425 239; www.dunbrody.com; tours daily 9am–6pm), docked to the east of the river, a full-scale replica of a sailing ship built in 1845 to transport emigrants to North America. On board, actors tell the stories of the passengers, who travelled in this 'coffin-ship' in order to escape the Great Famine. It is both entertaining, and a sobering reminder of the ordeal suffered by over 2 million

Jerpoint Abbey.

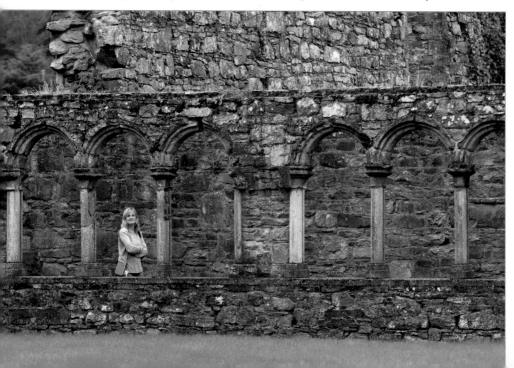

people who emigrated from Ireland in that era.

Clonmel

From Kilkenny, follow the N76 south to **Clonmel** ⑰, a busy Tipperary market town on the River Suir. The area to the north and east of the town is known for its apple orchards, and Clonmel is the centre of the Irish cider-making industry. However, travel to the south, and you will find another kind of scenery altogether.

The **Nire Valley Drive** is a signposted circular route of about 23 miles (37km) that travels along the edge of the **Comeragh Mountains to Ballymacarbry**, and the **Nire Valley**, returning to Clonmel through **Clogheen**. This is not for the fainthearted; the roads are narrow, sometimes steep, and there are several hairpin bends, but the forest and bog land scenery is magnificent. Ballymacarbry is a good base from which to follow the various waymarked trails in the area.

The Rock of Cashel

From Clonmel, head northwest on the R688 to **Cashel** ⑱. A cluster of romantic-looking, grey, turreted buildings stands on a limestone outcrop rising (200ft) 60 metres above the Tipperary plain, and absolutely every tour bus stops here. It will greatly enhance your visit if you can avoid the crowds by visiting at lunch time or in the late afternoon.

The **Rock of Cashel** (tel: 062-61437; www.cashel.ie) was probably once a centre of Druidic worship. By the 4th century AD Cashel was the ceremonial centre of the Kings of Munster. It was here, legend has it, that St Patrick baptised King Aengus (see margin).

The largest building on the rock, the shell of **St Patrick's Cathedral**, built in the Gothic style, was in use from the 13th to the mid-16th centuries when it was desecrated in Oliver Cromwell's campaign. **Cormac's Chapel** is a simpler building dating

from 1127, before the Norman invasion, with a high, corbelled roof similar to those found in early saints' cells in Glendalough and Dingle. Cormac's Chapel is generally considered one of the greatest achievements of native Irish church architecture. The entry archway is a fine example of the Hiberno-Romanesque style of architecture. The broken sarcophagus within the chapel is believed to be Cormac's final resting place. Don't miss the medieval paintings showing through the old plasterwork.

Spend some time lingering at Cashel, absorbing its unique atmosphere, and enjoying memorable views of the surrounding countryside. Rather than visiting the two heritage centres, concentrate on the Rock. Take a quick look at the town and maybe a light snack at the **Cashel Palace Hotel**, a red-brick, Queen Anne-style bishop's palace built in 1730. Note also the well-preserved wooden Victorian shop fronts across the road.

Cahir ⑲ (pronounced '*care*') situated on a hill above the River Suir, has a certain faded charm, due chiefly

St Patrick's Cathedral on the Rock of Cashel.

to the well-proportioned Georgian houses in its Mall and main square. It is known chiefly for its antique shops and its castle. **Cahir Castle** (tel: 052-744 1011) is a massive limestone fortress dating from the mid-12th century set on a rock in the River Suir. There is an informative guided tour, but avoid the audio-visual display. Walk up the hill beside the castle to the attractive main square. About a mile outside Cahir on the Clonmel road (also accessible by footpath from the castle car park) is the **Swiss Cottage** (tel: 052-744 1144; www.heritageireland. ie; closed mid-Nov–Mar), a thatched *cottage orné* built in 1810 to amuse the Earls of Glengall. It allowed its lordly aristocrats to play make-believe as 'humble folk' for a day. To enhance the fantasy, hidden doorways were built to allow servants to bring food and drink without being seen.

Walkers might like to detour northwest on the N24 for 14 miles (22km) to **Bansha**, and on to Tipperary town and the **Glen of Aherlow** (www.aherlow. com), an excellent area for hiking with marked trails of various lengths. The Glen, which is partly wooded and runs alongside the Aherlow River, has great views of the Galtee mountains (sometimes spelt Galty), and is a good base for getting off the beaten track. The Glen of Aherlow leads to **Kilfinane** 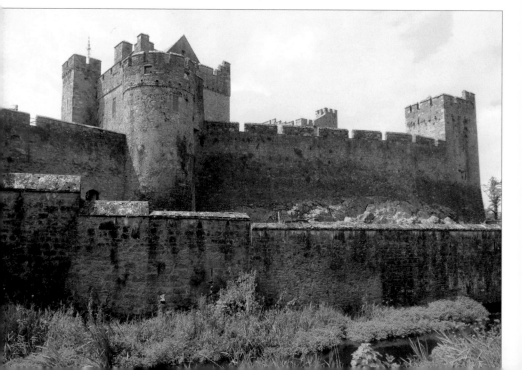 ❷⓿ at the heart of the Galtee and Ballyhoura Mountains. Its main feature, the Kilfinane Moat, is an ancient, flat-top mound encircled by three ramparts.

The Ballyhoura Way

The 56-mile (90km) **Ballyhoura Way** (www.ballyhoura.com) is a marked footpath through north Cork and County Limerick to Tipperary town. Some sections have been waymarked as loop walks varying in length from 2 miles (3km) to 12 miles (20km), with a map board at the starting point of each walk. This is beautiful, unspoilt countryside, a mixture of pasture and woodland, with medieval and megalithic monuments.

From Kilfinane, continue driving west joining the N20 and turning south for Cork, or head south and join the N8 for Cork. Either way, Cork city is about one hour's drive.

Cahir Castle.

Horse-drawn Caravans

Slow travel doesn't get much slower, but these holidays appeal to anyone, from students to retired executives, who are looking for relaxation.

Holidays in horse-drawn caravans have been available for the last 50 years. The caravans are of the type traditionally used by Travellers, since the 19th century – barrel-topped and brightly painted.

Operators offering these holidays at first bought caravans from the Travellers, and made modifications to them. That supply dried up, however, as the real 'travelling people' moved into modern caravans, towed by cars, or settled into houses. Today operators have the caravans made in the traditional style.

Today just a handful of operators in the Republic – in counties Mayo and Galway in the west, in Laois in the Midlands and Wicklow on the east coast – offer this kind of horse-drawn holiday. Clients come from all over the world, with 85 percent as online bookings. Most people do this as a one-week holiday.

It can be a relaxing way of seeing a small area of the country. You clop along at about a mile an hour, so you only travel about 10 to 15 miles each day. You see and smell everything around you – the birds and animals, the hedges and fields. Maps with descriptions of interesting features to look out for en route are supplied. It's more about enjoying the experience than reaching a destination.

The caravans usually sleep four people – some can fit an extra berth – and are well equipped. Operators offer either fixed routes or will arrange alternatives in advance. Overnight stops are made at farms, pubs, guesthouses or hotels.

Holidaymakers are sent on their way after receiving instructions and practice in leading and driving the horse. The instructor will travel with them on the road until they feel confident and relaxed and will also meet up with them at their first overnight stop to help them unharness, and again the next morning before they head off. The horses used are quiet and are well-used to their line of work.

On a practical note

Expect to pay around €850 low season to €1080 per caravan per week (four people) depending on the region. A fifth person costs around 15 percent more. There is a charge of about €21 per night per caravan per overnight stop which covers grazing, showers, etc. Oats for the horse are supplied.

Taking it slowly through the countryside.

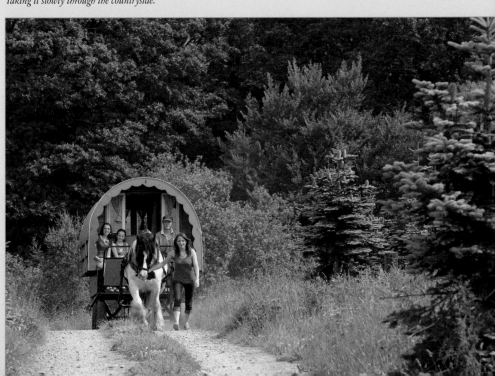

Cork's Huguenot quarter.

CORK AND SURROUNDINGS

After experiencing Cork's gentle charms, you can explore the port of Cobh, visit an innovative wildlife park and aim to acquire eloquence (while abandoning dignity) by kissing the Blarney Stone.

Pride of place runs deep amongst the natives of **Cork ❶**, an attitude ably underlined by its natives repeated reference to their city as 'the real capital.' Renowned as much for the singsong lilt of their accent as for their traditional determination to usurp Dublin at commerce, culture and sport, the friendly population need little prompting to extol their proud birthright. The Cork catchphrase 'Up the Rebels!' – recalling the city's contrarian political past, in which it frequently backed the minority (usually losing) side – is still used at sporting events.

Growing immigration

With a population of around 123,000, Cork has long divested itself of its sleepy second-city status with multinationals setting up business operations combined with a growing influx of immigrants from Europe, Africa and East Asia. The result is a cosmopolitan city bristling with tapas bars, busy restaurants and festivals of which the Cork Jazz Festival (www.corkjazzfestival. com) in October and International Choral Festival (www.corkchoral.ie) in May reign supreme.

Lying at the mouth of the River Lee, the city's historic centre is formed on an island created by two channels of the river. Easily walked from end to end over a day, it allows the visitor

easy access for sightseeing, shopping and idle strolling within convenient distance of any car park.

Founded by St Finbar in the 6th century, the name 'Cork' derives from the Irish *Corcach Mór Mumhan*, translated as the 'great marsh of Munster.' The place was prone to flooding and allowed early civilisation to flourish only on marshy islands joined by bridges.

Over the centuries, Cork, like much of Ireland, was invaded by the Vikings, the Normans and the English – as well as an episode of the Black Plague in

Main Attractions

St Finbar's Cathedral
University College, Cork
English Market
Rory Gallagher Piazza
Opera House
St Anne's Church
Cork City Gaol
Blarney Castle
Fota Wildlife Park
Cobh

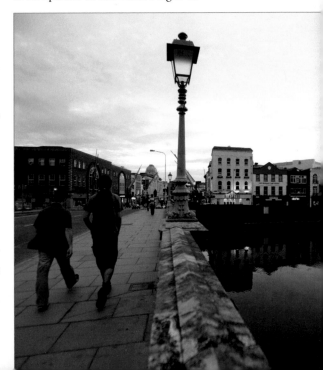

Cork occupies an attractive riverside setting.

1349 that almost wiped out the city. The McCarthy's of Desmond, a native tribe who grasped power in the 12th century, are credited with constructing the first city walls, built in the present-day Shandon area. Over the centuries, these defensive structures were extended to make Cork one of the great walled cities of Ireland's medieval period.

Cork was at its most affluent in the 18th century, when its butter market was a source of vast wealth. Much of the best architecture – as seen in the wide streetscapes of the South Mall, Grand Parade and the North Mall – dates from this period. In the 18th and 19th centuries – the era of the 'merchant princes' – Cork's more affluent citizens lived in its waterside suburbs or on the high ground to the north of the city to avoid the diseases endemic in its marshy centre, where slaughter houses and tanneries proliferated. Nowadays people still prefer to live outside the city, commuting from its pleasant hinterlands, and the city centre itself has a very low population, measured in the

hundreds. However, some 350,000 people live within a 45-minute journey of Cork city in attractive seaside locations such as Cobh and Kinsale, or satellite towns such as Midleton, Ballincollig and Carrigaline. The total student population is around 25,000 (University College and Cork Institute of Technology combined), a figure which will not surprise anyone who has seen the young people pouring out of the city's bars and discos at closing time on the weekends. With traditional manufacturing industries like Ford and Dunlop long since closed, the city and its hinterland are now home to high-tech pharmaceutical and computer multinationals such as Pfizer and Apple.

Cork's tenure of European Capital of Culture in 2005 prompted a redesign of the city's St Patrick's Street and Grand Parade by the Barcelona architect Beth Gallí, giving a pedestrianised focus with her pavements of polychromatic stone and futuristic street lights. The most successful of several regeneration projects is the area between Patrick Street and the

Sculpture on St Finbar's Cathedral.

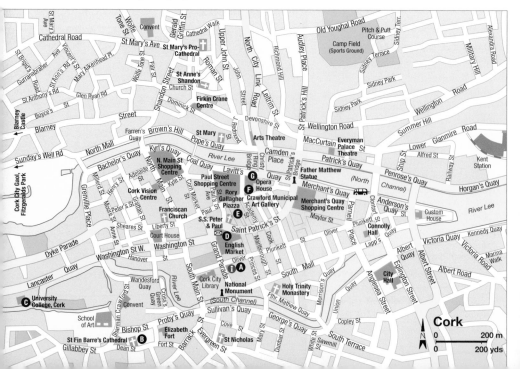

river, around Paul Street and Corn-market, the latter having a lively Saturday street market. Outdoor bar and café tables under awnings in these pedestrianised areas, where buskers abound, has created an unusually lively streetlife.

The city centre

Cork's narrow lanes, half-hidden flights of steps and unexpected plazas lend themselves to lazy strolls or determined one-day sightseeing excursions. The city centre is often likened to Venice and Rome for its many bridges and steep hills, but, as in Venice or Rome, any geographical confusion that may occur will usually be solved by walking a straight line to a major landmark.

Start at the **Tourist Information Office Ⓐ** (tel: 021-425 5100; www.discoverireland.ie/Places-To-Go/Cork; free) on **Grand Parade**. Take a look across the street at a terrace of three elegant Georgian houses with slate-hung, bow-fronted windows, typical of Cork's 18th-century prime. In the southwest, across the south channel of the River

Lee, you can see the spires of **St Finbar's Cathedral Ⓑ** (www.cathedral.cork.anglican.org; free), where the city began as a monastic school in about AD 650. Both the cathedral, and the bridge across the Lee are built of characteristic white limestone. The compact but ornate cathedral, designed by William Burges, who also contributed the stained glass, sculptures, mosaics and metalwork for the Gothic Revival style interior, dates from 1865. It has been restored to a high gloss: don't miss the golden angel on top of the exterior of its rotunda.

Washington Street, which reaches Grand Parade in a T-junction, leads, after a 10-minute walk, to the campus of **University College, Cork Ⓒ** The Visitor Centre (tel: 021-490 3000; http://www.ucc.ie/en/visitors/centre; free) is located in the north side of the 19th-century Tudor-Gothic style Quadrangle, adjacent to a display of ancient Ogham Stones – gravestone-like rock tablets with varying sequences of short lines etched along one side, recording events and occasions in an ancient language known

University College, Cork.

St Finbar's Cathedral.

THE CORK ACCENT

The singsong qualities of the Cork accent can often prove a tricky hurdle for the visitor to overcome, especially when combined with the speed of speech generally acknowledged the fastest in the country. With a rich vein of slang running through daily discourse, the need for a polite 'pardon me?' will be frequent. Given the multitudes of invaders through the centuries, Viking, Norman, Elizabethan and Huguenot, to name but a few, Corkonians have assimilated a lexicon all of their own.

Cork Slang, Like by Seán Beecher, on sale at local bookshops (www.cork-slang.com), provides a good introduction. Thus you will learn that a *flah-bag* is a promiscuous woman, a *masher* is an attractive man, *langers* is drunk, *scauld* is tea and *meejum* is a measure of stout.

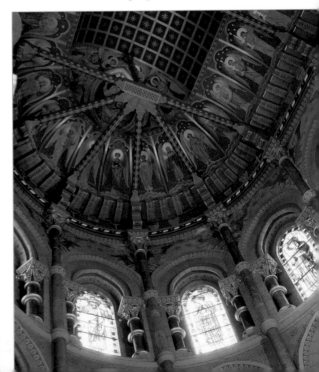

As well as the meats and fish, Cork's English Market now has wine merchants, bakers and other artisan food producers – putting it on most foodies' must-see lists. While there, pause for a break at the first-floor Farmgate Café (inexpensive), one of the city's liveliest lunch spots, perfect for people watching.

Shopping at Princes Street Market.

as Ogham. Known locally as UCC, the college has 15,000 students. The new buildings on campus have been cleverly integrated to create a second focal area with a 21st-century identity. The **Honan Chapel**, a Hiberno-Romanesque chapel dating from 1916, which showcases Celtic Revival arts and crafts, forms part of this vista. The campus has several other interesting buildings, notably the **Lewis Glucksman Gallery** (www.glucksman. org), a boldly designed art gallery with its top floor among the tree tops, which has won several architectural awards. Professor George Boole, whose Boolean Logic has become the basis of modern day computer science, spent much of his working life at UCC.

Back at the Tourist Information Office on Grand Parade, walk a few steps to the left for a look at **South Mall**, Cork's business area in the city's 18th-century prime. It is now the legal and banking district. Prior to its 18th century development, 'The Mall', as it is known locally, was a waterway where merchant ships moored and the

flights of stone steps still visible on its north side recall its maritime past.

The English market

Leaving the river to your back, walk along the Grand Parade to Cork's indoor food market, the **English Market** Ⓓ (www.englishmarket.ie; free), which extends across a whole city block. This huge market, with its ornate Victorian cast-iron frame, is one of the city's showpieces, where over 150 stalls of artisan food makers, continental delis and organic farmers sell their wares alongside traditional fishmongers, beef, lamb and pork butchers and poulterers. At the Princes Street end of the market there is a top-lit piazza with a central fountain. A bronze plaque commemorates the visit of HM Queen Elizabeth II in 2011. The Farmgate Café in the balcony above sources all its ingredients from the market. Note the stall at the door with a display of tripe (cows' intestines) and *drisheen* (blood sausage), and the buttered eggs (the shells rubbed with butter to preserve their freshness) sold in the piazza.

St Patrick's Street

Follow Grand Parade into the graceful curve of **St Patrick's Street**, Cork's main shopping street. The major department store **Brown Thomas** has a good stock of Irish crystal. Look up, because above the modern shop fronts many of the buildings on Patrick Street (as it is generally called) have retained 18th- and 19th-century features. After lunch you'll hear a unique Cork phenomenon – cries of 'Eeeechooo!' from vendors of Cork's evening paper, the *Evening Echo*. A bronze statue of this quintessential Cork symbol, 'the Echo boy', stands at the junction of Patrick Street and Cook Street.

About 20 yards/metres along St Patrick's Street, on the left-hand side, a pedestrian alleyway next to the Body Shop leads to the **Rory Gallagher Piazza** E, a pedestrian square popular with buskers, named for the Cork-raised rock and blues guitarist who died in 1995. This area is the closest Cork gets to a 'left bank', with a cluster of design conscious home furnishing stores, fashion and vintage clothing boutiques and trendy cafés.

Turn right on to Paul Street for the **Crawford Municipal Art Gallery** F (tel: 021-480 5042; www.crawfordart gallery.ie; Mon–Sat 10am–5pm, Thu until 8pm; free). It has an interesting permanent collection, in which most major 20th-century Irish artists are represented, and a good collection of topographical paintings of Cork in its 18th- and 19th-century prime. It also mounts and hosts touring exhibitions in an extension, built in 2001, which wraps around the existing red-brick building, using the same material, in an adventurous design by Dutch architect Eric van Egeraat.

The **Opera House** G (www.corkopera house.ie), just around the corner in the direction of the river, dates from 1965, and was recently given a stylish facade and a pedestrianised forecourt. To the right is St Patrick's Bridge, and straight ahead is the modern Christy Ring Bridge. Both lead from the central island of Cork to the northside.

Cross the Christy Ring Bridge, and climb the hill to O'Connell Square

The Firkin Crane Centre.

A river view in Cork.

Blarney Castle.

Cork's Opera House.

and the **Firkin Crane Centre** (tel: 021-450 7487; www.firkincrane.ie; free) Part of the centre, a classical rotunda attractively built in cut limestone, is used for dance performances, and part houses the **Shandon Craft Market**. It dates from the 18th century when much of Cork's wealth derived from the exporting of butter. Butter was packed in wooden barrels known as firkins, which were weighed here by a crane. Learn more next door at the **Cork Butter Museum** (tel: 021-430 0600; www.corkbuttermuseum.com).

St Anne's Church

Across the road is **St Anne's Church** (www.shandonbells.org; free) whose steeple is the city's iconic landmark. Erected in 1847, it is topped by a large salmon-shaped weather vane above the four-sided clock predating London's Big Ben (1858). The clock was known as 'the four-faced liar' due to a peculiar quirk of its machinery that allowed four different times to be displayed. This malfunction was corrected some years ago, much to the chagrin of locals.

Built in 1722, the steeple is of red sandstone faced with white limestone, a popular combination in local architecture, known as 'streaky bacon', from which the colours of the Cork hurling and football teams are taken. A climb to the belfry (fee) rewards visitors with the chance to play a tune on the famous Shandon Bells – an exercise that will allow your inexpert rope pulls to echo discordantly across the city. Past the bell loft, stairs leads to the tower's terrace and stunning views on all sides.

The old prison

A 20-minute walk starting at the North Mall beside the river at the foot of Shandon Street, uphill into Sunday's Well Road leads to **Cork City Gaol** (tel: 021-430 5022; www.corkcitygaol.com; free), a 19th-century prison recreated in all its miserable conditions. With wax figures crouched in the tiny cells and the sounds of dragging chains, the atmosphere is sobering and perhaps not suitable for very young children. The building also houses a fascinating (but rather underpromoted) **Radio Museum** in the former studio of Cork's first radio station, with numerous genuine artefacts, providing a history of the early days of radio broadcasting.

Walking back toward the city centre, cross the River Lee on Daly's Bridge, a pedestrian suspension structure known locally as 'the shaky bridge', to **Fitzgerald Park**. Set beside the river, the 18-acre (7-hectare) landscaped municipal park is a popular oasis. **Cork Public Museum** (tel: 021-427 0679; Mon–Fri, 11am–1pm & 2.15–5pm (4pm Sat), Sun 3pm–5pm, closed Sun Oct–Mar; free) is housed in a Georgian house and contains historical artefacts relating to the city's history.

Blarney Castle

A visit to **Blarney Castle ❷** (tel: 021-438 5252; www.blarneycastle.ie; daily 9am–sundown, Sun until 5.30pm in summer) makes a pleasant half-day outing. Don't be put off by Blarney's reputation as a tourist trap. The castle is surrounded by well-tended gardens, two rivers, a 'Druid' grotto and parkland (don't miss the lake), and the experience is humorously presented tongue-in-cheek as a load of Blarney.

The castle is not furnished, nor, like many castles of its age, is it a ruin. It is basically a 15th-century fortified home, and the staircase is narrow so that it can be defended by one man holding a sword. Kissing the **Blarney Stone** is supposed to bestow the gift of eloquence. The word Blarney has entered the English language to mean 'smoothly flattering or cajoling talk', but the origins of the strange tradition are obscure.

Having ascended the castle's many steps to the stunning vistas offered by the rooftop viewing point, those who would romance the Stone are held by the waist while leaning over the battlements to offer puckered lips upon the legendary surface. There is no charge, but most people are so happy to survive the ordeal, they gladly pay €10 at the exit for a souvenir photo.

Fota Wildlife Park

The east side of Cork Harbour is formed by three islands, **Little Island**, **Fota Island** and **Great Island**, all connected by causeways. The road from Cork to Cobh brings you past the walls of the 780-acre (315-hectare) **Fota Estate. Fota Wildlife Park** ❸ (www.fotawildlife.ie; tel: 021-481 2678; free) aims to breed certain species that are under threat in the wild. Giraffe, zebras, ostrich, oryx and antelope roam freely in grassland, monkeys swing through trees on lake islands, while kangaroos, wallabies, lemurs and peacocks have the complete freedom of the park. Fota is the world's leading breeder of cheetahs, one of the few animals here that must be caged.

The freely accessible **Fota Arboretum** is beside the Wildlife Park, behind Fota House (tel: 021-481 5543; www.fotahouse.com; free). The house, built as a shooting lodge, was enlarged in 1820 to a symmetrical neoclassical design. The arboretum has a beautiful collection of mature trees. Many of these specimens were introduced

Giraffe roam freely in Fota Wildlife Park.

There is no dignified way to kiss the Blarney Stone.

St Colman's Cathedral.

*Cheetah family at
Fota Wildlife Park.*

from Asia, Australia and the Americas during the 19th century.

The Cove of Cork

Cobh ❹ (pronounced 'cove') was a small fishing village, referred to as the Cove of Cork. It grew in importance as a British naval base during the18th and 19th centuries thanks to its natural deep-water harbour. The fine cut-stone buildings on the two main islands in its harbour were built by the British Navy during the Napoleonic Wars (1792–1815). In Victorian times Cove became Queenstown, and after Independence reverted to its original name in Irish transliteration.

Cobh is attractively located on a steep slope with a Victorian-style promenade, and panoramic south-facing views of Cork harbour. It is a popular commuter town, linked by rail to the city. Visitors are attracted by its maritime history as the last – and first – European port of call for transatlantic shipping. Between 1848 and 1950 about 2.5 million adults and children emigrated through the port. Their transport ranged from convict transports and the 'coffin ships' of the famine years, overcrowded and unseaworthy, to the luxury of White Star and Cunard liners. Cobh was the last port of call of the *Titanic* in 1912, and it was to Cobh that most of the bodies recovered from the torpedoing of the *Lusitania* in 1915 were brought. The Titanic Experience Cobh (tel: 021-481 4412; www.titanicexperiencecobh.ie) occupies the former offices of the White Star Line, and is an interactive exhibition leading to the actual dock from which passengers embarked on the tenders that carried them out to the liners. The old railway station is now the Cobh Heritage Centre (tel: 021-481 3591; www.cobhheritage.com; daily 9.30am–5.30pm; free). The history of emigration from Cobh is covered in **The Queenstown Story**, an imaginative audio-visual exhibition. Allow at least an hour.

A large, Gothic-revival church, **St Colman's Cathedral**, was built in granite between 1868 and 1915. From its parapet you can see Roches Point in the south, which marks the harbour entrance, and the open sea beyond.

Cork and Surroundings

0 20 km
0 20 miles

ATLANTIC OCEAN

THE SOUTHWEST

This is where the Atlantic Ocean first touches
Europe, and the mild climate enhances the
spectacular scenery of the Wild Atlantic Way.

Cork and Kerry, Ireland's most
southwesterly corner, offer an
attractive combination of sea
and mountain scenery, interspersed
with lively small towns and villages – Kinsale, Clonakilty, Kenmare,
Killarney and An Daingean/Dingle.
Life is taken at a slower pace herea-
bouts, and old fashioned courtesies
survive: for example, on the smaller
back roads it is still the tradition for
passing cars to salute one another, so
do not be surprised if strangers wave
at you. People find it quite natural to
strike up conversations, just because
you happen to be in the same place at
the same time. Here, a friendly infor-
mality prevails.

Touring the southwest

Bring strong walking shoes and waterproof jackets. The further west you go,
the more likely you are to encounter
rain, as the clouds scud in from the
Atlantic, but it is seldom continuous
heavy rain, and the showery weather
typical of Killarney and Dingle often
alternates with sunshine, creating
some magical light effects, including
numerous rainbows.

The rich farming country on the
fertile plains of the Rivers Lee and
Bandon give way to more rugged, hilly
land, the closer you get to the coast.
More than 600 miles (1,000km) of
coastline include impressive slate and

sandstone cliffs, long sandy beaches
and rocky inlets, and easily accessible offshore islands, with abundant
wildlife. This is beginning of the Wild
Atlantic Way, a 1600 mile (2600 km)
route that stretches up as far as the
northern headlands. Because of the
proximity of the Gulf Stream, parts
of the coast of west Cork and Kerry,
including Glengarriff, Killarney and
Sneem, are frost-free year round, and
have lush, sub-tropical vegetation.

An added bonus throughout
the region is the high quality of its

Main Attractions
Kinsale
Glandore
Mizen Head
Bantry Bay
Glengarriff
Killarney
Ring of Kerry
Valentia Island
Dingle
Tralee

Riding the Atlantic waves.

Kinsale's harbour.

natural produce – farmhouse cheeses made from the milk of cows grazing on fertile green fields, locally reared beef, pork and lamb, freshly caught fish and shellfish, local honey, home-grown potatoes, salads and vegetables (increasingly organic) will impress foodies with their flavour and freshness. All of these products can be found in specialist food shops and at farmers' markets and are sourced for the best local restaurants.

The pleasures of the southwest are chiefly rural. Most people who visit the area come for the outdoors and the scenery. The lakes and mountains of Killarney can compete with the best

Europe has to offer, while the **Ring of Kerry** presents a succession of spectacular seascapes. The less-frequented **Beara Peninsula** is preferred by walkers and cyclists who enjoy the relative lack of traffic and the simple B&B accommodation available. The West Cork coast also has its champions: relatively small scale cliffs and hills, miles of fuchsia hedges dripping with dark red, honey-scented flowers, clashing exuberantly with swathes of sprawling purple heather.

The most popular part of the west among visitors is the western tip of the Dingle Peninsula, a largely Irish-speaking area rich in prehistoric and

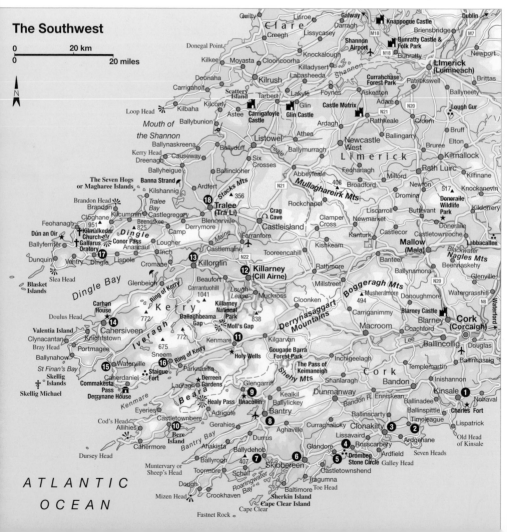

The Southwest

early Christian remains, with some of the world's best coastal scenery and the country's best traditional music.

Kinsale

Kinsale ❶, 12 miles (19km) south of Cork Airport on the R600, is the big success story of Irish tourism. Once a run-down fishing port, it is now a wealthy resort with so many restaurants that it's known as 'the gourmet capital of Ireland'. It is situated at the top of a fjord-like harbour where the River Bandon runs into the sea. Craft shops, galleries, restaurants and antique shops abound. While the south-facing slopes of the inner harbour have been marred by up-market housing developments, including a series of large apartment blocks known locally as 'Heineken Heights', the outer harbour is mercifully unspoilt.

The **Old Courthouse** in Market Square dates from 1600. In 1706 a Dutch-style gabled frontage and octagonal clock tower were added. The Courthouse contains the **Kinsale Regional Museum** (tel: 021-477 7930;

free), whose exhibits include mementoes of the *Lusitania*, sunk 14 miles (23km) off the coast by a German submarine in 1915. The inquest into the sinking was held here.

Also of interest nearby are the 12th-century **St Multose Church** and the 16th-century restored **Desmond Castle** (tel: 021-477 4855; Apr–mid-Sept daily 10am–6pm), which houses the International Museum of Wine. (Many emigrant Irish families from the 17th century onwards got involved with the wine trade in Europe, Australia and the US.) Originally built as a custom house, from the mid-18th century Desmond Castle was used as a prison, and it is known locally as the French Prison after a tragic fire in which 54 prisoners, mainly French sailors, died. **Charles Fort** (tel: 021-477 2263; daily May–Sep 10am–6pm; mid-Mar–Apr & Oct Sat–Sun 10am–6pm; charge), a five-minute drive down Kinsale Harbour, is a star-shaped fort enclosing 9 acres (3.5 hectares) of ground, and was built in 1677. Because it is overlooked by high ground, it was never a great success militarily, and its working life

FACT

On 7 May 1915 the Cunard liner Lusitania was torpedoed ten miles off the Old Head of Kinsale; 1,198 of the 1,959 people aboard died. A stone memorial beside a Napoleonic signal tower on the Old Head commemorates the tragic event.

Kinsale.

Charles Fort.

as a recruit training centre ended in 1921 when the IRA burnt it down. There is good cut-stone work on many buildings, and wonderful sea views. On the outer harbour side of the fort an attractive footpath runs along beside the sea towards the harbour mouth for about 1 mile (2km; free).

Courtmacsherry Estuary

Leave Kinsale by crossing the River Bandon to the west. The R600 runs along the edge of the **Courtmacsherry Estuary** which in winter months is home to great flocks of plover, oyster catchers and curlew. In the summer, cormorants, egrets and herons should be easy to spot.

The distant view of **Timoleague** ❷ is dominated by the grey stone ruins of the waterside 12th-century **Timoleague Franciscan Friary** (www. timoleague.ie). Until the 16th century the monks were wine importers. The ruins are freely accessible. There are some garish modern graves inside, but the tall Gothic windows framing views of the estuary offer an irresistible photo opportunity. The

Drombeg Stone Circle.

interior walls of Timoleague's tiny 19th-century **Church of Ireland** are entirely covered by a mosaic mural in the decorative style favoured by the Oxford Movement. The 20th-century Hiberno-Romanesque-style **Church of Our Lady's Nativity** contains some fine stained-glass windows by the acclaimed Dublin artist, Harry Clarke (1889–1931).

Clonakilty and environs

Arriving at **Clonakilty** ❸, take the bypass and park in one of the designated areas to explore the colourful and compact town centre on foot. **Emmet Square** is lined by tall Georgian houses. The **General Post Office** is in a small 19th-century church. Note the hand-painted shop signs above wooden shop fronts, which have been revived in recent years. The **West Cork Model Railway Village** (tel: 023-883 3224; www.modelvillage.ie) in the old railway station at the east end of town is a 1:24 scale model of the towns of Bandon, Kinsale, Clonakilty and Dunmanway, as they were in the 1940s, and of the long closed West Cork Railway.

Historians will like the eclectic **West Cork Regional Museum** (Old Methodist School, Western Road; tel: 023-883 3115; May–Oct), which has memorabilia of the West Cork patriot Michael Collins (see page 48) among its extensive collection. Collins's birthplace, a dignified memorial featuring the walls of the family farmhouse and a bronze statue, is signposted 6 miles (9km) west of Clonakilty, just beyond **Lissavaird**.

The **Michael Collins Centre** (tel: 023-884 6107; www.michaelcollinscentre. com; Jun–Sep, Mon–Fri 10.30am–5pm, Sun 11–2pm or by appointment) is 2 miles/3km outside Clonakilty off the R600 Timoleague road. It offers an audio-visual display, photo and militaria exhibition featuring the local hero, and can organise guided tours (in your own car, or tour bus) of the somewhat scattered sites associated with Collins. Lectures and other events mark the anniversary of his death on 22 August 1922, in an ambush at nearby **Béal na Blath**.

Continuing west on the N71, the road crosses a wide sea inlet at **Rosscarbery ❹**. This was an important monastic centre from the 6th to the 12th centuries. The protestant Cathedral Church of St Fachtna (1612) is the smallest cathedral in Ireland and has been attractively renovated. The pretty village square, on a hill above the main road, with craft shops, bars and cafés is worth exploring.

Turn left just beyond Rosscarbery on to the R597 Glandore road. From June to September this little road, and many others like it around west Cork, are lined by tall hedges of *Fuchsia magellanica*, a shrub with bright red bell-shaped flowers imported from Chile in the 19th century. It has adapted so well to the climate that it grows wild in profusion.

About 2 miles (3.5km) along is the road to the **Drombeg Stone Circle** (free), one of the most complete and most impressively situated of the region's early Iron Age remains. The circle is oriented to the winter solstice. If it's cloudless on 21 December, it is an impressive sight as the last rays of the sun travel through a cut in the distant mountains and land on the flat stone at the far side of the circle.

Michael Collins, two weeks before his assassination in 1922.

FUCHSIA BRANDING

A green logo featuring a fuchsia flower and the words 'A place apart – West Cork' is part of a regional branding exercise designed to enhance the area's reputation for high-quality food, accommodation and craft products. Those sanctioned to use the fuchsia logo must adhere to strict quality criteria, and reflect local characteristics including environmental quality, and an awareness of the richness and diversity of local heritage. The fuchsia sign on a menu guarantees the best regional ingredients. Producers include Castletownbere's Shellfish de la Mer, luxury cakes from Coolmore Foods, wild smoked salmon from Ummera Smoked Products, West Cork Bakery's handmade bread, Skeaghanore Duck from Ballydehob (very flavoursome) and Follain Teo's high-fruit preserves, relishes and marmalade.

In winter **Glandore** ❺, a tiny village built on the south-facing slope of a protected harbour, with a year-round population well below 100, will be virtually empty, while in summer it will be teeming with wealthy visitors and their yachts. This lovely spot is known locally as Millionaire's Row. **Union Hall,** on the opposite side of Glandore Harbour, is a small fishing village. The brightly painted trawlers moor nearby at **Keelbeg Pier**. Note the characteristic multicoloured houses: it's said this tradition began when fishermen used whatever was left over from the annual painting of their boats to brighten up their houses. The custom has been enthusiastically adopted by developers of new holiday homes, but you will quickly learn to distinguish the real thing.

Castletownshend

Castletownshend is signposted from Union Hall on an attractive back road which passes through **Rineen**. Castletownshend may be the prettiest village in west Cork, but it is also the least typical. Wander along its two streets,

Brightly coloured buildings in Skibbereen.

noting its large, well-designed three- and four-storey houses, often stone-built and neoclassical. These belonged to 'planter' families – Protestant English ex-soldiers who were given lands in the area in the late 17th century.

A wall plaque in **St Barrahane's Church** enlarges on their history. Behind the church are the graves of Edith Somerville (1858–1949) and her writing partner, Violet Martin (1862–1915). As Somerville and Ross, they are best known for a series of comic sketches of Irish country life, *Some Experiences of an Irish RM* (Resident Magistrate). They also wrote a well-received novel, *The Real Charlotte*. There's a wonderful view of the sheltered anchorage from their graves.

Skibbereen

Skibbereen ❻ is a market town built in a solid bourgeois style in the 19th and early 20th centuries. Symptomatic of the changes that have taken place in rural Ireland since the economic boom, it now has a tiny (but very welcome) bypass, in the form of a ring road studded with supermarkets and DIY warehouses.

The **Skibbereen Heritage Centre** (tel: 028-40900; www.skibbheritage.com; free), on Upper Bridge Street makes a good attempt to explain the causes of the Great Famine of 1845–7 that took the lives of over 10,000 people in the area.

Baltimore, 8 miles (13km) south of Skibbereen, is a popular sailing and holiday village on **Roaringwater Bay.** The bay covers an area between Mizen Head in the west and Baltimore in the east, which is known for its numerous rocks and islands. In good visibility, the **Fastnet Rock Lighthouse**, can be seen on the horizon some 14 miles (23km) to the south.

Baltimore is also the base for the mail boats and ferries servicing Roaringwater Bay's two largest inhabited islands, Cape Clear and Sherkin. **Sherkin Island** is only a quick hop (tel: 087-911 7377; http://sherkinisland.eu for ferry details). The ruins of a 15th-century Franciscan friary stand just beside the pier on Sherkin. The island is 3 miles long and 1.5 miles wide (5

by 2.4km) with several pleasant sandy beaches, and good peaceful walking on its quiet, almost traffic-free roads. It's popular for day trips.

Birdwatching centre

Cape Clear Island is reached by a thrilling 45-minute boat ride through the rocks of Roaringwater Bay (tel: 028-39159; www.cailinoir.com). There is usually a boat out at 11am, returning at 4pm. Cape Clear (pop. 120) is an Irish-speaking island about 3 miles long by 1 mile (5 by 2km). There are three pubs, a youth hostel, a campsite, a bird observatory, a heritage centre and plenty of simple accommodation. Cape Clear's Bird Observatory often reports landings of rare migratory birds, and the appearance of large flocks. Cape hosts a storytelling festival every September.

The N71 west leaves Skibbereen beside the banks of the **River Ilen**. Keep an eye out to the left for your first panoramic view of Roaringwater Bay and its numerous islands.

Ballydehob ❼ is a lively, brightly painted village built on a hillside,

The Baltimore Beacon warns ships of the treacherous coast.

BALTIMORE'S BOATING TRADITION

From May to September, Baltimore's fleet of gaff-rigged wooden sailing boats can be seen in the harbour. A group of enthusiasts rescued the bones of an old sailing ship rotting in the mud, and used it as a template to revive the area's traditional mackerel boats. These were built for speed, to get the catch back into port ahead of the pack, and provide exciting sailing. The boats, which were in use up to the 1950s, are built in a traditional yard at Oldcourt (just outside Baltimore) by Liam Hegarty and Fachtna O'Sullivan, whose families have been building boats here for generations.

There are now about 40 sailing vessels in the fleet, of various designs, and several canoe-like currachs, traditionally built of tarred canvas on a wooden frame. The smaller 'towelsail' yawls were used for crab fishing in inland waters, and are designed to navigate shallow rocky coves. The 'towelsail' was a sail hung over the body of the boat to create a tent (*teabhal* in the local Irish dialect, pronounced 'towel') for the crab fishermen who spent many nights aboard.

The boats celebrate the start of the season every year on the last weekend in May with mussel eating and net mending competitions in the Baltimore Seafood and Wooden Boats Festivals (www.baltimorewooden boatfestival.com). In summer the fleet, a much-loved spectacle and emblem of maritime heritage, travels to regattas along the Cork coast.

Jazz festival in Ballydehob.

Bantry House.

apparently in the middle of nowhere. There is a pleasant walk along its disused railway viaduct, a relic of the short-lived West Cork Railway. The village is a popular retreat for city folk – English, Dutch, German and even Irish – seeking a better quality of life.

Continue on the R592 towards Schull. In good weather you will see **Mount Gabriel** (1335ft/407 metres) on your right. The two white balls on its summit guide transatlantic air traffic. While Ballydehob has a reputation for being arty, **Schull**, 3 miles (5km) down the R592, is the heart of fashionable west Cork, a summer resort for wealthy Dubliners. Walk down to the pier for another look at Roaringwater Bay, and then explore its one main street, checking out its restaurants, bookshops and craft boutiques.

Mizen Head

Leave Schull on the R592 to travel to the tip of the **Mizen Peninsula**. The road passes rocky, rugged bits of low-lying coast. About 4 miles (7km) west at **Altar**, there is a megalithic tomb on the left, known locally as

the Altar Rock. The **Mizen Head** is a dramatic spot with wild Atlantic waves pounding the rocks even in the calmest weather. The lighthouse signal has been automatic, and the station unstaffed since 1993. The **Mizen Head Visitor Centre** (tel: 028-35115; www.mizenhead.net; mid-Mar–Oct daily 10.30am–5pm, Nov–mid-Mar Sat–Sun 11am–4pm) is located in the lighthouse keeper's house on an island at the tip of the peninsula. To reach it you must cross a concrete suspension bridge while the waves swirl around 150ft (45 metres) below. It's worth bringing a camera.

The **Sheep's Head Peninsula** is a thin finger of land dividing Dunmanus Bay from Bantry Bay to the north. From Goleen or Schull, follow the R591 to Durrus, and follow signs for the Sheep's Head Drive (50 miles/80km), which leads to the N71, and Bantry town. The peninsula is small and sparsely populated, with most people living in scattered farmhouses. There is a timeless air about the gorse and heather of the heathland, and the rough green fields with grey stone walls. The marked Sheep's Head Way walking trail of over 60 miles (100km) has been designed with loop walks of one to two hours; maps are available locally. The views to the north and south are superb. Stop at the Tin Pub in Ahakista to experience old-style hospitality, then explore the nearby megalithic stone circle, signposted as part of the waking trail. Near Kilcrohane is a plaque commemorating the novelist J.G. Farrell (*Troubles, The Siege of Krishnapur*) who was swept out to sea while fishing from the rocks in 1978, shortly after moving to live in the area.

The shores of Bantry Bay

The town of **Bantry** ❽ is distinguished only by its setting on the shores of **Bantry Bay**. **Bantry House and Gardens** (tel: 027-50047; www. bantryhouse.com; Mar–Oct daily 10am–6pm; café, craft shop), a short walk from the town centre, is a large, mid-18th century mansion with a magnificent setting overlooking the famous bay (which is 4 miles/6.4km wide). The gardens have recently been replanted with some striking contemporary effects enhancing features such as an ancient wisteria trained on a circular trellis.

Inside, there is a fine collection of treasures, including Aubusson carpets, Gobelin tapestries, Russian icons, Chinese lacquer and a mixture of French and Irish 18th-century furniture.

Head inland from Bantry via **Kealkil** to visit **Gougane Barra**, a deep tarn which is the source of the River Lee. The lake is surrounded on three sides by steep precipices, which run with cataracts after heavy rain. **St Finbar's Oratory**, a small stone-built chapel (a 20th-century replica) on an island in the lake, can be reached by a causeway. This is believed to be where St Finbar lived in the 6th century before founding his monastery in Cork city. A pilgrimage is still held on the first Sunday after St Finbar's Feast Day, 25 September. There's something special about the place, particularly if you arrive early, before the majority of day trippers.

Glengarriff

The N71 climbs above Bantry Bay into open, more rugged country, offering ever-changing views across the bay. **Glengarriff ❾**, a wooded glen with a sheltered harbour warmed by the Gulf Stream, has an especially mild climate, with an average annual temperature of 52°F (11°C). Azaleas, rhododendrons, magnolia and camellias grow in abundance. **Glengarriff Bamboo Park** (tel: 027-63975; www.bamboo-park.com; daily 9am–7pm) has walks through over 30 different species of bamboo and palm trees with superb sea views.

Glengarriff village is teeming with craft shops, serving coaches en route to Killarney. Take a ferry from the pier to **Ilnacullin Gardens** (tel: 027-63040; Apr–Oct) on **Garinish Island**, five minutes offshore. Allow about an hour and a half. Don't miss the formal Italian Garden, with colonnades and a terrace heightening the contrast between the classical man-made

Glengarriff.

TIP

Maps with a funky Red Fish logo are available locally on Beara entitled "A Grand Day Out". Follow the trail to discover thirteen attractions including gardens, craft and art galleries and restaurants displaying the sign of the Red Fish.

beauty of the garden and the wild mountain scenery that surrounds it. Alternatively, for the same fare (€12) you can take a boat trip around the harbour without landing on the island. Except in very bad weather, you will see families of basking seals on the rocks between the mainland and the island.

The Ring of Beara

The **Ring of Beara** is less well known than its neighbour to the north, the Ring of Kerry, yet it also offers impressive scenery. It is a favourite haunt of walkers, cyclists, birdwatchers and people who enjoy natural beauty. Although the drive covers only about 68 miles (110km), much of it is on narrow, winding roads, so allow a full day.

The **Beara Peninsula** stretches for about 30 miles (48km) southwest from Glengarriff, forming the north side of Bantry Bay. The **Caha** and **Slieve Miskish** mountains run down the centre of the peninsula, and the road around it is mainly on a narrow coastal plain.

A shorter route to Kenmare, avoiding the Ring of Beara, can be taken

Killarney landscape.

at Adrigole, about 12 miles (19km) beyond Glengarriff. The R574 climbs north across the peninsula in a series of small but sharp hairpin bends, leading to the **Healy Pass** (1,083ft/330 metres). Stop here to enjoy a panoramic view of Bantry Bay to the south, with the Kenmare River and the MacGilligcuddy Reeks in the north. Turn right at Lauragh on to the R571 Kenmare road.

Many would consider **Castletownbere ⑩**, with a population of about 850, little more than a village. However, it is a busy working port, home to Ireland's largest white fish trawling fleet. Get a feel for the place by walking along the quays and admiring the brightly coloured fishing fleet. The film director Neil Jordan, who has a house nearby, is one of several international celebrities to have fallen for the charms of this remote spot. **MacCarthy's Bar** in the main square will be familiar to readers of Pete MacCarthy's humorous travel book of the same name: he is pictured on its cover having a pint with a nun. It is a traditional bar-cum-grocery shop, and still does a roaring trade supplying victuals to the town's many trawlers.

Leave town on the R575 for **Allihies**. After about 5 miles (8km) a sign on the left indicates the Dzogchen Beara Retreat Centre (tel: 027-73032; www.dzogchenbeara.org), a Buddhist mediation centre with hostel, and in summer a café. Visitors are welcome to join daily meditation at their cliff top centre, or simply enjoy the gardens and sea view.

Allihies village is a straggling line of brightly coloured cottages set between sea and hills (now augmented by replica cottages, mainly second homes), and was built for the copper miners working in the hills behind it. The sandy beach at **Ballydonegan** was formed of spoil from the mines. The **Allihies Copper Mine Museum** (tel: 027-73218; www.acmm. ie; café) explains the history of mining in the area, from the Iron Age to the arrival of Cornish miners in the 19th century, and the subsequent departure of many miners for Butte, Montana when the mines closed in the 1950s. Walk up to the abandoned mines (marked by tall brick chimneys) and enjoy the views of sea and wild hillside. You can walk from here to the next village, **Eyeries** (7 miles/11km), on a grassy footpath that forms part of the Beara Way. Even if you only walk a few miles of it, the peace and isolation will be memorable.

The road between Allihies and Eyeries, another village of small, brightly coloured houses, is one of the highlights of the Ring of Beara. In good weather the **Iveragh Peninsula** is clearly visible to the north, across the **Kenmare River**, as are the conical shaped **Skellig Rocks** off its tip. You will get a closer look at these rocky islands from the Ring of Kerry.

Derreen Gardens (tel: 064-668 3588) were planted 100 years ago beside Kilmakilloge Harbour, a sheltered inlet on the south shore of the Kenmare River. The woodland gardens run down to the water's edge and contain many azaleas and rhododendrons, massive stands of bamboo and groves of New Zealand tree ferns – all of which thrive in the mild air warmed by the Gulf Stream.

Kenmare ⑪, an attractive little town backed by hills, has a good selection of shops and restaurants. Guided boat trips of the Bay are run from Kenmare Pier by Seafari Seal and Eagle Watching Cruises (tel: 064-668 3171; www.seafariireland.com; mid-Apr–Sept). The **Kenmare Heritage Centre** (tel: 064-6641233; Apr–Sept) explores themes of local interest, including lacemaking. Sheep are still traded from makeshift pens at the traditional Friday market.

Killarney drinking hole.

Killarney

Killarney ⑫ may be the most commercialised area in the Southwest, but it is still possible to avoid the crowds and enjoy the lakes and hills. The romantic scenery of boulder-strewn, heather-clad mountains, deep blue lakes dotted with wooded islands and wild woodland has been preserved

TIP

When visiting Killarney National Park keep an eye out for wildlife. A herd of over 500 red deer roam freely, mainly in the mountain areas of Torc and Mangerton, and also in Muckross and Knockreer Estates. The best time to spot them is early morning. White-tailed sea eagles are being reintroduced: the first 75 chicks took flight in 2007 after an absence of over 100 years. When mature, the wingspan is up to 8ft (2.5 metres).

within a large national park. Avoid the town by day. Killarney isn't a great place to shop for crafts, as it caters chiefly for the first-time visitor, but it is always useful to visit the Tourist Information Office beside the central car park for details of special events, festivals, guided walks, and Gaelic Games (hurling and football).

Enjoying a visit to Killarney is largely a matter of attitude. You won't appreciate Killarney from the inside of a car. One great pleasure here is the damp woodland aroma that permeates the mild air. As in the rest of Kerry, it is important not to be put off by rain. Any weather, good or bad, tends not to last long around here. In fact, the lakes of Killarney look especially good when seen through a light drizzle.

Arriving from Kenmare, you may decide to stop on the N71 and climb the path beside the **Torc Waterfall** to enjoy the view.

Killarney National Park

A nice contrast to the wildness of Torc can be found across the road in **Muckross Park**, a neatly trimmed lakeside

area with gravel paths that forms the nucleus of the **Killarney National Park Ⓐ**. This is a car-free zone, and it is a good place to take a ride on one of Killarney's famous jaunting cars (open horse-drawn carriages). The drivers (jarveys) are traditionally great talkers. Don't be surprised if you hear a phone ring during your quaint ride; the jarveys use their mobile phones to line up their next customer. Jarveys are now obliged to use 'dung catchers' on their horses when driving through Muckross Park.

Muckross House Ⓑ (tel: 064-667 0144; www.muckross-house.ie), built in the 19th century in the Elizabethan style, houses a folklore and farming museum. You can admire the rhodo-dendrons and azaleas in the formal gardens free of charge.

Muckross Traditional Farms Ⓒ (optional joint ticket with Muckross House) is a largely outdoor attraction with a healthy walk between three different-sized farms, all inhabited by chatty, well-informed guides (disguised as farmers), illustrating farming methods before electricity and

Red deer in Killarney National Park.

the internal combustion engine. This may be your only chance to get up close to a pair of Irish wolfhounds: huge but gentle creatures who live on the middle farm.

Ross Castle Ⓓ (tel: 064-663 5851; Apr–Oct; free) is a 14th-century castle keep that has been fully restored and furnished. You can hire a rowing boat here, and take a picnic over to **Innisfallen Island** Ⓔ about 1 mile (1.6km) offshore. The wooded island has the remains of an abbey founded about 600AD, which is famous for the *Annals of Innisfallen*, a chronicle of world and Irish history written in this remote and beautiful spot up to 1320 by a succession of monastic scribes.

Consider taking an organised half-day coach-horse-and-boat trip through the **Gap of Dunloe** Ⓕ, a narrow mountain pass formed by glacial action. The organised trip has the advantage of allowing you to travel through the Gap on foot or horseback and then go back to town by boat without having to retrieve your car.

The Gap itself is an unpaved path that stretches for 4 miles (6.4km) between the **Macgillicuddy's Reeks** and the **Purple Mountain** Ⓖ, which gets its name from the heather that covers it in the autumn. There is no motor traffic, but in summer there is a constant stream of ponies, jaunting cars and pedestrians. The scenery is first-rate, with a chain of five small lakes beside the road, and massive glacial boulders, but don't expect solitude.

The Ring of Kerry

You can drive non-stop around the 112 miles (180km) of the Ring of Kerry in under four hours, but allow a full day as you will want to make several stops. The Ring of Kerry is justifiably famous for its combination of lush, sub-tropical vegetation and rugged seascapes. In July and August the narrow two-lane road can be clogged by a slow procession of tour buses and RVs. If traffic and commercialism bother you, do the

Ring of Beara instead, or go straight to Dingle.

Killorglin ⓭ is a busy village which makes the most of its strategic position on the road between Killarney and Dingle. Its focal point is now a modern square at the top of the town, a product of recent redevelopment. It is famous for the Puck Fair – Ireland's oldest fair, dating back to pagan times – from 10–12 August. On the first day, a mountain goat is crowned King Puck, garlanded with ribbon, and installed on a tall throne overlooking the town, where it stays until the evening of the third day. Horse trading in the traditional manner is still a feature, along with plentiful free entertainment. There are good walks nearby in Glenbeigh Woods and on Rossbeigh, 3-mile (5km) long sandy beach.

Cahersiveen ⓮ (pronounced 'cah-her-sigh-*veen*') is the chief market town for the Iveragh peninsula, but don't expect a buzzing metropolis. Note the 'ghost hotel', long untenanted, the remnant of an over-optimistic investment during the economic boom. **The Barracks** (tel: 066-947 2777; www.

TIP

Fed up with driving? Several companies run day trips around the Ring of Kerry by mini-bus, including Kenmare Coach and Cab, tel: 064-664 1491, www.kenmarecoachandcab.com; and O'Connor Autotours, Killarney, tel: 064-663 1052, www.oconnorautotours.ie.

The Ring of Kerry.

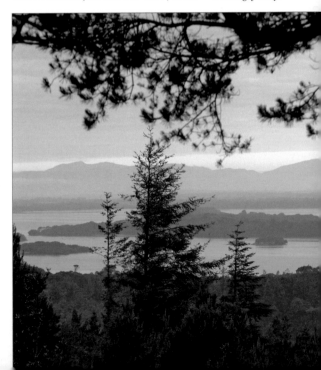

oldbarrackscahersiveen.com) is a community-led heritage centre occupying an exotic-looking, white-turreted building. The story goes that it should have been built in India, on the Northwest Frontier, but the plans were mistakenly sent to Ireland. In fact its architect, Enoch Trevor Owen, habitually built in what he called the Schloss style, and looked at from another angle, his design suits the hill-backed location very well. But why spoil a good story? Nowadays it houses an amusing and informative series of exhibitions.

Follow the sign outside The Barracks to the pier. The prettiest part of Cahersiveen is its backside, which overlooks the wide estuary of the River Ferta and the green hills beyond.

Valentia Island

Look out for signs to the Valentia Island car ferry (April–Sept daily 8.15am–10pm) about 3 miles (5km) west of Cahersiveen. This lands you in **Knightstown** at the eastern tip of **Valentia**, a sleepy place, eerily quiet, with a couple of bars. The island is 6.75 miles (11km) long and 1.7 miles

(3km) broad, a quiet place with a population of about 700. Its relative lack of traffic and wonderful sea views make Valentia a good destination for walkers; maps are available locally; don't miss the Tetrapod footprints near the Slate Quarry, made by a precursor of the dinosaur. The original transatlantic cable connecting Europe with Newfoundland was laid from here between 1857 and 1865. Valentia is connected to the mainland by a causeway at **Portmagee**. The **Skellig Experience** (tel: 066-947 6306; Apr–Nov), beside the causeway, is an uninspiring visitor centre. Opt instead for a boat trip to the islands (tel: 066-947 6214; www.skelligrock.com May–Oct). Bear in mind that all the boats are open, the water can be rough, and bad weather leads to cancellations, sometimes for days on end.

Skellig Michael, the largest of the three islands, was inhabited by monks from the 7th until the 12th centuries. It rises in a cone shape to a double peak 712ft (217 metres) high. A flight of 600 steps lead to the monastery, built of dry stone with no mortar. Enthusiastic guides, all trained archaeologists, live on the island from June to August, to supervise visitors and tell them the island's history.

A scenic drive

If the weather is good, take the scenic road from Portmagee to Waterville through **Ballynahow**, along an impressive arc of coast and mountains with the best views so far of the Skelligs.

Rejoin the main Ring road just before Waterville. **Waterville** ⑮ is a popular base for golfers, who like the famous links, and anglers who have a choice of deep-sea fishing in Ballinskelligs Bay or angling on Lough Currane, half a mile inland.

The next stretch of road is one of the most scenic stretches, winding along the edge of **Ballinskelligs Bay** through rocky coastline backed by rugged green hills. **Derrynane House**

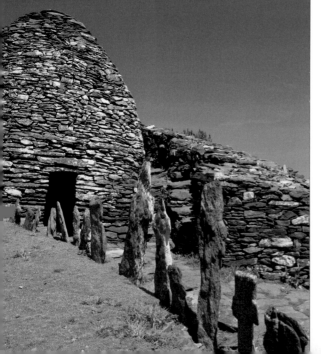

Beehive stone huts and a gravestone shaped like a human figure are part of the ruins of St Finian's Abbey on Skellig Michael.

(tel: 066-947 5113; May–Oct) is a mile beyond **Caherdaniel**. The house belonged to Daniel O'Connell (1775–1847), remembered chiefly for his campaign for Catholic emancipation (granting civil rights to Catholics), in 1829. The 320 acres (130 hectares) of woods surrounding the house (year-round; free) have pleasant walks and access to an attractive sandy beach.

Castlecove is a small, friendly place with good sandy beaches. A narrow lane beyond the church climbs 1.75 miles (3km) to **Staigue Fort**. This is a well-preserved example of a prehistoric stone fortress, dating from 1500 BC. It consists of a circular dry-stone wall, 115ft (35 metres) in diameter, varying in thickness from 13ft to 5ft (4 to 1.5 metres). A series of steps in the walls lead to a platform with good sea views. The landowner requests a small donation.

Sneem ⑯ is another pretty village, laid out English-style around a village green beneath a semi-circle of low mountains. Some of the charm has been lost following over-intensive development of holiday homes. Turn your back on these and walk down the road beside the Blue Bull (signposted 'Pier') past an attractive communal garden. Looking back through the reeds you can appreciate Sneem's sheltered location between the sea and the hills.

Sneem marks the start of the most sheltered part of the Ring of Kerry's coast. Here you will see lush, subtropical growth – wild rhododendrons, azaleas, camellias and bamboo – evidence of the benign effect of the Gulf Stream. The N70 continues past Parknasilla, a large hotel resort with pleasant walks in its wooded waterside grounds, on to Kenmare, where the N71 leads to either Killarney or Glengarriff.

The Dingle Peninsula

The weather can make or break a visit to **Dingle ⑰** (now signposted as An Daingean by government decree: you will not see any signposts directing you to Dingle; see page 197). If the sea mist is down, consider postponing your trip. At Killorglin take the N70 to Castlemaine, and in Castlemaine

TIP

Brandon Bay at the north side of the Dingle Peninsula, is a popular surf and windsurfing destination. It's fun to watch, or you can learn the sport at Jamie Knox Watersports; tel: 066-713 9411, www.jamieknox.com.

Dingle harbour.

take the R561, which gives good views across the bay of the coast of the Iveragh peninsula. **Inch** has 4 miles (6.5km) of sandy beach backed by dunes. There is safe swimming and the surf is suitable for beginners. The beach is also popular with shore anglers and walkers. There is free parking, and a couple of simple cafés.

Dingle has a population of about 1,500, which can treble in summer. Its tourism was boosted by the filming of *Ryan's Daughter* in 1969. Since 1985, a wild dolphin, Fungi, has been entertaining visitors with his playful antics, and townsfolk recently erected a bronze statue of him on the pier. Skippers tout for business, offering 'money-back if no dolphin sightings' deals.

Dingle, where you will hear the Irish language spoken in everyday dealings, is very popular with visitors, and offers good restaurants and lively music pubs. A triangular 10-minute walk from the pier area, up Green Street (the best place for craft shops), down Main Street and back along the Mall to the pier takes you past most of the shops, pubs and restaurants.

An Diseart (Green Street; tel: 066-915 2476; www.diseart.ie; grounds free) is a huge 19th-century convent, converted into an Institute of Spirituality and Celtic Culture. Its walled gardens and graveyard create an oasis in the town centre, and the building has beautiful stained-glass windows in pre-Raphaelite style.

Continue west on the R559. Between **Ventry** and Slea Head there are over 400 *clocháns* ('beehive' huts). The farmers charge you a nominal sum to visit them. These small conical huts of unmortared stone are not prehistoric, as the farmers claim; the oldest date from the early Christian period, the 5th to 8th centuries, and were used by hermit monks. Others were built within the past 100 years or less to house farm implements: there is little timber in these parts, so it is cheaper to build with stone. Dunbeg Fort (tel: 066-915 9755; www.dunbegfort.com) just beyond Ventry, a properly excavated Iron Age promontory fort dating from about AD 800, built on a cliff edge, and the adjacent Visitor Centre (included in charge), are worth

Slea Head.

a visit, as are the *clocháns* half a mile further on, which look out to the Skellig Rocks. The road then climbs westward around Eagle Mountain to **Slea Head,** and has good panoramas.

The Blasket Islands

The group of seven rocky islands offshore are the **Blasket Islands**. The **Great Blasket,** the largest one, is about 4 miles (7km) long and 0.75 mile (1.5km) wide. It was inhabited until 1953. The islanders were great storytellers and have made a lasting contribution to Irish literature. **The Great Blasket Centre** (tel: 066-915 6444; closed Nov–Mar) tells their story using many old records and photographs. Below Mount Eagle is the village of **Dunquin**, a scattered settlement whose harbour was once the landing point for the islanders. Stop at Dunquin Pier, and walk down the steep, concrete path.

Boats go to the island regularly in the summer (tel: 086 335 3805; www.blasketislands.ie; Easter–Sept daily). The crossing takes 20 minutes, but until the long-promised new pier is built, landing is by transfer to dinghy, so you must be fit and agile. There are frequent crossings between 10am and 4pm, weather permitting, or you can opt for a two-and-a-half hour eco-tour around the islands.

On towards Tralee

Gallarus Oratory (well signposted) is an extraordinary little building of unmortared 'dry' stone, which probably dates from the 8th century. It is in the shape of an inverted boat, with a door at the west and a window in the east wall. It remains as dry and solid as the day it was built, and is very dark inside.

Avoid the **Conor Pass** in bad weather – take the N78 through Annascaul instead. The drive is hairraising in all weathers as you climb steeply to 1,496ft (456 metres) above sea level.

Both roads meet at Camp on the N86 Tralee road

Tralee ⓲ (pop. 22,750) is the county town of Kerry, but don't expect a lot. While it may seem like a booming metropolis after a few days in Dingle, Tralee is essentially

The rose garden in Tralee's town park.

Summer comes to Ventry Strand.

DINGLE'S FIGHT TO SAVE ITS NAME

A new law in 2005 decreed that all Irish-speaking places must use the Irish-language version of their place name, and that only the Irish-language version can appear on legal documents, maps and signposts. The Dingle Peninsula is known as Corca Dhuibhne (pronounced '*corka guiney*') in Irish, but Irish is spoken only at the far western tip of the peninsula, which is where the new legislation comes into effect. But the people of Dingle Town, officially within the Irish-speaking area, are reluctant to lose a name that they consider is effectively an international brand name, worth millions to its thriving tourist industry. Many refused to call their town An Daingean.

A local plebiscite was held in 2006. It favoured the bilingual name Dingle Daingean uí Chúis (the fortress of O'Cush – pronounced '*dangan ee quish*'), but the central government argued that complex legislation would be needed to create an exception to the rule protecting Irish-language place names – and anyway the Minister refused to make any exceptions. Meanwhile, the name 'Dingle' was used by most local businesses, and the same government's tourist publications, while the legal arguments continued in Dublin. The Irish-language sign for An Daingean at the town's entrance was defaced by graffiti to read DINGLE. Another case of "Only in Ireland"…

a quiet market town. In August it comes to life briefly for the **Rose of Tralee Festival**, a beauty and personality pageant. The town's most attractive area is near the museum: the **Town Park** and **Denny Street**, with its nicely proportioned Georgian houses. The park is the headquarters of **Siamsa Tíre** (tel: 066-712 3055; www.siamsatire.com), Ireland's national folk theatre, which stages nightly performances in summer.

The enjoyable **Kerry County Museum** (tel: 066-712 7777; http://kerry museum.ie) is in a neoclassical building at the top of Denny Street. The country to the north of Tralee is the flatter, more sheltered part of Kerry. Take the R551 north from Tralee to **Ardfert**, a small village with the impressive ruins of a large 12th-century cathedral (tel: 066-713 4711; May–Sept; ruins: free).

Access to the long sandy beach at **Banna Strand** and a monument commemorating Roger Casement's landing from a German submarine in 1916 can be had about 2 miles (3km) north of Ardfert.

Ballybunion

The road continues to **Ballybunion**, a small seaside resort famous for its championship golf course, dramatic cliff walk and sandy beaches. Beside **Lady's Strand** is Ballybunion Seaweed Baths (tel: 068-27469; Jun–Sep), where farmers came to ease their aching bones after harvest time A warm seawater bath is still a great tonic, especially on a rainy day.

Listowel, a quiet little place, with a large main square, is known for **Listowel Writers' Week** (http://writers week.ie) which takes place every June. The remaining 15.3m-tall towers of its 13th century Listowel Castle (tel: 086-385 7201; June–Aug, daily 9.30am–5.30; guided tour only; free) can be climbed by an external staircase, giving views of the River Feale and the town square below. There is an attractive walk along the riverside. From **Tarbert** on the banks of the Shannon Estuary a car ferry runs to Killimer in Co. Clare (www.shannonferries.com), providing a scenic alternative to a long detour through Limerick.

Festival time in Tralee.

The Irish Language

Even though the most famous Irish writers wrote in English, Irish is the Republic's official language. But how many people can speak it fluently?

From the foundation of the Irish Free State back in 1922, enormous efforts were made to encourage everyone to learn and use the language – including making it compulsory at school and awarding extra marks for answering in Irish in examinations.

The Gaeltacht

The new Irish State also designated geographical areas, most along the western seaboard, as the Gaeltacht. Within them, people use Irish all the time, and residents receive grants from the government to promote the language and cultural heritage. There are sizeable Gaeltacht areas in counties Donegal, Mayo, Galway and Kerry as well as smaller parts of counties Cork, Waterford and, the only inland area: Meath. Generations of Irish teenagers have spent part of their summer on subsidised holidays in these areas – sent home if they speak English.

Visitors from overseas can also spend their holidays in Gaeltacht areas, learn some Irish, and enjoy pubs with traditional music sessions and céilís (literally translated as 'dance gatherings'). Check out www.oideasgael.ie.

Such is human nature that compulsory Irish at school had the opposite effect to its intent on the general population of the Republic. While everyone educated here has some knowledge of the language, until recent decades they usually denied they did, while using some words in conversation: craic (fun) probably the most commonly heard.

Attitudes to the language have changed over the last two decades, particularly in the Republic. A grassroots movement developed to increase the number of all-Irish schools – gaelscoileanna – where all subjects are taught through that language. Since the 1980s the number of schools has grown – by 2015 there were 305, both at primary and secondary level, with over 43,000 students. In County Cork, for example, there are 21 all-Irish primary schools – there was only one until the 1980s.

Irish-language media

There's been an Irish language radio station since 1972, Raidió na Gaeltachta, run by State broadcaster RTÉ, joined by the television service TG4 in 1996. There's also the Dublin community radio station Raidió na Life, and BBC Northern Ireland provides about 40 hours a week of radio in Irish. The weekly newspaper Foinse (meaning 'source') is available free every Wednesday with the Irish Independent newspaper, and has a readership of 195,000, many of whom are keen to practise their language skills. The 2011 Census revealed that use of the language is dropping in Gaeltacht areas from 70 percent in 2006 to 68.5 percent. However, it also showed that among the general population 1.5 million claim they can speak it, though only 77,185 use it daily and how well people speak it is another matter. The growth of all-Irish schools and the daily viewer figures for TG4 of more than 800,000, despite huge competition from overseas channels, show that an enthusiasm for the language survives. And on road signs in the Republic it shares equal billing with English.

The popular slogan 'Guinness is good for you' in Irish.

Grazing by the river.

LIMERICK AND THE SHANNON REGION

Within easy reach of Limerick is a region of ruined castles, a dramatic coastline, spectacular caves and the eerie moonlike landscape of the Burren.

The counties of Clare and Limerick constitute most of this prosperous region. Golfing, fishing, walking and surfing are amongst the main activities. The Cliffs of Moher rise almost vertically out of the sea and north of them lies the mysterious Burren, home to a remarkable variety of Alpine and Mediterranean wild flowers.

Limerick city

Limerick ❶ is a modern city (pop. 56,800, with another 91,500 living in the suburbs) with a medieval core on King's Island. It is more than 1,000 years since Viking traders established a sheltered seaport at the head of the Shannon estuary. But even today the city is full of historical reminders.

The bulk of the city lies to the east of the River Shannon, and footpaths give access to the wide, fast-flowing Shannon, its best asset. The city's high level of crime, reflected in feuds and drug wars, has given the tourist authorities a headache, but a regeneration programme is helping local communities tackle social problems.

An attractive riverside path, the Spokane Walk, skirts the Shannon and leads from the Tourist Information Office at Arthurs Quay Park, and over a steel footbridge to King

John's Castle, so that the entire medieval quarter can comfortably be visited on foot while enjoying riverside views. Pubs and cafés with outdoor tables and a thriving weekend farmers' market add to the lively ambience.

The **Tourist Information Centre** Ⓐ (20 O'Connell St; tel: 061-317 522; www.limerick.ie; Mon–Sat 9am–5pm; free) offers details of historical guided city tours, including *Angela's Ashes* walking tours of locations in Frank McCourt's memoir.

Main Attractions

King John's Castle
St Mary's Cathedral
Bunratty Castle
Ennis
Kilrush
Lahinch
Cliffs of Moher
Lisdoonvarna
The Burren

The Curragower Bar, Clancy's Strand.

King John's Castle

To get a feel for the history of the place it's best to start in the medieval quarter. The top attraction here is the 13th-century **King John's Castle B** on King's Island (tel: 061-360 788; www.shannonheritage.com; May–Sept 9.30am–5.30pm, shorter hours in winter). The castle is one of Ireland's most impressively sited Norman fortresses, with curtain walls and drum towers surviving. Climb one of the round towers for an excellent view of both river and town. An audio-visual display recounts Limerick's history from its foundation by the Vikings in 992 AD.

Limerick's castle is one of Ireland's most impressive fortresses.

Look into the elegant **Bishop's Palace C** (Church Street, King's Island; tel: 061-313 399; www.limerick civictrust.ie; Mon–Fri 10am–1pm, 2–4.30pm), the former Palace occupied by the Church of Ireland Bishops from 1661 to 1784, which has been restored by the Limerick Civic Trust and is now its headquarters. Walking tours of Georgian Limerick depart from here; phone for details. The Palladian-style Palace houses a Hall of Fame Room comprising portrait drawings of 23 local people honoured for their outstanding achievements. One of these is Richard Harris, a rugby star turned actor, who enjoyed a cinema career spanning 50 years and was winning a new generation of fans in the Harry Potter films when he died in 2002.

A short walk across Thomond Bridge takes you to the **Treaty Stone** , a rough-hewn limestone block raised on a pedestal. Tradition has it that on this rock the Treaty of Limerick was signed in 1691 marking the surrender of the city to William of Orange. The treaty demanded that the government promised to respect Catholicism, but it was rejected by the English and Irish Parliaments, allowing Limerick to be dubbed the 'City of the Broken Treaty'. The Latin inscription on the stone is taken from Virgil's description of Troy: 'It was an ancient city, well versed in the arts of war.'

Back across the river and in Castle Lane, the **Limerick City Museum** is based in a granary-style building housing more than 40,000 objects illustrating historical aspects of the city and surrounding areas (tel: 061-417 826; http://museum. limerick.ie; Mon–Fri 10am–1pm & 2.15–5pm; free).

Limerick's cathedral

A short distance along Nicholas Street is what many regard as the *pièce de résistance* of the city's sights – **St Mary's Church of Ireland Cathedral** (tel: 061-310 293; www.cathedral. limerick.anglican.org; free). Founded by King Donal Mór O'Brien on the site of his palace, it is the oldest building in daily use in Limerick and there is at least one daily service. Built in the form of a cross, it incorporates both Romanesque and Gothic styles.

The Romanesque West Door is magnificent, the black oak misericorde (mercy) choir stalls are carved with animal features, and there's a pre-Reformation altarstone, a leper squint window, and stained-glass windows. The Cathedral hosts many civic and musical events and has an unbroken tradition of choral music for more than 800 years.

Hunt Museum

From the Cathedral, cross over the Matthew Bridge and on Rutland Street you will come immediately to the former Custom House, now

George's Quay and the Locke Bar.

TIP

While walking around Limerick, you may be lucky enough to see 'gigs', the specially trained trotting horses that are ridden around the streets in preparation for race meetings, and which cause additional headaches for motorists in the traffic-choked streets.

St Mary's Church of Ireland Cathedral.

the **Hunt Museum G** (tel: 061-312 833; www.huntmuseum.com; Mon–Sat 10am–5pm, Sun 2–5pm). This superb private collection contains 2,000 original works of art and antiquity. They range from the 9th-century enamel Antrim Cross, to Egyptian, Roman and Etruscan pieces, Chinese porcelain, works by Picasso, Renoir and the great Irish artists Jack B. Yeats and Roderic O'Conor. The collection was assembled by John Hunt, a medievalist, and his wife Gertrude, and left to the nation on his death in 1976.

Limerick is full of delightful architectural surprises. From Rutland Street, a brisk 20-minute walk through the main shopping area (allow more time for window shopping) along O'Connell Street leads to the spacious streets of the Georgian area, a district known as **Newtown Pery**. Turn a corner in this area with its well-ordered geometry and you'll be enchanted by a church, a square or a terrace of houses with brightly painted doors and semi-circular fan-lights.

The Crescent and St John's Square

The Crescent H consists of elegant four-storey houses and has been well restored. Now mostly offices, they are occupied by accountants, solicitors and the like. From here Barrington Street leads to Pery Square and the **People's Park I** where workers bask on the grass at lunchtime with their sandwiches. No. 1 Pery Square, one of a fine terrace of houses built around 1830 overlooking the park, has been restored and is now a boutique hotel with a popular bar and bistro. Another, the **Georgian House and Garden** can be visited on the Limerick Civic Trust's walking tour, or by appointment with the Trust (see page 202).

Make a short detour down Parnell Street and along Upper and Lower Gerald Griffin streets to take in the exquisite **St John's Square J**. This 'square' is in fact a three-sided terrace of houses with a basement and three bays. The mid-18th-century houses are the earliest Georgian development in Limerick and were originally occupied by the gentry as town houses during the winter.

Art galleries

Music and the arts are flourishing in Limerick and the city hopes to be named European City of Culture in 2020 (www.limerick2020.ie). The **Belltable Arts Hub K** (69 O'Connell Street, tel: 061-774 774; www.limetreetheatre.ie; Mon–Sat noon–5.30pm; free) has contemporary exhibitions and a theatre. The **Limerick City Gallery of Art L** (tel: 061-310 633; www.limerickcity.ie/lcga; Mon–Sat 10am–5.30pm, late opening Thu till 8pm, Sun noon–5.30pm; free) in Pery Square was once a Carnegie Library. Its permanent collection of Irish art ranges from the 18th century to the 21st, and there is a handy coffee shop. The gallery is the focal point of a city-wide Biennial of Contemporary Art

– EVA (www.eva.ie) – a major event on Ireland's visual arts calendar.

The university

The **University of Limerick** (www. ul.ie) in the suburbs at Plassey, has established a reputation as Ireland's leading university in industry-led research. It is a showcase for contemporary Irish architecture and sculpture, and hosts concerts and musical events ranging from pop to classical.

Apart from its vibrant artistic side, the city is renowned for its passion for sport and one game in particular. For more than 100 years rugby has been part of the lifeblood of Limerick and has been played by all sections of the population. Some wags joke that the city has three cathedrals: St Mary's, St John's and Thomond Park, the 'cathedral' of rugby fans, not just in Limerick, but throughout the entire Province of Munster.

Rugby is the game of the people, stirring passionate support and local loyalties. The oldest senior club, Garryowen, has even given its name to the game's international vocabulary – the Garryowen, called after the traditional attacking ploy: the 'up and under'.

Shopping centre

Many familiar chain stores have branches in Limerick. The liveliest part of the shopping district is the pedestrianised Cruise's Street area, off O'Connell Street. At numerous cafés, many with outdoor tables you can choose from the usual range of espressos, mochas, cappuccinos or lattes. You will also stumble across antique dealers, barbers, victuallers and saddlers, and Fox's Bow, an alleyway with quirky shops. The restored **Milk Market** ⓝ, at Corn Market Row, comes alive every Friday, Saturday (the busiest day, open from 8am–3pm) and Sunday. A great range of food is on offer: cheeses, fish, seaweed, sausages, jams, chutney and breads, as well as organic farm produce. Sunday is the day for antiques, books, CDs, and vintage clothing. A canopy provides protection against the weather.

Milk Market.

MULTICULTURAL LIMERICK

In Limerick you are likely to hear Polish, Russian or Estonian spoken as much as English. It is home to Ireland's second largest Polish community after Dublin, with an estimated 10,000 living and working in the city. There are numerous shops selling Polish food, drink, newspapers and magazines. The Polish in Limerick have their own website, http://PolskiLimerick.com.pl, and the local newspaper, the *Limerick Leader*, runs a weekly column in Polish. A Polish Arts Festival (http://polishartfestival. ie) takes place every year, too.

There is also a large African community, from Nigeria, Ghana, Somalia, the Congo and elsewhere. The churches established by African Christians hold lively Sunday services, which is a welcome new component of the city's culture.

Heritage on view at Adare.

Lough Gur.

South of Limerick City

Attractions to the south include museums, visitor centres and charming villages. **Lough Gur** ❷ (tel: 061-385 186; www.loughgur. com; 10am–5pm, closed Oct–Apr), 12 miles (19km) south of Limerick on the N24-R514 near Bruff, is one of Europe's most complete Stone Age and Bronze Age sites. It has a horseshoe-shaped lake, rich in bird-life. The **Grange Stone Circle** is 150ft (45 metres) across and contains about 100 boulders. More than 20 other stone circles, tombs, hut foundations, lakeside dwellings and ring forts have been excavated beside Lough Gur.

An interpretative centre built in the form of Neolithic huts houses a collection of artefacts and has an audio-visual presentation introducing the site. Guided walks can be booked in advance.

Adare ❸, 10 miles (17km) southwest of Limerick, is one of Ireland's prettiest villages. Several of its stone-built cottages are thatched, and they all have colourful front gardens.

Adare is noted for its antique dealers, but don't expect bargains.

The **Adare Heritage Centre** (tel: 061-396 666; www.adareheritagecentre. ie; daily 9am–6pm; free, charge for exhibition) has a Tourist Information Centre (tel: 061-396 255) with free maps of the village, and a helpful history display. The 14-arch bridge over the River Maigue dates from medieval times and leads to the Augustinian Friary built in 1315, and now Adare's Anglican church. The cloisters were converted into a mausoleum for the Earl of Dunraven in 1826 and the church was restored in 1852. A metal stile beside the church leads to a charming riverside walk of about a mile, which loops back to the village centre down Station Road.

Opposite the Augustinian Friary is the entrance to the lovely Adare Manor, now an American-owned luxury hotel, **Adare Manor and Golf Resort**. It has twice hosted the Irish Open golf tournament and is regarded as one of Ireland's finest parkland courses. However, only

CITY OF SIEGES

Limerick was besieged three times in the 17th century as Britain strove to subdue the Irish. The first blockade, in 1651, was led by Oliver Cromwell as part of a merciless campaign after the execution of Charles I. By the time the citizens surrendered five months later, 5,000 had died of disease or starvation.

The other two sieges, in 1690 and 1691, were linked to William of Orange's campaign to secure the English throne against the Catholic James II. After James fled to France, many of his supporters holed up in Limerick. William's first siege failed to dislodge them. The following year a more determined siege sapped the citizens' morale and they signed the Treaty of Limerick, which promised religious liberty and restoration of property but was not honoured.

golfers and hotel guests can pass the security barrier.

Adare Manor was the seat of the Earls of Dunraven, who built the picturesque thatched cottages that line the village for their workers. The original 18th-century manor was enlarged in the Gothic Revival style in the mid-19th century. In its grounds are the ruins of the 14th-century **Desmond Castle** and of a 1464 Franciscan Friary, accessible by a separate entrance.

Flying Museum

On the south bank of the Shannon Estuary, **Foynes** ❹ played an important part in aviation history. In the late 1930s flying boats would land on the sheltered stretch of the Shannon between Foynes Island and the shore, having made the transatlantic crossing from Newfoundland. The award-winning **Foynes Flying Boat Museum** (tel: 069-65416; www.flying boatmuseum.com; mid-Mar to Nov daily 9am–5pm) commemorates those days with models and photographs, and includes the original

terminal building, radio room and weather forecasting equipment - the only such museum in the world.

Shannon Crossing

There is a pleasant drive along the flat wooded shores of the wide Shannon estuary to **Tarbert** ❺, where a car ferry will take you across the Shannon Estuary in 20 minutes to Co. Clare. The ferry is often accompanied by a pod of about 100 bottlenose dolphins, whose presence will be announced over the loudspeakers.

North of Limerick City

This is castle country, with ruined stumps of crumbling tower houses dotted around the place. There were once more than 420 tower houses in the Shannon area. Few are as imposing or as carefully restored as Bunratty whose rectangular 15th-century keep is surrounded by four corner turrets, each topped with battlements and a set of flags.

Bunratty Castle and Folk Park ❻ (tel: 061-361 511; www.shannon heritage.com; daily) is strategically

Foynes Flying Boat Museum.

Adare Manor.

placed on the road between Shannon Airport and Limerick city. It contains furniture and paintings from the 15th and 16th centuries. The Folk Park behind it consists of 25 acres (10 hectares) of reconstructed and fully furnished farmhouses, cottages and shops, as they would have appeared to a visitor to mid-western Ireland in the late 19th century. There is even a village street with blacksmith, pub, drapery, print works and post office. **Durty Nelly's**, an old-world Irish pub next door to the village, has been copied all over the world.

Another corny but enjoyable experience is the medieval Irish banquet, a purely tourist-oriented but good-natured event – essentially a meal with Irish cabaret during which the guests are serenaded by Irish colleens – which takes place twice nightly at Bunratty and at the nearby **Knappogue Castle** (tel: 061-360 788) at Quin to the north of Bunratty. Knappogue is a 15th-century Macnamara stronghold, also restored and furnished in period.

The Craggaunowen Project

The **Craggaunowen Project** ❼ (tel: 061-360 788; Easter–Sept daily 10am–5pm) is built in the grounds of another castle, a 16th-century tower house. The project has reconstructed authentic replicas of dwelling places in prehistoric and pre-Christian Ireland. On an island in the lake, reached by means of a footbridge, is a *crannóg*, a fortified dwelling of clay and wattle. A small ring fort, which shows how a farmer would have lived in the 5th or 6th centuries, has been built. Also at Craggaunowen is the traditionally built boat in which the writer and adventurer Tim Severin sailed to Nova Scotia in 1976, retracing the legendary 6th-century voyage of St Brendan, and making a plausible case for its historical reality.

To escape from the beaten path of the castle trail, consider an outing to **Scarriff** ❽, a quiet little town set on high ground overlooking Lough Derg. It is a rural backwater, popular with visitors in summer and sleepy in winter, which has a reputation for traditional music. **Drewsborough House**

near **Tuamgraney**, to the south of Scarriff, is the birthplace of the novelist Edna O'Brien who has written scathing descriptions of the inhabitants of this area which was considered remote 50 years ago.

Both Scarriff and Tuamgraney are on the scenic drive that goes all the way around **Lough Derg** ❾, a wide, almost sea-like part of the Shannon River, which is popular with watersports enthusiasts. It is worth taking in at least the 5-mile (8km) stretch northeast to **Mountshannon**, a neat 18th-century village. Offshore you can visit **Holy Island**, an uninhabited 49-acre (20-hectare) island that had a 7th-century Christian settlement. There are the remains of five churches and a 79ft (24-metre) high round tower. **St Conran's Church** in Tuamgraney is based in a 10th-century church that is the oldest church in continuous use in Ireland.

Ennis

Ennis, a busy market town 23 miles (37km) west of Lough Derg, has an inviting cosiness, partly due to its size and human scale but also because a bypass has diverted much of the traffic. Ennis prides itself as being "Ireland's friendliest town". The Tourist Information Office (tel: 065-682 8366; www.visitennis.com) is on Arthur's Row, off O'Connell Street.

The same building is shared with the **Clare Museum** (tel: 065-682 3382; www.clarelibrary.ie; Jun–Sep Mon–Sat 9.30am–5.30pm, Oct–May Tue–Sat 9.30am–5.30pm; free), which tells the story of 6,000 years of history through the *Riches of Clare* exhibition.

Ennis Friary (tel: 065-682 9100; www.heritageireland.ie; Apr–Oct 10am–6pm) is a Franciscan Friary founded by the O'Brien Kings of Thomond in the 13th century. The well-preserved ruins consist of a nave, chancel, belfry and cloister.

Ennis is known as a centre for traditional Irish music and dance. Performers and students (many of them youngsters) flock to the Fleadh Nua (www.fleadhnua.com) a competitive festival for musicians and dancers held annually at the end of May. Traditional musicians gather in the local pubs and hold impromptu music sessions year round too, all of which can be enjoyed for the price of a drink - ask locally where to go. More formal, ticketed events, and the finals of the Fleadh Nua are held at **Glór Theatre** (Friar's Walk; tel: 065-684 3103; http://www.glor.ie; free). The striking modern building hosts well-known touring acts on the Irish music scene, locally produced drama, and there is a craft gallery and coffee shop onsite, too.

Kilrush

Moving down to the coast, **Kilrush** ❿ is 5.5 miles (9km) west of Killimer where the car ferry from north Kerry docks. Kilrush, with a population of 2,650, is the biggest town on the coast of west Clare. It was designed by a local landlord in the 18th century to complement his estate.

The style chosen for the town is pleasantly neoclassical, with wide

EAT

For connoisseurs of the kitsch, Bunratty Castle's Medieval Banquets, held twice nightly at 5.30pm and 8.45pm for up to 141 people, take some beating. Goblets of mead precede the spare ribs with honey and whiskey sauce, and medieval madrigals aid the digestion. Prices start at around €60 for an adult. Details: www.shannon heritage.com.

Bunratty Castle.

streets and a main square big enough to accommodate horse fairs. Traditional livestock fairs (mainly horses, donkeys and sheep, with side stalls) are held in the square on the first Thursday of March, June and October.

The ruins of the Vandeleur family mansion, which was destroyed by fire in 1897, are at the centre of the 420-acre (170-hectare) Kilrush Forest Park. The **Vandeleur Walled Garden** (Vandeleur Demesne, Killimer Road; tel: 065-905 1760; www.vandeleurwalledgarden.ie; Apr–Sep Mon–Fri 10am–5pm, Sat–Sun noon–5pm, Oct–Mar Mon–Fri 9.30am–4.30pm) is enclosed behind old stone walls at the centre of a woodland estate, and has a courtyard with a coffee shop and a Victorian-style glasshouse displaying unusual and tender plants.

A 15-minute boat ride from Kilrush Creek Marina (Griffin Boat Hire; tel: 065-905 1327; Apr–Oct daily) will take you to **Scattery Island** which has a 6th-century monastery founded by St Senan, the remains of five churches and a round tower The monastery was plundered by Vikings

before being recaptured by Brian Ború. There is a Visitor Centre on the island, and guided tours are available free. Dolphin-watching cruises run by the **Shannon Dolphin and Wildlife Foundation** (Kilrush Creek Marina; tel: 065-905 2326; www.shannondolphins.ie; June–Sept) operate daily in summer, weather permitting, to watch families of bottlenosed dolphins playing in the estuary. Another firm, Dolphin Discovery (tel: 065-905 1327; www.discoverdolphins.ie) also operates from Kilrush Marina in the summer.

Kilee ⓫, 8.5 miles (13km) to the west, is on the Atlantic coast of Clare, as opposed to the banks of the Shannon Estuary, and has a sandy beach. The village has been rather overwhelmed by bland developments of holiday homes (it is traditionally a favourite weekend spot for Limerick City people), but its centre retains an old world charm. There is a scenic drive south to Loop Head lighthouse, a round trip of about 34 miles (55km). At **Carrigaholt** ⓬ a 16th-century tower house stands beside the pier with good views from its top

Pale sandy beach in Lahinch.

floor across the Shannon Estuary to north Kerry.

Lahinch

The west-facing beaches, where long rolling waves break on the sand after their Atlantic crossing, are popular with water sport enthusiasts all the way up the coast to **Lahinch** (sometimes spelt Lehinch) also famous for its golf links. This part of the west Clare coast has become the haunt of some of the world's leading surfers because of the immense size of its waves. A 'new' wave Aill na Searrach (the leap of the foals), and with the nickname Aileens, was first successfully surfed in 2005 and has attracted many of the world's leading surfers. Aileens is hidden at the base of cliffs and rises to epic proportions of up to 25ft (8 metres). Those hoping to conquer it do so with the help of a jet-ski. The Clare waves suit surfers of all abilities when conditions are right and it is the country's fastest-growing sport. For an updated daily surf report visit www.lahinchsurf shop.com; for general information on surfing in Ireland contact the Irish Surfing Association; tel: 096-49428; www.isasurf.ie.

From Lahinch, **Ennistymon** ⓮, 2.5 miles (4km) inland is a charming, old-fashioned resort town on the Cullenagh River, which has retained many original wooden shop fronts and some friendly pubs. The river has a series of waterfalls visible from its seven-arched bridge.

The Cliffs of Moher

Towering to 650ft (214 metres) high and stretching for 5 miles (8km), the **Cliffs of Moher** ⓯ on the west coast of Clare have always been a popular destination. But with upwards of 1 million visitors a year tramping across them, erosion began to set in calling for an extension of old paths, elevated viewing platforms, more seating and the ecological reconstruction of the cliff wall and grass.

For those who wish to keep dry and warm, the whole experience can now be enjoyed in the sparkling New Visitor Experience (tel: 065-708 6141; www.cliffsofmoher.ie; daily 9am–dusk; free, Atlantic Edge exhibition, charge, and €6 charge per vehicle for parking; ATM facilities).

The centre was 17 years in the planning and cost more than €31 million. It is largely hidden from view as it has been subsumed into the contours of the landscape and covered by a hillside. As you approach, the building appears to be in darkness – the idea being to create a dimly lit cave-like effect.

Doolin Cave

Just over 3 miles (5km) away you come to an experience that should feature on the itinerary of every tourist to County Clare: **Doolin Cave**, Pol an Ionáin 'the ivy cave' (tel: 065-707 5761; www.doolincave.ie; daily mid-Mar–Oct, 9am–5pm; weekends off season). One of the world's biggest freestanding stalactites, 'The Great Stalactite', opened in 2006 after a

Cliffs of Moher Visitor Experience.

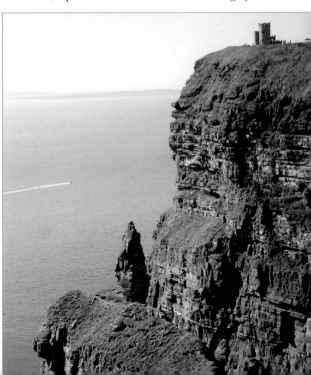

The Cliffs of Moher.

The Cliffs of Moher

The Visitor Experience exhibition will teach you all about the ridged Cliffs of Moher, a protected haven for many species of seabirds.

Formed by layers of siltstone, shale and sandstone, the Cliffs of Moher have long been recognised and protected. In 1988 the area around them was designated as a Refuge for Fauna and the following year became a Special Protection Area for birds. The layering of rock has led to the development of narrow horizontal ledges that provide nest sites for seabirds including fulmars, guillemots, razorbills and puffins. The area is Ireland's most accessible breeding site of puffins, and hundreds of pairs of these comic-looking birds nest there. The designation includes the cliffs, cliff-top maritime grass and heath, and a 200-metre zone of open water.

Moher Ranger tours

For the real elemental experience and to properly feel the gustiness of the wind on your face and

It's a long way down.

see the waves booming below, you should walk up to the edge. With binoculars you can look across to Liscannor Bay or pick out the Aran Islands. Friendly and knowledgeable 'Moher Rangers' will guide you round and explain the significance of the site, taking you up to O'Brien's Tower built in 1835 by Cornelius O'Brien, a descendant of Brian Ború, the High King of Ireland. The best time to spot the sea birds is at the height of the breeding season from early May to the end of July. You should have fine views of puffins wheeling in to land and be able to pick out rows of guillemots and kittiwakes crouched precariously on ledges.

Interpretive centre

The Visitor Experience's exhibition area features the Atlantic Edge (an optional multimedia exhibition) incorporating the themed zones of ocean, rock, nature and man. It includes the Ledge, computer-generated images of life above and below water that lets you see close-up the natural world from a bird's-eye perspective. You can also take a Clare journey with a high-definition cinematic aerial tour of varied landscapes tracked on a map of the county.

A touch screen displays the changing earth over geological time; there are views of cave interiors and explanations of Clare's underground rivers. The human history of life has not been neglected and a rich fund of legends from the area are told through taped interviews and displays. It's a long way from the 1950s when a local guide, Dinney McMahon, realised he could make a living from trading to tourists at the cliffs. He sold postcards, tin whistles and *shillelaghs* (traditional knotty walking sticks with a large knob at the end, made out of wood, also known as blackthorn sticks), and charmed visitors with stories of local gods as well as the habits of the birds. He died of a heart attack at 80 while making his way to his stand on the cliffs; a memorial stone marks the spot.

One of Europe's busiest tourist attractions, the cliffs are worth a half-day visit. If you enjoy walking, follow the 5-mile (8km) waymarked trail from Doolin (part of the Burren Way), and experience the cliffs in the old-fashioned, pre Visitor Centre mode. This is one of Ireland's most popular locations, as the numerous clips on YouTube confirm, and always manages to stir something within the imagination. In high season, get there early before the crowds.

15-year battle over planning permission. The stalactite – it's more than 600,000 years old – was discovered by two English cavers in 1952 and is an extremely popular draw.

A minibus driver brings you the short distance to the entrance where you are given a hard hat and torch before descending 125 steps to experience a stunning subterranean world and a memorable sight. The visitor is plunged into darkness and then in a flash the subtly lit stalactite appears before you in the main chamber. The stalactite hangs more than 20ft (7 metres) from the ceiling and weighs in at 10 tons – and it is still developing. The cave tour takes one hour and numbers are limited to 20.

Doolin

Doolin ⓰ (also called Roadford on some maps) consists of a long straggle of B&Bs, hostels and hotels, several restaurants, craft shops and three pubs. The pubs are renowned for traditional music. Some young musicians spend the whole summer camping here, learning from their elders.

Lisdoonvarna

Moving inland to **Lisdoonvarna** ⓱, if you visit the Burren Smokehouse (tel: 065-707 4432; www.burrensmokehouse.ie) you will be shown an exhibition kiln and smoke box with a short audiovisual presentation of the smoking process in action. The town developed as a spa centre for tourists due to the healing properties of its sulphurous spring water (the baths, alas, are no more). Today its main claim to fame is its **Matchmaking Festival** in September when shy farmers meet women under the direction of Willie Daly, matchmaker, horse whisperer and publican (his bar is at 1 Main Street, Ennistymon). The festival now offers a matchmaking website and speed dating (www.matchmakerireland.com).

Music is a permanent soundtrack to the lives of the people of Clare. The next village on the southern fringe of the Burren, **Kilfenora** ⓲ is famous for the Kilfenora Ceilí Band, a group of local traditional musicians which celebrated its 100th anniversary in 2009, and tours throughout Ireland and to the UK and USA. It is also

Doolin coastline.

The Cliffs of Moher are Ireland's most visited natural attraction.

The Burren.

the home of the **Burren Centre** (tel: 065-708 8030; www.theburrencentre. ie; mid-Mar–Oct 10am–5pm; charge to exhibition). A multi-dimensional exhibition tells the story of the Burren and there is an informative video presentation. The centre also houses a tourist information point, exhibition area, craft shop and tea rooms.

Next door to the centre it is well worth a look at the 12th-century **St Fachtnan's Cathedral** with its fine collection of medieval High Crosses. A sloping glass roof has been installed on the north chapel to protect the crosses from the elements. Information panels outline the details of the crosses, the most famous being the impressive Doorty Cross with its bishop holding his hand up in blessing.

The Burren

Travelling east from Kilfenora you come to the beautifully proportioned ruin of **Leamaneh Castle** where you turn north entering the hauntingly magical kingdom that is the **Burren ⑲**.

This is botanical holy ground of a high order, a meeting place of plants from the Arctic, the Alps and the Mediterranean. Over 70 percent of Ireland's native flora is found here, including 24 species of orchid and 25 types of fern. The best-known flower in this wild rock garden is the spring gentian *(Gentiana verna)* a dazzling small blue plant that can be seen in April and May. Search hard and you will find it growing alongside brightly coloured magenta geraniums, early purple-orchids and swathes of creamy mountain avens all sprouting from the grykes (vertical crevices that lie between the pavement). The clints are the glacially polished horizontal surfaces that you walk across and which occasionally wobble.

The Burren is renowned as a place of geological and archaeological wonder. Miles of gunmetal grey ancient stone walls thread in all directions. Everywhere there are giant boulders – glacial erratics – that were dropped by the glacier. These rock refuges are part of the topographical outdoor decor of the place and have stood for 15,000 years.

Spend just a short time here and you will be enthralled. You will quickly realise why the Burren means 'rocky place'. It is a Karst landscape (from an area in the former Yugoslavia with similar terrain) hewed from stone: stone monuments, stone cottages, stone fields, pavement, rocks and walls. With a patina all its own, it feels unlike anywhere else in Ireland – almost a different country.

Carron

Follow the road from Leamaneh Castle to **Carron** where you will see a *polje*, a geological term for a depression in the limestone and where a turlough, or seasonal lake (full of fresh water in winter and entirely dry in the summer) is to be found. Carron has the **Michael Cusack Centre** (tel: 065-708 9944; www.michaelcusack.ie; Apr–Oct, Mon–Sun 10am–5.30pm). Cusack was the founder of the world's largest amateur sporting organisation, the Gaelic Athletic Association. The 19th century herdsman's cottage where Cusask grew up has been fully restored. The centre tells the story of his life from his humble origins in Carron through his travels and careers. Nearby, the Burren Perfumery & Floral Centre (tel: 065-708 9102; www.burrenperfumery.com; daily, May, June and Sept 10am–6pm, July–Aug 10am–7pm, Oct–Apr 10am–5pm; café; free) highlights the sensory side of the Burren and serves delicious home baking and other organic food.

Now retrace your route back to the main road and you will come to **Caherconnell Visitor Centre** (tel: 065-708 9999; www.burrenforts.ie; Mar–Oct Mon–Sun 10am–5pm, July–Aug 10am–6pm).

This centre explains the circular and walled farmsteads found throughout the Burren that are known locally as 'Cahers'. There are more than 500 of them, including the spectacular Cahercummaun. The best preserved is found at Caherconnell.

Poulnabrone

A short distance north you will see from the road what is unquestionably Ireland's best known, most-visited and most-photographed megalithic burial tomb, the **Poulnabrone** (the pool of the sorrows) portal dolmen with its huge capstone. Ancient, baffling, yet strangely familiar as its image is reproduced all around you on postcards, T-shirts, book covers and holiday brochures; it was built about 4,500 years ago.

Each day numerous tour coaches stop at this dolmen which, although now roped off for protection, is in its natural state. A timeline on a signboard interprets its significance and puts it in context with information on the surrounding flora.

The dolmen was excavated in 1986 and the remains of 22 bodies – 16 adults and 6 children, male and

TIP

Doolin Ferries (tel: 065-707 445; Easter–Oct; www.doolinferries.com) runs a service from Doolin Pier to the three Aran Islands, and also offers a tour of the Cliffs of Moher. The Cliffs of Moher Cruises also operate daily services to one of the three Aran Islands, Inis Oirr, as well as a Cliffs of Moher cruise. The cruises leave from Doolin Pier and Liscannor, subject to tides and weather conditions (tel: 065-707 5949, daily Apr–Oct; www.mohercruises.com).

Irish dancing sculpture in Lisdoonvarna.

female – were discovered. The bodies were reckoned to be at least 1,500 years old.

Aillwee Cave

Follow a twisting road with hairpin bends down Ballyallaban Hill for 3 miles (5km) and you come to another underworld adventure, **Aillwee Cave** (tel: 065-707 7036; www.aillweecave. ie; daily 9.30am–5.30pm, July–Aug 10am–6.30pm), discovered around 1940 by a herdsman. Guides accompany you on a 35-minute tour through caverns, over bridged chasms, under weird formations, past pale threads of straw stalactites hanging down alongside waterfalls. The Burren Birds of Prey Centre (same contact details) is located at the cave, and puts on flying displays of falcons, hawks and owls.

Ballyvaughan

Picturesquely sited **Ballyvaughan** ⑳ (pop. 220) is the best base for exploring this unique landscape. The village has two hotels, pubs and cafés and a bicycle hire business – one of the best

Dunguaire Castle.

ways of appreciating the Burren is on two wheels.

Each May, Ballyvaughan hosts **Burren in Bloom** (www.burreninbloom. com), a month-long programme of talks and tours. Illustrated talks on the flora, birdlife, archaeology and geology as well as history and folklore tours, ghost tours of Aillwee Cave, workshops, concerts and traditional music nights are all on the packed itinerary.

Before heading north out of the Burren it's worth a short detour off the main road to explore the well-preserved ruins of **Corcomroe Abbey**. Now roofless, this Cistercian abbey was built shortly after 1195 in a serene valley near Bell Harbour. According to legend, the stonemasons who built it were executed when they had finished their work to prevent them building a more beautiful church elsewhere.

Kinvarra

There is a pleasant scenic drive along the south shore of Galway Bay to **Kinvarra** ㉑, a charming fishing village at

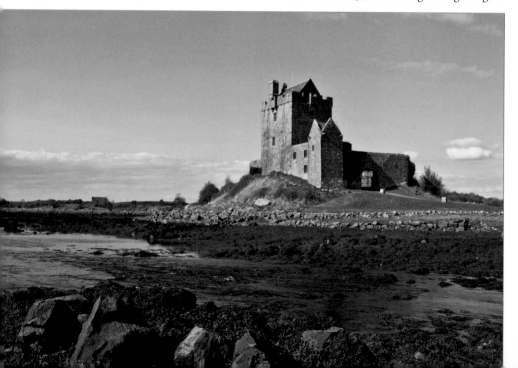

the head of Galway Bay with a grassy quayside and an alternative spelling of Kinvara. It is popular with visitors who enjoy its old-fashioned pubs and modern restaurants. The highlight of the year is the annual Cruinniú na mBád in mid-August, 'the gathering of the boats'. In this festive regatta, traditional Connemara sailing craft – the famous brown-sailed Galway Hookers, which were once used to carry turf across the bay – race against each other in a grand spectacle.

In spring, the Fleadh na gCuach, 'the cuckoo festival', a traditional Irish music event, attracts large crowds.

The floodlit **Dunguaire Castle** (tel: 061-360 788; May–Oct) is a four-storey tower house built by the shore in 1520. At night this lonely sentinel is used for medieval banqueting, hence the floodlighting. A recent addition to Kinvarra is **Murphy Store,** (tel: 091-637 760) a 200-year-old listed building on the quayside that has been restored from dereliction. Originally used as a grain store, it is now a coffee and craft shop specialising in seaweed-based products from Ireland's west coast. The work of local artists and potters is also on display.

In the centre of Kinvarra, it's well worth visiting a small café and gallery run by **Burrenbeo** (www.burrenbeo. com), an information and education resource, with a good selection of books on the Burren.

Yeats associations

The final leg of a Shannon journey takes the visitor to **Gort**, a pleasant market town with a large main square, on the main road from Ennis to Galway. It is known locally as 'Brazil', as it has a large community of Brazilian residents, mostly from the same area in northeast Brazil, who came to Ireland originally to work in the meat-processing industry. Gort Forge is mentioned by the poet W.B. Yeats, who restored the nearby castle, **Thoor Ballylee ㉒** a 16th-century tower house that was the summer home of the

Nobel prize-winning poet from 1917 to 1928.The tower, has been damaged by floodwater, and is no longer open to the public. But you can still follow the signposts from the N18 (5km/3 mi) and enjoy its secluded location in a wooded area beside a stream.

The tower house, which Yeats bought for £28, was discovered for the poet by his benefactor, Lady Gregory (1852–1932), herself a playwright and collector of folklore. Her house at **Coole Park ㉓** (Coole Park Visitor Centre; tel: 091-631 804; www.coolepark. ie; daily Apr–May and Sept Mon–Sun 10am–5pm, June–Aug 10am–6pm, park grounds: 8.30am–7.30pm, June–Aug 8.30am–9pm; grounds free), 2 miles (3km) northwest of Gort was demolished in 1947, but its grounds are now a nature reserve.

In the walled garden stands a great copper beech tree, the famous 'Autograph Tree' on which Lady Gregory's guests – Yeats, the playwrights George Bernard Shaw, J.M. Synge and Sean O'Casey, the poet John Masefield and the painter Augustus John – carved their initials.

Kinvarra.

THE BURREN

North Clare contains a strange landscape, a treeless limestone plateau that's a place of pilgrimage for botanists and geologists.

A frustrated general serving Oliver Cromwell, one of the many ruthless invaders from across the Irish Sea, famously condemned this bleak place as having 'not enough wood to hang a man, not enough water to drown him, not enough clay to cover his corpse.' The view probably hasn't changed much in 350 years, but now the Burren (meaning great rock) is a national park. It covers 200 sq miles (500 sq km) of lunar-like limestone formation with delicate flora and fauna of Arctic, Alpine and Mediterranean origin, brought to the area by migrating birds. Here you will find, in seasonal abundance – but protected by the State – orchids, the purple bloody cranesbill and azaleas. The Burren is also an area of potholes, seasonal lakes, caves and streams.

The view from Corkscrew Hill

Properly appreciating the extraordinary nature of the place requires some study. The Burren Experience, on the northside of Ballyvaughan village, on the Kinvarra road, gives an introduction, but a finer overview can be had at the original Burren Centre, to the south in Kilfenora village. A good overall view of this 'stony district' can be had from the so-called 'Corkscrew' Hill on the road linking Ballyvaughan with Lisdoonvarna, but by far the best way to explore the fissured terrain is on foot.

Scattered throughout the region are tombs, chambers and dolmens of the Stone Age – notably, near Corkscrew Hill, the famous Poulnabrone Dolmen, dating from 2,500 BC.

This bleak limestone terrain had its origins 70 million years ago when shells of marine animals were compacted on the seabed and later pushed above the waves by geological shifts. A soft rock, the limestone has been eroded by wind and rain, creating cracks and crevices which both drain off rainwater and provide shelter for the remarkable variety of fauna.

The Burren is home to many plants which flourish in its apparently inhospitable landscape. They are nurtured by a unique combination of soil, heat and moisture.

Carron, east of the Burren, means the Cairn and has yielded up useful archaeological evidence of Bronze Age life. The stones that today form walls to keep the wind at bay were then used to construct a great cairn 8ft high and 50ft in diameter (2.4 by 15 metres) which protected the bodies in the burial mound. At Kilnaboy, in the upland part of the Burren, is the great stone fort of Cahercommaun (7th–10th centuries).

Poulnabrone Dolmen.

THE TOMBS THAT HAVE DEFIED TIME

Poulnabrone Dolmen dates from 2,500 BC and is a striking example of the many ancient monuments which are particularly common in this part of Ireland because of the ready availability of limestone slabs. Its name means 'pool of sorrows'. Because its massive capstone is set at an angle, it has been fancifully been called a launching pad for a Stone Age missile.

Such single-chambered portal graves were originally covered with a mound of earth and stones, and are a testament to the great reverence the Neolithic people had for their dead.

Passage-graves, in which the burial chamber was reached through a passage, reveal sophisticated building techniques and often-intricate abstract carvings. Some of Europe's most spectacular examples can be seen at Newgrange, west of Drogheda in Co. Louth.

Stone circles, which served as prehistoric temples, are probably related to the megalithic tombs. Some of the most impressive can be found at Lough Gur in Co. Limerick and near Hollywood in Co. Wicklow.

The commonest monument is the ring fort – about 30,000 survive. These were circular stone defences surrounding dwellings or royal seats.

It's surprising to find small green fields in such a stony landscape. But sheep farmers know how to survive the bleak winters in the west of Ireland. Animal farming flourishes due to the Burren's mineral wealth, which has especially helped horse breeding.

On the road through the Burren from Kinvarra lies the ruined Corcomroe Abbey, founded by Cistercian monks around 1195. Although Henry VIII dissolved the monasteries in 1554, the abbey's remoteness allowed the monks to remain for many years.

Co. Clare is very much part of the western seaboard, from its natural boundary of the Shannon estuary to its northern border with Galway. The full force of the Atlantic can be felt here and lighthouses played a vital part in warning ships clear of the treacherous coastline. At Spanish Point, near the village of Milltown Malbay, some ships from the Spanish Armada sent to invade England were wrecked in 1588.

GALWAY AND THE WEST

Beyond the liveliness of Galway city lies Connemara's wild, romantic landscape. Here Irish is still spoken and the beauty of the rural countryside with its vast skies and empty hillsides is spellbinding.

The short-lived boom in the Irish economy led to rapid development in many parts of the west of Ireland, including Galway city, which had long been a quiet backwater. These days Galway city, with a population of 76,800 is surrounded by a dual-carriageway ring road, which boasts 16 roundabouts, and the ring road is frequently grid-locked. But as most people live in new suburbs, the city's historic centre and docks remain relatively unscathed.

Galway ❶ has developed a unique personality, combining a strongly Irish identity with cosmopolitan influences, epitomised by the broad cultural mix of the Galway Arts Festival. Being a compact city with quaint shops and numerous pubs in a largely pedestrianised historic centre, Galway has become a popular party destination. The party often starts on the train, with beer and card games, as those who arrive by rail will notice. Spanish teenagers, Irish hen parties and couples on a city break all enjoy the unique atmosphere. Seafarers also like Galway, and it has twice been the final port of call for the Volvo Ocean Race, a 39,000-mile (62,800km) ocean-racing marathon that ends in a massive party.

The medieval city

The city lies on the northeastern shore of **Galway Bay**. Unlike Dublin, it wasn't conquered by the Vikings but was invaded by the Anglo-Normans in the 13th century. It developed strong trading links with France and Spain, rather than England and Wales, which has contributed to its unique character.

The medieval city grew up on the eastern bank of the River Corrib, inside the stone walls between 1232 and 1243, developing as a thriving port for wine, spices and fish. It became known as the 'City of the Tribes' because of the influence of 14 wealthy Anglo-Norman merchant

Main Attractions

Eyre Square
Lynch's Castle
Galway Races
Lough Corrib
Aran Islands
Clifden
Kylemore Abbey
Westport
Achill Island

View of the Long Walk, Galway.

The Quincentennial Fountain is a representation of the sails of the Galway hooker, a traditional fishing boat unique to Galway.

families who ruled it as an independent city-state. These families held power in the town and county for many centuries. Each family had its own street and mansion with stone-faced designs. Remnants of the buildings and the stonework can be seen on a walk around the city.

The modern city

The logical starting point, and the place where people travelling by bus and train arrive, is **Eyre Square**. The square, Galway's focal point and main public park, was presented to the city in 1710 by Mayor Edward Eyre. In 1963 it was where the US president John F. Kennedy made a speech after receiving freedom of the city. The square has been re-landscaped in a €10 million project, with a sweeping walkway, giving the city's iconic central point a much-needed facelift.

Fourteen flags, each one representing one of the Tribes, now fly along one side of the square. The adjacent **Quincentennial Fountain Ⓐ**, was erected in 1984 to celebrate the 500th anniversary of Galway

becoming a city. The fountain is composed of sheets of iron depicting the area's distinctive sailing boats, the Galway hooker.

Browne's Gateway Ⓑ, the entrance to the town house of a merchant family originally built in 1617, is a cut-stone doorway and window, and stands beside the flags.

The **Fáilte Ireland Tourist Information Centre, Ⓒ** (Forster Street tel: 091-537 700; www.galwaytourism. ie; Mon–Sat 9am–5pm; free) just off the eastern corner of Eyre Square, is well stocked with booklets, maps, postcards and gifts.

Galway is compact enough to not lose your bearings. The most notable ecclesiastical building is the Anglican Cathedral, the **Collegiate Church of St Nicholas Ⓓ** (tel: 091-564 648). Built around 1320, it is the largest parish church of the medieval period in Ireland. Christopher Columbus is reputed to have prayed here in 1477 before setting off on his voyage of discovery.

Outstanding features of interest inside the church include the

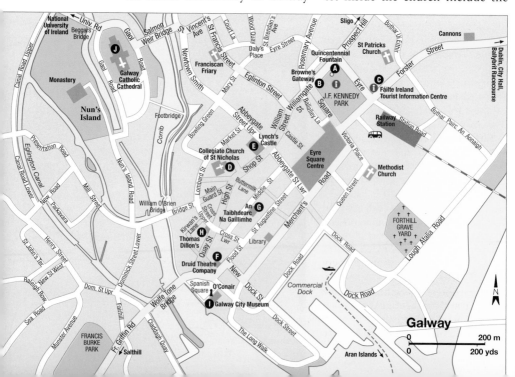

Galway

0 — 200 m
0 — 200 yds

Crusader's Tomb dating from the 13th or early 14th century with an inscription in Norman French, and a carved Baptismal Font of the late 16th or early 17th century. The Saturday morning **farmers' market** (http://galwaymarket.com) beside the Collegiate Church of St Nicholas is not to be missed. It is reputed to be one of the liveliest in the country, with organic vegetable growers from Connemara sharing space with sushi-makers, purveyors of Indian street food, flowersellers, wood turners and knitwear stalls, while buskers entertain with juggling and music.

Lynch's Castle

Another historic building is **Lynch's Castle E** in Shop Street. This was the town house of the premier Tribe and is now a bank displaying in its foyer a series of wall panels telling the story of the castle. The castle – in fact a fortified town house – dates from the 15th century. The imposing smooth stone facade is decorated with carved panels and stonework, as well as gruesome gargoyles that include a lion devouring another animal, and a monkey and child. Inside, a reproduction of a 1651 map shows the symmetrical yet simple layout of the streets.

Traditional shops

A stroll around the streets is an assault on the senses, particularly the smells and sounds. The streets that coalesce – **William, Shop, High** and **Quay streets** (the latter leading down to the Spanish Arch) are lined with dozens of restaurants and pubs, many with outdoor tables

The survival of smaller independently owned businesses is part of the appeal. In Galway the usual corporate giants sit cheek by jowl with traditional, family-run shops: drapery stores, cheesemongers, bakers, barbers, bespoke tailors and shops selling shooting and fishing tackle.

For more than 60 years, for example, the family-run **Ó'Máille's** (16 High Street; tel: 091-562 696; www. omaille.com) has specialised in handwoven tweed, including hand-knitted Aran sweaters. Its claim to fame is that it produced the costumes for John Ford's classic 1952 film *The Quiet Man*, filmed in the village of Cong, about an hour's drive north of Galway (see page 26).

Charlie Byrne's (The Cornstore, Middle Street; tel: 091-561 766; www. charliebyrne.com) is a sprawling shop that stocks a huge selection of new and old books.

The centre of the city also buzzes with chic cafés, bakeries and bustling pubs. **Griffins Bakery** (21 Shop Street, 091-563 683; www.griffinsbakery. com), for example, was established in 1876. Using traditional recipes, the naturally fermented breads are baked fresh each day at the back of the shop. A popular speciality is whiskey brack (whiskey-marinated fruit bread).

The arts

Galway has a strong artistic and literary tradition, as evidenced by its rash

Open-air chess.

of festivals. The city's most celebrated drama group, the **Druid Theatre Company** ⑤ in Chapel Lane, presents work by Irish playwrights and has built up an international reputation. The National Irish Language Theatre, *An Taibhdhearc* ⑥ (pronounced 'thive-arc'), is based in Middle Street, and holds summer shows and traditional singing and drama. For details of forthcoming events, visit www.antaibhdhearc.com.

The Galway Races

The Arts Festival is closely followed by the **Galway Races** (tel: 091-753 870; www.galwayraces.com), a week-long extravaganza running from late July to early August that brings thousands of people to the city in search of *craic*: after a day at the races the tradition is to party all night. Accommodation at this time is scarce, and prices shoot up: if you're not a racing fan, avoid Galway in race week. The races are held at **Ballybrit Racecourse** 3 miles (5km) to the east of the city near Galway Airport.

The Claddagh Ring

Across the Corrib River, on the other side from the city, was the **Claddagh**, the original Irish settlement situated outside the city walls. There's little trace of the old thatched cabins in the area's current modest housing, but the fishing village gave its name to the **Claddagh Ring.** This was a traditional ring with two hands holding a heart that wears a crown. The heart represents love, the crown is loyalty and the hands symbolize friendship. According to tradition, the rings were handed down from mother to daughter.

One of Galway city's oldest shops, **Thomas Dillon's** ⑧ (1 Quay Street; tel: 091-566 365; www.claddaghring.ie), established in 1750, sells fine gold and sterling silver examples of the ring. At the back of the shop, the small **Claddagh Museum** tells the story of this ring that is now a much sought-after fashion accessory and a symbol of romance.

Galway City Museum

Galway City Museum ① (Spanish Parade; tel: 091-532 460; www.galway

Gargoyle at Lynch's Castle.

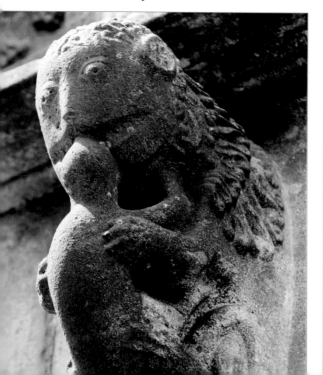

FESTIVAL FEVER

The Galway Arts Festival (www.giaf.ie), is held during the last two weeks in July. This dynamic mixture of drama, music, poetry and dance showcasing local and national culture kicks off with a parade led by the flamboyant street theatre company, Macnas, whose name means 'joyful abandonment'. While the Cúirt International Festival of Literature (www.galwayartscentre.ie), in late April, offers a cross-section of contemporary writing. It has hosted an impressive array of international talent including the Nobel Prize winners J.M. Coetzee, Nadine Gordimer, Derek Walcott and Seamus Heaney. Galway's compact city centre practically guarantees that you will be rubbing shoulders – or sharing a bar counter – with other festival goers and the big names, giving the experience an extra edge.

citymuseum.ie; Tue–Sat 10am–5pm; Sun noon–5pm Apr–Sep, free), a fine building on the city side of the Spanish Arch that was another product of the boom years. The ground floor covers the contemporary city, emphasising the arts scene, and two upper floors focus on medieval and post-Famine Galway.

The Spanish Arch

The only remaining gate of the walls that surrounded the ancient city, the sturdy **Spanish Arch,** still stands beside the **Fishmarket.** It took its name from the former trade with Spain and leads through to the **Long Walk** where small ships and boats are berthed and where you may sometimes see a flotilla of swans.

The Fishmarket is an outdoor area used 100 years ago to load kelp on to carts to be sold as fertiliser. Nowadays this grassy open space with welcoming benches is a popular place for tourists to rest and young people to congregate, often entertained by the city's ubiquitous buskers.

The Catholic Cathedral

From the Spanish Arch a pleasant riverside path will take you to **Galway's Catholic Cathedral ❶** (www. galwaycathedral.org) – or, to give it its full magisterial title, the **Cathedral of Our Lady Assumed into Heaven and St Nicholas.** Built between 1959 and 1965, the Cathedral with its copper dome has an impressive variety of interior art. The last great building to be built of natural stone in Ireland, its stained-glass windows depict John F. Kennedy, Christ rising from the dead and the Irish patriot Padraig Pearse.

A sight not to be missed on the river beside the Cathedral is the **Salmon Weir Bridge ❿** built in 1819. Lying north of the Church of St Nicholas, it is the last bridge upstream before the waters of the **Corrib River** open out into the lough. At the right time of year (generally early spring but sometimes later too) hundreds of fish wait under the shadow of the bridge before making their way upstream to spawn in Lough Corrib.

The Spanish Arch.

Galway Arts Festival exhibition.

TIP

Wood Quay near Galway's Salmon Weir Bridge is the departure point for the Corrib Princess (tel: 091-592 447; www.corrib princess.ie; May–Sept 2.30pm and 4.30pm, July and Aug also 12.30pm, 1.5-hour duration), an enclosed launch that cruises up the river along a lovely stretch of water to Lough Corrib.

Salthill

Galway's small neighbour **Salthill** ❷ is just 2 miles (3km) along the coast, and offers an escape from the city streets as well as tremendous views of the wide expanse of **Galway Bay.** This resort was built in the early years of the 19th century. The walk from the city to the end of the promenade, where you must kick the rock before turning back, is a traditional, often bracing, Sunday afternoon activity for Galway residents.

As befits such a place, it has its quota of amusement arcades, discos and a fairground. **Leisureland** (Salthill promenade; tel: 091-521 455; www.leisureland.ie; free) is a family entertainment and amusement complex with three swimming pools and a waterslide. It is also used for concerts, exhibitions and conferences.

Atlantaquaria (Toft Park, Salthill; tel: 091-585 100; www.national aquarium.ie; Mon–Tue 10am–5pm, Sat–Sun 10am–6pm, adult €12.00, child €7.50), the country's national aquarium, is a good place to spend an hour on a rainy day and get acquainted with some of the 170 species of marine and freshwater life including seahorses, stingrays and the angel shark. The estuary exhibit shows the fish that make the mouth of the Corrib River their home.

Connemara

Connemara, Galway City's hinterland, is full of lakes, bogs and mountains, but almost empty of people. Traditionally, its farming and fishing communities clustered around the coast, while its interior was inhabited chiefly by sheep farmers. Until Clifden was built in the mid-19th century, Connemara did not even have a town. It has always attracted visitors, especially painters who have found inspiration in the light and landscape. Two extensive ranges of mountains, the **Twelve Pins** (also known as **Twelve Bens**) and the **Maumturks,** dominate the views and suit all levels of walkers.

The visitor does not have to travel far from the city before entering the Irish-speaking area known as the

Entertainment at the King's Head pub, Galway.

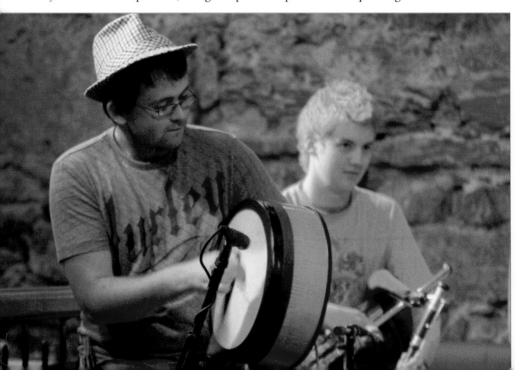

Gaeltacht. The road signs are in Irish only. One of the first places you will come to is **Bearna** (Barna), which has a lively hotel, The Twelve, and a golf club with an 18-hole championship course. Much new housing, most of it architecturally undistinguished, has been built along this stretch of coast, which is now a commuter belt; if such developments offend, take the inland N59 road via Oughterard, turning off for Roundstone west of Recess. The coast road wends its way around bays and inlets and through a series of former fishing villages which become more picturesque the further you get from the city, including **An Spidéal** (Spiddal), **Casla** (Costelloe), **Scrib** (*Screeb*), **Cill Chiarain** (Kilkieran), **Caiseal** (Cashel) and eventually **Roundstone** (www.roundstone.ie). The latter is a pretty holiday resort with a sheltered harbour for fishing and sailing boats, a little gem of a place which has attracted many artists and writers. Here you re-enter the non-Gaeltacht part of Connemara before completing the journey to Clifden, the 'capital of Connemara'.

In both **Spiddal** ❸ and **Roundstone** ❹ local crafts thrive. **Spiddal Craft & Design Studios** (tel: 091-553 376; www.ceardlan.com; free) offers visitors the chance to see artisan craftworkers putting their skills on display and to buy directly from them. Workshops include candlemaking, leather work, pottery, screen printing, weaving and wood turning.

In a former Franciscan Monastery in Roundstone, a bodhrán-making business, **Roundstone Music, Craft & Fashion** (tel: 095-35808; www.bodhrán.com; daily; free) is a popular attraction.

Lough Corrib and Cong

If you chose the inland route (N59) to Roundstone via Oughterard, you will have distant views of **Lough Corrib** ❺, the Republic of Ireland's largest lake. Renowned for its salmon and brown trout, it also has a number of islands. You can take a day or evening cruise from Oughterard to **Cong** ❻ on the Mayo side of the lake, and sample its tranquillity from the water (tel: 094-954 6209; www.corribcruises.com).

Looking across Galway Bay towards the Aran Islands.

Galway Cathedral.

The West

Scale:
0 — 10 km
0 — 10 miles

ATLANTIC OCEAN

Sligo Bay

Stags of Broad Haven

Benwee Head
Portacloy
Downpatrick Head
Lenadoon Point
Easky
Aughris Head

Erris Head
The Arches 305
Belderrig
Glinsk
Céide Fields
Ballycastle
Rathlackan
Kilcummin
Rathlee
Templeboy
Sligo

Broad Haven
Knocknalina
Benmore 351
Creevagh
Killala
Killala Bay
Enniscrone
Owenbeg
Knockalongy 543

Doonamo Fort
Annagh Head
Belmullet
Barnatra
Glenamoy
Moyne Abbey
Rosserk Friary
Corbally
Slieve Gamph or Ox Mts
512
Sligo

Corraun Point
Bunnahowen
Slieve Fyagh 331
Belville
Ballina (Béal an Átha)
Bunnyconnellan
416
Masshill

Mullet Peninsula
Drumreagh
Carrowmore Lake
Bangor Erris
Doobehy
Eskeragh
Crossmolina
Mullany's Cross
Corlee
N17

Inishkea North
Tristia
Bellacorick
Errew Abbey
N26
Foxford

Inishkea South
Fallmore
Bellacorick
Slieve Car 720
Keenagh
Derreen
698
Nephin 804
Lough Conn
Pontoon
Lough Cullin
Callow
Charlestown
Moy
Longford

Doohooma
Shranamanragh Br.
Nephin Beg 628
Nephin Beg Range
Glennamong 628
Castlehill
Birreencorragh
Furnace Lough
Beltra Lough
Beltra
Ross West
Strade
N5
Ireland West Airport Knock
Swinford

Blacksod Bay
Ridge Point
Slievemore 671
Croaghaun 667
Dugort
Keel
Cashel
Achill
Corraun Peninsula 521
Srahmore
Lough Feeagh
Croaghmoyle
Castlebar (Caisleán an Bharraigh)
National Museum of Country Life
Turlough
Balla
Kiltamagh
N17
Knock
Ballyhaunis

Achill Head
Dooagh
Dooega
Ashleam Bay
Carrickkildavnet Castle
Cloghmore
Corraun Hill
Rockfleet Castle
Burrishoole Abbey
Newport
Clew Bay
Westport House
Westport
Cloonkeen
Balla
Ballintubber Abbey
Plains of Mayo
Ballynastangford
Brickeens

Achill Island
Bolinglanna
Newport Bay
Westport Bay
Murrisk
Croagh Patrick 763
Knappagh
Killavalley
Lough Carra
Claremorris
Ballindine
Cloonfad

Clare Island
Ballytoohy
461
Kilsallagh
Kilgeever Abbey
Croagh Patrick
Carrowkennedy
Partry
Moore Hall
Ballygarries
Milltown
N17
Dunmore
Carrowntanlis

Inishturk
Louisburgh
Roonah Quay
Emlagh Point
Kinnadoohy
Cregganbaun
Sheeffry Hills Doo Lough 761
Delphi
Tourmakeady
Lough Mask
Ballinrobe
Kilmaine
Neale
Foxhall
N17

Inishbofin
Bofin
Oceans Alive Visitor Centre
Cashleen
Ballynakill Harbour
Mweelrea Mts
Killary Harbour
Salrock
Aasleagh
Devil's Mother
648
Leenone
Bennacunneen 578
Maumtrasna
Maum
Clonbur
Cong
Ashford Castle
Cong Abbey
Shrule
Caherlistrane
Tuam

Aughrus More
Cleggan
Letterfrack
Kylemore Abbey
Connemara National Park
Finnisglin
Leckavrea Mt 612
Curraun
Lough Corrib
Ross Abbey
Greenfield
Headford
Moneen
Knockmoy Abbey

Kingstown
Streamstown
Clifden
The Twelve Pins 728
Recess (Sraith Salach)
Maam Cross
Oughterard
Aughnanure Castle
Knockferry
Cloonboo
Ardnasodan
Turloughmore

Mannin Bay
Connemara Heritage & History Centre
Dan O'Hara Homestead
Toombeola
Shannawona
346
Rosscahill
Tullokyne
Claregalway
N17

Ballyconneely
Errisbeg 300
Roundstone
Casheen
Derryrush
Gortmore
Screeb
Galway
Moycullen
Carnmore
M6
Athenry

Slyne Head
Callow
Glinsk
Pearse's Cottage
Rosmuck
Kinvara
Salthill
N17

Ballyconneely Bay
Mace Head
Cerna
Kilkieran
Bealadangan
Costelloe
Rossaveal
Inverin
Spiddal
Barna
Galway (Gaillimh)
Oranmore
Clarinbridge

St Macdara's Island
Mweenish Island
Lettermore Island
Casheen Bay
Lettercallow
Carraroe
Ballynahown
Galway Bay
Aughinish
Carrowmore
N18
Kilcolgan

ATLANTIC OCEAN
Lettermullan
Gorumna Island
Cashla Bay
North Sound
Dunguaire Castle
Ardrahan

Inishmore
Onaght
Oghil Church
Oghil
Black Head
Fanore
Corcomroe
Coole Park
Kinvara
Thoor Ballylee

Dún Aengus Fort
Temple Benen
Killeany
Foul Sound
Ballyvaughan
Aillwee Cave
Gort

Aran Islands
Inishmaan
Inisheer
Fardurris Point
Slieve Elva 345
The Burren
Poulnabrone
Caherconnell
Boston
Lough Cutra

Lisdoonvarna
Doolin
Doolin Cave
Leamaneh Castle
Burren National Park
Tubber
Killeen

Clare
Kilfenora
Limerick
M18

To reach Cong by car, drive around the lake via Maam Cross and Clonbur, a scenic hour's drive of 48km (30 miles). While Cong is best known for its associations with John Ford's film *The Quiet Man*, it is also a tranquil lakeside village surrounded by a wealth of archaeological remains including stone circles and burial mounds. There are also the remains of a 12th-century Augustinian abbey (village centre, freely accessible) with fine cloisters and a stone fishing hut. You can walk the mile from the abbey to Ashford Castle (www.ashfordcastle. com), one of Ireland's great castle hotels, on a lakeside path. The original building dates from the 12th century, but the existing castle, a splendid turreted affair, was built by the Guinness family in 1857 as a holiday home.

The Aran Islands

During a holiday in Connemara, a side trip to the **Aran Islands** ❼ is regarded as *de rigueur*. Aran Island Ferries (tel: 091-658 903; www.aranisland ferries.com), operates daily services from **Ros a' Mhil** (Rossaveal) on the Connemara coast, with a bus link to Galway City. An air taxi service to the three islands is run by Aer Arann Islands (tel: 091-593 034; www.aerarann islands.ie) from Connemara Regional Airport, a 45-minute drive west of Galway city. The flight takes less than 10 minutes; the ferry journey to Inisheer (the furthest island) is one hour. The three Aran Islands – **Inishmore, Inishmaan** and **Inisheer** – contain many pre-Christian and early-Christian remains. Visitors should carry waterproof clothes and wear shoes suitable for uneven terrain.

Inishmaan and Inisheer are small enough to walk. The best option on Inishmore, the biggest island, is to hire a bicycle in **Kilronan,** the main village: you can even opt for an electric bike if the hilly terrain is daunting. (tel: 099-61132; www. aranislandsbikehire.com) You can leave your luggage at the Inishmore Tourist Information Office (Kilronan, tel: 099-61263), which can also help you find B&B accommodation.

Fishing is still important to the islanders, but tourism has been

Roadside scenery near Roundstone.

Connemara is characterised by lakes, bogs and mountains.

Inishmore landscape.

growing significantly. As many as 2,000 day-trippers a day in peak season can visit Inishmore, which has a permanent population of 900.

You can cycle or take a minibus to **Dún Aengus** stone fort on Inishmore, one of Europe's finest prehistoric monuments. Perched on the edge of a vertical 200ft (60-metre) cliff, it consists of four semi-circular defensive walls. The experts have failed to date Dún Aengus with any accuracy: some say 4,000 BC and others 1,000 BC. But, apart from its historic interest, the view from its ramparts is one of the most striking imaginable. On a clear day the sweep of coastline from Kerry and Clare to the south, as well as the length of Galway to the western extremity of Connemara is visible.

Clifden

Clifden.

Back on dry land, **Clifden** ❽ the region's principal town, is a lively spot with a good choice of hotels, Bed & Breakfast accommodation and restaurants, and is one of the best places to buy traditional tweed.

In August the town hosts the Connemara Pony Show, an annual highlight based around these small sturdy local ponies.

Connemara National Park

Connemara National Park (Letterfrack; tel: 095-41054; daily, visitor centre charge, park freely accessible) is an unfenced nature reserve covering 5,000 acres (2,000 hectares) and is rich in wildlife. A series of summer programmes serves up an enticing choice of walks, talks and special events.

Nearby, hidden away in the hillside beneath the Twelve Pins, is the restored cottage of Dan O'Hara, a tenant farmer evicted because he was unable to pay his rent and who has been immortalised in song and story. The cottage is now part of **Connemara Heritage & History Centre** ❾ (Lettershea; tel: 095-21246; www.connemaraheritage. com; Apr–Oct daily; free) and gives visitors an insight into the life of a farmer in the west of Ireland just before the 1845 potato famine. The centre provides an audio-visual tour

INSPIRED BY ARAN

The Aran Islands have long attracted artists, novelists, poets, philologists, antiquarians and film-makers. Robert Flaherty's 1934 film *Man of Aran* made the islands known to a worldwide audience. The playwright John Millington Synge wrote his book *The Aran Islands* while living on Inishmaan, where he also heard the plot of his most famous play *The Playboy of the Western World*.

Inishmore has produced an internationally known writer, Liam O'Flaherty. Born in the shadow of Dún Aengus, he is famous for his nature stories and as author of the novel *The Informer* (filmed by director John Ford in 1935 and starring Victor McLaglen).

Irish is the daily language of the people of Aran, but most are equally fluent in English.

of Connemara through the ages with reconstructions of a *crannóg* (prehistoric artificial island home) ring fort and *clochán* (a dry stone hut).

Kylemore Abbey

The road between Letterfrack and Leenane features one of Ireland's most photographed buildings – the dramatically sited **Kylemore Abbey** ⑩. This late 19th-century limestone and granite building was erected by a Liverpool merchant as a gift to his son, and, until 2009 was run by the Benedictine nuns as a boarding school for girls. The miniature Gothic chapel, craft shop and restaurant are all open to the public (tel: 095-41146; www.kylemoreabbeytourism. ie open daily; charge for gardens).

The next village is **Leenane,** situated dramatically at the mouth of **Killary Harbour,** Ireland's only fjord, and marking the separation of counties Galway and Mayo. Its **Sheep & Wool Centre** (tel: 095-42323; www.sheepandwoolcentre.com; free) has live breeds, demonstrations of spinning and weaving, a

multilingual historical video and, of course, a gift shop.

A choice of roads here will take you up to **Westport,** either via the spectacular **Doo Lough Pass** to **Louisburgh** or directly along the N59.

Croagh Patrick

Looming ahead you will see the unmistakable cone of **Croagh Patrick** ⑪, Ireland's holy mountain. The Reek, as it is known, is climbed in honour of St Patrick by more than 30,000 pilgrims – many of them barefoot – on the last Sunday in July. Some set out before dawn and many are still descending as darkness falls. The Visitor Information Centre (Murrisk; tel: 098-64114; www. croagh-patrick.com; free) at the base of the mountain contains fascinating information about the archaeological discoveries on the summit. The remains of a dry stone oratory were carbon-dated to between 430 AD and 890 AD. Across the road from Croagh Patrick, on the banks of Clew Bay, are the ruins of **Murrisk Abbey** (1456).

The much photographed Kylemore Abbey.

Children enjoying the swan boats at Westport House & Country Park.

View of Croagh Patrick.

Clare Island

Clare Island ⓬ (www.clareisland.info) is well worth visiting to learn the seafaring exploits of Grace O'Malley, or Granuaile (1530–1603), a pirate queen who preyed on cargo vessels; late in her life she journeyed to London to do a deal with Queen Elizabeth I, negotiating in their only common language, Latin. Clare Island has a population of about 350 and holds much interest for the botanist. It measures 3.5 by 1.5 miles (5.5km by 2.5km) and has a small hotel and some B&Bs. There is a ferry service (tel: 098-23737; www.clareisland ferry.com) that takes 15 minutes from Roonagh Harbour, Louisburgh.

Westport

Picturesquely situated on the Carrowbeg River, **Westport** ⓭ a busy market town with colourful shop fronts, that attractively combines the old and the new, is designated as one of Ireland's heritage towns. It was recently voted 'Best Place to Live in Ireland' by readers of *The Irish Times*. A walk around the streets exploring its tree-lined riverside mall, fine Georgian buildings and octagon, on a network of interlinking footpaths will explain why. The town's quays, a ten-minute walk from its centre, are on Clew Bay, and the old warehouses have been nicely developed as tourist accommodation. This is the place for spectacular sunsets, to be watched, perhaps, from the terrace of one of the two waterside pubs. Don't miss **Clew Bay Heritage Centre** (tel: 098-26852; www.museumsofmayo.com; free) at The Quay for a look back at the way people lived.

One of Ireland's most historic homes, **Westport House & Country Park** (The Demesne, Westport; tel: 098-27766; www.westporthouse.ie; Mar–May, 10am–4pm, June, July–Aug 10am–6pm, Oct 10am–4pm) is set in magnificent parkland on the outskirts of Westport and has attractions for children of all ages. It is owned by direct descendants of Grace O'Malley.

Achill Island

In 1910 the Belfast artist Paul Henry set out for **Achill Island** ⓮ for two weeks. He was immediately captivated by its beauty, tore up his return train ticket, and stayed nine years. Henry described it as 'a windswept island at the back of beyond'. But he felt it 'talked' to him and that he had been carried there 'on the currents of life'.

Top to bottom, Achill Island measures just 15 miles (24km) by 12 miles (18km). It is joined to the mainland by a causeway built in 1888 but once you cross **Achill Sound** a feeling of isolation and otherworldliness persists in the stark landscape. The island is largely shaped by the wet Atlantic climate and it rains with a grim persistence. About 2,500 people live on the island. In the winter the caravan parks, B&Bs, craft and coffee shops are closed, the scattered villages deserted, the numerous clusters of new holiday homes empty, and the long sandy beaches at **Keel, Dooagh, Trawmore,** as well as the silver and golden strands in the remote north side are deserted apart from wading birds. This is the best time to visit when you share the tranquil beaches

with sanderlings, oystercatchers and golden plovers.

To get a feel for the past, take the narrow single-track road signposted to the **Deserted Village** on **Slievemore Mountain.** More than 70 roofless stone houses are all that remain of this village that in 1837 was the largest human settlement on the island. A single grassed-over street runs between the houses and even today there is a feeling of desolation about it.

The most scenic route on Achill is the **Atlantic Drive** that loops round the south of the island and takes in **Carrickkildavnet Castle,** a 15th-century tower house.

For more information, contact Achill Tourism (www.achilltourism.com; tel: 098-20400.) in Achill Sound.

The Mayo coast

Crossing back to the mainland again, continue along the remote north Mayo coast road and you will be startled by a pyramid-shaped building. This is the remarkable **Céide Fields** ⑮ (pronounced 'kay-jey') Visitor

Achill Island beach.

HEINRICH BÖLL

Achill Island has long had a magnetic pulling power for writers, poets and painters. The German writer Heinrich Böll, who won the Nobel Prize for Literature in 1972, spent 35 summers on Achill, visiting the island right up until his death, aged 67, in 1985.

Böll lived in a cottage in Dugort (*Dubh gort,* meaning black field and pronounced with a heavy local emphasis on the second syllable sounding like 'du-gort'). The cottage, where most of his novels were written, is now a residential retreat for international and Irish artists and writers. When he first came to Achill, Böll said he felt like he was 'playing truant from Europe'. His *Irish Journal, A Traveller's Portrait of Ireland* (1957) shows a warm affection for the area as well as the country itself.

The rugged cliffs at Benwee Head.

National Museum of Country Life.

Centre (Ballycastle; tel: 096-43325). An extensive stone-age monument, the site includes field systems, dwelling area and megalithic tombs dating back 5,000 years. The bog's rare wild flowers and the spectacular cliffs opposite the centre attract botanists, geologists and birdwatchers.

The neighbouring towns, **Killala** and **Ballina** ⑯, have their own particular charms for the visitor. Killala rises above a small harbour, its skyline dominated by a pencil-thin 10th-century round tower and the spire of the Church of Ireland. Ballina, with its streets sloping down to the River Moy, is the largest town in Mayo and is internationally renowned for salmon angling. The area attracts large numbers of visiting fishermen and women for both game and coarse angling.

Knock

An inland detour takes you to **Knock** ⑰ where in 1879 several people reportedly saw the Blessed Virgin silhouetted on the gable of the local church. The story is told by

Knock Folk Museum (tel: 094-938 8100; www.knockshrine.ie; May–Oct 10am–7pm, Basilica: all year; main pilgrimage season from the last Sun in Apr to the 2nd Sun in Oct; free).

The village is thronged year-round with shops selling souvenirs and religious artefacts. Holy water is offered free on tap: you'll need to bring your own bottle. One of Ireland's most popular pilgrimage places, it is visited by over 1 million people each year.

To end your cultural tour of the west with a reflective look at what life in rural Ireland used to be like, turn off the N5 to visit the award-winning **National Museum of Country Life** ⑱ tel: 094-903 1755; www.museum.ie; Tue–Sat 10am–5pm, Sun 2–5pm; free) at Turlough Park, 5 miles (8km) from **Castlebar**, Co. Mayo's capital. The museum, the first branch of the National Museum to open outside Dublin, houses the National Folklife Collection detailing the domestic lives of people who lived in rural Ireland between 1850 and 1950.

Shannonbridge.

INLAND IRELAND

Bogs, lakes and rivers dominate the countryside of these often overlooked counties in the middle of the country. Fishing and boating are the big attractions here, and the landscapes are seductive.

eography class for Irish primary school children traditionally reduced their country to a common item of domestic tableware – a saucer. With the outer rim representing the ragged, mountainous coastal regions, the Midlands were credited with the dubious honour of being Ireland's flat centre.

In a region marked by the relative absence of physical drama, where bog land and lake account for much of the terrain, the counties of Longford, Laois, Offaly, Westmeath, Roscommon, Cavan and Monaghan have long played second fiddle to the more popular tourist regions of the South and West.

However, bisected by the River Shannon, the region is rich in varied recreation options, from fishing on the many lakes, walking the Slieve Bloom hills, to exploring the slower pace of life in its sleepy towns and villages.

Echoes of the past

Perceived by many, including the Irish, as a rather dull part of the country, the Midlands are, in fact, one of the last remaining regions where the pace of life harks back to an Ireland of 30 years ago. The attendant bustle and ubiquitous traffic jams are happily still absent. Life here is still unhurried and friendly.

The inland counties offer much for the visitor – especially Clonmacnoise,

Ireland's most important and atmospheric monastic site. Grand mansions and castles pepper the region, and farmers' markets and espresso bars sit comfortably with centuries-old pubs and grocery shops as new blood mixes happily with old, unchanged ways.

From Ballinasloe to Clonmacnoise

Ballinasloe ❶, the chief town of east Co. Galway, has long been an important crossing place of the **River Suck**, and marks a kind of

Main Attractions

Clonmacnoise
Birr Castle
Lough Derg
Emo Court
Mullingar
Strokestown Park House and Famine Museum
Bellamont House
Castle Leslie
Patrick Kavanagh Centre

Clonmacnoise monastic site.

Inland Ireland

N

0   10 km

0   10 miles

border, more psychological than physical, between the west of Ireland and the Midlands. Every year during the first week of October Europe's oldest horse fair takes place here. Between Ballinasloe and Loughrea, off the M6, is the **Dartfield Horse Museum and Heritage Centre** (tel: 091-843 968; www.dartfield.com; daily 9am–6pm; free). The museum occupies a courtyard of the original Dartfield House. As well as an exhibition on the history of Irish horses and Connemara ponies, together with farm machinery and carriages, there are 350 acres to enjoy, and a walking tour to see a variety of animals including horses, deer and sheep. Horse riding is also available.

From Ballinasloe take the R357 to **Shannonbridge** ❷. This is the point where county Galway meets counties Offaly and Roscommon, and the River Suck flows into the River Shannon. There's a lot of bog in the Midlands, in various stages of development. The state-run Irish Peat Board, Bord Na Móna, who run the Blackwater Power Station,

closed the passenger railway line in November 2008 but they are working closely with the Irish Tourist Board (Fáilte Ireland) to develop eco-tourism in the bog land.

Clonmacnoise ❸ (tel: 090-967 4195; www.heritageireland.ie; daily) is one of Ireland's most important monastic sites, superbly located on a bend in the River Shannon. It was built on an esker, or natural gravel ridge, that overlooks a large marshy area. The monastery was founded in AD 545 by St Kieran and was the burial place of the Kings of Connaught and Tara. While it may appear remote today, in earlier centuries transport for pilgrims was easier by water than over land.

The earliest of the surviving ruins dates from the 9th century. The monastery was plundered from then onwards by the Irish, the Vikings and the Anglo-Normans until it was destroyed in the Elizabethan wars of the mid-16th century by the English garrison from Athlone. Yet there's still plenty to be seen. The Visitor Centre has a collection of carved

FACT

The great period of country house building in Ireland began in the early 1720s. English architects who had studied in Italy introduced Palladianism, and soon a diluted version of the style appeared everywhere, from village churches to farmhouses.

The gardens at Birr Castle and Demesne.

The Great Telescope at Ireland's Historic Science Centre.

Contestant at the Ballinasloe Horse Fair.

grave slabs dating from the 9th to the 12th centuries, as well as a helpful audio-visual presentation.

Among the older surviving buildings of the complex are the shell of a small cathedral, two round towers, the remains of eight smaller churches and several High Crosses. There are various doorways and chancel arches in the Irish Romanesque style. One of the churches, Temple Connor, was restored by the Church of Ireland in 1911 and is used for services.

Around Lough Derg

Head south for **Shannon Harbour**, the junction of the Grand Canal and the River Shannon, which is a popular mooring place for river cruisers. About 5 miles (8km) further south is **Banagher ❹**, another popular boating centre with a marina. This pretty, one-street village will be eerie and empty in winter, and bustling with river enthusiasts in summer.

The town has two notable literary connections, the first of which was Anthony Trollope, who worked in the area as a land surveyor in 1841 and penned his first novel, *The Macdermots of Ballycloran*, here. Charlotte Brontë spent her honeymoon in the area. A common Irish exclamation: 'That beats Banagher!' dates back to a period during the 19th century when the town was ruled by corrupt officials and gave rise to this definition of poor standards still in popular currency.

Signposted from the centre of the village and lying a mile or so outside it is the lovingly restored **Cloghan Castle** (www.cloghancastle.com; private hire only).

Birr

Birr ❺ is an attractive Georgian town, more or less in the centre of Ireland, dominated by **Birr Castle and Demesne** (tel: 057-912 0336; www.birrcastle.com; daily). As an estate town that grew in tandem with the castle, Birr is a good example of Georgian town planning, with many original entrance fanlights, door panelling and iron railings still intact.

The gardens of Birr Castle cover 100 acres (40 hectares) and have more than 1,000 species of trees and shrubs with an especially strong Chinese and Himalayan collection. In spring, magnolias, crab apples and cherries will be in flower; in the autumn, maples, chestnut and weeping beech supply colour. The box hedges subdividing the formal gardens are the highest in the world.

The 17th-century castle is private, but its stable block now houses a **Historic Science Centre** (tel. as above). The owners of Birr Castle, the Parsons family, later ennobled as the Earls of Rosse, have manifested a scientific bent for several generations. In the 1840s the 3rd Earl of Rosse built the Great Telescope which enabled him to see further into space than any of his contemporaries. The telescope, which has a 56ft (17-metre) tube and a 6ft (1.8-metre) mirror, was in use until 1908 and has been restored to working order.

Walk into town along **Oxmanton Mall**, a tree-lined thoroughfare that leads from the castle gates past a row of elegant Georgian houses. **Emmet Square** in the town centre is the location of one-time coaching inn **Dooly's Hotel** (dating from 1747; www.doolys hotel.com), which gave its name to the Galway Blazers when they set fire to it after a Hunt Ball in 1809, almost destroying the building.

Lough Derg

From Birr, head to **Borrisokane** and the eastern shores of **Lough Derg ⑥**. At Lough Derg the Shannon widens into a 50 sq mile (130 sq km) lake that is about 10 miles (16km) across at its widest point. This side is in County Tipperary and the west of the lake is in County Clare. The circular **Lough Derg Drive** (about 50 miles/90km; www.shannonregiontrails.ie) passes through a succession of pretty villages, but the lake itself is not always visible. The villages on this side of Lough Derg are peaceful, out-of-the-way places to stay that have been steadily gaining in popularity. Most visitors either have a boat of some kind or are interested in fishing – mainly coarse angling – on the lake. Others enjoy walking, both near the lake and on the other side of Birr in the waymarked trails of the **Slieve Bloom Mountains**.

Terryglass is one of the prettiest villages near Lough Derg, although you have to leave the main road to find the lake. **Dromineer** on the other hand is right on the water, and has a ruined castle on its pier. Many of the people you meet in the pubs will be temporarily living on river cruisers, which they own or have hired.

A very accessible range of low-lying hills perfect for either leisurely strolling or steep hiking, the Slieve Bloom Way is a 20-mile (32km) circular trail through mostly uninhabited landscape and hidden vistas. You can dip in and out of the trail at many points, but the villages of Cadamstown and Kinnity are ideal starting points.

Nenagh

Nenagh ⑦ is a Tipperary market town, bypassed by the busy Dublin-Limerick main road. All that remains of the original Norman settlement is the **Nenagh Castle Keep**, or 'donjon', with walls 20ft (6 metres) thick. It reaches to a height of 100ft (30 metres). Across the road in the **Governor's House** of the old town gaol is the **Nenagh Heritage Centre** (tel: 067-33850; www.nenagh.ie; free), which includes the condemned cells and execution room of the gaol, and a museum of rural life.

Roscrea ⑧, is an attractive little town, rich in heritage, bisected by the main road from Thurles to Athlone that cuts through the west facade of the 12th-century St Cronan's Abbey, which is all that remains, with a round-arched doorway containing a moulded figure of St Cronan.

Roscrea's 13th-century castle is a polygonal structure with two D-shaped towers. The gatehouse is topped by 18th-century gables and chimneys. It now houses the **Roscrea Heritage Centre** (tel:

The neo-Gothic St Mary of the Rosary Church, Nenagh, built in 1895.

Roscrea Castle.

Damer House.

0505-21850; www.heritageireland.ie; daily Apr–mid-Sept; charge also includes Damer House).

Damer House (Wed–Sun 11am–5pm), which stands inside the castle walls, is an elegant, 18th-century, three-storied house with a plain, symmetrical facade and a handsome pine staircase. It was completed in the 1720s and became a Bishop's Palace before being converted to a military barracks in 1798. It was very nearly demolished in the 1970s to make room for a car park but was saved through the vigilance of the Irish Georgian Society.

Emo Court

Travel east again, bypassing **Portlaoise**, to visit **Emo Court** ❾ (tel: 057-862 6573; house daily Apr–mid-Sept). This fine Georgian mansion was built in 1792 for the Earl of Portarlington in the Classical style by James Gandon, best known for Dublin's Four Courts and Custom House. It was restored and donated to the nation in 1996 by a private benefactor.

Walking the Slieve Bloom Way.

Approached via an avenue of splendid giant sequoia trees, the house is certainly worth a visit. Built over a 70-year period as a result of the 1st Earl's fluctuating financial fortunes, the house is the only large-scale domestic example of Gandon's work apart from the Custom House. Pride of place goes to the domed rotunda, designed by Gandon's successor, William Caldbeck, a mix of marble pilasters with gilded Corinthian capitals supporting the enormous blue painted dome which was inspired by Rome's Pantheon.

The gardens were created in two parts. The Clucker, named because it was once the site of the nun's quarters of an ancient abbey, is planted with azaleas, rhododendrons and Japanese maples. The Grapery is planted with trees and shrubs and leads down to the peaceful lakeside walk.

Nearby is **Coolbanagher Church,** also designed by Gandon, within which are the original 1795 architectural plans. An intricate 15th-century font from an earlier church has been incorporated. Close by is Gandon's mausoleum for Lord Portarlington.

Charleville Forest Castle

There is another interesting house in an entirely different style to the north near Tullamore, **Charleville Forest Castle** ❿ (tel: 057-932 3040; www.charlevillecastle.ie). The castle is gradually being restored by volunteers.

Designed by Francis Johnson, the architect responsible for many of Dublin's Georgian houses, this fine example of Gothic Revival style was commissioned by Baron Tullamore in 1812. With its flag tower and castellated turrets rising high over an estate of pleasant woodland walks and gardens, the house is built of grey limestone with an internal gallery complete with some intricate plasterwork running the entire length of the garden front.

Five avenues lined by Irish yew trees radiate from the house. The grounds contain many impressive trees including an oak believed to be 700 years old. Tullamore is also where Irish Mist and Tullamore Dew liqueurs are made. The drinks' histories and traditional distilling methods are explained in the **Tullamore Dew Heritage Centre** (tel: 057-932 5016; www.tullamoredew.com; daily; free).

Around Lough Ennel

Follow the N52 from Tullamore for 7.5 miles (12km) north to **Kilbeggan** ⓫. **Locke's Distillery** (tel: 057-933 2134; www.kilbeggandistillery.com; daily), advertised for miles around, is on the banks of the River Brosna, which is fed by springs from nearby Lough Ennel. It claims to have been the world's oldest pot-still distillery. After closing in 1957, it was reopened as a museum in 1987.

It is said that all good whiskey depends on the water that goes into the distillation process. The distillery was in use from 1757 to 1953 and much of the original equipment is still in place. There are enticing smells of malt and oak as you view the equipment, and a tasting.

The low-lying **Lough Ennel** can be seen from the N52 between Kilbeggan and Mullingar. It is a popular place for swimming, boating and fishing. The restored **Belvedere House and Gardens** (tel: 044-934 9060; www.belvedere-house.ie; daily) is remarkable for its beautiful setting, with terraced gardens descending in three stages to the shores of the lake.

Mullingar ⓬, the chief town of County Westmeath, is an important cattle-dealing centre with a pleasant, old-world ambience which is also popular with anglers. The Cathedral of Christ the King (Mary Street; tel: 044-934 8338; free) was completed in 1939 with a finely carved facade in the Renaissance style. Inside are mosaics by the Russian artist Boris Anrep. Tours are available from May–Sept; phone for details.

Around Lough Derravaragh

Tullynally Castle ⓭ (tel: 044-966 1159; www.tullynallycastle.com; gardens and tearooms daily Apr–Sept), to the north of Mullingar, just beyond **Castlepollard**, used to be known as

Locke's Distillery, fed by springs from Lough Ennel.

Locke's Distillery is the last remaining example of a small pot-still whiskey distillery in Ireland.

Pakenham Hall. This massive, grey stone, turreted house overlooking **Lough Derravaragh** has been the seat of the Pakenham family, now the Earls of Longford, since 1655. The current family includes the children of the late British peer Lord Longford: his historian son Thomas, and his daughters, biographer Antonia Fraser and novelist Rachel Billington. The castle is the home of Thomas Pakenham, and is not open to the public.

The original fort was converted into a two-storey house in the 18th century. A Gothic facade was added in the early 19th century, and in the mid-19th century Sir Richard Morrison designed the central tower and two wings. The landscaped gardens, which include a grotto, have spectacular views of Lough Derravaragh.

Multyfarnham, a 2-mile (3km) detour off the N4 Longford road, is a one-street town with some good old-fashioned pubs. Multyfarnham's **Cistercian monastery**, founded in 1306, has an attractive slender tower 88ft (27 metres) high. The abbey was restored by the Franciscans in 1973. Its stained-glass windows show the legend of the Children of Lir who were turned into swans and lived nearby on Lough Derravaragh. The Franciscans have built a life-size Stations of the Cross in a grove of evergreens beside a fast-flowing stream.

To the south of Longford off the R397, the **Corlea Trackway Visitor Centre** at Kenagh (tel: 043-332 2386; www.heritageireland.ie; Apr–mid Sept daily; free) interprets an Iron Age Bog Road dating from 148 BC – the largest of its kind ever to be uncovered in Europe.

Famine Museum

If you can only visit one stately home in the Midlands, then follow the N5 for 25 miles (40km) west of Longford to **Strokestown Park House and Famine Museum** (tel: 071-963 3013; www.strokestownpark.ie; closed Nov–mid-Mar except for pre-booked tours). The village leads to an imposing Georgian-Gothic arch, which leads to the house. The village, with its exceptionally broad main street, was laid out in the early 19th century to complement the new entrance. The house itself is a fine Palladian mansion designed by Sir Richard Cassels in the 1730s. The central block was the family's residence while the wings either side contained the stables and the kitchen areas. The kitchen is especially interesting. A gallery runs above it from which the lady of the house could oversee the staff without entering the kitchen itself. Each Monday morning she would drop a menu with instructions for the week's meals. Tunnels to hide the movements of tradesmen and servants link the main block of the house to the kitchens and stables. The walled garden has also been restored in line with horticultural practices of the 18th century.

The house, accessible by guided tour only (40 minutes), was at the centre of a large estate. It stayed in the Mahon family until 1979 when it was bought and restored by a local businessman.

Tullynally Castle.

Allow another hour for the **Famine Museum**, housed in the stable yard (see page 245).

West of Strokestown where the N5 crosses the R367 lies **Tulsk** and the **Cruachan Aí Visitors Centre** (tel: 071-963 9268; www.rathcroghan.ie; Mon–Sat all year and Sun June–Oct), which explores the archaeological, historical and mythological aspects of Cruachan, burial place of the Kings of Connacht.

Roscommon

Roscommon ⓰, to the south of Tulsk, is a pleasant market town built on a low hill in the midst of rich cattle and sheep country. **Roscommon Castle** (freely accessible), to the north of the town, is an impressive ruin on a green field site. It was originally a 13th-century Norman stronghold. It has massive walls defended by round bastions at each corner, and the mullioned windows can still be seen in some of the remaining walls.

Adjacent to the town are the remains of the 12th-century **Roscommon Abbey** founded by Felim O'Conor, king of Connacht, who was buried there himself in 1265. Eight sculpted figures represent the 'gallowglass' – professional soldiers for hire used extensively during the period. Much of the remaining structure dates from the 13th century.

Around Lough Ree

Thanks to the ring road around Athlone, it is possible to drive from Roscommon to **Glasson**, which is about 6 miles (10km) outside Athlone, without fighting Athlone's traffic. Glasson is one of a series of pretty villages on the eastern shore of **Lough Ree** ⓰, part of the River Shannon. There are good amenities for water sports, attractive country pubs and restaurants, and a series of lake shore and forest walks. The poet and dramatist Oliver Goldsmith (1730–74), best known for his 1773 comedy *She Stoops to Conquer*, is associated with this area.

The play's central device, by which a traveller mistakes a private home for a country inn, supposedly happened to Goldsmith at Ardagh House in Ardagh, which is now a school. The

Foxgloves in Co. Wicklow.

Jet-skiing on Lough Ree.

RECALLING THE FAMINE

The Famine Museum at Strokestown Park House presents a vivid display tracing the history of the family and the estate and links this to the national events in 1845–50 which led to Ireland's Great Famine and the resulting mass emigration or death of more than 2 million people – almost one-quarter of the population.

It balances the history of the big house with the experiences of the peasants who worked the land. Moving documents record the pleas made to the Mahon family by tenants starving as a result of a devastating potato blight, together with the response they received. The museum also aims to raise awareness of contemporary famine by demonstrating the link between the causes of the Great Irish Famine and that of famine in the developing world.

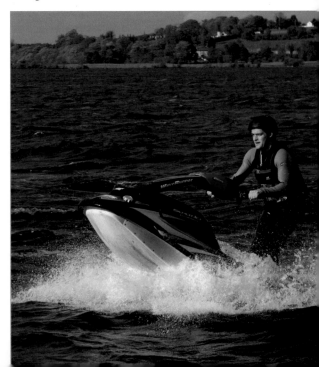

house where he grew up, Lissoy Parsonage, is now in ruins. The **Three Jolly Pigeons** pub (tel: 090-648 5162) on the Ballymahon road, is the headquarters of the annual Oliver Goldsmith Summer School. Though he rarely returned to his childhood county, his recollections of Longford are also thought to have influenced his epic poem *The Deserted Village*.

Athlone

Athlone ⓘ, which straddles the River Shannon at an important strategic point to the south of Lough Ree, has the distinction of being half in Co. Westmeath and half in Co. Roscommon. It is an important commercial centre, and the busiest town in the Midlands (www.athlone.ie).

Athlone Castle (tel: 090- 644 2130; www.athloneartandheritage.ie; daily, closed Mon Nov–mid–Mar) is a squat, 13th-century building, which was badly damaged in 1690 when the Irish made a stand here against the advance of Cromwell's forces. The castle has been beautifully restored and now has a €4.3m visitor centre on its long history, the highlight being the Siege of Athlone in 1690–1. The area behind the castle is being promoted as Athlone's 'Left Bank'. There are some nice town houses dating from the 18th and 19th centuries, several good restaurants and bars.

You will notice that even relatively modest restaurants in Athlone tend to have trilingual menus. This is because the town is very popular with holidaymakers on Shannon cruisers, most of whom eat ashore as often as they can. The nicest thing to do in Athlone is to take a boat trip up the Shannon to Lough Ree. Viking Tours Ireland (tel: 086-262 1136; www.vikingtoursireland.ie) have a replica Viking longboat, comfortably equipped with snack bar on board, that leaves regularly between Easter and August for a 90-minute cruise from the quay beside Athlone Castle.

Cavan's cruising

Across the border to the south of Enniskillen, landlocked Co. Cavan, emptied by emigration, bridges the two Irelands by providing the source of

Athlone.

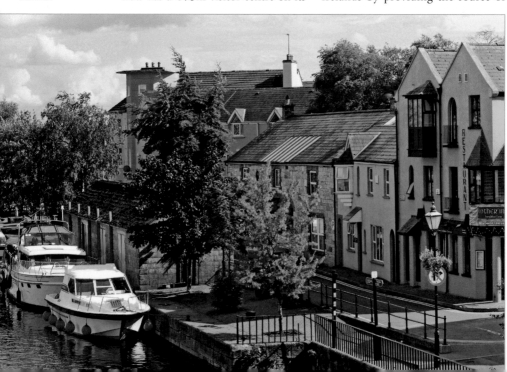

two great rivers: the **Shannon,** which flows south to the Atlantic, and the **Erne**, which flows north into Fermanagh's magnificent lakes. Both rivers are ideal for cruising. Most of the county's scattered towns and villages have small hotels, which cater for visiting fishermen. The Ballinamore-Ballyconnell canal linking the two river systems has been reopened and pleasure trips along the canal are in demand (Inland Waterways Association of Ireland; tel: 01-890 924 991; www.iwai.ie).

Cavan town ⑱, a busy market town and a popular destination for anglers, is a pleasant place to explore on foot with many unspoilt old pubs. It is the site of a 14th-century Franciscan friary, of which only a belfry tower remains. The Roman Catholic Cathedral, in contrast, dates from 1942.

St Feithlimidh's Cathedral (tel: 049-433 7168; guided tours on request; free) at Kilmore is just off the main Cavan-Crossdoney road, 3 miles (5km) west of Cavan town. It has been a place of worship for up to 15 centuries. The cathedral dates mainly from the 19th-century and is built in the Early Decorated or Middle Pointed style with a central tower that is finished by a distinctive four-sided pyramidal roof. Its Romanesque doorway dates from the early 13th century and came from a nearby priory on Trinity Island in Lough Oughter.

Killykeen Forest Park (tel: 049-433 2541; free) 5 miles (8km) from Cavan town, covers 600 acres (240 hectares) of mixed woodland overlooking Lough Oughter on the Erne river system and offering a picturesque landscape of lakes, islands and woodland. It is especially popular with fishing enthusiasts, as well as walkers, thanks to its forest paths and trails.

A bit further north just off the R201 near Milltown is Drumlane Abbey (www.drumlane.ie), located in a peaceful setting on the Erne River. The Augustinian St Mary's Priory was founded here in the 12th century, although the buildings possibly date back to the sixth century. There are remains of the round tower minus its roof, a church, graveyard and stone crosses.

Village Ireland tours

A tour going west and north from Cavan would take in **Arvagh**, a peaceful village 14 miles (22km) southwest on the R198 by Lough Garty; 17th-century **Cloughoughter Castle** on an island in Lough Oughter and nearby **Killeshandra**, a popular spot for anglers; **Dowra**, to the northwest on the R200 near the Black Pig's Dyke, thought to be an ancient frontier earthwork; **Swanlinbar on the N87**, with its faded, once-a-spa charms, on the Border; **Blacklion**, on Lough Macnean 33 miles (52km) northwest on the N3/R200, a hamlet surrounded by many prehistoric ringforts and cairns including a beehive-shaped sweat house, a Celtic form of Turkish bath; and **Butlersbridge**, 4 miles (6km) north on the N3 near which Ballyhaise House, now an agricultural college, has a rare 1733 oval saloon and two storeys vaulted over in brick.

Cavan town.

Angling near Cloughoughter Castle, on an island in Lough Oughter.

A tour going east and south would cover: **Cootehill**, 16 miles (26km) northeast on the R118 which has a splendid 1730 Palladian house, **Bellamont House**, built for the Coote family in Bellamont Forest. Often hailed as Ireland's loveliest 18th-century house, it was built by Sir Edward Lovett Pearce and inspired by Italy's Palladian villas. One of its most famous owners, Charles Coote, Earl of Bellamont, was known as 'the Hibernian seducer' because of his extramarital activities. He was eventually shot in the groin by Lord Townshend. A portrait by Sir Joshua Reynolds hangs in the National Gallery of Ireland. The house is privately owned but there are walking trails open to the public in Bellamont Forest.

Southeast 13 miles (21km) on the R192 to **Shercock**, is where the playwright Richard Brinsley Sheridan once lived; **Kingscourt**, whose Catholic church has some renowned stained glass; **Bailieborough**, on the R165, which has a fine main street; **Virginia**, 19 miles (33km) southwest

on the N3, planned as a garrison town in 1610 and now a handsome, peaceful place with Cuilcagh House, owned by playwright Tom McIntyre (private), where Dean Swift began *Gulliver's Travels*, 3 miles (5km) east; and **Ballyjamesduff**, where the award-winning Cavan County Museum in Virginia Road (tel: 049-854 4070; www.cavanmuseum.ie; Tue–Sat all year, Sun pm June–Sept; free) houses a collection of pre-Christian and medieval artefacts including the 1,000-year-old Lough Errol dugout boat and Lavey Sheela-na-gigs.

The Cavan Way

The Cavan Way provides a pleasant hill and valley walking connection between the Leitrim Way at Dowra and the Ulster Way at Blacklion village. The walk follows quiet valley and river-sided landscapes to the enclosed uplands of the river's source at the mystical Shannon 'Pot' (from the Irish *Lag na Sionna*, meaning 'hollow of the Shannon').

Walkers enjoy the upland section between the 'Pot' and Blacklion, which includes the forested Burren area and its cemetery of ancient tombs, stone megaliths and monuments. Cavan Tourism has more details (see page 248).

Mild Monaghan

To the northeast, in Monaghan, is the small agricultural town of **Clones** ⑲ (pronounced 'clone-ess'), whose most famous son is Barry McGuigan, the 'Clones cyclone' who became world featherweight boxing champion in 1985. The town's commercial centre is Fermanagh Street, signalling the town's former significance for the farmers of south Fermanagh.

But, just as partition destroyed its role as an important railway hub, so the Troubles initially hit trade as northerners became reluctant to cross the border. However, the two tills on most shop counters hint that the two different currencies – the British pound in Northern Ireland and the euro in the South – have encouraged a great deal of cross-border price comparing, especially on diesel and petrol.

The writer Patrick McCabe was born in Clones. His popular novels include *The Butcher Boy* and *Breakfast on Pluto*, both filmed by Neil Jordan.

Clones has an ancient lineage. The remains of a 12th-century Augustinian abbey (known as '**the Wee Abbey**') can be seen in Abbey Street. An ancient cross in the marketplace shows scenes from the Bible, such as the Fall of Adam and Eve and the Adoration of the Magi. The cemetery has a 9th-century **round tower**, 75ft (23 metres) high and rather dilapidated, and an early Christian carved **sarcophagus**, thought to be the grave of the founder, St Tiarnoch, the key to which can be obtained from nearby Patton's pub.

Several Georgian houses are a reminder of the town's 18th-century prosperity. Another sign of the vanished 'Ascendancy' era are the 'big houses', once the homes of the well-to-do Anglo-Irish, many of which have fallen into disrepair.

Monaghan is a quiet, trim county of snug farmhouses and tranquil market towns, and lakes and rivers

FACT

Monaghan's mix of monotonous low hills and poor small farms was well captured by the novelist and poet Patrick Kavanagh (1904–67), who grew up here on a farm at Inishkeen. A man whose acerbic wit spared little, including his native county, Kavanagh described Monaghan's natives as being 'locked in a stable with pigs and cows forever.' His 1948 book Tarry Flynn, later dramatised, achingly explores the repressed emotions of a young farmer in this area.

The 18th-century Hope Castle, set in Lough Muckno Leisure Park, was once a convent and is now a hotel.

Castle Leslie, where Paul McCartney got hitched to Heather Mills.

Church in County Monaghan.

that draw fishermen. Its administrative centre, **Monaghan** ⑳, 12 miles (19km) northeast of Clones, has a **Market House** dating from 1792, an imposing 19th-century Gothic Revival cathedral (**St Macartan's**) and a good **County Museum** (tel: 047-82928; www.monaghan.ie; Mon–Sat; free) highlighting prehistoric relics and local arts and crafts. The **Garage Theatre** (tel: 047-81597; www.garagetheatre.com), located in a disused ward of a psychiatric hospital, mounts excellent touring productions.

Rossmore Forest Park, 2 miles (3km) southwest of Monaghan town on the R189 to Newbliss, has several forest walks, a nature trail and a yew walk. The ruins of the 16th-century **Rossmore Castle** provide a viewing point to the surrounding countryside. The park contains examples of a wedge tomb and a court tomb dating 3,000 to 1,800 BC. The landscape has many drumlins (low rounded hills), laid down during the Ice Age over 10,000 years ago when boulder clay was deposited as small hillocks by moving ice.

Castle Leslie

To the north, 5 miles (8km) on the R185, by Glaslough, is the reputedly haunted **Castle Leslie** (www.castleleslie.com), home of the literary Leslie family and now a hotel with a thriving equestrian centre. Set on an estate of 1,000 acres (400 hectares), Castle Leslie is rich in Victorian splendour, both in its furniture and family portraits. Winston Churchill, a first cousin of the family, best known for its writers and eccentrics, was a regular guest.

To the south, east of **Newbliss**, 10 miles (16km) on the R188, at **Annamakerrig House** is the **Tyrone Guthrie Centre** (tel: 047-54003; www.tyroneguthrie.ie), an international haven for professional artists in all art forms. Six miles (10km) east is **Rockcorry**, where John Gregg invented Gregg's Shorthand, America's favourite.

Continuing along the R183 to **Castleblayney**, a town so steeped in the tradition of country music it has been called the Nashville of Ireland. It's a good centre for walking, fishing and golf, and is situated by the attractive Lough Muckno. Hope Castle (tel: 042-974 9450; free), built on the site of Blayney Castle in the 18th century, is now a leisure park.

Poet and novelist Patrick Kavanagh grew up 10 miles (16km) east of attractive **Carrickmacross**, at tiny Inishkeen, where a riverside museum, the **Patrick Kavanagh Centre** (tel: 042-937 8560; www.patrickkavanaghcountry.com; Tue–Fri 11am–4.30pm or by appointment; free) run by local volunteers, celebrates his work. While he spent most of his life in Dublin, the harsh isolation of his native county informed much of his work during his life. Mocked by the Dublin literary community of the time, Kavanagh, an irascible character, claimed, perhaps justifiably, that he was hated. When *The Irish Times* surveyed 'the nation's favourite poems', 10 of Kavanagh's poems were in the first 50. (See page 249.)

Traditional local lace is still made and sold in Carrickmacross (www.carrickmacrosslace.ie).

Rural Bungalows

Ireland's legendary green countryside is defaced by a rash of houses built with unsuitable materials and painted with more exuberance than taste.

Promotional photos of Ireland could lead visitors to believe that the majority of the rural population lives in small, two-room cottages nestling in the landscape. On the contrary, most country people have given up their dark, cramped accommodation in favour of something more commodious – and visible. From the 1960s, new homes began to appear, often next door to the old cottage. The preferred design was, at first, a modest bungalow, with larger windows, decent plumbing and perhaps an extra bedroom or two. Their owners, seized by fits of individuality, often painted the walls in colours that were unexpectedly cheerful (sometimes garish), or added panels of stone cladding.

Quirky pastiche

Over the years, rural homes have become larger and more embellished – although many retain the one-storey format. Some are garnished with Georgian porticoes and balustrades; others loop off into Spanish-arched verandas, while still others sprout eagle-topped gateposts and gold-tipped wrought-iron gates. Tyrolean bargeboards, Victorian lamp stands and fairy tale wishing wells have likewise found a place in the Irish countryside. The more exuberant homeowners have gone for a jolly *mixum gatherum* of the whole lot – causing architects and purists to despair.

Not only have many of the new houses turned their broad backs on the traditional designs, but they do not conform to the way that buildings have been placed in the Irish countryside since time immemorial. In the past cottages and farm structures were snuggled into the landscape unobtrusively – in the lee of a hill, in the fold between two fields, in the arm hold of a hedgerow. But the new residences are often displayed monumentally on the brow of a hill or dropped importantly into the middle of a plot, with little to no landscaping or thought to aesthetic appeal.

County council planning departments issue booklets on careful site selection and layout, and on appropriate design and materials, but this advice is blissfully ignored by many home builders. Indeed, the most famous catalyst for the new style residences was a pattern book called *Bungalow Bliss*, by Jack Fitzsimons, first published in 1971, and which ran to at least a dozen editions over 30 years. This and other pattern books include self-build designs that often pay no heed to traditional materials, form or scale.

Bungalow blight

Fitzsimons's book title has given rise to cries of 'bungalow blight' and 'bungalow blitz', in protest against the proliferation of single houses spreading ribbon-like along the rural roadsides of some counties. The National Trust for Ireland, An Taisce, is in constant battle with local authorities over the granting of planning permission for such 'one-off' houses. But some county councillors are reluctant to veto the building projects of their constituents. There is a visceral desire among many Irish to have a house of their own, and this is hard to disregard. An Irishman's home is all-important. It is definitely his castle – and it may equally be his Spanish hacienda, Texan ranch or Tudor mansion - it just might not be quite as stylish or pleasing to the eye.

A mountainside home.

Slieve League Cliffs, Co. Donegal.

THE NORTHWEST

The counties of Sligo, Leitrim and Donegal combine Stone Age burial sites, a craggy coastline, quiet fishing villages and echoes of William Butler Yeats.

S outhwestern Sligo, a land of bright lakes and dramatically carved valleys left behind when the last ice age retreated 10,000 years ago, wears its history on its sleeve. Huts from 2,000 BC cluster on a plateau high in the Bricklieve Mountains west of Lough Arrow.

To the west lie the passage tombs of Carrowkeel Cemetery where Stone Age farmers buried their dead. Cairn K catches the rising sun on the year's longest day, yet the main road to Dublin, the N4, is just a mile west. Across it and across Lough Arrow, south of Riverstown, is the 200ft (70-metre) unexcavated Heapstown Cairn. Almost every hilltop has a passage grave, every lake a defensive artificial island, a crannog, every river confluence a castle, a friary, a priory.

Ballymote

Along the R295, and 5 miles (8km) northwest from Carrowkeel, Richard de Burgo, the Red Earl of Ulster, has left us the 10ft (3-metre) walls and six towers of his castle, built in 1300, in **Ballymote ❶**. The ruins beside it are of a Franciscan friary where, in 1391, priests wrote the *Book of Ballymote 1*, which enabled scholars to interpret Ireland's ancient Ogham (pronounced 'oh-am') script. At **Collooney**, north again 5 miles (8km) stands a castle, site of a great battle when the English

fought off French troops supporting the 1798 rising.

Like bookends, the county begins and ends with seaside resorts. **Enniscrone** (or Innishcrone to some purists), on the shores of Killala Bay, is at the western end, and at the other is Bundoran, in Donegal. Both have been revitalised by the surfing community. Recall the pre-wet-suit days by visiting the seaweed baths at Enniscrone Kilcullen's Bath House (tel: 096-36238; http://homepage. eircom.net/~seaweedbaths/frame.htm;

Main Attractions

Sligo town
Lake Isle of Innisfree
Erne–Shannon Waterway
Carrick-on-Shannon
Bundoran
Donegal town
Glencolumbkille
Glenveagh National Park
Inishowen Peninsula

The dolmen at Carrowmore.

The Northwest

0 ____ 10 km
0 ____ 10 miles

ATLANTIC OCEAN

June–Sept daily 10am–8pm, Oct–May noon–8pm).

From Enniscrone, follow the surfers' coast through **Easky** with its 15th-century Rosalee Castle and two Martello towers built to repel Napoleon in the early 19th century. Alternatively take the road south from Easky, past the sparkling waters of Easky Lough deep into the Ox Mountains before joining the N17 at Tobercurry. Young children may wish to stop off at Lavagh, near Tobercurry, to visit **Gillighan's World** ❷ (tel: 071-913 0286; www.gillighans world.ie; May Sat–Sun noon–5pm, Jun Thu–Sun noon–5pm, Jul–Aug Tue–Sun 11am–6pm), an open-air park and pet zoo where you can explore the kingdom of the fairies with its miniature villages set in an enchanted glade.

Carrowmore

At **Carrowmore** ❸, 5 miles (8km) southwest of Sligo town, the 6,000-year-old Bronze Age graves of Ireland's largest Megalithic cemetery (Visitor Centre; tel: 071-916 1534; www.heritageireland.ie; May–mid-Oct daily) are easily approached, scattered across the tussocky fields. Above them, on the western horizon, on top of 1,078ft (328-metre) Knocknarea, is the vast cairn, 200ft long by 35ft high (70 by 11 metres), consisting of 40,000 boulders. It is named Mebh's (pronounced 'maeves') Cairn, supposedly for the 1st-century AD Mebh of Connaught whose lust for glitz, baubles and fine clothes would put many a modern royal princess in the shade. The advised approach is from the south.

Sligo town

Sligo town ❹ (pop. 19,000), best known for its associations with the poet, playwright and Abbey Theatre co-founder William Butler Yeats, is the county's tourist magnet. To the west lie miles of stretches of open beaches, and to the north mountains

rise like jutting tablelands dominating the skyline.

Founded by the Normans in the 13th century, Sligo flourished into a prosperous town and has Catholic and Anglican Cathedrals. **Sligo Abbey** was built for the Dominicans in 1252 and was burned in a fire in 1414. It was rebuilt and damaged by fire during the 1641 rebellion and is the only surviving medieval building.

Today the town, with its diverting narrow streets and traditional shop fronts, is the business hub of the northwest of Ireland and with contemporary hotels it is an ideal base for exploring the region. Like so many Irish towns, the waterfront has been developed and along Rockwood Parade cafés, bars and restaurants offer alfresco dining, allowing you to watch swans struggling against the strong current of the River Garavogue.

W.B. Yeats (1865–1948), who spent most of his childhood holidays here, is the main attraction and his legacy is to be found all around. The **Yeats Memorial Building** (Yeats Society; tel: 071-914 2693; www.yeatssociety.

TIP

Hargadon's at 4–5 O'Connell Street (tel: 071-915 3709, www.hargadons.com) is one of Ireland's most famous traditional pubs with much of its original wooden interior still in place. It also has an excellent restaurant (Mon–Sat noon– 3.30pm and 4–9pm) and a wine shop.

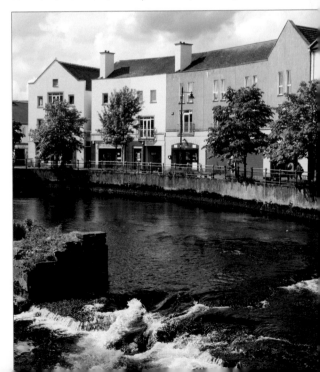

The Garavogue River in Sligo town.

com; Tue–Sat 10am–5.30pm) in Hyde Bridge, is the venue for the Yeats International Summer School in August. A permanent Yeats photographic exhibition is on display and the River Café offers refreshment. A bronze statue portraying the poet stands across the bridge. Upstairs in the Yeats Memorial Building, The **Sligo County Museum** (tel: 071-911 1850; www.sligolibrary. ie, Oct–Apr 9.30am–12.30pm Tue–Sat, May–Sept 9.30am–12.30pm & 2–4.50pm; free), housed in a former presbytery on Stephen Street contains Yeats's letters, a complete collection of his poems, photographs of his funeral, and his Nobel Prize citation.

The arts and theatre thrive in Sligo. The **Model**, home of the **Niland Collection** (The Mall; tel: 071-914 1405; www.themodel.ie), was once an imaginatively extended Model School, and now a unique gallery featuring a nationally significant art collection with works by Jack Yeats and Paul Henry. The town supports two theatres. **Hawk's Well Theatre** (tel: 071-916 1526; www.hawkswell.com) hosts visiting touring productions and

shows by local companies. It shares a building with the tourist information office (Temple Street; tel: 071-916 1201; www.discoverireland.ie/northwest; free). The **Blue Raincoat Theatre Company** (tel: 071-917 0431; www. blueraincoat.com) is based at the Factory Performance Space on Lower Quay Street.

Lissadell House

Head out of town and branch west, 4 miles (6km) along the northern shore of Drumcliff Bay to the extensively restored **Lissadell House** ❺, Ballinful (www.lissadellhouse.com; daily, 20 Mar–16 Oct 10.30am–6pm, adult €12, child €6), visible from several vantage points.

Designed in the neoclassical Greek Revival style, it was built of local cut grey limestone for the Gore Booths in 1833. By the end of the 20th century it had fallen into a dilapidated state, but even if the house were to crumble, Yeats has immortalised it: *The light of evening, Lissadell, / Great windows open to the south, / Two girls in silk kimonos, both / Beautiful, one a*

Lissadell House.

gazelle. The girls were poet Eva and her sister Constance, later to become Countess Markievicz, a friend of the Irish President Eamon de Valera who read her funeral oration. Constance, although sentenced to death for her heroic part in the 1916 Easter Rising, was the first woman to be elected to the British House of Commons. She never took the seat, preferring Ireland's equivalent, the Dáil. The neglect of the house was reversed in 2003 when the new custodians – Edward S. Walsh, a barrister from Dublin, and his wife, Constance Cassidy – bought the house for €4.55 million after the Government declined to buy it on behalf of the Irish State. The property has been meticulously restored. Visitors can now tour the house and gardens. There is also lots to keep children amused with a pet farm and the Saddle Room Magic Theatre. For art lovers there are regular art talks and workshops.

Lake Isle of Innisfree

Southeast of Sligo town, the R286 follows a signposted 'Yeats Country Drive' along the north side of beautiful **Lough Gill** ❻ swinging south at the elegant 17th-century lakeside **Parke's Castle**, (tel: 071-916 4149; Apr–Sept daily 10am–6pm) and then joins the R288 to **Dromahair** and the 15th-century Creevylea Abbey ruins.

The final stage of the journey, a visit to Yeats's Lake Isle of Innisfree, or a tour of Lough Gill can be taken by boat (tel: 071-916 4266; www.roseofinnisfree.com; 12.30, Easter–Sept) Innisfree is a tiny island, just a mile square, and poor weather can make it difficult to replicate Yeats's vision.

The Yeats brothers spent their holidays at windswept **Rosses Point**, 4 miles (6km) northwest on the R291. The view across to Knocknarea is inspiring; mid-channel is a seafarer's marker, the Metal Man – according to Yeats 'the only Rosses Point man who never told a lie.'

North of Sligo, 5.5 miles (9km) on the N15 is tiny **Drumcliff** ❼ at the foot of the majestic cliffs of Ben Bulben. Although he died in France, Yeats by his own request

The Yeats Room at the Sligo County Museum.

Drumcliff's Church of Ireland cemetery, resting place of W.B. Yeats.

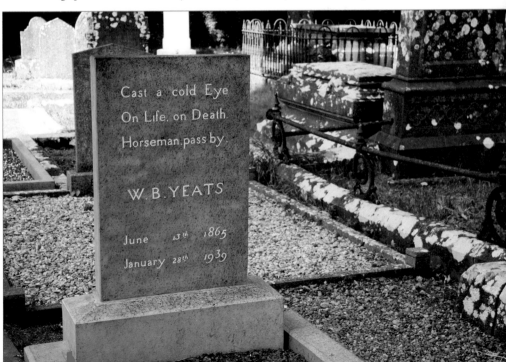

TIP

The Lough Gill is noted for brown trout and salmon. February, March and May are good months for salmon, while mid-May to mid-June is the best time for brown trout. There is public access to the lough from a pier on the south side of the mouth of the Garavogue River, at Innisfree pier and from the pier at Sriff Bay in the east.

was re-interred here in the dour little Church of Ireland's graveyard, citing the spot in his poem which begins: '*Under Ben Bulben's head*' and finishes with the celebrated words inscribed on his tomb '*Cast a cold eye / On life, on death, / Horseman, pass by!*'. The adjoining church has been restored.

The adjoining round tower is evidence of St Columba's AD 575 monastery, whilst on the 10th-century High Cross it is just possible to make out the bible stories of Cain and Abel, Adam and Eve. Glencar Lough, east on the N16 and half in county Leitrim, has a dramatic setting. Earlier literary diversions may be contemplated at Cooldrumman, halfway between Drumcliff and Lissadell. Here, in the Battle of the Books, AD 561, 2,000 monks of various factions, and their supporters, died in an argument as to whether St Finian was right in citing Derry's St Columba for breach of copyright.

Further north off the N15, turn west at Grange for superb **Streedagh Strand** with *Carriag na Spáinneach*,

Spaniard's Rock, where three ships of the Spanish Armada foundered in 1588. Most of the shipwrecked, cold and starving were put to the sword. Some re-grouped, joined the *Gerona*, only to suffer similar fates at Port na Spániagh, Dunluce, Co. Antrim. The little road east from Grange leads up Ben Bulben.

Mullaghmore ❽ is a harbour village, a picture postcard from some perfect childhood holiday. The large sandstone castle built on a rock overlooking the harbour, Classiebawn, was inherited by Edwina, wife of Lord Louis Mountbatten. On 27 August 1979, Lord Mountbatten, his sister-in-law, the Dowager Lady Brabourne, his grandson Nicholas and a local boy, Paul Maxwell, were killed when a bomb containing 50lbs (22.5kg) of gelignite exploded on their fishing boat. Three others were badly injured but survived. The IRA claimed responsibility; there was no local involvement. The Blue Flag (EU-approved for quality) beach is golden; bright boats rock by the pier and waves splash on Mullaghmore Head.

Looking towards Ben Bulben from Drumcliff churchyard.

W.B. YEATS

The son and brother of painters, Yeats (1865–1939) studied art in Dublin and London but became interested in mysticism, the supernatural and Irish nationalism. With Lady Gregory, an Anglo-Irish aristocrat, he founded the Abbey Theatre in Dublin at the same time as his unrequited passion for Maud Gonne, an English-born revolutionary and actress, inspired his early poetry. At 52, he married the 25-year-old Georgie Hyde-Lees, who was deeply into mysticism.

The drama of the 1916 Easter Rising encouraged his interest in politics and he became a senator in the Irish Free State's government from 1922 to 1928, serving as chairman of a commission on coinage. He was awarded the Nobel Prize for Literature in 1923. His status as a major English-language poet is assured.

Offshore is the low-lying unin-habited **Innishmurray Island**, 4 miles (6km) away with one of the most complete and visually exciting early Christian monastic settlements in Europe: the stunning remains of St Molaise's 6th-century monastery, and three churches within a 12ft (4-metre) -high dry-stone wall – just about the only survivors of Viking raids in the 9th century. If the cross-ing from Mullaghmore, or Rosses Point, was rough enough, travellers might seek out the island's other curiosity, its cursing stones. Boats to Innishmurray can be hired for day trips (www.sligoheritage.com).

Sligo Folk Park , (Millview House, Riverstown; tel: 071-916 5001; www.sligofolkpark.com; Jun–Aug Mon–Sat 10am–5.30pm, Sun noon–5pm; Sept–May Mon–Fri 10am–5pm) is worth a visit to see traditional craft demonstrations that include thatching, creel-making, butter-making and wood-turning, as well as a working forge. A museum is devoted to rural history with displays of farm implements.

Leitrim: rescued by water

North of Mullaghmore, Leitrim is allowed to just dip its toes into 2.5 miles (4km) of the Atlantic, before the shoreline reaches the **Drowse**, one of the best salmon rivers and the bound-ary with Donegal. Ten miles (16km) inland and Leitrim's border is with Fermanagh in Northern Ireland.

Another 20 miles (32km) east and its northern border is with Mona-ghan. At **Lough Allen** ❿ – its biggest lake, which divides the county into two topographical areas – there are scarcely 5 miles (8km) of Leitrim soil between north Monaghan and south Roscommon.

This tiny county of lakes and rushes, meandering rivers, bumpy roads, crumbling farmhouses, drumlins (low rounded hills) and neglected fields, often referred to as 'leaky Leitrim', once dismissed for its poverty, is now valued as a place that has retained the quiet charm of pre-Celtic Tiger Ire-land. The great famine of 1845–46 hit the county hard, and emigration has continued ever since. The unflinching novels of John McGahern (1934–2006)

Yeats' statue in Sligo.

The beach at Mullaghmore.

who lived and farmed at Feenagh near **Mohill** ⓫, catch the air of rural desperation that pervaded.

McGahern was one of the most important Irish writers since Samuel Beckett. With his sparse and incisive lyrical style, he was the master of precise language. His stories, set deep in the poor Leitrim soil, tap into the social and economic realities of Irish life in the 1930s and 1940s. 'There is nothing dramatic about the Leitrim landscape,' he once wrote, 'but it is never dull.' His last published book, the painfully recollected *Memoir* (2005), illuminated much of the fiction that preceded it. The writer and commentator Fintan O'Toole summed up John McGahern's legacy: 'He changed Ireland, not by arguing about it, but by describing it.'

Erne-Shannon Waterway

That quiet countryside and unspoilt environment so powerfully described in McGahern's books is now attracting visitors. Leitrim has much going in its favour. A glance at the map shows a necklace of lakes linking the rivers Shannon and Erne via the Ballinamore–Ballyconnell Canal – more prosaically marketed as the **Erne–Shannon Waterway**. From spring to winter, the banks of the lakes and rivers – where cows drink hock-high amongst the flag irises – are dotted with the big green umbrellas of visiting fishermen after bream, eel, perch, pike, roach and rudd.

Hired cruisers flying Austrian, British, Dutch, French and German ensigns ply the canal, their crews clinking their gin 'n' tonic glasses, their skippers nautical in caps, binoculars at the ready. Heron poise in the reed mace, great crested grebe dive before the bow wave. Amid the uncut water meadows, amateur botanists count sedges; birdwatchers tick off another species of warbler and cup their ear for the cry of corncrake and cuckoo.

Apart from the fishing, boating and birdwatching, tourists come for hill walking, horse-riding, cycling and traditional music. The new money has brought music back to the pubs, turned old market houses into heritage centres and tourist offices, and refurbished town piers and lake fishing stands. The Organic Centre in **Rossinver** offers courses in subjects ranging from 'plant to plate' and 'growing in polytunnels' (tel: 071-985 4338; www.theorganiccentre.ie).

At the southern tip of Lough Allen, **Drumshanbo** ⓬ dances to the beat of the *bodhrán* and banjo as well as the piper and fiddler. Music seeps from the pubs at all times of the year but two highlights are An Tóstal (www.antostalfestival.ie), held at the end of May, and in mid-July a week-long annual festival of song and dance, the Joe Mooney Summer School (www.joe mooneysummerschool.com).

Slieve Anierin (*Sliabh an Iarainn*, 'Mountain of Iron') lies northeast of Drumshanbo and the mountain takes its name from the fact that iron and coal were smelted from it. The mining on the nearby Arigna Mountains ended in 1990 but the memories are retained

A necklace of lakes link the rivers Shannon and Erne.

in the Arigna Mining Experience (tel: 071-964 6466; www.arignamining experience.ie; Mon–Sun 10am–6pm), which explains the social and mining traditions of the area. A 45-minute underground tour, led by ex-miners, shows what it was like to work in some of the narrowest coal seams in the western world. An exhibition area traces 400 years of mining history in the area and a DVD gives an insight into the mining process. A visit to the coffee shop is rewarded with stunning views of the natural surroundings.

Carrick-on-Shannon

The county town, **Carrick-on-Shannon** ⑬, (pop. 4,500) is a buzz of activity, much of it centred on the riverside and bustling marina with its opulent cruising boats, quality restaurants and luxury hotels. A walk around town with its attractive shop fronts is rewarding. Carrick boasts some striking architecture including the remarkable **Costello Memorial Church**, a tiny Catholic chapel on Bridge Street which is the smallest in Ireland and reputedly the second smallest in the world. The

tourist office is based in the Old Barrel Store, at the Marina (tel: 071-962 0170; www.leitrimtourism.com).

Drumsna, just southeast, where Anthony Trollope wrote his first novel, (see page 262), and Roosky 9 miles (14km) south again, have also found prosperity. **Lough Rynn Castle** (tel: 071-963 2700, www.loughrynn. ie), once home to the Earl of Leitrim, has now been converted into a luxury hotel where non-guests are welcome for afternoon tea and a stroll in the splendid gardens. It is 10 miles (16km) east of Carrick-on-Shannon. Ten miles (16km) to the northeast, **Carrigallen** has a flourishing theatre, the Corn Mill (tel: 049-433 9612; www.cornmill theatre.com).

The Leitrim Genealogy Centre (tel: 071-964 4012; www.leitrimroots.com) at Main Street in **Ballinamore** ⑭ will help those interested in delving into their Irish past. The staff will compile a family history report.

For another take on the past, visit the **Glenview Folk Museum** (tel: 071-964 4157; www.glenview-house.com; Apr–Oct daily; free) in Aghoo, just south of

Carrick-on-Shannon.

FACT

Anthony Trollope's first novel, The McDermotts of Ballycloran, is highly melodramatic, involving illegal distillers, a ruthless attorney, a wronged woman and a murder. Trollope himself said of it: 'As to the plot itself, I do not know that I ever made one so good, – or, at any rate, one so susceptible of pathos.' He thought it painted an accurate picture of what Irish life was like before the devastating 1846 potato famine.

Ballinamore. The museum houses a private collection of 3,000 agricultural items from the 19th and 20th centuries. Nearby, fragments of the old Sligo Leitrim and Northern Counties Railway, whose initials were interpreted locally as 'Slow Late and Never Completely Reliable', can be traced.

Donegal

The Atlantic storms into Donegal's rocky coves, rumbling round white boulders up in banks beside the sheep-cropped grass. Rusty winches, skeletal memories of long-lost fishing enterprises, paint red the stone of crumbling piers. Dreamers and poets, and stressed-out business executives from Continental Europe, put thatch back on the roofs of old stone cottages, whilst locals, seemingly with no planning constraints erect new bungalows higgledy-piggledy, despoiling (for the tourist) the silent landscape of empty valleys, purple mountains, rushing streams and towering sea cliffs.

Donegal's people, like Leitrim's, will argue that they are hard done by. In Donegal, tenuously linked to the rest of the Republic by a slender isthmus, they say Dublin forgets them. Certainly much of the county harks back to another age: tiny fields bound by dry-stone walls, the hay cut by scythe then tossed in cocks; a scattering of sheep, woolly dots on a distant, bare, impossibly steep, mountainside.

Bundoran

County Donegal contains seven Blue Flag beaches recognised for their safety as well as the quality and cleanliness of water and recycling facilities. The beaches start at **Bundoran** ⑮, which 30 years ago, was described in an architectural guide as 'a squalid place with little of interest'. In the intervening years the town has worked hard to clean up its act capitalising on its seaside location, marine wildlife and magnificent **Tullan Strand**. It is a popular centre for surfing, with many taking up the challenge offered by 'The Peak', a classic left-hander that runs to about 110 yards/metres and a bodyboarding wave known as three-D. Regular sea angling and sightseeing trips with whale, seal, porpoise and dolphin-watch cruises are available in the summer.

Amongst the family attractions are the **Waterworld and Seaweed Baths** (Sea Front; tel: 071-984 1172; www.waterworldbundoran.com; June–Aug daily noon–6pm, Apr–May Sat–Sun only, noon–6pm), with its wave pools, water slides and sauna and steam rooms.

Rossnowlagh ⑯, Bundoran's smaller quieter cousin round the coast to the north, is a base for surfers. The extensive Blue Flag beach is very popular with families and there are lifeguards on duty during the summer months.

In the one-time garrison town of **Ballyshannon** ⑰, where the waters of the Erne are tamed to produce hydro-electricity, pretty Georgian houses survive and literary folk commemorate the town's most famous son, poet William Allingham (1824–89) remembered for

Good surfing at Bundoran.

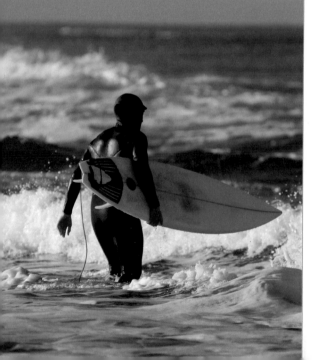

his verse *Up the airy mountain, / Down the rushy glen, / We daren't go a-hunting / For fear of little men.*

The more recent memory of another son of Ballyshannon, the rock musician Rory Gallagher (1948–95), is honoured at the annual **Rory Gallagher International Festival** (www.rorygallagherfestival.com) during the June Bank Holiday weekend, attracting up to 5,000 visitors to the town. Gallagher, who blazed a trail for rock bands, enjoyed a successful solo career selling millions of albums worldwide. His concerts have gone into the pantheon of rock history and his music is enjoying a resurgence of interest.

Inis Saimer, the little island situated in the Erne Estuary is said to be the spot where the first inhabitants of Ireland landed, led by a chieftain from Scythia (near modern Macedonia) around 2,700 BC.

The county town

Donegal ⑱, the lively county town, has a busy triangular 'Diamond' market square, congested with tourist traffic all summer. The town's history has a familiar ring. It has a notable castle (tel: 074-972 2405; www.heritageireland. ie Easter–mid-Sept Mon–Sun 10am–6pm, mid-Sept–Easter Thu–Mon 9.30am–4.30pm). Once an O'Donnell stronghold, it was redesigned, as was the town itself, by the Brookes, planters who took over the land after the O'Donnells were deported in the so-called 'Flight of the Earls' at the turn of the 17th century. In the now ruined O'Donnell-financed Franciscan abbey, south on the estuary of the Eske, monks compiled, in the 1630s, *The Annals of the Four Masters*, tracing Ireland's history back to the time of Noah's granny.

Complementary to tourism, the weaving and making up of tweeds is the main industry, and Magee's, the town's largest shop, is the industry's principal outlet. A mile south, **Donegal Craft Village** (tel: 074-972 2225; www.donegalcraftvillage.com; some workshops closed out of season; free) established in 1985, demonstrates weaving and other craftworks.

Three miles (5km) south of Donegal town, at **Laghy**, the R232 runs

St Patrick's Purgatory, Lough Derg.

DANIEL O'DONNELL

County Donegal's famous son Daniel O'Donnell is world renowned for his unique blend of country and Irish folk music. Born in Dungloe in 1961 and brought up in Kincasslagh, O'Donnell's success has been attributed to his close, friendly relationship with his huge fanbase, and his stage presence.

An initial career founded on a business studies degree was perhaps not the normal grounding for a music legend, but a portfolio of 20 UK Top 40 albums and 15 Top 40 singles unsurprisingly led to him receiving the award of an honorary MBE for services to the music industry in 2002. He has sold over 10 million records.

Today Daniel O'Donnell has returned to his homeland to live and will forever be held an icon in Irish culture.

TIP

Visitors interested in the influence of the Cistercian monks in Ireland can trace their history in the Abbey Water Wheels Visitor Centre at Assaroe, Rossnowlagh (tel: 071-985 1580; Easter week, June–Sept Mon–Sun 11am–7pm, Oct–May Sun only 2.30–7pm; free).

southeast for Pettigo from where the R233 bears north 3 miles (5km) across desolate bog land to **Lough Derg ⓳**, with its tiny Station Island, focal point for a major act of pilgrimage, St Patrick's Purgatory (see page 265). The island, now covered with buildings, looks from a distance like a Canaletto painting and the pilgrims commemorate the 40 days Ireland's saint spent on it, praying, fasting and expelling evil spirits. Many Irish Catholics, especially from the north and west, have spent the required three days of ritual there, walking barefoot, repeating prayers and consuming nothing but black tea and dry toast.

Pilgrims are increasingly coming for 'time': time to pray, time to reflect, time for themselves and time away from their hectic everyday world. An increasing number of men are visiting the island, marking a change from the popular belief that the women came to the island to pray for the men. Figures show that 20,000 pilgrims a year come to Lough Derg – not only from Ireland but also from 35 countries around the world.

Killybegs

The road west from Donegal town runs past Bruckless, where there are live oysters and mussels for sale, then through the fishing port of **Killybegs ⓴** where hefty trawlermen, drinking amongst the Victorian villas, give the town a raffish, frontier air. The Maritime & Heritage Centre (tel: 074-974 1944; www.visitkillybegs.com; Mon–Fri 9.45am–5.30pm; adult €5.00, child €4.00) in the carpet factory building combines the traditions of handknotting carpets and the history of fishing in Ireland's premier port. The centre has installed Ireland's only interactive Navigation Wheelhouse Simulator where one can step into the boots of a seafarer to steer a boat into the harbour.

Kilcar, 7 miles (11km) on along the craggy, beautiful coastline, is another vacation, traditional music and tweed centre somewhat overshadowed by **Ardara** 20 miles (33km) to the northeast. It is rewarding to continue further west over the steep Glengesh Pass through quiet **Carrick,** then turning south for the precipitous drive past

Killybegs harbour.

Teelin to Carrigan Head at the eastern end of 2,000ft (650-metre) **Slieve League** whose sheer cliffs – the highest marine cliffs in Europe – drop a scary 765ft (235 metres) into the indigo sea beyond. An alternative is to leave transport at Teelin, walking the signposted One Man's Pass in the same direction. The views from *Amharc Mór* are, when not shrouded in mists, spectacular – and vertiginous.

For those in need of a calming cup of coffee afterwards the **Slieve League Cultural Centre** houses a tea shop and craft gallery, as well as archaeological, geological and tourist information (tel: 074-973 9077; www. slieveleaguecliffs.ie).

Glencolumbkille

Glencolumbkille ㉑, further west in the lowlands at the head of Glen Bay, represents a landmark in the development of a particular kind of Irish tourism. The idea was devised here that the draughty, cold traditional thatched whitewashed cottage could be upgraded, given central heating, pine furniture, shower, television and fridge and clustered into a marketable group. Purists dismiss it, while its protagonists argue that it sustains life and employment in distressed rural communities. Four cottages in the **Folk Village Museum** (tel: 074-973 0017; www.glenfolkvillage.com; Easter–Sept Mon–Sat 10am–6pm, Sun noon–6pm) present traditional life over the centuries; one cottage, the Shebeen, sells seaweed and fuchsia wine.

Tiny **Port,** hard to reach in the next valley north, demonstrates what happens when a village dies, but most travellers continue northeast the 16 miles (26km) to **Ardara** ㉒, where the Heritage Centre (tel: 074-953 7905, http://www.ardara.ie; Easter–Sept daily 10am–6pm) has a tourist information point, then to Glenties, both awash in season with Northern Ireland's holidaymakers buying Guinness, tweeds, Aran sweaters, salmon flies for the Owena and Owentocker rivers, and tapping their toes to fiddlers.

Drive north of Ardara to the gloriously soft sandy beach at **Nairn** (known as Tramore strand) where sanderlings frequently perform like clockwork toys, and en route you will pass the wind turbine at the Dolmen Centre (Kilclooney, Portnoo; tel: 074-954 5010; www.dolmencentre.com; Mon–Fri 10am–4pm, 7–10pm; free), the first eco-tourism centre in Ireland, which uses the latest in green energy.

North, the N56 continues to **Dungloe,** capital of the Rosses, a raggedly charming peninsula of islands, trout lakes and inlets. From **Burtonport,** 4 miles (6km) northwest, a 25-minute ferry service (tel: 074-952 0532; www.arranmoreferry.com) runs to Arranmore island, 3 miles (5km) offshore, with its 900 souls, dry-stone walls, holiday cottages and an abundance of wildlife. There are a number of activities to enjoy on the island including excellent lake and shore fishing. A brisk walk can be combined with a stop at one of the island's six traditional Irish pubs renowned for their charming atmosphere. The west of the island has many marine caves and stacks carved from solid rock resulting in a spectacular cliff coastline, and there are great views of the mainland from Glen Head.

Ferries for bare and windswept **Tory Island** ㉓ (tel: 074-953 1320; www.toryislandferry.com), a popular tourist destination, run the 15-mile (24km) sea journey regularly from Bunbeg. Home once to Balor, the one-eyed God of Darkness, Tory gave its name (meaning outlaw) to Britain's right-wing political party when it opposed James II in 1680. The island's main village, West Town, has a 51ft (15-metre) round tower and the ruins of two churches. Corncrakes, almost extinct in the rest of Ireland, abound on Tory. This area, like Gweedore to the north, is traditionally Irish speaking.

The dramatic conical quartz mountain north of Dunlewey is **Errigal,** Donegal's highest at 2,466ft (752 metres). The peak south is Slieve Snaght, 200ft (70 metres) less. At the Dunlewey Visitor Centre (tel: 074-953 1699; www.dunleweycentre.com; mid-Mar–Nov Mon–Sun 10.30am–4.30pm; free) the traveller can regress to the mid-20th century within the cottage of Manus Ferry, a renowned Donegal weaver. Boat cruises are available on the lake and visitors are entertained with tall tales of the 'ghost' of the Green Lady.

Dunfanaghy

Twenty-one miles (37km) north on the N56, **Dunfanaghy** ㉔ is a popular resort, especially with golfers, but also offers opportunities for walking, cycling and horse riding. The Dunfanaghy Workhouse (tel: 074-913 6540; www.dunfanaghyworkhouse.ie; Apr Mon–Sat 9.30am–5.30pm, May–Jun & Sep daily 9.30am–5pm, July–Aug 9.30am–5.30pm, Oct–May Mon–Wed 9.30am–4.30pm; free), where people fled from the distress of the famine, was the scene of horrific suffering. Today part of the building has been turned into an interpretative centre and exhibition gallery.

Right next door, the long-established **Art Gallery** (tel: 074-913 6224, www.thegallerydunfanaghy.com) has been attracting visitors for many years, its walls decorated with some of the most evocative and moody images of Donegal captured by contemporary Irish painters.

Tory Island.

Round the coast, the **Falcarragh Visitor Centre** (*An tSean Bheairic*; tel: 074-918 0655; www.falcarraghvisitorcentre.com; Mon–Fri 10am–5pm, Sat 11–5pm; free), fuses culture, heritage, history and tourist information in a former police station.

From Falcarragh, travel southeast 8 miles (13km) along the R255 to walk through the 10,000 acres (400 hectares) of **Glenveagh National Park** ㉕ (tel: 074-913 7090; www.glenveaghnationalpark.ie; charge for castle). The park was given to the nation by Henry McIlhenny whose family made their fortune from Tabasco Sauce.

With its castle and its formal French and Italian gardens mixing with the wild mountains, the park has a further surprise in the Regency-style **Glebe House Gallery** (tel: 074-913 7071; http://glebegallery.ie; daily 11am–6.30pm, closed Fri June–Sept; free), which displays paintings by Degas, Renoir, Picasso and the primitive painters of Tory Island. Much photographed is **Gartan Lough,** 3 miles (5km) south via a narrow bog road. On the shores of Gartan Lough, **Colmcille Heritage Centre** (Churchill, tel: 074-913 7306; www.colmcilleheritagecentre.ie; Easter–Sept Mon–Sat 10.30am–5pm, Sun 1.30–5pm; free) tells the story of the saint through an audio-visual display.

Letterkenny ㉖, the prosperous county town on the River Swilly 10 miles (16km) to the southwest, is useful as a base. Its most prominent landmark is the Cathedral, built in modern Gothic style by local masons using Donegal stone.

A choice of routes

The traveller could turn southeast from Letterkenny and head through little-known east Donegal. If the mood takes you, a tour of the 18th-century courthouse and jail in **Lifford** (tel: 074-914 1733; www.liffordoldcourthouse.com; Mon & Wed 10am–2pm, Tue & Thu–Fri 10am–3.30pm) will fill you in on the severe punishment meted out and the grim conditions endured by the inmates.

At **Raphoe**, a well-signposted 20-minute drive from Letterkenny off the N13, those interested in archaeology will want to inspect the impressive 64-stone **Beltany Stone Circle,** a Celtic ritual site (tel: 074-912 1160). Back on the N13 travelling south, the road transverses the rugged Barnesmore Gap, a scenic mountain pass that cuts through the Blue Stack Mountains. For centuries the gap has been a strategic gateway between northern and southern parts of County Donegal, hence, up to about 1800, it was the notorious haunt of brigands and highwaymen.

To the north of Letterkenny a choice of routes presents itself. One option is to follow the N56 southeast from Dunfanaghy, then take the R245 north chasing the Atlantic Drive past the golfer's haven of Rosapenna around Mulroy Bay with its farmed mussel rafts and salmon cages. Continue around windswept Fanad Head, then south again to Rathmullan, from whence, in 1607, the leading clan chiefs took flight by ship for Spain. Their story is recalled in the **Flight of**

The castle at Glenveagh National Park.

WHERE

Tourism in the Inishowen area has been boosted by the Foyle Ferry between Greencastle and Magilligan Point in Co. Derry. A shuttle service operates on the route, weather permitting, from mid-March to September. (074-938 1901; www.loughfoyleferry.com). In summer a regular ferry service also operates across Lough Swilly from Buncrana on the west side of Inishowen across to Rathmullan on the Fanad peninsula. Both options avoid the long drive around the lough shores.

Malin Head.

the **Earls Heritage Centre** (tel: 074-915 8131; June–Sept Mon–Sat 10am–6pm, Sun 12.30–6pm).

Beyond, 7 miles (11km) southwest, is charmingly preserved, riverside **Ramelton,** in whose Heritage Centre you can find your local roots – should you have any – in Donegal Ancestry (tel: 074-915 1266; www.donegalancestry.com; June–Sept Mon–Sat 10am–1pm, 2pm–1pm, Sun noon–4pm; free): thence to Letterkenny again. From here it's a tempting run northwest, for 16 miles (26km), to the 4,000-year-old **Grianán of Aileach,** a spectacular circular stone enclosure atop an 800ft (240-metre) mound. Its name is translated, controversially, as 'sun-palace'.

Buncrana

Even more tempting now is the drive 40 miles (64km) north to Ireland's most northerly point, **Malin Head** on the **Inishowen Peninsula**. On the way there are a number of attractions to entice the visitor. Along the shores of Lough Swilly, military historians will want to see the Fort Dunree

Military Museum (tel: 074-936 1817; www.dunree.pro.ie; Mon–Sat 10.30am–6pm, Sun 1–6pm; adult 7. Child €5) near **Buncrana** which has a heritage centre with an underground bunker and an extensive collection of military artefacts and memorabilia.

Further along, near Ballyliffin, stop off at the **Doagh Island Famine Village** (tel: 074-937 8078; www.doaghfaminevillage.com; Easter–Sept daily 10am–5pm; adult €6, children free) where the charge includes a guided tour with tea and coffee, soda bread and biscuits for a thought-provoking look at the past.

The **Inishowen Maritime Museum and Planetarium** (tel: 074-938 1363; www.inishowenmaritime.com; Easter–Sept daily 9.30am–5.30pm, Winter Mon–Fri 9.15am–5.30pm) is drawing in visitors to Greencastle. As well as the emphasis on astronomy, dazzling laser light shows are performed live here every weekend in summer, accompanied by recorded traditional and modern Irish music.

Most of Buncrana's many pubs have live music at weekends.

Northern Ireland

0   10 km
0   10 miles

ATLANTIC OCEAN

Malin Head

Inishtrahull So

Ballyhillin

Urbalreagh

Glengad Head

Dunmore Hea

Kinnac

Bay

Doagh Island Famine Village

Malin

Carndonagh Cross

Gleneely

Stroov

Greencastle

Tory Island

West Town

Tory Sound

Fanad Head

Dunaff Head

Pollan Bay

Ballyliffin

Carndonagh

Clonmany

Glasmullan

Slieve Snaght

615

Castle Carry

Moville

Lough Foyle

Mag

Melmore Head

Atlantic Drive

Fortsalon

Inishbofin

Horn Head

Downings

Portnablagh

Cranford

Magheroarty

Dunfanaghy

Falcarragh

Ards Forest Park

Doe Castle

Glen Lough

Cresburgh

Rathmullan

Magherabane

Slieve Snaght 483

Scalp Mountain

Inch Island

Burnfoot

Muff

White Castle

Lima

Bloody Foreland

Brinlack

Gortahork

Gola Island

Muckish Mountain 670

Milford

Lough Fern

Termon

Speenage

Buncrana

Inishowen

Eglinton

Tormeady Point

Rosses Bay

Gweedore

Annagry

The Rosses

Errigal 752

Glenveagh National Park

Dunlewy

St Colmcille Oratory

Kilmacrenan

Ramelton

Grianán of Aileach

Earhart Centre

Derry

Ballykelly

Glenhead

Owey Island

Bunbeg

Loughanure

Slieve Snaght 663

Gartan L.

Church Hill

Ellistrin

Manorcunningham

New Buildings

A6

Ardmore

Ness Wood

Ballym

Aran or Aranmore Island

Burtonport

Ballintra

Dunloe

Letterkenny (Leitir Ceanainn)

St Johnston

N13

Claudy

Magheraroarty

Crohy Head

Commeen

Kingarrow

Rashedoge

Raphoe

Rossgeir

Dunnamanagh

Mountcastle

Park

Sperrin Mts

Doocharry

Fintown

Cark Mountain 366

Convoy

Lifford

Carnanreagh

Mount Hamilton

Gweebarra Bay

Lettermacaward

L. Finn

Finn

Drumnacross

Kilross

Rossgeir

Beltany Stone Circle

Strabane

Dergalt

Glenelly Valley

Sperri

Heritage

Centre

Portnoo

Nairn

Aghla Mt 596

Bellanamore

Welchtown

Castlefinn

Sion Mills

Plumbridge

Scotch Town

Dawros Head

Maas

Glenties

Commeen

Ballybofey

Cross Roads

Killen

Ardstraw

Gortin

Mullaghcarn 542

Greencastle

A505

Cre

Wellb

Beetling

Slievetooey 443

Ardara

Tangaveane

Lavagh More 672

Carnaween 521

Croaghnageer 547

Donegal

Castlederg

Newtownstewart

Drumlegagh

Killeter

Killen

Ulster American Folk Park

Gortin Glen Forest Park

Port

Glengesh Pass

Meentullynagar

Croagh

Letterbarra

Lough Eske

Blue Stack Mts

St Patrick's Purgatory

NORTHERN

Tappaghan Mt 336

Sixmilec

Glencolumbkille

Crove

Inver

Donegal

Lough Derg

Tievemore

Lack 336

Gortaclare

Omagh

Slieve League 601

Carrick

Killybegs

Bruckless

Laghy

Pettigo

Kesh

IRELAND

Dromore

Fintona

Garvaghy

Teelin

Kilcar

Mac Swyne's Bay

Doorin Point

Rossnowlagh

N15

Castle Caldwell

White Island

Boa Island

Castle Archdale Country Park

A32

Augher

Carrigan Head

Fintragh Bay

St John's Point

Belleek

R. Erne

Cliff's of Magho

Lower

Lough

Irvinestown

Killadeas

Kilskeery

Aughta

Donegal Bay

Ballyshannon

Bundoran

Mullaghmore Head

Mullaghmore

Kinlough

Lough Navar Forest Park

Tully

Erne

Killadeas

Tempo

Slieve Beagh 371

Em

Inishmurray

Streedagh Point

Cliffony

Creevykeel Court Cairn

Grange

Benbulben 526

Lough Melvin

Garrison

Derrygonnelly

Monea

Devenish Island

Enniskillen

Fivemiletown

Lissadell House

Rosses Point

Drumcliff

Dartry Mts

Glencar L.

Rossinver

Leckanarainey

Lough Macnean Upper

Castle Coole

A4

Ballyconnell

Raghly

Sligo Bay

Sligo (Sligeach)

Parke's Castle

Manorhamilton

Belcoo

Lough Macnean Lower

Macnean

Florence Court

A509

Maguiresbridge

Lisnaskea

Derrynawilt

Monag (Muineac

Strandhill

Knocknarea 328

Gill

Innisfree

Dromahair

Glenfarne

Marble Arch Caves

Florence Court Forest Park

Drumcard

Lough Erne

Newtownbutler

Clones

Smithbor

Dromard

Carrowmore

Ballysadare

Ballintogher

Drumkeeran

Dowra

Tiltinbane 592

Glengevlin 655

Derrylin

Swanlinbar

Teemora

Wattle Bridge

Swan

Cross Roa

Coolaney

Colooney

Derryhacreeve

Source of the Shannon

Slieve Rushen 405

Belturbet

Scotshouse

Bellamon House

Sligo

Ropefield

Sligo Folk Park

Heapstown Cairn

N4

Lough Allen

Ballinagleragh

Iron Mts

Benbrack 496

Bencroy or Gubnaveagh 519

Slieve Anierin 586

Ballyconnell

N3

Cootehil

Templehouse Lake

N17

Ballymote

Geevagh

Ballinamore

Garadice Lough

Killashandra

Doogary

Bellanacaroy

Tobercurry

Carrowkeel Cemetery 321

Castlebaldwin

Lough Arrow

Drumshanbo

Leitrim

Corrigeenroe

Roscommon

Garvagh

Carriggallen

Cornafean

Cavan (An Cabhán)

Canningstown

Cava

Bunnananddan

Ballinafad

Curlew Mts

Lough Key

Knockvicar

Carrick-on-Shannon

Drumsna

Cloone Grange

Arvagh

Cross Keys

Gorteen

Mayo

Lough Gara

Boyle

Lough Key Forest Park

N4

Longford

Garvah

R. Erne

Bellananagh

Athlone

Mapped numbered markers: ① Derry, ② Strabane, ③ Omagh, ④ Ulster American Folk Park, ⑦ Castle Coole, ⑧ Devenish Island, ⑨ White Island, ⑩ Cliff's of Magho, ⑪ Marble Arch Caves

REPUBLIC OF

NORTHERN IRELAND

Northern Ireland's traditional attractions are as alluring as ever with its gorgeous lakes and glens, stunning coastline and wealth of golf courses.

Both the Republic and Northern Ireland are part of the EU, and the peace process has bought more stability to a quiet rural area that has many scenic attractions and where political unrest was always a localised affair. In fact, it can be hard to tell when you've crossed the border but slowly you'll notice that post boxes and phone booths are no longer green but red, and prices have changed from euros to pounds...

The troublesome border

One reason it is so difficult to be sure of the border's exact location is that it snakes its way along 18th-century county boundaries through farming land that is sometimes bleak, more often beautiful. It takes little account of natural boundaries, such as rivers, or of the cultural differences that separate Republican-minded Roman Catholics and British-oriented Protestants. A priest may find part of his parish on one side of the border, the rest on the other. Houses straddle it so that, as the joke has it, a man may sleep with his head in the United Kingdom and his heart in the Republic of Ireland.

Political expediency accounts for the absurdities. It had been intended to redraw the border rationally after partition in 1920, and a Boundary Commission was set up to advise. But in the end the British and Irish

governments, hoping to avoid further trouble, suppressed the commission's report and left things as they were. Had they decided differently, much of the subsequent conflict might have been averted.

It should be noted that the terms 'Ulster' and 'Northern Ireland' are not synonymous. Whereas the ancient Irish province of Ulster consisted of nine counties, the new state of Northern Ireland, popularly known as Ulster, consisted of only six: **Antrim, Down, Armagh, Derry, Fermanagh**

Main Attractions

Derry City
Ulster-American Folk Park
Enniskillen Castle
Mourne Mountains
Downpatrick
Strangford Lough
Mount Stewart
Ulster Folk and Transport Museum
Causeway Coastal Road
Giant's Causeway

Dual signage in Armagh.

Derry's symbolic Hands Across the Divide sculpture by Maurice Harron.

and **Tyrone**. Yet the three counties that went to the Republic – **Donegal**, **Cavan** and **Monaghan** – are still bound to the other six by firm family and trading ties. To many locals, the border is an abstraction, or perhaps an approximation: the states it divides do not agree about its length, the Republic claiming it is 280 miles (448km) and Northern Ireland authorities adamant that it is 303 miles (485km).

Old Derry's walls

Across the border from Donegal, is the county of Londonderry and its famously friendly chief city, Northern Ireland's second, whose very name has long been a bone of contention for its main two communities. Catholics refer to Derry, for both county and city, while Protestants stick to Londonderry, with officialdom increasingly resorting to the clumsy **Derry-Londonderry** ❶ in a nervous effort to maintain neutrality For its year as the inaugural UK City of Culture in 2013 adopted the slogan 'Let's make it LegenDerry', but its official title was the hyphenated

Derry-Londonderry. The year 2013 was also the 400th anniversary of the building of the 20-ft-tall walls that still surround the city. Derry-Londonderry has undergone considerable development since 1998, which was crowned in 2011 by the spectacular €14.5m **Peace Bridge** ❹, a graceful self-anchored suspension bridge for cyclists and pedestrians. The beautiful bridge across the River Foyle has transformed Derry's skyline, and is seen as a symbolic unification of all communities living in the city. Its citizens take a matter-of-fact approach to its troubled history, and enjoy explaining its complex loyalties to visitors.

There has been a renaissance in community activity, especially in the arts, and it has made great efforts to oblige the visitor with an annual calendar of attractions and festivals such as the massive Halloween Carnival, and the City of Derry Jazz and Big Band Festival in April/May. As with many border towns and cities in Northern Ireland, you'll find a general acceptance of euros if you're travelling from the Republic.

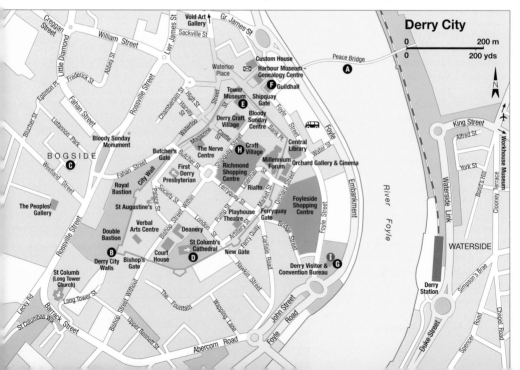

Derry City

The city's growth was financed by London guilds, which in 1613 began creating the last walled city in Europe. Its purpose was mercantile success and you can still see traces of its former economic confidence in the ornamental facades of the old shirt-making factories, which provided the city with its livelihood for generations.

The **Derry City Walls** (www.derryvisitor.com; free access), 20ft (6 metres) thick and complete with watchtowers and cannon such as the 18-pounder **Roaring Meg** (dating from 1642), are marvellously intact.

The Bogside

Two 17th-century sieges failed to breach the walls, earning the sobriquet 'maiden city'. Some say the city still has a siege mentality; a theory reinforced by the IRA's daubed slogan 'You are now entering Free Derry'. This was the name given to the **Bogside** ⓒ, a densely populated Roman Catholic housing estate, when its inhabitants barricaded it against the police in 1969. Their grievances were old ones. After Ireland's partition in 1920, the city's governing Unionists had fixed constituency boundaries to ensure a 'permanent' majority for themselves in what was a mainly nationalist area – an artificial majority that wasn't overturned until the mid-1970s. Feeling isolated from the prosperous eastern counties, Derry's citizens built up both a wonderful community spirit and a resentment that finally boiled over. A good way to experience the political history of the Bogside is to visit the **The Peoples' Gallery** (46 Derry Street; mobile tel: 075 1405 2481; www.bogsideartists.com; free), in the centre of the area. Guided tours of all 12 murals by the artists who created them can be booked in advance. For more on the people's story of the civil rights movement, visit the Museum of Free Derry (tel: 028-7136 0880; www.museumoffreederry.org; Mon–Fri 9.30am–4.30pm, Apr–Sept Sat 1–4pm, also July–Sept Sun 1–4pm).

The most famous siege – which is still commemorated by Protestant marches today – took place in 1689, when the Catholic forces of James II blockaded the Protestant supporters of William of Orange for 15 weeks, almost forcing them into submission. About 7,000 of the 30,000 people packed within the city's walls died of disease or starvation. One member of the besieged garrison chillingly recorded the selling prices of horseflesh, dogs' heads, cats and rats 'fattened by eating the bodies of the slain Irish'.

The city's eventual relief is depicted on the siege memorial window of **St Columb's Cathedral** ⓓ (London Street; tel: 028-7126 7313; www.stcolumbscathedral.org; donation) a graceful 17th-century Anglican church built in 'Planter's Gothic' style. The chapter house contains siege relics. Outside the walls, off Bishop Street Without, **St Columba's Long Tower Church** (tel: 028-7126 2301; free), built 1784, and known just as Long Tower Church, has a lavish interior.

The Planter's Gothic-style St Columb's Cathedral.

Celtic, a Scottish football team, has a historic connection with the people of Ireland.

Derry's Guildhall.

Celebrating Hallowe'en in downtown Derry.

The award-winning **Tower Museum** ❸ (tel: 028-7137 2411; www.derrycity.gov.uk/museums; daily 10am–5.30pm, adult £4.00 child £2.00) skilfully uses audio-visuals and photography to tell its story from both sides of the sectarian divide. There's also an exhibition on the recovery of a ship from the 1588 Spanish Armada, wrecked off Donegal's coast.

The Guildhall

Streets from the city's original four gates (Shipquay, Ferryquay, Bishop's and Butcher's) converge on The Diamond, a perversely square-shaped market place at the top of Shipquay Street, the steepest main thoroughfare in Ireland. At the bottom of the street, the **Guildhall** ❺ (Guildhall Square; tel: 028-7137 7335, www.derrycity.gov.uk/Guildhall; daily 10am–5.30pm; free), one of those Tudor-Gothic structures popular in Northern Ireland, clearly shows the influence of the London merchants.

Behind the Guildhall is Derry Quay, celebrated in song by hundreds of thousands of emigrants who sailed down the Foyle from here, bound for a new life in America.

Across the river, is the old **Workhouse**, which opened in 1840 and was once home to 800 inmates. It was open right up until 1948, when it became a hospital. In later years, it operated as a museum.

There are now various tours to guide you around the city and its environs. The best place to enquire about these and all other tourist information is the **Derry Visitor and Convention Bureau** ❻ (44 Foyle Street; tel: 028-7126 7284; www.derryvisitor.com; free), who also run their own walking tours of the city.

VOID (Patrick Street; tel: 028-7130 8080; www.derryvoid.com; free) showcases both established Irish and international artists in some eight exhibitions a year in its two galleries and six studios, while the **Verbal Arts Centre** (Stable Lane and Mall Wall, Bishop Street Within; tel: 028-7126 6946; www.verbalartscentre.co.uk) is the only centre in Ireland dedicated to storytelling, both verbal and written. Many in the city's resurgent arts community have links to the **Nerve Centre** (7–8 Magazine Street; tel: 028-7126 0562; www.nervecentre. org), which also stages live music and film festivals, and arts activities. A dynamic programme of events from drama and dance to comedy and musicals is hosted at the **Millennium Forum** (tel: 028-7126 4455; www. millenniumforum.co.uk) and the renovated **Playhouse** (tel: 028-7126 8027; www.derryplayhouse.co.uk).

Shoppers will find plenty to keep them occupied but perhaps the most engaging destination is the Derry **Craft Village** on Shipquay Street, a historic reconstruction of an 18th-century street and a 19th-century square with artisan craft shops, restaurants, bars, exhibitions and live music.

Small-town Tyrone

Thirteen miles (21km) southwest of Derry city, in county Tyrone on the A5 is **Strabane** ❷, a border town paired with Lifford on the Donegal side. In the 18th century Strabane was an important centre for publishing. John Dunlap, printer of America's Declaration of Independence, trained in **Gray's Printing Press** (49 Main Street; tel: 028-8674 8210; restricted opening times, call for details). It's worth the effort if for its intriguing display of ink, galleys, presses and the story of Dunlap's emigration. In Dergalt, 2 miles (3km) to the southeast, signposted off the B47, is a whitewashed cottage, the **Woodrow Wilson** Ancestral Home (tel: 028-7138 4444; www.derrystrabane.com; July–Aug Tue–Sun 2–5pm; free).

Sion Mills, 3 miles (5km) south of Strabane, is a village whose name betrays its origins. The linen-workers' old cottages are charming. The Parish Church of the Good Shepherd is a striking Italian-style edifice, contrasting with the modern architecture of St Teresa's Catholic Church, whose facade displays an image on slate of the Last Supper.

As you drive into **Omagh** ❸, the county town of Tyrone, 16 miles (25km) along the A5, the religious fragmentation of Northern Ireland is immediately apparent. On the right is the Presbyterian Church (Trinity); on

TIP

At the Tower Museum is the Derry Genealogy Centre (tel: 028-7137 7331; www.derry.roots ireland.ie), which will, for a fee, assist those tracing their roots in Co. Derry and the Inishowen Peninsula of Donegal.

Peace Bridge, Derry.

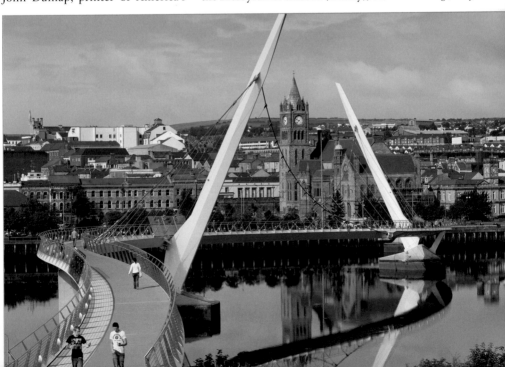

Ulster-American Folk Park.

the left, the Methodist Church; next, St Columba's Church of Ireland; then the Gothic spires of the Roman Catholic Church of the Sacred Heart, a poor man's Chartres Cathedral. There are many more. The joining of the rivers Camowen and Drumragh to form the Strule make the location pleasant enough, but Omagh is more a town for living (and praying) in than for visiting. Locals still recall the Saturday afternoon in August 1998 when a maroon Vauxhall Astra exploded in the town, killing 29 people. In its shops, alongside the usual linen souvenirs, are plaques and statuettes made of turf (peat). This is cut from the **Black Bog** between Omagh and Cookstown, 27 miles (43km) to the east.

American connections

During tough times in the 1800s, the area's strong Scots-Presbyterian work ethic spurred many to seek their fortune in America. The results were remarkable and Northern Ireland claims that 11 US presidents have had roots in the province: Andrew Jackson, James Knox Polk, Andrew Johnson, James Buchanan, Ulysses S. Grant, Chester Alan Arthur, Grover Cleveland, Benjamin Harrison, William McKinley, Theodore Roosevelt and Woodrow Wilson. Many Americans visit to seek out ancestral homes.

The Mellon banking family of Pittsburgh, having traced their roots to 4 miles (6km) north of Omagh, off the A5, endowed the **Ulster-American Folk Park** ❹ (tel: 028-8224 3292; nmni.com/uafp; Mar–Jun & Sep Tue–Sun 10am–5pm, Jul–Aug daily 10am–5pm, Oct–Feb Tue–Fri 10am–4pm, Sat–Sun 11pm–4pm; free) on the site at Camphill as part of Northern Ireland's contribution to the bicentenary of America. To illuminate the transition made by the 18th-century emigrants, craftsmen's cottages, a schoolhouse, a blacksmith's forge and a Presbyterian meeting-house from the Old World have been rebuilt on a peat bog alongside log cabins, a Pennsylvania farmstead and a covered wagon from the New World. Peat is kept burning in the cottages, and there are demonstrations of candle-making, fish-salting and horse-shoeing as well as periodic 'living history' recreations of battles between redcoats and native Americans. An indoor exhibit recreates the main street of an Ulster town 100 years ago, its hardware shop displaying foot warmers and lamp wicks. A replica of an emigrant ship links the continents. There's not a whiff of Disney, due to the attention to detail, though the American 'half' looks more prosperous than the original settlers found it. The award-winning park has a number of annual celebrations, including Fourth of July and an Appalachian and bluegrass festival.

A Centre for Migration Studies on the site has a reference library open to the public for research and staff will help with enquiries about migration history.

Relics of old industries

There's nothing Northern Ireland likes better than history, and almost every village in Tyrone – Castlederg, Donaghmore, Fivemiletown, Newtownstewart – has its heritage centre. One of the more interesting is along the A505 from Omagh. The An Creagan

Visitor Centre in **Creggan** (tel: 028-8076 1112; www.an-creagan.com; free), at the foothills of the blue-tinged Sperrin Mountains, hosts an interpretative exhibition of the area, craft shop, bar/restaurant, self-catering cottages and regular cultural events.

Dungannon

In and around **Dungannon** ❺, 13 miles (21km) south of Cookstown and once the seat of the great O'Neill clan, there are several attractions. One of the more atmospheric places to shop here is the Linen Green (1 The Linen Green; tel: 028-8775 3761; www.thelinengreen.co.uk; Mon–Sat 9.30m–5.30pm) in Moygashel, on the fringes of the town. Based in an old linen mill, it includes brands such as Foxford, Anthologie Homeware and Newbridge Silverware. Less than 2 miles (3km) from Dungannon is the village of **Castlecaulfield**, created in the 17th century by Sir Toby Caulfield as part of the Ulster Plantation. It contains the remains of his mansion, where Oliver Plunkett is said to have preached.

Old advertisement at the Ulster-American Folk Park.

The bluegrass festival at Ulster American Folk Park.

FACT

Just a few miles east of Dungannon, Peatlands Park is rich in insects, particularly butterflies, moths, dragonflies and damselflies. Many woodland and wetland birds and several species of waterfowl nest here. Grey squirrels, badgers and hares are also here, while lizards and newts can be found in the open bog areas.

Beaghmore is a complex of early Bronze Age megalithic features, stone circles and cairns.

Signposted from the M1 motorway, exit 13, 7 miles (11km) east of Dungannon, is **Peatlands Park** (tel: 028-3839 9195; open access to pedestrians at all times; car park: April–May & 16th Sept–Oct daily 9am–7pm, June–15th Sept daily 9am–9pm, Nov–Mar 9am–4.30pm) is a preserved Irish bog with over 16km (10 miles) of marked pathways to explore.

Take the A45 from Dungannon and on the outskirts of Coalisland you will find **the Coalisland Enterprise Centre**, with its celebration of the Irish bog, the Island Turf Crafts Gift Shop And Visitor Centre (tel: 028-8774 9041; www.islandturfcrafts.com; Mon–Fri 9.30am–5.30pm, Sat 10.30–5pm). There's an indoor bog, a museum exploring Ireland before and after the Ice Age and a shop selling turf crafts. Also at the Enterprise Centre is the **Irish World** genealogy centre (tel: 028-8774 6065; www.irish-world.com), which offers a range of services to people tracing ancestors in Tyrone and Fermanagh, and the **Craic Theatre Company** (tel: 028-8774 1100; www.craicartscentre.co.uk). Perhaps

Northern Ireland's only (non-council-owned) community theatre, Craic stages everything from Shakespeare to musicals, plus visiting productions from the likes of Dubbeljoint at its 200-seat theatre.

Main Street Cookstown

Twenty-five miles (40km) east of Omagh, **Cookstown** ❻, the exact middle of Northern Ireland, is renowned for its main street, 2 miles (3km) long and 160ft (50 metres) wide, and can be located from miles away by the 200ft (61-metre) spire of the Gothic-style Catholic church. The town has a strong tradition of nationalism, often refined in its many old-fashioned pubs. Local livestock sales give a good insight into the rough amiability of the rural Ulster character. Four miles (7km) west, the water-powered **Wellbrook Beetling Mill** (tel: 028-8675 1735; www.nationaltrust.org.uk; Mar–Sep Sat–Sun 2–5pm, adult £5.00, children free) has demonstrations of linen processing by costumed guides. Three miles north of Cookstown, at Moneymore, is a rare treat for lovers of historic costumes. A National Trust property, the 17th-century **Springhill House** (tel: 028-8674 8210; www.nationaltrust.org.uk; Grounds year round daily 10am–5pm; House mid-Mar–June Sat–Sun noon–5pm, July–Aug daily noon–5pm, Sept Sat–Sun noon–5pm; adult £5.00, child £2.27) has acquired an award-winning collection of costumes dating from 1690 to the 1930s. The impressive grounds, which house a children's adventure playground, are open daily all year. Look out for the allegedly friendly ghost, Olivia Lenox-Conyngham, a one-time inhabitant of the house.

Many Neolithic graves and stone circles are sprinkled around both towns. The best are at **Beaghmore** (free access), 10 miles (16km) west of Cookstown, off the A505. Villages such as **Clogher** and **Coagh**, **Moneymore** and **Pomeroy** are noted for fine traditional musicians and a variety of

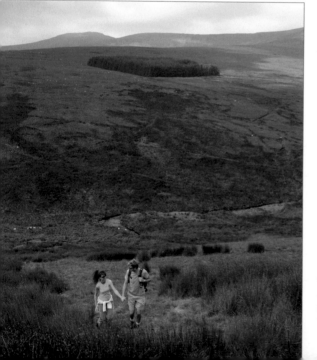

ecclesiastical architecture. There's a run-down air about some, the result of chronic unemployment. But it's as well to remember writer John Broderick's advice in *The Pilgrimage*: 'The city dweller who passes through a country town and imagines it sleepy and apathetic is very far from the truth: it is watchful as the jungle.'

The poet Seamus Heaney is celebrated near his native village at the 17th-century fortified house Bellaghy Bawn (Bellaghy; tel: 028-7938 6812; www.doeni.gov.uk/niea; Sun noon–4pm). Much of Heaney's poetry derives its imagery and colloquial language from his rural upbringing in this part of Northern Ireland.

Ulster's Lakeland

To the southwest, **Fermanagh**, adjacent to Monaghan and Cavan, has many things in common with them, particularly its tempo. Politically it is part of Northern Ireland and is the province's lakeland playground: a third of it is under water. But political divisions are less of a barrier these days: the restoration of the Ballinamore–Ballyconnell cross-border canal means that you can now travel all the way here from Limerick by inland waterway.

Enniskillen

The county town, **Enniskillen** ❼, a Protestant stronghold since Tudor times, is built on an island between two channels of the River Erne as it flows from **Upper** to **Lower Lough Erne**. In summer, pleasure boats (*MV Kestrel*, Round O Quay; tel: 028-6632 2882; www.ernetoursltd.com; June–Aug daily 2.15 and 4.15pm, May, Sept, Oct on Tue, Sat, Sun; with exceptions) ply the lakes, and visitors cruise them in hired craft (Manor House Marine, Killadeas; tel: 028-6862 8100; www.manor marine.com).

The town's strategic importance is shown by **Enniskillen Castle** (tel: 028-6632 5000; www.enniskillencastle.co. uk; July–Aug Mon & Sat–Sun 2–5pm Tue–Fri 10am–5pm, May–June & Sept Mon & Sat 2–5pm Tue–Fri 10am–5pm, Mon–Sat, Oct–Apr Mon–Fri 2–5pm). The earliest parts date from the 15th century and the imposing

TIP

The best introduction to Seamus Heaney's rich and allusive poetry is through his early collections *Death of a Naturalist* (1966) and *North* (1979). In 1999 he published an acclaimed translation of the Old English heroic poem *Beowulf*.

Uncrowded cruising on Fermanagh's lakes.

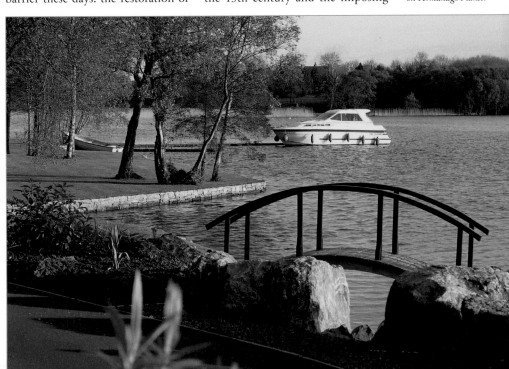

water gate from the late 16th century. The castle houses two museums, one specialising in prehistory, the other in military relics.

Enniskillen is rich in small bakeries and butcher's shops, and there's a gossipy atmosphere as farmers mix with townsfolk in **Blakes of the Hollow** (http://blakesofthehollow.com), one of the North's finest pubs. A secret is soon shared in such a place. Confusingly, the main street, best viewed from the head of the 108 stairs of **Cole's Monument** (Forthill Park; tel: 028-6632 3110; May–Sept Sat–Sun 1–3pm) changes its name six times between the bridges at either end. One of the best-preserved towns in Northern Ireland, Enniskillen has several appealing areas, not least the **Buttermarket** (Mon–Sat 10am–5.30pm) in the centre, a restored 19th-century courtyard specialising in crafts and art galleries.

A true taste of the region's flavour can be gained by circling Lower Lough Erne by road or by boat. **Devenish Island ❽** (Centre open Easter–August daily 10am–6pm; www.discovernorthern ireland.com/Ferry-to-Devenish-Island) is reached by ferry from Trory Point, signposted 3 miles (5km) north of the town at the A32/B82 junction. It is the best known of the lough's 97 islands because of its elaborate, well-preserved round tower, which you can climb by internal ladders. Close by are the decorative ruins of the 12th-century Augustinian abbey of St Mary.

Ten miles (16km) northwest of Enniskillen, **Castle Archdale Country Park** (tel: 028-6862 1588; www. ni-environment.gov.uk/archdale; Visitor Centre Sun noon–4pm, park: daily 9am–5pm; free) has pony trekking, boating and 230 acres (90 hectares) of lovely parkland with walks and cycle rides. The Archdale Centre is in the last remaining part of Archdale Manor House, the courtyard buildings. A ferry departs from Castle Archdale Park Marina (tel: 028-6862 1892, www.castlearchdaleboathire.com; Mar–Jun & Sep Sat–Sun 10am–6pm, July–Aug daily 10am–6pm) for **White Island** with its 12th-century church along one wall along which are lined up eight mysterious pagan statues, discovered only in the 20th century.

Fishing by Enniskillen Castle.

Their origins fox experts; some speculate that seven may represent the deadly sins.

A few miles on, past the village of **Kesh** is the strangest of all local stone figures: the two-faced Janus on **Boa Island ⑨**, which is joined to the mainland by a bridge at each end (see box).

Following the lough's shoreline, you reach **Pettigo**, an old plantation town once the railhead for pilgrims visiting the holy sites at **Lough Derg**, across the border in Co. Donegal. The River Termon, running through Pettigo, marks the border and is said to be stuffed full of bilingual trout. It is also said that when a man had his skull fatally cracked during a fist fight in the middle of the bridge a surveyor had to be called to determine whether he had died within the jurisdiction of the Northern police or the Republic's gardaí. An oak tree on one side of the bridge was planted in 1853 to mark the British victory at Sebastopol. A statue on the other side commemorates four IRA men who died fighting the British in 1922.

Castle Caldwell

Castle Caldwell (tel: 028-6634 3165; daily dawn–dusk; free access), on the A47 4 miles (6km) east of Belleek, a ruined 17th-century castle by the loughside nearby, has become the centrepiece of a working forest, popular with picnickers and bird watchers. It's one of a number of areas where modern growth is being cut back and ancient woodland regenerated. A fiddler who, the worse for drink, fell off a barge and drowned is remembered on a fiddle-shaped monument with a cautionary verse that ends: *On firm land only exercise your skill. There you may play and safely drink your fill.*

The border touches the River Erne again at **Belleek ⑩**, where anglers assure you that you can hook a salmon in the Republic and land it in Northern Ireland. It was after inheriting nearby Castle Caldwell estate in 1849 that John Caldwell Bloomfield discovered all the requisite ingredients to make pottery. He located his new company in Belleek in 1857 (it celebrated 150 years in 2007), and with many changes of ownership since,

The two-faced Janus carving on Boa Island.

ANCIENT MONUMENTS

In most countries, a find such as the ancient Janus statue on Boa Island would have been turned into a major tourist attraction. Here, you have to watch for an easily missable road sign pointing to 'Caldragh Cemetery' (free access), then tramp through cowpats down a farm lane until you come across a field full of overgrown, moss-covered gravestones, in the middle of which lurks the inscrutable Celtic figure. The lack of refurbishment makes the place feel splendidly eerie; you notice the figure's sexual arousal and the hollow in its head and wonder whether that hollow once held sacrificial blood.

A second Janus figure was discovered on the little island of Lustybeg, near the small village of Kesh. There are holiday chalets for hire on this island.

Belleek Pottery.

Marble Arch Caves.

Belleek Pottery is still thriving. Today, the Visitor Centre (tel: 028-6865 9300; www.belleek.com/uk/belleek-visitors-centre; July–Sept Mon–Sat 9am–6pm, Sat 10am–6pm, Sun noon–6pm,Oct–Dec & Mar–June Mon–Fri 9am–5.30pm, Sat 10am–5.30pm, Sun 2–5.30pm, Jan–Feb Mon–Fri 9am–5.30pm; tours every half-an-hour 9.30am–4pm; free) at the distinctive 1893 factory building is one of Ireland's most popular attractions with a museum, showroom, tearoom and audio-visual display.

You can take the scenic drive back to Enniskillen along the south side of the lough, stopping 5 miles (8km) northwest of Derrygonnelly on the A46 at **Lough Navar Forest Park** (tel: 028-6634 3165; daily 10am–dusk; free access), where a lookout point offers a panorama of five counties. Peregrine falcons and merlins are among various birds flying overhead, while plentiful deer herds graze. Two monuments here commemorate the crew of two American seaplanes that crashed locally during World War II. At **Tully**, off the A46, 3 miles (5km) north of the village,

is one well-preserved 17th-century castle (Sun noon–4pm; free) whilst at **Monea**, 7 miles (11km) northwest of Enniskillen on the B81, is another with free access at all times.

Marble Arch Caves

'Over 300 million years of history' – impressive even by Irish standards – is the slogan used to promote **Marble Arch Caves** (Marlbank, Florencecourt; tel: 028-6634 8855; www.marblearchcaves.net; Mar–June and Sept daily 10am–4.30pm, July–Aug 10am–5pm), a network of limestone chambers containing remarkable stalactites. A 75-minute tour includes an underground boat journey. The 'Moses Walk' is so called because the dammed walkway has been created through a lake, with more than a metre of water on either side.

Twelve miles (20km) southwest of Enniskillen, the caves are reached by following the A4 southwest for 3 miles (5km), then following signposts after branching off on the A32 towards Swanlinbar. The complex includes car parking, souvenir shop and restaurant and you can get information on the nearby **Cuilcagh Mountain Park**, designated alongside Marble Arch Caves as a Unesco Global Geopark.

Florence Court

Florence Court (tel: 028-6634 8249; www.nationaltrust.org.uk; house: May–Sept daily 11am–5pm, Mar–Apr and Oct Sat–Sun only, with exceptions, grounds: daily 10am–dusk) is a beautiful 18th-century mansion 4 miles (6km) back. Contents include fine rococo plasterwork and 18th-century furniture. The grounds include an ice house, a water-powered sawmill, a walled garden, extensive park and woodland and a yew tree reputed to be the parent of all Irish yew trees. You can sample home-made delights served in the Stable restaurant.

Two miles (3km) southeast of Enniskillen on the A4 is Ireland's finest classical mansion, **Castle Coole** (tel: 028-6632 2690; www.nationaltrust. org.uk; June–Aug daily 11am–5pm, mid-Mar–May and Sept Sat–Sun only, with exceptions, grounds: daily 10am–dusk). Completed in 1798, it is a perfect example of late 18th-century Hellenism and has furniture dating from before 1830. A state bedroom is presented as it was for George IV. The park lake's graylag geese were established here 300 years ago.

County Armagh

To the east is County Armagh, known as the Apple Orchard of Ireland, and during the 1980s and '90s, its southern acres – thanks to terrorist activity near its border with the Republic – by the less inviting sobriquet of Bandit Country.

Its county town of **Armagh** ⑫ (always called a city despite a population of just over 15,000) symbolises many of Northern Ireland's problems. Its two striking cathedrals – one Protestant, one Catholic, both called **St Patrick's** – sit on opposite hills like, someone once said, the horns of a dilemma. The two communities live mostly in separate parts of the city, with little interaction.

Armagh is known for its dignified Georgian architecture. At one end of an oval **Mall** – where cricket is played in summer – is a classical courthouse, at the other a jailhouse. The Ionic-pillared **County Museum** (The Mall; tel: 028-3752 3070; www.armagh.co.uk; Mon–Fri 10am–5pm, Sat 10am–1pm, 2–5pm; free) contains many local artefacts, as well as records of Ireland's worst railway disaster, which happened in 1889 just outside Armagh; 80 Sunday School excursionists died when 10 uncoupled carriages ran down a steep incline into the path of a following train.

The Planetarium

Access is free into the gardens of the 1790 Observatory that accommodates Ireland's main **Planetarium** (tel: 028-3752 3689; www.armaghplanet. com; Mon–Fri 1–5pm, Sat 11.30am–5pm, pre-booking essential for shows). Astronomical shows have been enhanced by a major refurbishment to the Digital Theatre,

WHERE

Armagh's location makes it a good base from which to explore the southern part of Northern Ireland. It is 37 miles (60km) from Belfast, 81 miles (130km) from Dublin, and a 45-minute drive from Belfast International Airport.

St Patrick's Roman Catholic Cathedral, Armagh.

TIP

The Book of Armagh, written in 807 by the scribe Ferdomnach, is a precious historic record because of the information it provides about the elusive St Patrick. Touch screens in St Patrick's Trian exhibition allow visitors to question three people who were connected with the book and discover how to make medieval inks and a quill pen.

Armagh Observatory.

including the world's most advanced digital projection system. There are interactive exhibitions and an outdoor Astropark with scale models of the planets, too and it also hosts regular activities.

Somehow the contemporary design of the **Market Place Theatre and Arts Centre** (Market Street; tel: 028-3752 1821; www.marketplacearmagh.com) sits comfortably within Armagh's historic centre. It is one of Northern Ireland's most important venues for drama, music and comedy and also has a popular bar and restaurant.

The Palace Demesne covers 70 acres of beautiful parkland, where the original palace building and stables, designed by Thomas Cooley in 1768, take centre stage. Today, it is a public park in the town centre that hosts many events.

In the city centre is **St Patrick's Trian** (English Street; tel: 028-3752 1801; Sept–June Mon–Sat 10.30am–5.30pm, July–Aug until 8.30pm, Sun 2–8.30pm). This explains St Patrick's connections with the city, including the 9th-century *Book of Armagh* (see

margin) and also has an interesting craft shop.

Two miles (3km) west of the city, off the A28, is the high-tech **Navan Centre** (tel: 028-3752 1801; www.armagh.co.uk; Apr–Sep daily 10am–4pm, Oct–Mar 10am–pm), celebrating Emain Macha, Ulster's Camelot around 600 bc. Until restored, it was a neglected hilltop; now it comes complete with hands-on exhibits and audio-visual interpretation facilities. Access to the hilltop is free.

Armagh's villages

The city is surrounded by neat villages, reached through a network of pleasant lanes, some of which host the local sport of road bowling, culminating in the Ulster Finals (see page 93). In May, the countryside around **Loughgall** is radiant with apple blossom. In the village the **Dan Winter Ancestral Home** (9 The Diamond, Derryloughan Road; tel: 028-3885 1344; www.danwinterscottage.com; Mon–Sat 10.30am–5.30pm, Sun 2–5.30pm, Jul–Aug until 8.30pm; free) recounts the founding of the Orange Order. Lovers of art should investigate the quaint **Dispensary House Gallery** (88 Main Street; tel: 028-3889 2010; Mon, Wed–Sat 2–5pm; free).

Crossmaglen, a village at the heart of this fiercely republican area – known as Bandit Country during the Troubles – has a large market square, containing a striking bronze monument to the IRA; this village was in the front line of many battles between the IRA and the security forces in the 1970s and '80s. Remarkably, after enduring many sectarian murders, Crossmaglen has begun promoting tourism with some degree of success.

But it's the beauty of the Ring of Gullion, and the mystical **Slieve Gullion**, source of myths like Deirdre of the Sorrows, which is the focus of modern tourism. There are fine walks, and cycle rides, around **Slieve Gullion Forest Park** (tel: 028-3755 1277; Easter–Sept 10am–dusk; free), where a forest drive winds up to two mountain-top Stone Age cairns. In the vicinity are three trails, also for walking or cycling, around Mullaghbane, Forkhill and Creggan, which trace the history of local 18th-century Ulster poets. Traditional music can be enjoyed at pubs, such as the Welcome Inn in **Forkhill**, on Tuesdays from 9pm.

Portadown and Lurgan

Between Armagh and Belfast is a chain of towns built on commerce. **Portadown** ⓭, 10 miles (16km) to the northeast, has found its role scaled down from that of a major railway junction to a prosperous market town noted for rose growing and coarse fishing. Linen manufacturing has diminished, as it has in **Lurgan**, 6 miles (10km) further along the A3. In the 1960s it was decided to link the two towns to form the 'lineal city' of **Craigavon**, thereby reducing congestion in Belfast; but the new city's population didn't arrive in the expected numbers and civic pride has kept the separate identities of Portadown and Lurgan very much alive despite the

mushrooming between them of housing estates, schools and roundabouts.

Lough Neagh's wildlife is well explained in the **Lough Neagh Discovery Centre** (tel: 028-3832 2205; www.oxfordisland.com; daily 9am–5pm, with exceptions; free). The best way to explore the Lough is on board *The Maid of Antrim*, which departs from various points from April until October (tel: 028-2582 2159, www.lough neaghcruises.co.uk).

Seven miles (11km) west of Portadown, off the B28 are two National Trust mansions. 17th-century **Ardress House** (Annaghmore; tel: 028-8778 4753; www.nationaltrust.org.uk; July–Aug Thu–Mon 1–5pm) has a fine collection of 18th-century furniture. Another National Trust property, the 19th-century **Argory** (144 Derrycaw Road, Moy; tel: 028-8778 4753; house: July–Aug daily noon–5pm, mid-Mar–June, Sept–Oct Thu–Sun noon–5pm, grounds: daily 10am–5pm) has delightful grounds and a tearoom featuring great local baking. The house has been well refurbished.

Traditional crafts at the Navan Centre.

Brontë Homeland

Banbridge , 10 miles (16km) south of Lurgan, has a peculiar main street, bisected by an underpass taking through traffic, with sections of road on either side serving a collection of small shops. Just outside the town, off the dual carriageway, the Outlet shopping centre is among the biggest in Northern Ireland.

To its southeast, off the B10, is 'Brontë Homeland', promoted from the **Brontë Homeland Interpretive Centre** (Church Hill Road, Rathfriland; tel: 028-4062 3322; mid-Mar–Sept Fri–Sun noon–4.30pm, other times by appointment), a confusingly signposted trail invented by the tourist authorities to capitalise on the fact that Patrick Brontë (or Brunty or Prunty), father of the novelists Charlotte, Emily and Ann, was born in a cottage at Emdale, 3 miles (5km) southeast of Loughbrickland. The family's fame was cemented in Yorkshire, not in Emdale, and there's nothing here to conjure up the claustrophobia of *Wuthering Heights* or *Jane Eyre*. But the drive through country lanes so narrow that the hedges almost meet is worth taking and, if you lose track of Patrick Brontë's trail on Ballynaskeagh Road, or Ballynafern or Lisnacroppin, it doesn't much matter.

The river valleys are peppered with the tall chimneys of disused linen mills so for access to the history and impact of what was the province's major industry go northwest along the Lagan valley to the impressive **Irish Linen Centre and Lisburn Museum** (tel: 028-9266 3377; www.lisburnmuseum.com, Mon–Sat 9.30am–5pm; free) with its hand-loom weaving workshop. A range of damask table linen is sold in the museum shop with a flax flower pattern designed by the museum staff.

Newry

With its key location equidistant between Dublin and Belfast the newly appointed city of **Newry** , 19 miles (10km) to the southwest of Banbridge, was bound to prosper once the peace process began. Newry's two huge shopping centres, the Quays and Buttercrane, are the hubs of a city that

Loyalist marching band.

View of Lough Neagh.

attracts large numbers of cross-border shoppers hoping to make some savings due to the different tax systems. Newry and Mourne Museum and the tourist information centre are to be found in the restored 16th-century **Bagenal's Castle** (tel: 028-3031 3182; www.bagenalscastle.com; Mon–Sat 10am–4.30pm, Sun 1.30–5pm; free) and its adjoining warehouse. Exhibitions explore the history of the area and building, and there are a café and shop too.

From Newry you can drive 12 miles (19km) north on the A27, or walk or cycle along towpaths, to the **Scarva Visitor Centre** (tel: 028-3883 2163; www.banbridge.com; Tue–Sat 10am–4pm; free), which explains the building of the canal and its uses. Four miles (6km) west of Newry, on the A25, the thatched 18th-century **Derrymore House** (tel: 028-8778 4753; www.nationaltrust.org.uk; grounds dawn to dusk) recalls a more sheltered world.

Warrenpoint

From Newry it's 5 miles (8km) southeast to the pretty seaside resort of **Warrenpoint** ⓰, overlooking Carlingford Lough. Its Maiden of the Mourne festival each August is a poor copy of the 'Rose of Tralee', but Warrenpoint's 'Blues in the Bay' (http://bluesonthebay.co.uk) held annually in late May is one of the best blues festivals in the UK. A few minutes around the coast, **Rostrevor**, sheltered by hills, is a smaller but prettier resort town with more of a Victorian atmosphere.

A steep half-mile walk up the slopes of **Slievemartin** (1,595ft/486 metres) brings you to **Cloghmore**, a 'Big Stone' supposedly hurled by the Irish giant Fionn MacCool at a rival Scot. The geological explanation for this misplaced piece of granite is more mundane, having to do with glacial drift.

Skirting round the **Mourne Mountains**, past 14th-century **Greencastle**, takes you to the active fishing village of **Kilkeel**, capital of the so-called 'Kingdom of Mourne'. Despite its idyllic location between mountain and sea, there is little to recommend the charmless Kilkeel to the visitor, except perhaps the restored Hanna's Close holiday cottages (tel: 028-4176 5999, www.mournecountrycottages.com) on the outskirts of town, an ideal base from which to explore the Mournes.

There's a choice here: you can proceed along the coast via **Annalong**, a smaller fishing village with old cottages as well as a **corn mill** and **harbour** (tel: 028-4175 2256; Apr–Oct 2–5pm) with a waterwheel dating from 1830, or you can turn inland into the Mournes. The Mourne Mountains meet the sea at Newcastle.

Meandering in the Mournes

The Mournes are 'young' mountains (like the Alps) and their chameleon qualities attract walkers. One moment the granite is grey, the next pink. You walk by an isolated farmhouse, and within moments are in the middle of a wilderness. One

The Legananny Dolmen is near Banbridge. It can be found off the B7, 7 miles (11km) south of Dromara, signposted from Dromara and Castlewellan. Entrance is free.

The Mourne Mountains meet the sea at Newcastle.

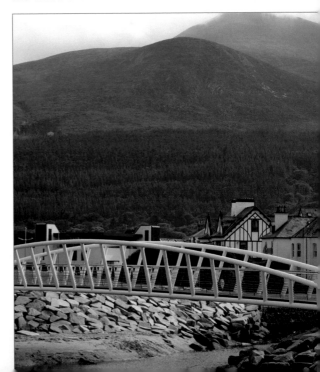

The Marching Tradition

Parades and bunting, bands and bibles... it's hard to escape these provocative rituals during July and August. What lies behind them?

Northern Ireland is unique in its flourishing popular culture: there are bands in every village and every housing estate, and nowhere else in the UK do normally discreet citizens sing and dance in the streets.

The main Orange procession, which celebrates the 1690 Battle of the Boyne in which William III (William of Orange) cemented the Protestant heritage, takes place on 12 July. On 13 July, the Black Men (the Orange Order's elite) dress up in period costume to re-enact King Billy's routing of the Catholic King James II in the 'Sham Fight' at Scarva, County Down. On 12 August the 'Apprentice Boys' march through Derry City in memory of 13 apprentices who closed the city's gates against the forces of James II. While quiet church parades and processions occur throughout the year, this prolonged marching season throughout the summer can lead to provocation and an increase in sectarian violence.

The very loud Lambeg drum.

The Green Orangemen

Lady's Day, in honour of the Madonna, Mary Mother of God, is held on 15 August by the Ancient Order of Hibernians, sometimes known as the Green Orangemen. (Green symbolises Catholic Ireland, orange Protestant Ulster.) Like their Orange counterparts, the Hibernians mix prayer with pageantry.

Now that the Troubles have ceased, such pageantry is slowly becoming less political and more of a tourist attraction. Traditionally it appeared to Catholics a sign of 'triumphalism' and to Protestants as another nationalist provocation.

A big investment

Flautist James Galway started his career in a Belfast band, and there can be few parts of Europe where such a high percentage of the population plays an instrument. In late spring and early summer, motorists driving through the leafy lanes of Ulster must be prepared to round a corner to find the road blocked by columns of men in bowler hats solemnly drumming and tootling their way to a local band contest. Scottish and Gaelic pipers compete with ecumenical harmony, at their own expense and 'for the glory of it', in villages and towns throughout summer. With a set of pipes costing £1,500 or so, there may be £2.5 million worth of pipes keening at a typical contest.

minute, the Mournes justify all the songs written about them; the next, they become plain scrubland and unexceptional hills. The weather has a lot to do with it.

Off the B27 the remote **Silent Valley Mountain Park** (daily 10am–dusk) cradles a large dam, which supplies Belfast and Co. Down with water. In the heart of the Mournes, this beautiful and tranquil spot is ideal for picnics and hiking, and there is an innovative exhibition in the modern information centre.

Slieve Donard, the highest peak at 2,796ft (850 metres), has exhilarating panoramic views.

As you reach the foothills of the Mournes, turn right just before Hilltown towards **Newcastle** ⓲. This is east Down's main resort, with a fine, sandy beach, an inordinate number of cake shops and the celebrated Royal County Down Golf Club, one of the world's top 10 links courses. Home to the famous Slieve Donard Hotel and adjacent to the tranquil Murlough nature reserve, Newcastle has undergone a serious makeover, including a smart promenade, but even that can't quite remove its old-fashioned seaside resort atmosphere.

Several forest parks – **Donard, Tollymore, and Castlewellan** – are good for riding (by pony or bicycle). This is an area that invites you to unwind, that doesn't understand people in a hurry.

Five miles (8km) inland from Newcastle, **Castlewellan** is a picturesque village with a wide main street. Nine miles (14km) to the west, **Rathfriland** is a steep-streeted plantation town with livestock sales and views of the Mournes.

As an alternative to heading into the Mournes from Newcastle, one can continue round the coast, via, at **Dundrum,** Ireland's finest Anglo-Norman castle to **Ardglass**, where several smaller, ruined castles hint at its strategic importance in the Middle Ages to unwelcome kings visiting from Britain. A source of wonderful local seafood, Dundrum has two excellent restaurants to enjoy it, the Buck's Head and Mourne Seafood Bar.

TIP

The minor roads and lanes that criss-cross the Mournes included many marked cycle trails. For a list of suggested itineraries, such as the Beetler's Trail and the Poet's Trail, visit www.visitmourne mountains.co.uk.

Castlewellan Park.

Pony trekking at low tide, Newcastle.

St Patrick's grave in Down Cathedral – though the saint's last resting place is a matter of dispute.

Downpatrick

Seven miles (11km) inland to the northwest is **Downpatrick** ⑱, which has a Georgian air and a cathedral supposedly built on the site of St Patrick's first stone church. The saint himself is said by some to be buried here. You can follow Patrick's story in a high-tech interactive exhibition with audio-visual film at the **St Patrick Centre** (St Patrick's Square, tel: 028-4461 9000; www.saintpatrickcentre.com; June–Aug daily 9.30am–6pm, Apr–May and Sept Mon–Sat 9.30am–5.30pm, Sun 1–5.30pm, Oct–Mar Mon–Sat 10am–5pm), itself the hub of Downpatrick's famous week of celebrations around St Patrick's Day, 17 March. A hundred yards or so away the atmospheric **Downpatrick and County Down Steam Railway** (tel: 028-4461 5779; www.downrail.co.uk) runs weekends between June and September and special holidays.

Down County Museum (The Mall; tel: 028-4461 5218; www.downcounty museum.com; Mon–Fri 10am–5pm, Sat–Sun 1–5pm; free) housed in an old gaol, explores the local heritage.

The Christian theme continues, off the A7 a mile northwest at riverside Cistercian **Inch Abbey** (www.doeni. gov.uk/niea). The **Struell Wells** (free access), off the B1, 1.5miles (2.5km) east of the town, are evidence of pagan worshippers long before Christianity.

North of the town there begins a prosperous commuter belt, populated by well-spoken professionals who put their money into making their homes ever more comfortable. The source of their prosperity and the commercial magnet to which they are drawn each working day lies to the north: Belfast.

Comber

Comber ⑲, 17 miles (27km) to the north at the head of Strangford Lough, was a linen town and still has a working mill. The town centre retains its old character, despite the developers, with cottage shops and a square. **Castle Espie** (Wildfowl and Wetlands Trust; tel: 028-9187 4146; daily 10.30am–dusk), on the shores of Strangford Lough, is base for Ireland's largest collection of ducks, geese and swans.

The conservation area of **Strangford Lough** is noted for its myriad islands, most of which are sunken drumlins (low rounded hills), the smooth glacial hillocks that characterise Co. Downs landscape. There are rocky shores on this side of the lough at places like **Whiterock Bay. Mahee Island,** accessible by bridge, has a golf course and the remains of **Nendrum Abbey** (Visitor Centre: tel: 028-9181 1491; www.doeni.gov.uk/niea; Easter–Sept daily 10am–6pm, Oct–Easter noon–4pm; free), an early monastery.

The Ards Peninsula

You can reach the **Ards Peninsula,** a 23-mile (37km) -long finger dotted with villages and beaches, by means of a regular car ferry that chugs a slanted course from **Strangford ⑳**, 8 miles (13km) from Downpatrick, across to Portaferry. The Vikings are said to have had a trading post at Strangford in the 9th century. Nearby is **Castle Ward House** (tel: 028-4488 1204; www.nationaltrust.org.uk; house; mid-Mar–Oct daily 11am–5pm, grounds: daily 10am–4pm, Apr–Sept until 8pm), an

18th-century Georgian mansion, once the home of the Lord of Bangor. Overlooking the lough, the house has two 'fronts' in differing styles (classical and Gothic) because the Lord and his Lady had diverging tastes. There are wildfowl in the 700-acre (280-hectare) grounds, and the **Strangford Lough Wildlife Centre** (tel: 028-4488 1411; www.strangfordlough.org) is located at the water's edge. There's also a Victorian laundry, two small 15th-century castles and an adventure playground for children.

The ferry across the mouth of the lough deposits you at Portaferry, where the sunsets are as fine a sight as anywhere in the world and where the local lobster and the **Exploris** (Castle Street; tel: 028-4272 8062; www.exploris.org.uk; Mon–Sat 10am–5pm, Sun noon–5pm, with exceptions), Northern Ireland's only sea aquarium, are not to be missed.

Nine miles (14km) north of Portaferry along the A20 is the one-street town of **Kircubbin**, a boating centre with a small pier jutting into Strangford Lough. Two miles (3km) inland

Strangford Lough.

The Exploris aquarium charts the marine life of Strangford Lough and has a seal rehabilitation centre.

Donaghadee.

takes you to the **Kirkistown Circuit**, a wartime airport and the home of car racing in Northern Ireland. Motor sport has a keen following in Northern Ireland; motorcycle racing and rallying can take place on public roads closed by Act of Parliament for the events.

Four miles (6km) further north on the A20 in the pretty village of **Greyabbey** is the site, with 'physic garden', of a Cistercian abbey dated 1193, and one of the most complete of its type in Ireland (tel: 028-9181 1491; www.doeni.gov.uk/niea; Easter–Sept daily 10am–6pm, Oct–Easter Sun only noon–4pm; free).

Two miles (3km) north of the village is another National Trust treasure, **Mount Stewart** (tel: 028-4278 8387; www.nationaltrust.org.uk; gardens: daily 10am–6pm, house: mid-Mar–Oct Thu–Tue 11am–6pm). It is an 18th-century house, which has several fine gardens and a mild microclimate that fosters delicate plants untypical of the area. The rhododendrons are particularly fine, and the gardens contain a variety of statues of griffins, satyrs, lions and the like. The **Temple of the Winds**, an 18th-century folly in the grounds, was built by James Stewart, a rival of Robert Adam, and is modelled on another in Athens. It offers a splendid view of the lough.

Newtownards

Newtownards ㉑, a sprawling commuter town at the head of Strangford Lough, belies its name; it's an old town, dating back to the 17th century. It was an old market town and still is a bustling shopping centre with a blend of traditional shops and a covered shopping centre. There is a fine sandstone town hall and other buildings of historical interest include **Movilla Abbey** on the site of a 6th-century monastery about 1 mile (1.6km) to the east of the town.

The **Somme Museum** (233 Bangor Road, tel: 028-9182 3202; www.irishsoldier.org; Apr–Jun & Sep–Nov Mon–Thu 10am–4pm, Sat 11am–4pm, July–Aug Mon–Sat 10am–5pm, Dec–Mar Mon–Thu 10am–4pm, first Sat of the month 11am–4pm) reconstructs elements of the 1916 battle in which many Ulstermen died.

Overlooking the town is **Scrabo Tower** (Scrabo Country Park; tel: 028-9181 1491), a 19th-century memorial to the third Marquess of Londonderry, offering vistas of the lough and the soft-hilled countryside and good walks in the nearby **Killynether Wood**.

Donaghadee ㉒, 8 miles (13km) to the east, is notable for its much-painted harbour and lighthouse, and summer boat trips (Nelson's Boats; tel: 028-9188 3403) up Belfast Lough and to **Copeland Island** (a bird sanctuary), just offshore. The twisting road passes 18th century **Ballycopeland Windmill** (Millisle; tel: 028-9181 1491; visitor centre: July–Aug daily 10am–5pm; free) and quiet beaches at **Ballywalter** and **Ballyhalbert**, and the fishing port of **Portavogie**, which has occasional evening quayside fish auctions.

Bangor

Bangor ㉓ was originally a small seaside resort, noted for its abbey. The expensively rejuvenated seafront still has to gentrify some of its fast-food bars and souvenir shops to do justice to the marina packed with yachts and cruisers. Rowing around the bay in hired punts and fishing trips from the pier are evergreen attractions. The town has a leisure centre with heated swimming and diving pools. For some reason, perhaps the bracing sea air, Bangor is favoured by evangelists who trawl for souls along the sea wall by the little harbour.

The **North Down Heritage Centre** (Town Hall, Castle Park Avenue; tel: 028-9127 1200; www.northdownmuseum.com; Tue–Sat 10am–4.30pm, open Mon Jul–Aug 10am–4.30pm, Sun noon–4.30pm; free) Housed in the converted stables and laundry of Bangor Castle it contains some interesting treasures ranging from ancient manuscripts to a display on locally born songwriter and artist, Percy French (1854–1920), who wrote 'The Mountains of Mourne' among other famous songs.

The old Bangor has been overgrown by acres of housing developments

Mount Stewart.

Ulster Folk and Transport Museum.

Seaside fun at Bangor's Pickie Pool.

Cushendun.

and shopping centres, many of them inhabited by people who work in Belfast. It is a busy town with a weekly open-air market, plenty of pubs and eating places, and parkland. The best beach is nearby **Ballyholme Bay**, a sandy arc which can become very crowded.

If you leave Bangor by the A2, a detour to the right will take in the beaches of **Helen's Bay**, the nearby wooded **Crawfordsburn Country Park** (tel: 028-9185 3621; free) and the picturesque village of **Crawfordsburn** with its charming **Old Inn**. Such havens are unusual so close to a city the size of Belfast.

The 'Gold Coast'

The A2 from Bangor to Belfast runs through what locals enviously describe as the 'Gold Coast'. This is stockbroker country, where lush lawns meet mature woodland. Hillside sites, overlooking the shipping lanes, have traditionally lured the well-heeled. **Cultra,** 6 miles (10km) from Bangor, has leafy lanes and the resplendent **Culloden Estate & Spa**. They go in

for yachting, golf and horse riding around here.

Holywood, an ancient religious settlement a mile further on, enjoys a quiet prosperity since it was bypassed. Nothing much happens here, apart from summer jazz and rumours of the odd dance around the Maypole, but it has pleasant craft shops and art galleries, and good pubs and restaurants.

Nearby, at Cultra Manor is the award-winning **Ulster Folk and Transport Museum** ❷❹ (tel: 028-9042 8428; http://nmni.com/uftm; Oct–Feb Tue–Fri 10am–4pm, Tue–Sun, Sat–Sun 11am–4pm, Mar–Sep Tue–Sun 10am–5pm, adult £11, child £6), which brings social history to life. Farmhouses, cottages, churches and mills have been painstakingly reconstructed – often brick by brick from their original locations. Freshly made soda bread, a local speciality, is sometimes baked over a traditional peat fire. On another part of the site the Transport Museum is also fascinating; exhibits range from horse-drawn chariots right up to a prototype of the ill-fated Belfast-built DeLorean sports car. There is a *Titanic* exhibition and the state-of-the-art X2 Flight Exhibition, where you can simulate flying.

From here it's a straight run into Belfast (see next chapter).

North of Belfast

If you aren't in the mood for city life, however, a good ring-road system will take you through the city to the north shore of Belfast Lough and the suburbs of **Whiteabbey** and **Green-island,** with some opulent housing.

Carrickfergus ㉕, 12 miles (19km) north from Belfast along the A2, is yet another market and dormitory town. Its big synthetic-fibre plants are empty now – a contemporary monument to its industrial past. The imposing 12th-century Norman **Castle** (The Marine Highway; tel: 028-9335 1273; Easter–Sept daily 10am–6pm, Oct–Easter until 4pm) beside the harbour, scene of gunrunning exploits early in the 20th century, still attracts attention for its authenticity. It is a real castle in every sense, with a portcullis, ramparts, chilling dungeons, cannons and a regimental museum in the keep. Looking to the new age of leisure, the town's **marina** has 300 berths. The parish church of St Nicholas (with stained-glass windows to Santa Claus) is 12th-century.

In Antrim Street, **Carrickfergus Museum & Civic Centre** (tel: 028-9335 8049 www.doeni.gov.uk/niea; daily, 10am–4pm; free) displays treasures excavated in Carrickfergus and provides general historical information about the town. **Flame, The Gasworks Museum,** (Irish Quarter West; tel: 028-9336 9575; www.flamegasworks.co.uk; May–Aug daily 2–5pm, Sept Mon–Fri 2–5pm, free) is Ireland's last surviving preserved gasworks.

A mile to the east at Boneybefore, the **Andrew Jackson Cottage** and **US Rangers Centre** (tel: 028-9335 8241; www.carrickfergus.org; May–Oct Thu–Sat 11am–3pm, Sun 1–4pm, Nov Apr Fri–Sat 11am–3pm) is a reconstruction of the thatched cottage home of Andrew Jackson, the seventh President of the United States. There is a museum dedicated to the elite US Rangers army unit in the grounds.

The countryside north of Carrickfergus becomes rich meadowland, with the sleepy seaside town of **Whitehead,** base for the Railway Preservation Society of Ireland on Castleview Road, from where occasional steam excursions run. The town nestles at the mouth of the lough, with a seashore walk to the Black Head lighthouse.

Beyond this begins the peninsula of **Island Magee**, with unspoilt beaches and caves, which wraps around Larne Lough. From here, the road runs into unlovely **Larne** ㉖, a port with frequent ferries to and from Stranraer in Scotland (70 minutes away).

The Causeway Coastal Road

The rewards of continuing along the coast are spectacular views of brown moorlands, white limestone, black basalt, red sandstone and blue sea

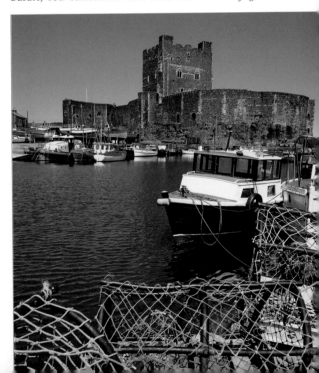

Carrickfergus Castle.

FACT

It was in Larne's harbour that Ulster Unionists, opposed to a Roman Catholic-dominated united Ireland, unloaded a large consignment of German-made rifles in 1914. It was probably only the intervention of World War I that postponed bitter conflict in the province of Ulster.

along the **Causeway Coastal Road**. A notable engineering achievement, it is explained in the Larne Tourist Information Centre (tel: 028-2826 2450; www.midandeastantrim.gov.uk; Oct–May Mon–Fri 9am–5pm, Sat 10am–4pm, Jun–Sep Mon–Fri 9am–5pm, Sat 10am–4pm, Sun 11am–3pm; free). The road, designed in 1834 by Sir Charles Lanyon as a work of famine relief, opened up an area whose inhabitants had previously found it easier to travel by sea to Scotland than overland to the rest of Ireland.

At various points, you can turn into one or other of Antrim's celebrated nine glens – **Glenarm, Glencloy, Glenariff, Glenballyeamon, Glenaan, Glencorp, Glendun, Glenshesk** and **Glentaisie** – and into another world. It's a world of weather-beaten farmers in tweeds; a world of sheep sales conducted by auctioneers who talk like machine guns; a world with a baffling dialect that turns a ewe into a 'yow' and six into 'sex'; a world where poteen, the 'mountain dew', is distilled in lonely places. It's not hard to track down this illicit (and potentially

lethal) alcohol. 'It's floating about,' they'll tell you. 'In fact it's practically running down the streets.'

Ballygalley ㉗, at the start of the famous scenic drive, has a 1625 fortified manor house (now a hotel) and, inland from the coast road, a well-preserved old mill and pottery. **White Bay** is a picnic area around which small fossils can be found. **Glenarm** has a beautiful park adjoining a fussy castle, home of the Earls of Antrim. **Carnlough** has a fine harbour and, running over its main street, a white bridge built in 1854 to carry limestone from the quarries to waiting boats. The Londonderry Arms hotel (also 1854) retains the charms of an old coaching inn. An eponymous literary summer school at **Garron Tower**, 5 miles (8km) north, celebrates John Hewitt, an acerbic dissenter poet.

The village of **Waterfoot** is the entrance to **Glenariff Glen**, a deep wooded gorge dubbed by Thackeray 'Switzerland in miniature'. Wild flowers carpet the upper glen in spring and early summer, and rustic footbridges

Carrick-a-Rede Rope Bridge.

carry walkers over the Glenariff River, past postcard-pretty waterfalls.

About 1.5 miles (2km) to the north, **Cushendall**, 'capital of the glens', was created largely by a wealthy 19th-century landowner, Francis Turnly. His most striking structure was the four-storey red sandstone **Curfew Tower**, built as 'a place of confinement for idlers and rioters'. The village has a good beach and is a popular sailing centre. Just to the north is **Layde Old Church**, dating back to the 13th century and containing some ancient vaults. Six miles (10km) further on, **Cushendun** ② is a village of Cornish-style white cottages, graceful old houses and friendly pubs, has been captured on countless canvases and is protected by the National Trust.

The northern coast

Crossing the towering **Glendun Viaduct** (1839), just before arriving at Ballycastle, one passes the ruins of **Bonamargy Friary**, founded around 1500. A vault contains the massive coffins of several MacDonnell chieftains who stood out successfully against the forces of England's Queen Elizabeth I.

The best time to visit **Ballycastle** ② is during the **Auld Lammas Fair**, held on the last Monday and Tuesday of August. Then this unspoiled town turns into one throbbing market place as farmers with impenetrable accents bring their livestock in from the glens and hundreds of stalls sell souvenirs, bric-a-brac, dulse (dried, edible seaweed) and yellowman (a sweet confectionery). It's great fun – an authentic folk event that owes nothing to the manipulations of tourist boards.

The **Ballycastle Museum** (tel: 028-2076 2942; www.discovernorthernireland.com; Apr, May & Sep Fri–Sat 10am–6pm, Sun noon–4pm, July–Aug daily 10am–6pm; free) concentrates on the folk and social history of the Glens. It is housed in an 18th-century courthouse and market building.

Rathlin Island

A seafront memorial marks the spot where, in 1898, Guglielmo Marconi

The Giant's Causeway

ROPE BRIDGE

A highlight of the Antrim coast is just west of Ballycastle. The Carrick-a-Rede Rope Bridge, a pedestrian suspension bridge over an 18-yard/metre channel, leads to Carrick Island, and an Atlantic salmon fishery. With a wooden floor, the bridge bounces as it swings in high winds, causing shrieks from thrill-seekers. Spare a thought for the salmon fishermen who traversed this chasm daily in the course of their work on a far flimsier structure than today's bridge.

Fortunately no accident ever occurred on the bridge and old photographs show people performing stunts, such as riding a bicycle across and doing handstands on a chair.

Once across on Carrick Island the view is fantastic and complemented by an array of diverse seabirds.

first seriously tested wireless telegraphy. He made his historic transmission between here and **Rathlin Island** ㉚, 8 miles (13km) off the coast towards Scotland's Mull of Kintyre. The boomerang-shaped island, whose population has slumped from 2,000 to 80 since 1850, makes its living from farming and fishing and attracts geologists, botanists and birdwatchers; there is a reserve (tel: 028-2076 3948) managed by the Royal Society for the Protection of Birds, an estimated 250,000 birds of 175 species.

A ferry (tel: 028-2076 9299; www.rathlinballycastleferry.com; daily year round; reservations advised) makes the journey from Ballycastle in 45 minutes. There is one pub, a hotel, guesthouse and youth hostel – but no policeman, and no need for one.

Five miles (8km) west, off the A2, is the **Carrick-a-Rede Rope Bridge** (tel: 028-2076 9839; www.nationaltrust.org; daily, Mar, Jun–Sep, Nov–Dec 9.30am–6pm, Apr–May, Sep–Oct 9.30am–7pm Jan–Feb 10.30am–3.30pm, adult £5.00, child £3.00), 65ft (20 metres) wide swinging over a 80ft (24-metre) chasm to an island salmon fishery (see page 299).

The Giant's Causeway

The **Giant's Causeway** ㉛, is an astonishing assembly of more than 40,000 basalt columns, mostly perfect hexagonals formed by the cooling of molten lava. Nowadays it attracts some 750,000 visitors a year. Dr Samuel Johnson, when asked by his biographer James Boswell whether this wonder of the world was worth seeing, gave the immortal reply: 'Worth seeing? yes; but not worth going to see.' It was a shrewd judgment in the 1770s when roads in the region were primitive enough to turn a journey into an expedition; indeed, the existence of the Causeway hadn't been known at all to the outside world until a gadabout Bishop of Derry stumbled upon them in 1692.

Today this geological curiosity disappoints some visitors, who expect the columns to be bigger – the tallest, in the **Giant's Organ**, are about

Atlantic views from Whitepark Bay, 7 miles (11km) west of Ballycastle.

Dunluce Castle.

39ft (12 metres) or who find their regularity diminishes their magnificence. Northern Ireland's only Unesco World Heritage Site, the visitor centre was rebuilt at a cost of £18.5m, with a glass front and a glass roof, and 186 basalt columns made from locally quarried stone. Admission includes a one-hour guided tour of the spectacular exhibition on all aspects of the Causeway. There is a park-and-ride service from Bushmills with discounted entry, or park at the **Giant's Causeway Visitor Centre** (44 Causeway Road; tel: 028-2073 1855; www.giantscausewayofficialguide.com; daily Nov–Jan 9am–5pm, Feb–Mar & Oct 9am–6pm, Apr–Jun & Sep 9am–7pm, July–Aug 9am–9pm, Nov-Feb to 4.30pm; adult £8.50, child £4.25) 2 miles (3km) north of Bushmills on the B146. At busy times of the year book an entry time online in advance of your visit. From the centre it is a 20-minute downhill walk to the main part of the Causeway; minibuses are available – a popular option on the way back up.

One of the most pleasant ways to reach the Giant's Causeway from Bushmills is on the Giant's Causeway and Bushmills Railway **steam train**, which operates daily July, August and Easter (tel: 028-2073 2844; www.free webs.com/giantscausewayrailway; Sat–Sun Mar–Oct).

Bushmills distillery

The Old **Bushmills Distillery** ㉜ (Distillery Road; tel: 028-2073 3218; www.bushmills.com; guided tours, Mar–Oct Mon–Sat 9.15am–4.45pm, Sun noon–4.45pm, Nov–Feb Mon–Sat 10am–4.45pm, Sun noon–4.45pm, adult £7.50, child £4.00), a couple of miles away, boasts the world's oldest whiskey-making licence (1608). Old Bushmills, Black Bush and Bushmills Malt, made from local barley and the water that flows by in St Columb's Rill, can be tasted after a tour. Connoisseurs tend to prefer the classic Black Bush to the more touted (and expensive) malt. The main difference between Scotch whisky and Irish whiskey, apart from the spelling, is that Scotch is distilled twice and Irish three times.

About 2 miles (3km) along the coast road are the romantic remains of **Dunluce Castle** (tel: 028-2073 1938; Apr–Sept daily 10am–6pm, Oct–Mar 10am–4pm). Poised on a rocky headland besides sheer cliffs, the 14th-century stronghold is huge and dramatic. It was abandoned in 1641, two years after part of the kitchen collapsed into the sea during a storm, carrying many servants to their death. In the graveyard of the adjacent ruined church are buried sailors from the Spanish Armada galleass *Girona*, which was wrecked on nearby rocks in 1588 with 1,300 men on board and was located on the seabed in 1967. Many of the *Girona*'s treasures are in Belfast's Ulster Museum.

Portrush and Portstewart

Next along the coast are two seaside resorts. **Portrush** ㉝ is the brasher,

Bushmills Distillery.

WHERE

Long-distance walkers
can pick up the North
Antrim Coast Path at
Portstewart Strand. It
forms part of the Ulster
Way and extends
eastwards for 40 miles
(64km) to Murlough Bay.

tackier, offering amusement arcades, burger bars, karaoke pubs, souvenir shops, guest-houses, a children's adventure play park, boats trips for sea fishing and viewing the Causeway and two championship golf courses. **Portrush Countryside Centre** (Bath Road; tel: 028-7082 3600; Easter–Sept daily 10am–6pm, Oct–Easter Sun only noon–4pm; free) has rock pool animals in a touch tank.

Portstewart, the quieter of the two resorts, is a tidy Victorian town with a huge strand, popular with anglers for its fine beach casting.

Nearby **Coleraine** is a busy market town, enlivened by also being home to the North Coast campus of the University of Ulster, a striking modern campus in 312 acres of landscaped parkland, with over 5,200 full time students.

A choice of routes

Here, you can either continue westwards towards Derry City or south towards the international airport and Belfast.

Oxford Island.

Along the first choice, the A2 towards Derry City, on a windswept headland is **Downhill Demesne** ❸ (tel: 028-2073 1582; www.nationaltrust.org.uk; grounds: dawn–dusk, house: Easter–Sept daily 10am–5pm), concealing the ruins of Downhill Castle and Hezlett House, and Mussenden Temple, perched precariously on a cliff, which housed an eccentric bishop's library and possibly his mistress; it was inspired by the temples of Vesta at Tivoli and Rome. Downhill Forest has lovely walks, a fish pond and waterfalls.

The alternative route is southwards through the relatively prosperous farming country 'east of the **Bann**'. This long, under-used river, which flows from the southeast of the province through Lough Neagh and into the Atlantic near Portstewart, is a rough and ready political dividing line between the western counties of Londonderry and Tyrone, with their preponderance of nationalists and Roman Catholics, and the eastern counties of Antrim and Down, with their Unionist/Protestant majority.

In a thriving market town like **Ballymoney** ③⑤, 17 miles (27km) southwest of Ballycastle, archaic words that would have been familiar to Shakespeare crop up in conversation – a legacy of the Scots Presbyterians who settled in the 1800s.

As elsewhere in Ulster, churches loom large. There's one on each of the four roads leading into a small village like **Dervock**, for instance, 4 miles (6km) north of Ballymoney and ancestral home of America's President William McKinley (assassinated in 1901). **Ballymena** ③⑥, 19 miles (30km) southeast of Ballymoney, is the staunchly Protestant business centre of **Antrim** ③⑦. The county town, 11 miles (18km) to the southeast, offers more to see. There's an almost perfectly preserved round tower, more than 1,000 years old, in **Steeple Park**.

The **Antrim Castle Gardens,** (tel: 028-9448 1338; www.antrim.gov.uk; free) are laid out like a miniature Versailles and run down to the shore of Lough Neagh. The Garden Heritage Exhibition in the restored Clotworthy House explains the history of the gardens and the family who created them. Don't miss the Garden Coffee Shop and the garden-themed Visitor Shop.

Lough Neagh

Lough Neagh (pronounced '*Nay*'), 17 miles long and 11 miles broad (27 by 18km) is the largest inland sheet of water in the British Isles. Legend has it that the warrior giant Finn McCool created the lake by scooping up a mighty handful of earth to fling at a rival Scottish giant (he missed, and the rock and clay fell into the Irish Sea to create the Isle of Man). Due to the lough's marshy edges, it has few access points – a reason, perhaps, why it is still one of Western Europe's most important bird habitats.

The **Lough Neagh Discovery Centre** on Oxford Island (see page 287) runs audio-visual shows about the wildlife and has a gift shop and café. There is sailing and water-skiing, with marinas at **Oxford Island** (south shore) and **Ballyronan** (west shore).

A large eel fishing industry is based at **Toome**. Until it became a fishermen's cooperative, gun battles used to take place on Lough Neagh between the police's patrol boats and the vessels of organised poachers.

The atmospheric, **Patterson's Spade Mill** (751 Antrim Road, Templepatrick; tel: 028-9443 3619; www.nationaltrust.org.uk; June–Aug Sat–Wed 11am–6pm, Apr–mid Sept Sat–Sun 11am–6pm) is the last working water-powered spade mill in the British Isles. And you can buy a spade, always remembering the Ulster saying about people who 'dig with the other foot' – a reference from the days when the shapes of spades were very localised and a stranger's home and therefore, by inference, his religion could be told from the cut of his spade.

Centre on Oxford Island (see page 287)

The Mussenden Temple.

Stormont Parliament Buildings.

BELFAST

A popular short break destination, this is a city of unexpected charms, mixing splendid Victorian architecture with genuine hospitality.

Belfast's dominant Victorian and Edwardian architecture resembles more a northern English city, such as Leeds or Liverpool, than the softer Georgian elegance of Dublin, just a hundred miles south. But Northern Ireland's capital has other attributes. A low-rise, open city, framed between lofty green Cave Hill and the great blue bowl of Belfast Lough, it is dotted with lovely parks and open spaces and, for a major city, is surprisingly easy to get around and out of, into the beginning of Northern Ireland's beautiful rural hinterland.

Above all, it's the people of Belfast who remain its great attraction. Despite preconceptions to the contrary, Belfast people remain among the friendliest you will meet, with an easy and down-to-earth sense of humour. And, ironically, it is precisely that synthesis of Ulster Scots and native Irish, so long a source of division, that gives the people of Belfast their distinct personality.

Belfast sells itself today as the birthplace of the legendary *Titanic*, whose luxurious embellishment symbolised the apex of Belfast's Edwardian heyday as one of the world's greatest shipbuilding ports, and whose watery fate prefigured Belfast's own long industrial and manufacturing decline. Now the city, rejuvenated with the help of huge investment

from the UK government, has been enjoying a renaissance as a short-break destination.

The city centre

The city radiates out from City Hall and the magnificent Victorian streetscape of Donegall Square. North of the square is a largely pedestrianised shopping area, leading to the Cathedral Quarter, Belfast's cultural district. Frequent bus services (Metro Bus 26, 26b or 26c) and a signposted footpath lead east across the River

Main Attractions

City Hall
Crown Liquor Saloon
Albert Memorial Clock
Titanic Belfast
Royal Botanic Gardens
Ulster Museum

Ulster Hall.

Belfast

0   500 m

0   500 yds

Lagan to the newly developed Titanic Quarter. To the south of Donegall Square, Great Victoria Street has several notable buildings, and leads to Shaftesbury Square, gateway to the University district.

The **Visit Belfast Welcome Centre** ❶ (9 Donegall Square; tel: 028-9024 6609; http://visitbelfast.com; free) is a good place to pick up information leaflets and the multilingual staff can advise on everything from attractions and events to restaurants and bars and accommodation, not just for Belfast but Northern Ireland as a whole.

Around the corner is the **City Hall** ❷ (Donegall Square; tel: 028-9027 0456; www.belfastcity.gov.uk/cityhall; tours: Mon–Fri 11am, 2pm, 3pm, Sat noon, 2pm, 3pm; free). Dubbed a 'Wrenaissance' building due to its shameless borrowing from St Paul's Cathedral in London, it is at the heart of Belfast. Famed for its marbled halls, its plush Council Chamber has resounded to some of the liveliest debate in the history of public affairs. The portraits of the lord mayors in the corridors tell their own story of Belfast's divided history, a long line of formally dressed unionists eventually reaching the first Catholic (SDLP) lord mayor in 1997. Not until 2002, with Sinn Féin's informally attired Alex Maskey, do you find a republican.

There is a coffee shop and an exhibition area. The surrounding gardens are a favourite summer lunchtime spot. Its many monuments include Thomas Brock's frumpy statue of **Queen Victoria** and his marble figure of **Thane,** a memorial to the victims of the sinking of *Titanic* in 1912. The **Titanic Memorial Gardens** (2012) has the names of all victims inscribed on bronze plinths and is on the east side of City Hall. City Hall's gardens are the venue for many annual events.

On the south side of City Hall remain several buildings from Belfast's linen era, including Yorkshire House, formerly a linen warehouse, now a chic hotel, **Ten Square** ❸ at 10 Donegall Square South whose Linenhall Street facade has some interesting carvings.

City Hall in winter.

LANYON'S LEGACY

Charles Lanyon (1813–89), an English architect, carpetbagger and engineer, conferred on Belfast's new bank buildings the majestic solidity of the palazzi of northern Italy. He understood the essence of the architectural faddishness and caught the spirit of early Victorian righteousness.

His neoclassical Crumlin Road Gaol promises unbridled retribution. Queen's University's faux Elizabethan design unashamedly appropriates Oxford's Magdalen. His Doric facade of the Union Theological College promises dour Presbyterianism. His Palladian Custom House intimidates. He was responsible for 14 churches. Although a philanderer who openly bought election votes, Lanyon was knighted, became the city's mayor and also one of its Conservative MPs.

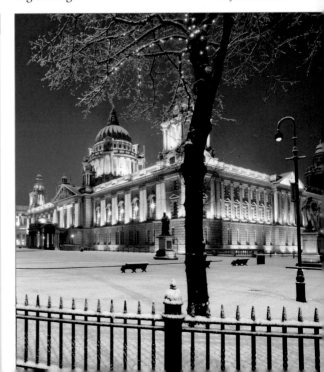

Belfast's Turbulent History

The history of Ireland's only industrial city is brief by European standards, but it is a stormy one of power struggles in factories and politics.

Belfast could barely be said to have existed before the arrival of Arthur Chichester at the very end of the 16th century. Tasked with the anglicisation of the fiercely Irish province of Ulster, Chichester defeated the rebellious Hugh O'Neill, last of the great Irish Chieftains, and cleared the land of its original owners. By introducing English and Scottish settlers, he changed the nature of Ulster forever.

Chichester built a striking timber castle in 1611 (which later burnt down) and developed a small 'towne of good forme' around it. For almost two centuries, Belfast grew slowly, handicapped by a corrupt and incompetent corporation. Despite a growing importance as a trading port, the town did not register its first major shipbuilder until the arrival of William Ritchie (whose

Belfast's High Street in around 1910.

first dry dock, dating from 1796, can be seen near Clarendon Dock).

It was not until the 19th-century industrial revolution, when Belfast added world-leading roles in shipbuilding, engineering and various kinds of manufacturing to its existing pre-eminence in the linen industry, that the now populous town hit its stride. It was now that the buildings that dominate Belfast today began to take shape as the great industrialists and entrepreneurs turned to architects such as Sir Charles Lanyon to reflect the town's increasing prestige in a more permanent way. Lanyon himself was responsible for many of Belfast's most iconic buildings (see page 307), including Queen's University, the Union Theological College and Crumlin Road Gaol.

Unionist power base

Despite a growing Catholic population, God's blessing seemed still to have a strong Protestant bias in the city. While many thousands of Catholics had flocked to the linen mills of west Belfast during the 19th century, power remained in the hands of Belfast's unionist ascendancy (a power base locked in by the partition of Ireland in 1920).

By the 1870s, a young William Pirrie had added his insatiable ambition and extraordinary abilities as a salesman to the firm of Edward Harland and Gustav Wolff, who were on their way to becoming the world's greatest shipbuilders from their fast-expanding base at Queen's Island.

Following Queen Victoria's conferring of city status on Belfast in 1888, Belfast Corporation invited designs for a new city hall to be built on the site of the old White Linen Hall. The competition was won by Alfred Brumwell Thomas, an Englishman who happily admitted his debt to Christopher Wren and London's St Paul's Cathedral. Similarly clad in finest Portland stone, City Hall was adorned with marble from the same quarry that supplied classical Rome and no expense was spared to impress. When the building opened in 1906 critics of its budget-busting extravagance were silenced and the ambition of the new city, now with a population of 450,000, appeared to have no limit. In fact, Belfast was already nearing the apex of its prestige.

Today, tourism chiefs have divided Belfast into a series of quarters and though boundaries tend to be vague, each has a distinct personality.

Ulster Hall

Also in Linenhall Street, the style of this part of the Linen Conservation Area is typified by the work of the celebrated architect Charles Lanyon (see page 307) at Nos **35–37**. Running parallel on the west side is Bedford Street, home to the distinguished **Ulster Hall ❹** (No. 30; tel: 028-9033 4400; www.ulsterhall.co.uk). Built in 1862 as a music hall, it now hosts rock and classical concerts, and cultural events; restored to its Victorian splendour, it has become home of the Ulster Orchestra.

Around the corner at 24 **Alfred Street** is the Catholic **St Malachy's Church ❺** (www.saintmalachysparish. com), noted for its red brick Tudor-style exterior and delightful fan-vaulted ceiling, famously described as an upside down wedding cake. The church, dating from 1844, was reopened after an extensive restoration in March 2009.

Grand Opera House

Despite damage from bombs and planners, **Great Victoria Street**, which runs south from the city centre to Shaftesbury Square, contains several of Belfast's best-known buildings. Before heading south, walk north to College Square East for a view of the beautifully proportioned classical facade of one of the city's finest buildings, Sir John Soane's dignified red brick **Royal Belfast Academical Institution ❻**, a prestigious non-denominational grammar school for boys, commonly known as 'Inst'. The baroque Portland stone building to the north, now part of **Belfast Metropolitan College**, has one of the last working steam-engine-powered ventilating and heating systems.

The street's highlights start at the corner with Howard Street, with the twin-domed **Grand Opera House ❼** (tel: 028-9024 0411; www.goh. co.uk) designed by theatre architect Frank Matcham. The building – with its plush brass and velvet, gilded elephant heads supporting the boxes, and excellent acoustics – was extensively refurbished and extended in 2006. Thanks to its now

The Crown Liquor Saloon, preserved by the National Trust.

Belfast in 1911, with Titanic in the background.

Festival time at the Albert Memorial Clock.

extended wing space, the venue where Luciano Pavarotti made his UK debut and Sarah Bernhardt, Orson Welles and Laurel and Hardy all appeared, can now house the grandest West End productions.

Diagonally opposite the Opera House, you can't help but notice the Tudor Gothic bulk of the **Presbyterian Assembly Rooms** now given over to an elegant shopping centre, the Spires Mall. Also on this side of the road, it's worth taking time to enjoy Guinness and oysters at one of the world's most beautiful Victorian pubs, the **Crown Liquor Saloon** ❽, (tel: 028-9024 3187; www.nicholsonspubs.co.uk), which was elegantly restored by the National Trust on the advice of John Betjeman. Its tiling and stained-glass windows were the work of some of Italy's finest craftsmen, in Belfast to work on Catholic churches and the White Star liners, in the 1880s.

Across the road from the Crown Liquor Saloon is a landmark familiar to the many journalists who visited Belfast during the Troubles:

the **Europa Hotel** ❾. Ironically, Belfast's first luxury hotel, built to a grand scale on the site of the Great Northern Railway Station (opened in 1971) can claim to be the most bombed hotel in Europe having been targeted 11 times since then by the IRA. A photographic timeline was installed to mark the hotel's 40th anniversary. The Italian marble lobby dates from a refurbishment in 2008. Nowadays the Lobby Bar and the Piano Lounge are atmospheric spots for a drink or afternoon tea and champagne.

Great Victoria Street meets the Dublin Road, which runs parallel to it, at **Shaftesbury Square** ❿, gateway to the university district. The Dublin Road, like many student neighbourhoods, is well endowed with small ethnic restaurants, fast food outlets and cheerful, noisy pubs.

Linen Hall Library

Back in the city centre, walking east along **Wellington Place**, is the **Linen Hall Library** ⓫ (17 Donegall Square North; tel: 028-9032 1707;

ARISTOCRAT OWNERS

The industrial revolution was facilitated by a change in land ownership. Until the mid-19th century, Belfast was the only Irish town to be run as a private fiefdom by a single family, lying as it did within the Donegall estate in Co. Antrim, owned by the descendants of British administrator Arthur Chichester.

The first Marquis of Donegall, though he lived in England, was enlightened enough to fund fine public buildings and insist on decent architectural standards. His spendthrift son, who succeeded to the estates in 1799, continued this policy but ran up such huge debts that he was forced to start selling off leases. By 1855 virtually the whole town had been sold to tenants or rich speculators. The family's legacy lies in the number of Belfast streets named after them.

www.linenhall.com; Mon–Fri 9.30am–5.30pm, Sat 9.30am–4pm; free). It is Ireland's last public subscription library. As well as the definitive collections – Troubles, Northern Ireland theatrical, C.S. Lewis and Irish Studies – it also has a pleasant café and literary-themed shop. To step into the history of Belfast and the collections of the Linen Hall Library, take a guided tour (Tue and Fri 11.30am, £3.50).

To the north is Donegall Place, with its streetscape of British chain stores. Off it, past Castle Junction, west down Bank Street, is **Kelly's Cellars** ⑫ Nos 30–32; tel: 028-9024 6058, www.kellyscellars.com), dating from 1720. Though considerably refurbished, the bars retain much of the charm, which appealed to Henry Joy McCracken and other Protestant leaders of the United Irishmen as they plotted here in 1798. It is also known for excellent Irish traditional music sessions held Monday to Thursday evenings.

Across High Street, you can take two routes. The first, north, brings you to **Rosemary Street** where, at **No. 33, William Drennan**, founder of the United Irishmen was born and where, at **No. 41**, is the 1783 **First Presbyterian Church** ⑬, the oldest place of worship within the city, its congregation once included *Titanic* designer Thomas Andrews, no doubt attracted by its charming boat-like interior. One of Belfast's oldest thoroughfares, Rosemary Street also hosts that shrine to freemasonry, the **Provincial Grand Lodge**. A plaque on the wall commemorates radical Belfast Presbyterian Henry Joy McCracken who worshipped in the church that once stood here.

Further up Royal Avenue the red sandstone **Belfast Central Library** ⑭ (tel: 028-9050 9150; www.ni-libraries.net/libraries/belfast-central-library; Mon & Thu 9am–8pm, Tue, Wed & Fri 9am–5.30pm, Sat 9am–4.30pm; free) is a good place to start for those wishing to research Belfast or Northern Irish history and culture, with extensive collections and a wide range of periodicals and newspapers going back to the 19th century.

Titanic Belfast.

Linen Hall Library.

A Titanic Belfast exhibit.

High Street

The other route takes you up High Street from the junction with Victoria. At **No. 105** is the striking portico of the magnificent 1816 **St George's Church** ⓘ (tel: 028-9023 1275; http://stgeorges.connor.anglican.org; free), which was transported by canal from the house of the eccentric Earl Bishop of Derry. At Queen's Square, across Victoria Street, the **Albert Memorial Clock** ⓘ was, until its restoration, threatening to rival the Leaning Tower of Pisa, while the renovated **McHugh's Bar** (www.mchughsbar.com) claims to be housed in Belfast's oldest surviving building.

Around the corner, Lanyon's glorious **Custom House**, where Anthony Trollope once worked, looks over what is now Belfast's premier public space. Since its transformation in 2005, **Custom House Square** has become a premier outdoor venue, used for all kinds of events from carnivals to live music.

Titanic Quarter

Donegall Quay ⓘ is the place to catch the Lagan Boat Company's fine tours (see page 313) and to see local sculptor John Kindness's now famous **Big Fish**, a 32ft (9.8-metre) salmon whose ceramic 'skin' tells the history of Belfast.

Across the River Lagan, at the gateway to the Titanic Quarter, the **Odyssey Arena** ⓘ (Queen's Quay; tel: 028-9045 1055; www.odysseyarena.com) is home to the Belfast Giants ice hockey team and is a venue for sporting events and pop concerts. The Odyssey Pavilion (www.odysseypavilion.co.uk) hosts the interactive discovery centre for family fun, **W5** (tel: 028-9046 7700; www.w5online.co.uk; Mon–Fri 10am–5pm, Sat 10am–6pm, Sun noon–6pm; adult £8.50, child £6.50) with nearly 200 interactive exhibits. There is also a bowling alley; cinemas, and a number of cafés, bars, restaurants and nightclubs.

The city's newest and most talked-about attraction is the **Titanic Belfast** ⓘ visitor centre (tel: 028-9076 6386; www.titanicbelfast.com; daily Apr–May & Sep 9am–6pm, Jun–Aug 9am–7pm, Oct–Mar 10am–5pm;

adult £17.50, child £ 7.25; book online to skip the queues). Opened in 2012, the 100th anniversary of the doomed liner's launch and sinking, the centre tells the liner's story and also brings to life the wider theme of Belfast's industrial heritage. Civic pride is evident in the scale of the Titanic building. Clad in diamond glazing, the bow-shaped facade of the six-storey building reflects the lines of the ship. Its shard-like appearance is created from 3,000 different-shaped panels, each folded from silver anodised aluminium sheets into asymmetrical geometries, which catch the light like a cut diamond.

A short walk from the Titanic Belfast is the **Titanic Dock and Pump House** (tel: 028-9073 7813; www.titanicsdock.com; Mon–Thu 10.30am–4.30pm, Fri 10.30am–4.30pmSun 10am–4.30pm; adult £5.00, child £3.50), for many visitors the most memorable of Belfast's Titanic-related attractions, and an amazing piece of industrial archaeology. The 900-foot long (274m) dry

dock where the Titanic was built is reached by steps leading 44 feet (13.5 metres) to the floor of the dock, retracing the physical footprint of the ship. It took 500 men seven years to build it, working here in all weathers. When full the dock held 21 million gallons of water. Guided tour by private arrangement; the café and visitor centre is housed in the original pump house.

Waterfront Hall

Back on the west bank of the Lagan is the copper-domed **Belfast Waterfront Hall** ❷⓿ (2 Lanyon Place; tel: 028-9073 7813; www.waterfront.co.uk), a forerunner of Belfast's renaissance when built in 1997 and a venue for top international performers.

Beside the Waterfront Hall is the Hilton Hotel; across the road the neoclassical 1933 **Royal Courts of Justice**, fashioned from Portland Stone.

At the corner of Oxford Street and May Street, **St George's Market** ❷❶, Ireland's oldest covered market, has been elegantly refurbished and now

Waterfront Hall.

FACT

'She was alright when she left here' was a popular T-shirt slogan in 2012. Many of Belfast's current residents are descendants of the people who built the Titanic, and civic pride at the achievement continues to be strong.

has many stalls selling superb locally produced food, including cheeses, organic meats, fish and seafood, and plants at the Friday **Variety Market** (6am–2pm) and the Saturday City Food, **Craft and Garden Market** (9am–3pm). The Sunday **Food, Craft and Antique Market** (10am–4pm) has many of those food stalls plus books and antiques, with a special emphasis on local arts and crafts.

Head down May Street and turn right into Victoria Street, where you will see the spectacular glass dome of Belfast's biggest and most impressive shopping centre, the **Victoria Square**.

On the other side of Victoria Square is the triangular **Bittles** bar, with its literary paintings and, nearby, the **Kitchen Bar**, one of Belfast's most famous traditional pubs. Further along Victoria Street is the excellent **Malmaison Belfast hotel** ㉒ (Nos 34–38), with its dramatic Gothic meets Alice in Wonderland decor, housed in two Victorian warehouses famous for their exterior carvings.

Queen's Quarter

Based around Sir Charles Lanyon's distinguished Queen's University, Queen's Quarter is a curious mixture of student haunts, elegant academia and Belfast's designer-label heartland, the Lisburn Road. **Queen's University** ㉓, its blue-tinged red brick at its best near dusk, is one of Lanyon's delights, appropriating the Tudor of Oxford's Magdalen College. There are over 100 listed buildings around the campus and surrounding area and it's worth picking up the 'Walkabout Queen's' leaflet from the **Queen's Welcome Centre** (tel: 028-9097 5252; www.queenseventus. com; Mon–Fri 8.00am–5pm; free) to help you on a signposted tour. In particular, search out the Great Hall, which Lanyon based on the medieval great halls of the Oxbridge universities. Also check out the **Naughton Gallery** (tel: 028-9097 3580; www. naughtongallery.org; Tue–Sun 11am–4pm; free) in the Lanyon Building, which houses the university's own extensive collection and hosts interesting touring exhibitions.

Inside Belfast Waterfront Hall.

You can find the best of world cinema at the **Queen's Film Theatre** near Queen's University (20 University Square; tel: 028-9097 1097; www.queensfilmtheatre.com), which now has two screens and a comfortable bar/lounge. Opposite the University's lawns stands its modernised **Student's Union**. Nearby is the delightful Italianate deconsecrated wedding cake, **Elmwood Hall**, which hosts concerts.

Northwards down University Road from Queen's is a selection of atmospheric cafés and restaurants. Writer and poet Ciaran Carson and many of Belfast's lively younger writers teach creative writing across the road at the **Seamus Heaney Centre for Poetry** (tel: 028-9097 1070; http://www.qub.ac.uk/schools/SeamusHeaneyCentreforPoetry), which organises literary events such as poetry readings, book launches, summer schools and talks.

Royal Botanic Gardens

South of the University, the **Royal Botanic Gardens** ㉔ (tel: 028-9031 4762; www.discovernorthernireland.com; 7.30am–dusk; free) contain another Lanyon gem, his restored curvilinear **Palm House** (Apr–Sept 10am–5pm, Oct–Mar 10am–4pm ; free). In the **Tropical Ravine** (currently closed due to renovation), water drips from banana leaves in a miniature sunken rainforest.

On the park's Stranmillis Road boundary, the **Ulster Museum** ㉕ (in the Botanic Gardens; tel: 0845-608 0000; http://nmni.com/um; Tue–Sun 10am–5pm; free), which features a 75ft (23-metre) -high atrium that leads into fascinating history, art and science galleries. The Belfast-born artist John Lavery (1856-1941) left a major bequest of his work to the museum, which is on permanent display. The museum also has an enclosed rooftop gallery to house its glass, jewellery and Belleek collections. Allow at least half a day.

Further south takes you to the pleasant village atmosphere of Stranmillis and the site of the **Lyric Theatre** ㉖ at 55 Ridgeway Street,

Botanic Gardens.

TIP

Taxis operate from 'taxi ranks' and do not stop when hailed. One of the main taxi ranks in Belfast city centre is in front of City Hall and there are further ranks at the airports and main stations. There are two types of taxi: London-style hackneys and saloon car 'radio cab' companies such as Value Cabs (tel: 028-9080 9080; www.valuecabs. co.uk), or fonaCAB (tel: 028-9033 3333; www. fonacab.com).

(tel: 028-9038 5685; www.lyrictheatre. co.uk), where Ulster-born actor Liam Neeson first trod the boards. Neeson was one of the chief fundraisers for the 390-seat venue completed in 2011 that graces the riverside site. Designed by Dublin architects O'Donnell + Tuomey, the unusual building was a response to the sloping parkland site and the brick streetscape of Belfast. The auditorium's interior uses iroko wood and specially fired brick. It has won many architectural awards.

North from Queen's again is the heavily student-influenced **Botanic Avenue**, home to excellent cafés and some of Belfast's best-value food at **The Other Place** (No. 79; 028-9024 9709). The excellent crime bookshop **No Alibis** (No. 83; tel: 028-9031 9607; http://noalibis.com), known for book launches and a regular haunt of Belfast writer Colin Bateman. The focus of the street is the all-purpose Madison's (Nos 59–63; www.madis onshotel.com), a lively hotel, bar, bistro and nightclub with an up-front decor worthy of Barcelona.

At the meeting point of Lower Crescent Street and University Road is the **Crescent Arts Centre** ❷ (2–4 University Road; tel: 028-9024 2338; www.crescentartscentre.org; free), a 19th-building of Scrabo stone, which houses a lively community arts centre. Left up University Road are two of Belfast's most enduring restaurants, Italian cuisine Belfast-style at **Villa Italia** (Nos 37–41; tel: 028-9032 8356, http://villaitaliarestaurant.co.uk) and **Buskers Retaurant** (No. 44; see page 321).

Cathedral Quarter

Gradually Belfast's historic Cathedral Quarter is becoming a cultural and entertainment district to rival Dublin's Temple Bar. Beginning in the city centre where Bridge Street meets Waring Street is the Soviet-themed **Northern Whig** with its chunky sofas and fine range of vodkas.

Opposite, the historic 1769 **Exchange and Assembly Rooms** ❷ (converted to the Northern Bank by Sir Charles Lanyon) hosted a famous

A Belfast blues band play the Kitchen Bar.

harp festival attended by rebels Wolfe Tone (who disapproved) and fellow United Irishman Henry Joy McCracken.

Across Donegall Street, the lovely facade of the Four Corners building has been preserved as a Premier Inn. Worth visiting on Waring Street is the **Royal Ulster Rifles Museum** ㉙ (No. 5; tel: 028-9023 2086; www.armymuseums.org.uk; Mon–Fri 10am–12.30pm, 2–4pm, Fri until 2.30pm).

Take a left down Donegall Street, passing two fine pubs, the traditional **Duke of York** (7–11 Commercial Court; tel: 028-9024 1062) and the **John Hewitt** at 51 Donegall Street (tel: 028-9023 3768), a superb community-run pub which features live music and is a key venue in the area's excellent Cathedral Quarter Arts Festival each April.

Also on Donegall Street, **Belfast Exposed** at Exchange Place (tel: 028-9023 0965; www.belfastexposed.org; Tue–Sat 11am–5pm) hosts contemporary photo exhibitions and allows access to its digital archive of 250,000 images of Belfast.

St Anne's Cathedral

Further along, the neo-Romanesque **St Anne's Cathedral** ㉚, dates from the beginning of the 19th century but wasn't completed until 2007 when its striking stainless steel 'Spire of Hope' was added. Check out the mosaic roof over the baptistery, composed of 150,000 pieces of glass. The famed unionist leader Edward Carson is interred here. Opposite, Writers' Square contains sculptural pieces by John Kindness and Brian Connolly, and during the festival hosts musical and comedy events. On the cathedral's east side in Talbot Street is the **Northern Ireland War Memorial** (www.niwarmemorial.org; Mon–Fri 10am–4pm), which gives an in-depth account of wartime Northern Ireland. To the rear, St Anne's Square is home to the **MAC** ㉛ (tel: 028-9023 5053; www.themaclive.com; daily, 10am–7pm; free), short for Metropolitan Arts Centre, Belfast's multi-million pound state-of-the-art facility for visual and performing arts. With two theatres, three art galleries, ancillary spaces, café and bar,

St Anne's Cathedral.

Stormont Parliament Buildings.

C.S. Lewis mural.

the opening of this landmark building in 2012 marked an important new stage in the on-going development of the Cathedral Quarter.

Donegall Street continues past the junction with Royal Avenue and on to **St Patrick's Cathedral** ㉜, where society painter Sir John Lavery used his beautiful wife Hazel (rumoured to have had an affair with Irish rebel leader Michael Collins) as the face of Madonna in his famous triptych of St Patrick.

Returning east from Donegall Street, along the atmospheric cobbled Hill Street, is one of Belfast's finest pubs, **The Harp Bar** (No. 35; see page 321), while the **Black Box** (Nos 18–22; tel: 028-9024 4400; www.blackboxbelfast.com), a dedicated performance space for new theatre, music and comedy, is another key venue for the Cathedral Quarter Arts Festival, the Belfast Film Festival and many others.

At the junction across the road at the corner of Waring Street and Skipper Street (named for being the lodging place for captains of ships tied up in nearby High Street when the River Farset ran through), is **The Spaniard tapas** bar (tel: 028-9023 2448, www.the spaniardbar.com).

Just along Waring Street is the area's new social hub, the **Merchant Hotel** ㉝ (Nos 35–39), converted from one of Belfast's finest buildings, the 1860s Ulster Bank. The sumptuous five-star hotel, Belfast's finest, radiates luxury from the Great Room restaurant where Ireland's largest chandelier hangs beneath a glass cupola to its 26 lavish rooms and five suites. Wander in for a look at the chandelier, (the restaurant is in the main lobby), and make a point of sampling one of its bars: for all its luxurious trappings, the hotel, like Belfast, is a democratic place, and all are welcome. The adjoining New York-style Cloth Ear pub and opulent Ollie's nightclub in the basement are also part of the hotel, and well worth sampling.

Opposite the Merchant is **Cotton Court**, the home of **Craft NI**. In the same building you can visit the ground-floor gallery of the

Belfast Print Workshop (tel: 028-9023 1323, http://bpw.org.uk), which has free exhibitions of leading print artists.

East Belfast

Not yet designated a quarter but the largest district of the city, it was here that three of Belfast's most famous sons were born: singer Van Morrison, footballer George Best (after whom Belfast City Airport is now named) and C.S. Lewis. 'Jack' Lewis, author of the *Chronicles of Narnia*, who was baptised at **St Mark's Church** on the Holywood Road by his formidable grandfather, the Rev Thomas Hamilton, is now celebrated with his own festival in December (www.eastside-arts.net). Ken Harper of **Harper Taxi Tours** (tel: 028-9074 2711, mobile 07711-757 178; www.harpertaxitours.com) will guide you on tours exploring locations relevant to each of the three or all.

Stormont

East Belfast's most famous building is the grand **Parliament Buildings** , Stormont, off the Upper Newtownards Road, now again the home of the rejuvenated Northern Ireland Assembly. Visitors don't have access to the building but can walk the 300 acres (120 hectares) of grounds (daily 7.30am–dusk; free), including the impressive one-mile driveway.

Though not exactly dominating the tourist map, east Belfast has some much-visited attractions to offer. Watching sweets and chocolates made in the traditional way will tempt children to **Aunt Sandra's Candy Factory** (60 Castlereagh Road; tel: 028-9073 2868; www.auntsandras.com; daily 10am–6pm, tour charge).

On the outskirts of Belfast, **Dundonald Ice Bowl** (111 Old Dundonald Road; tel: 028-9080 9100; www.theicebowl.com) has Ireland's only Olympic-sized ice rink, one of the biggest indoor play centres in Ireland and 30 state-of-the-art bowling lanes. Adjoining is the American-style mini golf centre the **Pirates Adventure Golf Course** (111a Old Dundonald Road; tel: 028-9048

FACT

Though lack of resources still affects both Belfast communities, this seems more evident in the Shankill, a heartland of loyalism. Compared with the more cohesive and vibrant republican community on the Falls, there is a listlessness and lack of bustle. This is typified by the two summer festivals, with the nationalist West Belfast Festival (Féile an Phobail), claiming to be Europe's biggest community festival, dwarfing the more modest Shankill version.

City bus preserved at the Ulster Folk and Transport Museum.

Murals are a reminder of Belfast's recent history as a bus passes Sinn Féin's headquarters on the Falls Road.

0220; www.piratesadventuregolf.com; daily 10am–10pm), while a short walk away is **Streamvale Open Farm** (38 Ballyhanwood Road; tel: 028-9048 3244; www.streamvale. com; 17 Mar–Halloween Mon– Sat 10.30am–5pm, Sun 2pm–5pm) offering lots of farm animals for children to meet.

Gaeltacht Quarter

This is essentially the nationalist part of west Belfast (omitting the Protestant Shankill area) and is focused on the **Falls Road**. A good introduction to the people and area is to take one of the cheap, shared black cabs that drive along the Falls Road from their HQ at Castle Junction (TaxiTrax; tel: 028-9031 5777).

In ascending order up the Falls Road, you should begin your tour at the 1866 **St Peter's Cathedral** ❸ (Peter's Square; tel: 028-9032 7573, www.stpeterscathedralbelfast.com), whose two great towers with rising spires were used as sightlines by German bombers in the war. The first flax spinning mill in west Belfast,

Conway Mill (5–7 Conway Street; tel: 028-9032 9646; www.conwaymill. org; free) hosts a Saturday market from 10am to 3pm, as well as community and cultural events. The lovely French-Gothic style **Clonard Church** (1 Clonard Gardens; tel: 028-9044 5950) is notable for its remarkable Rose Window, organ and mosaics.

The Irish language arts centre **An Cultúrlann McAdam Ó Fiaich** (216 Falls Road; tel: 028-9096 4180; www.culturlann.ie), with an Irish language book and gift shop, hosts Irish music and theatre and art exhibitions. It has a good-value restaurant, too.

One of the best ways to understand Belfast's rather turbulent history is to investigate **Belfast City Cemetery**, just off the Falls Road. Here are buried the powerful unionists who made modern Belfast. Over the road, in the **Milltown Cemetery** is the famous 'Republican Plot' where hunger striker Bobby Sands is buried. He died in 1981 while on hunger strike at HM Prison Maze.

Shankill and North Belfast

The rundown Shankill area lacks the vitality of nationalist west Belfast but Shankill Road itself is worth visiting for the famous political murals and the 'shamrock church', **St Matthews** ㊱. Take the Belfast Black Taxi Tour (tel: 028-9064 2264, www.belfasttours. com), to gain a deeper understanding of the issues.

Parallel to the Shankill Road is the **Crumlin Road**, highlighted by Lanyon's imposing **Crumlin Road Gaol** ㊲, which was restored in 2007. An underground tunnel connects it with Lanyon's **Courthouse** across the road.

Further towards the city centre is the most elegant Georgian building **Clifton House** (2 North Queen Street; tel: 028-9089 7534 for group tours), opened in the 1770s as the Belfast Poor House.

Down in the docks area of north Belfast is another Lanyon building the nautically themed **Sinclair Seamen's Church** ㊳ (Corporation Square; tel: 028-9071 5997). Its pulpit is shaped like a ship's prow and its bell is from the ill-fated HMS *Hood*, sunk by the *Bismarck* in 1941 with the loss of more than 1,400 lives. Further north is the Italianate Harbour Office, which leads into attractive tree-lined riverside plazas at the recently developed Clarendon Dock.

Outside Belfast

Seven miles (11km) east of Belfast on the main A2 road towards Holywood is the excellent **Ulster Folk and Transport Museum** at Cultra (see page 297).

To the north of the city centre, a 30-minute bus ride away, is the Scottish Baronial-style sandstone **Belfast Castle** ㊴ (tel: 028-9077 6925; Sun & Mon 9am–6pm, Tue–Sat 9am–10.30pm; free), built in 1870 as an aristocratic residence with fine views of the city, and **Cave Hill Country Park**. The **Belfast Zoo** (off Antrim Road; tel: 028-9077 6277; daily, Oct–Mar 10am–4pm, Apr–Sept 10am–6pm) built into Cave Hill, is known for its wonderful conservation policies.

Belfast Castle.

Workers outside City Hall, Belfast.

TRAVEL TIPS
IRELAND

Transport

Getting There 324
  By Air.................................... 324
  By Sea................................. 324
  By Bus................................. 325
Getting Around....................... 325
  Public Transport 325
  Private Transport................ 325
  Car Rentals......................... 325
  Cycling 325

A – Z

Accidents and Emergencies .. 326
Accommodation 326
Budgeting for Your Trip 326
Children.................................. 327
Climate................................... 327
Clothing.................................. 327
Crime and Safety.................... 327
Customs and
  Entry Regulations............... 327
Disabled Travellers 328
Electricity 328
Embassies and Consulates ... 328
Events 328
Gay and Lesbian Travellers 330
Health and Medical Care 330
Liquor Laws 330
Maps 330

Media 330
Money 331
Opening Hours........................ 331
Postal Services....................... 331
Public Holidays 331
Religious Services 331
Smoking.................................. 332
Telephones 332
Time Zone 332
Tourist Information 333

Further Reading

Irish Classics........................... 334
Contemporary Fiction
  and Poetry 334
History.................................... 335
Biography................................ 335
Memoirs and Journalism 335
Current Affairs........................ 335
Genealogy............................... 335
Architecture 335
Art and Decorative Arts 335
Cookery................................... 335
Drama 336
Folklore 336
Music 336
Travel 336
Landscape and
  Topography......................... 336
Other Insight Guides 336

TRANSPORT

GETTING THERE AND GETTING AROUND

GETTING THERE

By Air

Irish Republic

There are three major international airports in the Republic of Ireland, at Dublin, Cork and Shannon.

There are regular bus services from **Dublin Airport** (tel: 01-814 1111; for detailed transport information and links see www.dublin airport.com) by Dublin Bus, Airlink and Aircoach to the city centre, rail and bus stations taking about 40 minutes, departing every 10 minutes, less frequently from 9pm to 7am. The bus from **Cork Airport** (tel: 021-431 3131; www.corkairport.com) to the city takes about 10 minutes. From **Shannon Airport** (tel: 061-712 000; www.shannonairport.com) there is a regular bus service to Limerick city operating between 7am and midnight. It takes about 30 minutes.

Frequent flights from UK airports also arrive at regional airports such as Kerry, Galway, Waterford

Dublin's trams offer a quick way of getting to outlying areas.

and Knock. There are connections from Dublin and/or Shannon to many destinations in Britain and Europe. Low-cost airlines cover many destinations in eastern and southern Europe.

For flights to the United States from Dublin and Shannon, passengers clear US immigration before boarding the plane, enabling them to proceed straight to the baggage carousel and Customs at their destination.

Ryanair (www.ryanair.com) flies to Dublin, Cork, Knock, Kerry and Shannon from London Gatwick, Luton and Stansted and several provincial cities, while Aer Lingus (www.aerlingus.com) has flights from London Heathrow and Gatwick, Liverpool, Birmingham and Bristol to Dublin, Cork, Knock and Shannon. Other key airlines include **British Airways** (www.britishairways.com) and flybe (www.flybe.com).

Northern Ireland

Northern Ireland has two major airports: **Belfast International** (tel: 028-9448 4848; www.belfastairport.

co; a 30- to 40-minute bus ride from town; 24-hour service) and **George Best Belfast City Airport** (tel: 028-9093 9093; www.belfastcityairport. com), a short bus or taxi ride from the town centre.

Belfast International has services to New York (Newark) with **United**, and to many UK cities and European capitals with Easyjet (www.easyjet. com). George Best Belfast City serves the UK via **Aer Lingus, flybe and British Airways** airlines.

By Sea

Main ferry routes include Dublin to Holyhead (Wales) or Liverpool (England); Rosslare to Pembroke or Fishguard (Wales), Roscoff and Cherbourg (France); Larne to Fleetwood, Cairnryan or Troon (Scotland); Belfast to Stranraer (Scotland). Many routes vary by season; seas are rough in winter. **Irish Ferries** (tel: 08717-300 400; www.irishferries.com). *Services:* Holyhead–Dublin North Wall (3 hours 15 minutes) two crossings daily; Holyhead–Dublin fast service (1 hour 49 minutes) four crossings daily; Pembroke–Rosslare (3 hours 45 minutes). Also offers sailings every second day between Rosslare and Roscoff and Cherbourg.
Stena Line (tel: 01-204 7700, www.stenaline.co.uk, in Dublin, 08447-707 070 in the UK). *Services:* Holyhead–Dublin (3 hours 15 minutes); Fishguard–Rosslare (3 hours 30 minutes or 2 hours); Liverpool–Belfast (8 hours); Cairnryan–Belfast (2 hours 15 minutes).
P&O Irish Sea Ferries (tel: 01-407 3434; www.poirishsea.com in Dublin, 0871-664 2121in the UK). *Services:*

Cairnryan–Larne (1 hour 45 minutes); Troon–Larne (1 hour 49 minutes, mid-Mar–mid-Oct); Liverpool–Dublin (7 hours 30 minutes).

By Bus

Bus companies run through services from various points in England and Wales via the ferries. The ride to Galway from London, for example, takes around 17 hours by **Eurolines**, tel: 01-836 6111 in Dublin or 08717-8181718, www.eurolines.ie.

GETTING AROUND

Public Transport

In the Republic, there are two national service providers: Bus Éireann Expressway (serving provincial areas nationwide) and Iarnród Éireann (operating inter-city trains as well as the DART, the Dublin Area Rapid Transit system). Integrated information on public transport in Ireland by bus, rail and taxi, including door-to-door journey plans can be found on the website of the National Transport Authority, www.transport forireland.ie. The National Journey Planner App for web or Smartphone can be downloaded free from the site above, or download it free from your app store.

Express and local bus timetables are also sold in newsagents. Once off the main routes, small towns and villages may only be served by a couple of buses a week. For information on Expressway services, tel: 01-836 6111 (Bus Eireann, www.buseireann.ie). For information on bus travel within Dublin tel: 01-873 4222 (Dublin Bus, www.dublinbus.ie). The city's bus service can be maddeningly unpredictable. The LUAS tram system (tel: 1-800-300 604; www.luas.ie) offers a handy connection between Connolly and Heuston train stations. **Citylink.ie** (091-564 164, www.citylink.ie,) is a private bus company linking Cork to Galway and Clifden via Shannon Airport and Dublin to Galway via Athlone, with free on-board Wi-Fi on most services. **Aircoach.ie** (tel: 01-844 7118; www.aircoach.ie) has daily services from Dublin Airport to Belfast (2 hours), and via the city centre to Cork (3 hours).

Trains radiate from Dublin on different lines. A line links Limerick and Galway via Ennis, and there are commuter lines from Cork to Cobh

and Midleton, and from Dublin along the coast. Booking online with Irish Rail can lead to great savings if you can travel on off-peak trains. Dublin-Cork, for example, is €10 each way off-peak, compared to the regular fare of €65 return. For information on rail travel, tel: 01-836 6222 (Iarnród Éireann, www.irishrail.ie).

Eurail passes are valid for bus and train travel in the Republic, excluding city services. Reduced-rate Rambler passes provide unlimited travel on buses and/or trains, excluding city services, for either 8 or 15 days. Tickets can be bought from any bus or train station in the Republic, or through a travel agent abroad.

In Northern Ireland, trains run from Belfast northwest to Derry via Ballymena and Coleraine; east to Bangor; and south to Dublin via Newry. Buses are operated by the state-owned Ulsterbus. For bus/rail information, call Translink in Belfast, tel: 028-9066 6630 (www.translink.co.uk).

Private Transport

Driving

Outside the cities the roads are still amongst the least congested in Europe, although it's hard to believe this when stuck in a traffic jam in Dublin's ever-expanding suburbs or on the ring roads of Galway, Cork or Killarney. Drive on the left is the rule on both sides of the border, although there is a predilection in some rural areas for the middle of the road. All passengers, front and back, must wear seat belts.

In the Republic, the speed limit is displayed in kilometres per hour: 45kmh, 60kmh or 80kmh (28mph, 37mph or 50mph) in urban areas, and 80kmh or 100kmh (50mph or 62mph) on National routes (green signposts), with 120kmh (75mph) permitted on motorways. Barrier-free tolling is operational on certain motorways including Dublin's ring road, the M50; see www.eflow.ie for further information. On-the-spot fines can be issued for speeding offences. Drink driving laws are strict. It is an offence to drive with a concentration of alcohol exceeding 50mg per 100ml of blood.

In Northern Ireland, speed limits are displayed in miles per hour. The limit for country roads is 60mph (96kmh), and 70mph (113kmh) is allowed on motorways and dual-carriageway trunk roads.

Car Rentals

Irish Republic

At the height of summer, hire cars can be hard to find, so book in advance. If you're heading west, the smaller the car, the better – the most alluring lanes are the narrowest. Shop around – rental prices are lower outside the Dublin area. You must be over 23 with two years' full licence and under 76 to hire a car in the Irish Republic. **Alamo/Europcar/National Car Rental**, Arrivals Hall, Dublin Airport, tel: 1800-301 401 in Ireland, 061-206 088 in Ireland. www.ireland carhire.ie.
Avis, 1-890-405 060 in Ireland, Dublin Airport, tel: 01-605 7500; Shannon Airport, tel: 061-715 600; Cork Airport, tel: 021-432 7460; Killarney (Kerry Airport), tel: 01-605 7500; www.avis.ie.
Hertz Rent-a-Car, Dublin Airport, tel: 01-844 5466; Shannon Airport, tel: 061-471 369; Cork Airport, tel: 021-496 5849; www.hertz.ie.

Northern Ireland

Avis Rent-a-Car, Great Victoria Street, Belfast, tel: 084 4544 6036; Belfast International Airport, tel: 084 4544 6012; Belfast City Airport, tel: 084 4544 6028; City of Derry Airport, tel: 0781-621 3522; www.avis.co.uk.
Budget, Belfast, tel: 028-9023 0700; Belfast City Airport, tel: 028-9045 1111; Belfast International Airport, tel: 028-9442 3332. www.budget.ie.
Europcar, Belfast City Airport, tel: 0871-384 3425; Belfast International Airport, tel: 028-9445 9644; www.europcar.co.uk.
Hertz Rent-a-Car, Belfast International Airport, tel: 028-9442 2533; Belfast City Airport, tel: 028-9073 2451; www.hertz.co.uk.

Cycling

Cycling is enormously popular in Ireland. Throughout Ireland, Rent-a-Bike dealers hire out sturdy Raleigh Tourer bicycles, which can sometimes be delivered to airports. Expect to pay about €80 a week for rental. For a list of Raleigh Rent-a-Bike dealers, see www.raleigh.ie. In Dublin, visitors can buy a three-day ticket and avail of the city's bike-sharing scheme. See www.dublin bikes.ie. For cycling events around the country see www.ireland.com/cycling.

A – Z

A HANDY SUMMARY
OF PRACTICAL INFORMATION

A

Accidents and Emergencies

For **emergency services**, such as police, ambulance, fire service, lifeboat and coastal rescue, tel: 999 in Northern Ireland and either 999 or 112 in the Republic. The **Samaritans**, who help lonely, depressed and suicidal people, can be contacted on 1850-609 090 and in Northern Ireland on 028-9066 4422. See www.samaritans.org for your local branch.

Other Useful Numbers

Aids Helpline Dublin, tel: 1800-459 459 and Belfast, tel: 0800-137 437.
Alcoholics Anonymous, Dublin, tel: 01-842 0700; Belfast, tel: 028-9043 4848.
Drug Treatment Centre, tel: 01-648 8600, www.addictionireland.ie.
Poisons Information Service, Dublin, tel: 01-809 2566, www.poisons.ie.
Rape Crisis Centre, Dublin, tel: 1800-788 888 and Belfast, tel: 028-9032 9002.
Tourist Victim Support, Dublin, tel: 01 661 0562, Belfast +44 2890 244039.

Accommodation

It is possible to pay as much as €350 or more for a room in a top-rated hotel, or as little as €30 each for 'bed and breakfast' in a family home which takes visitors. Expensive is not necessarily better, of course, but generally speaking the more you pay, the more facilities are on offer. Most B&Bs have 'en-suite'

rooms with a shower or bath, as well as TV, phone and Wi-Fi. Some – especially farmhouses – offer first-class food. Prices vary. Both the Irish Republic and Northern Ireland classify hotels on a star rating. Guesthouses is a category for B&Bs with over five rooms. Some, but not all, have restaurant facilities. Guesthouses are not licensed to sell beer and spirits (unless the guesthouse is also a pub), but some have wine licences.

Hostels

The Irish Youth Hostel Association (An Oige) 61 Mountjoy Street, Dublin 7, tel: 01-830 4555; www.anoige.ie, has 24 hostels in the Republic, with fees varying from €15 to €25 per person per night, with a €2 discount per night for members. Hostels in Northern Ireland are run by Hostelling International Northern Ireland (www.hini.org.uk). Members of the International Youth Hostel Federation can use any of these.

Independent Holiday Hostels of Ireland (IHH) is an umbrella organisation for about 125 privately owned hostels. Like An Oige, these are relaxed places, with no curfews. Bed linen is supplied, but towel hire is usually extra. As well as traditional dormitory accommodation, many also have private double and family rooms, and offer cooked breakfast as an optional extra, as well as kitchen facilities. For a brochure, contact the IHH Office, PO Box 11772, Fairview, Dublin 3, tel: 086-2158786 www.hostels-ireland.com.

All independent hostels are privately owned, and can vary from scenic organic farms to a tiny townhouse stacked with bunk beds. The one drawback is a tendency to

overcrowding in July and August and at festival times. Some hostels prefer not to belong to any organisation, and may not have been inspected for compliance with fire regulations.

Budget Accommodation

The Irish student and youth travel company USIT runs Kinlay House year-round centres in Dublin (tel: 01-679 6644) and Cork (tel: 021-450 8966). Prices start at around €16. During the long vacation from mid-June to mid-September, they also offer self-catering apartments in UCD Village, Belfield Campus, Dublin 4 (tel: 01-269 7111). Brookfield Holiday Village, also offer apartments at College Road, Cork (tel: 021-434 4032; www.brookfieldvillage.ie) with prices starting at €25.

Self-catering Accommodation

This is available in houses, cottages (some thatched), apartments, caravans and even a few castles. If you are looking for a 'traditional Irish cottage' be warned that many are newly built in artificial 'clusters', and used solely for holiday rentals. Be sure you are getting what you want when you book. If touring the Republic, you can ask one of the local tourist offices to book ahead for you; a small charge is made for telephone costs.

B

Budgeting for Your Trip

Ireland is in the Eurozone, and has relatively high levels of VAT at 23 and 13.5 percent (17.5 percent in Northern Ireland). Restaurant meals, pub prices, wine, sweets and even newspapers all come under the 23 percent band, making everyday life more expensive than in many other European countries. Two people should budget using the guidelines below (though variables in meals and hotels can cause prices to rise considerably). Prices in Dublin will be higher than in rural areas. Most hotels and some B&Bs outside Dublin raise their rates in July and August. Major sporting fixtures, bank holidays and other big events also mean rises.

Double room per night in a three-star hotel: €60–120
Simple lunch for two: €16–24
Two-course dinner for two: €40–55
Car hire per week: €190
Miscellaneous (drinks, tips etc.): €30 per day (for two).

C

Children

Irish people love children, and give them a warm welcome. Baby supplies are easily obtained from supermarkets and smaller stores. Children are usually welcome at hotels and B&Bs, and most can supply special cots or babysitting services. Many hotels allow children under a certain age to stay in their parents' room at no extra charge, but the age limit varies. Most middle-range restaurants can supply highchairs, and there is usually a children's menu. The bigger restaurants and pubs should have nappy-changing facilities. Some of the grander establishments will only accept children over a certain age, usually about 12. Children are usually welcome in pubs frequented by visitors, but expected to be under the control of an adult at all times. Some landlords like children to be off the scene by early evening, and the law prohibits under-18's on any premises that serve alcohol after 9pm. Young people cannot drink alcohol until they are 18, and photo ID should be carried. During holiday periods, there are plenty of child-oriented activities designed by museums, local festivals and outdoor centres – Tourist Information Centres will have full details. Look out for family tickets, offering good-value deals.

Climate

Although Ireland lies at roughly the same northerly latitude as

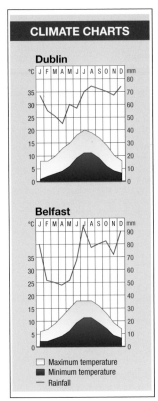

CLIMATE CHARTS

Dublin

Belfast

☐ Maximum temperature
■ Minimum temperature
— Rainfall

Newfoundland, it has a mild, moist climate, because of the prevailing southwesterly winds and the influence of the warm Gulf Stream along its western coast. As no part of the island is more than 70 miles (110km) from the sea, temperatures are fairly uniform over the whole country.

Average air temperatures in the coldest months, January and February, are mainly between 4°C and 7°C (39–45°F). The warmest months, July and August, have average temperatures between 14°C and 16°C (57–61°F), but occasionally reaching as high as 25°C (77°F). The sunniest months are May and June, with an average of between 5.5 and 6.5 hours a day over most of the country. The sunniest region is the extreme southeast.

Parts of the west of the country, with annual rainfall averaging 59ins (1,500mm), are twice as wet as the east because of the prevailing Atlantic winds.

Clothing

Casual clothing is acceptable almost everywhere in Ireland, including smart hotels and restaurants. Because of

the unpredictability of the weather, pack an umbrella, some rainproof clothing and a warm sweater, even in summer. But bring the suntan cream as well: when the summer sun shines, the ozone-laden winds from the Atlantic can intensify the burning effect of its rays.

Crime and Safety

While rural Ireland is generally a low-risk area for crime, visitors are often considered easy pickings. Hired cars are easy targets for criminals, and thefts from cars are commonplace in Dublin, other major towns and cities, and also in the car parks of visitor attractions. Never leave anything in sight in your car. Pickpockets operate in small gangs in central Dublin.

If you should have a bad experience, **Crime Victims Helpline** (tel: 1850-211 407, www.crimevictims helpline.ie) provides invaluable help.

Customs and Entry Regulations

Citizens of many countries do not require visas. EU citizens do not need a passport to enter Ireland, but most air and sea carriers require some form of photo identification, and some insist on a passport. Non-UK nationals must have a valid passport or national ID card for stays of up to three months.

If you are coming from outside the Eurozone, you must now fill in a customs declaration form for cash sums of over €10,000 taken into or out of the Republic of Ireland.

If you are arriving in Ireland from another EU country, you can bring in the following items without paying further duties, as long as they are for personal use: 800 cigarettes 200 cigars, 1kg of tobacco, 110 litres of beer, 90 litres of wine, 10 litres of spirits and 20 litres of fortified wine.

Residents of non-European countries can bring in 200 cigarettes or 50 cigars or 250 grams tobacco, plus 1 litre of spirits or 2 litres of fortified red wine, and 2 litres of wine plus 60ml perfume, 250ml eau de toilette and up to €175 worth of all other goods.

The customs restrictions between the Republic and Northern Ireland are normally limited to animals and agricultural products. There are no longer any border security checkpoints.

For more customs regulations information, visit www.revenue.ie.

D

Disabled Travellers

Ireland is still introducing facilities such as ramps and accessible toilets for people with disabilities. Public transport also lags behind, especially outside Dublin. However, visitors with disabilities often find that peoples' helpfulness makes up for the lack of amenities. The key organisation to contact for practical information, including wheelchair sales and rental, parking permits and holidays is the **Irish Wheelchair Association**, Ara Cuchulainn, Blackheath Drive, Clontarf, Dublin, tel: 01-818 6400, www.iwa.ie.

The official government body responsible for the rights of people with disabilities is **National Disability Authority**, 25 Clyde Road, Ballsbridge, Dublin 4, tel: 01-608 0400 (www.nda.ie). They will have up-to-date information on disability issues. The Head Office of **Fáilte Ireland** can advise on attractions and accommodation suitable for disabled visitors (88–95, Amiens Street Dublin 1, tel: 01-884 7700, www.discover ireland.ie).

In Northern Ireland the campaigning body **Disability Action** also offers practical advice. (2 Annadale Ave, Belfast, tel: 028-9029 7880 www.disabilityaction.org).

E

Electricity

220 volts AC (50 cycles) is standard. Hotels usually have dual 220/110 voltage sockets for electric razors only. To use their own small appliances, visitors may need a plug adaptor (best purchased in their home country) to fit Ireland's 3-pin flat or 2-pin round wall sockets.

Embassies and Consulates

Dublin

Australia: Fitzwilton House, Wilton Terrace, Dublin 2; tel: 01-664 5300; www.ireland.embassy.gov.au.
Britain: 29 Merrion Road, Dublin 4; tel: 01-205 3700, www.british embassyinireland.fco.gov.uk.
Canada: 7–8 Wilton Terrace, Dublin 2; tel: 01-231 4000, www.canada.ie.
US: 42 Elgin Rd, Dublin 4; tel: 01-668 8777; http://dublin.usembassy.gov.

South Africa: Earlsfort Terrace, Dublin 2, tel: 01-661 5553 http://south african.embassydublin.com.

Belfast

American Consulate General, 223 Stranmillis Road, Belfast, tel: 028-9038 6100, http://belfast.us consulate.gov.

Events

The number of events and festivals, big and small, increases every year. There are folk festivals, music festivals, oyster festivals, walking festivals, regattas, angling competitions, drama festivals, sporting competitions of all kinds, beauty contests, song contests, parades, car rallies, boat rallies, literary festivals, jazz festivals, agricultural shows, horse shows, commemorations, celebrations, hunt meetings, marathons, summer schools, community festivals, *ceilís*… the list seems endless. The biggest growth area is arts festivals – theatre and film in winter, and multidisciplinary summer events, including the Cork Midsummer Festival (June), Galway Arts Festival (July) and Kilkenny Arts Festival (August).

In many cases, dates and venues are variable and some festivals – particularly the smaller, local ones – may appear and disappear from year to year according to the availability of funds, enthusiasm or organisers.

Here is a small selection, listed in calendar order. Exact dates often vary, and local tourist offices can provide precise dates and details.
Temple Bar Traditional Irish Music & Cultural Festival, in unique historical venues, Dublin. January. Out to Lunch Arts Festival, Black Box, Belfast. January
Six Nations Rugby Championship (Ireland versus England, Wales, Scotland, France, Italy). Home matches at Lansdowne Road, Dublin. February/March.
Audi Dublin International Film Festival. Irish premieres of a selection of Irish and international cinema. Mid-February.
Tedfest, Celebration of Father Ted TV show, Aran Islands, Co Galway. February
St Patrick's Day. Festival of Ireland's national saint. Celebrated throughout Ireland and much of the world, notably in New York City. 17 March.
World Irish Dancing Championships. Attracts over 4000 international competitors. Early April, venue varies.

Mountains to the Sea Literary Festival, Dun Laoghaire, Co Dublin. March
Irish Grand National. This steeplechase (a race over jumps) is the ultimate test for Ireland's finest sports horses, and a thrilling spectacle. Fairyhouse. Easter Monday.
The Cathedral Quarter Arts Festival. Lively celebration of the arts in Belfast's vibrant 'left bank' district. First two weeks in May.
Belfast City Marathon road race. Some 3000 runners take to the streets. May.
Northwest 200: fastest motorcycle road race in Britain or Ireland. Along the Portrush–Causeway Coast, County Antrim. May.
Feile na Bealtaine/Dingle Peninsula Arts and Political Festival, Dingle Peninsula, Co. Kerry. Bilingual festival of culture and debate. Throughout May.
Ballymaloe Literary Festival of Food and Wine, Ballymaloe House, Co Cork, May.
Kinsale Sevens by the Sea, Kinsale, Co. Cork. Europe's largest rugby 7s festival takes place on the May Bank Holiday weekend.
Ballyhoura International Walking Festival. Guided walks for all levels of hill walkers in the rolling country of the Cork-Limerick-Tipperary border. Early May.
Balmoral Show of the Royal Ulster Agricultural Society, Belfast. Mid-May.
Beatyard, Dun Laoghaire, Co. Dublin. Open-air music and entertainment. May.
Listowel Writers' Week, Listowel, Co. Clare. Large friendly literary festival, readings and workshops popular with aspiring authors. Late May/June.
The Cat Laughs Comedy Festival, Kilkenny. International festival of stand-up comedy, with over 50 comedians hoping to bring a smile to the medieval city of Kilkenny. June bank holiday – late May to early June
Music in Great Irish Houses Festival: held in various mansions near Dublin. Early June.
Bloomsday Literary Festival, Dublin. Held on the date on which Joyce's *Ulysses* takes place. Once principally for Joyce buffs, now a city-wide celebration with free street entertainment, including breakfast some years. 16 June.
Walk the Glens, Glens of Antrim. Walking festival in an area known for breath-taking scenery. Early June.

Rory Gallagher Tribute Festival, Ballyshannon, Co Donegal. June.
Bulmer's Forbidden Fruit, Royal Hospital, Kilmainham, Dublin. Electronic dance festival. June
Dubai Duty Free Irish Derby. One-mile flat-race for three-year-old colts is the highlight of the most glamorous festival weekend in the Irish racing calendar. Held at the Curragh. Late June.
Hay Festival Kells, Co Meath. Offshoot of the famous Hay Festival in Wales. June
Westport Festival of Music and Food. Westport, Co. Mayo. Family-friendly two-day celebration in Mayo's most charming town. Late June.
Irish Oaks, the Curragh. Equivalent of the Derby for fillies. Early July.
West Cork Chamber Music Festival, West Cork Literary Festival. Culture reigns in Bantry town for the last week in June and first in July as the highly esteemed music festival is succeeded by internationally known writers at the literary event.
Kinsale Arts Festival – the seaside town plays host to an arts extravaganza with many family-friendly events. And street entertainment. Late June.
Willie Clancy Summer School, Miltown Malbay, Co. Clare. Seaside celebration of traditional Irish music, workshops and performances. Pioneered the revival of set dancing. July.
Orangemen's Day. Marching with Lambeg drums followed by bonfires all over Northern Ireland. 12 July.

Rose Week. The rose garden at Sir Thomas and Lady Dixon Park is one of the best in the world, Belfast. July.
Galway Arts Festival. Massive celebration of international and Irish theatre, film, art, literature and music precedes the races to create a mighty buzz. Mid-July.
Féile an Phobail. West Belfast's massive community festival with concerts, debates, tours, exhibitions and street theatre. July–August.
Galway Races. Heady, often hilarious, holiday horse-racing festival packs the city to bursting point. Late July/August.
Ulster Festival of Steam & Transport, The Showgrounds, Ballymena, Co. Antrim. Up to 30 vintage steam engines assemble. Early August.
Yeats International Summer School. Sligo. Enthusiasts from all over the world come to listen, learn and explore Yeat's much-loved Sligo. Late July to early August.
Dublin Horse Show, RDS, Ballsbridge. Greatest event in the show-jumping calendar. August.
Puck Fair, Killorglin, Co. Kerry. Ancient pagan festival at which a goat is crowned and horses are traded in the traditional manner amid much merry-making. August.
Kilkenny Arts Festival, Ireland's answer to the Edinburgh Festival with big international names from the worlds of drama, music and visual arts. Mid-August.
The Auld Lammas Fair, Ballycastle, Co. Antrim. The North of Ireland's most popular old fair, at which you traditionally 'treat your Mary Ann

to some dulse and Yellow Man. To find out more, go to Ballycastle, last Monday and Tuesday in August.
Ulster Grand Prix (motorcycling). The world's fastest road race, near Belfast. August.
Merriman Summer School, Lisdoonvarna, Co. Clare. A stimulating week of intense intellectual debate about the nation's culture, continued in the pub into the night. Mid-August.
Fleadh Ceoil na Eireann. A massive all-Ireland festival of Irish music, song and dance, centred on competitions. Venue variable. August.
Rose of Tralee Festival, Tralee, Co. Kerry. Party atmosphere as young women of Irish origin from around the world compete in a pageant based on personality; its popularity amazingly endures, even among the younger generation. Late Aug.
Electric Picnic, Stradbally, Co. Kildare. Ireland's biggest open-air music and arts festival. Early September.
Matchmaking Festival, Lisdoonvarna, Co. Clare. Good-natured low-key event in small, friendly town, mainly for the more mature soul-mate seekers. September.
Hurling and Gaelic Football: All-Ireland finals, Croke Park, Dublin. The highlight of the year for followers of the Gaelic Athletic Association and all lovers of fast ball games. September.
Galway Oyster Festival, Galway city. Celebration of the new season for the native bivalve, traditionally accompanied by stout and soda bread. Late September.
National Ploughing Championships. Venue variable. One of Europe's biggest agricultural shows with livestock arena, food and lifestyle villages. Late September.
Dublin Theatre Festival. Late September/October.
Banks of the Foyle Halloween Carnival, Derry City, Co. Londonderry. Halloween events for all the family; spectacular carnival parade. October.
Cork Jazz Festival, Cork City takes over the city, with top names concerts and free pub jazz. October Bank Holiday.
Wexford Festival Opera. The small coastal town hosts two weeks of full-scale productions of lesser-known operas, as it has done for over 60 years. Late October–November.

St Patrick's Cathedral, Dublin.

Dublin City Marathon. The big one for Irish runners, with a large international contingent, too. Late October.

Belfast Festival, Queen's University, Belfast. Ambitious, event-packed two weeks of music, drama, folksong, cinema, with many international participants. Late October/early November.

Bram Stoker Festival. A celebration of the legacy of the Dublin-born gothic author and creator of Dracula, Dublin, Late October.

Leopardstown Christmas Festival, Dublin: top-class National Hunt meeting over 4 days at the end of December. Traditional for Christmas get-togethers.

G

Gay and Lesbian Travellers

There should be no major problems for gay and lesbian travellers in Ireland. Be as safety-conscious as you would in any foreign city or country. But Ireland has only become an inclusive, non-discriminatory society relatively recently, and the best advice is 'don't flaunt it'. The development of the Irish gay scene is recent, and most openly gay Irish are young. Discrimination does still exist, and you are more likely to encounter it the further you get from Dublin, Galway and Cork cities. Gay men looking for a double room may find that all rooms in the B&B have suddenly been booked. Openly gay couples may attract unwanted attention in small-town pubs.

The following Lesbian and Gay Resource Centres offer advice and contacts:

Dublin: Outhouse, 51 Capel Street, Dublin 1, tel: 01–873 4932, www.outhouse.ie.

Cork: www.gaycork.com is Cork's LGBT portal.

Belfast: Queer Space, Old War Memorial Building, 9–13 Waring Street, Belfast City Centre (near St Anne's Cathedral, opposite the Premier Inn), www.queerspace.org.uk.

Gay Switchboard, Dublin, tel: 01-872 1055, www.gayswtchboard.ie offers information and advice.

Information on bars, clubs accommodation and friendly contacts can be found at www.gcn.ie, a lively gay magazine and information service based in Dublin's Temple Bar area.

H

Health and Medical Care

Medical Services

Medical insurance is highly advisable for all visitors. However, visitors from EU countries are entitled to medical treatment in Ireland, North and South, under a reciprocal arrangement.

With the exception of UK citizens, visitors from EU states should obtain form E111 from their own national social security office. These forms entitle the holders to free treatment by a doctor and free medicines on prescription. If hospital treatment is necessary, this will be given free in a public ward. UK visitors need only go to a doctor (or, in an emergency, a hospital), present some proof of identity (e.g. driving licence) and request treatment under EU health agreement.

L

Liquor Laws

The legal drinking age is 18, but some pubs will only serve patrons over 21 carrying photo identity. Pubs in the Republic of Ireland are open seven days a week, from 10.30am. Opening time is at the discretion of the landlord, and can vary from 12.30pm to 4pm or 6pm depending on local trade. Closing time, in contrast, is defined by law, but can vary depending on what sort of licence the pub has. Normal closing time is 11.30pm, but this can extend to 3am on Fridays and Saturdays and during festivals. Sunday opening hours are 12.30pm to 11pm. You are allowed half an hour 'drinking up time' after the official closing time, before you have to leave the premises. All bars in the Republic of Ireland are smoke-free, but heated outdoor 'smoking decks' are often provided. All pubs close on Good Friday and Christmas Day, but hotel bars are open for guests. Persons under the age of 18 are not allowed in the bar areas of licensed premises after 9pm (May to September until 10pm). Persons aged 18 to 21 can be required to produce evidence of age in order to remain in the bar area after those hours.

Opening hours in Northern Ireland are, generally, 11.30am to 11pm Monday to Saturday and 12.30pm to 11pm Sunday. Many pubs have extended opening hours at weekends.

M

Maps

If you intend to do the sort of driving that takes you off the main routes, it is worth buying the Complete Road Atlas of Ireland (Ordnance Survey Ireland and Ordnance Survey of Northern Ireland) which sells for about €9.99. Cyclists and walkers may want smaller scale maps: these can be bought locally from Tourist Information Centres, newsagents and bookshops. Insight Fleximaps to Ireland and Dublin are laminated for ease of use and durability.

Media

Magazines

Hot Press is a lively local pop culture paper. Totally Dublin (www.totallydublin.ie) is a freesheet and website covering Dublin's lively cultural scene, 'high and low'. The Irish Arts Review is a quality glossy magazine published four times a year covering all aspects of fine and decorative arts in Ireland. The Irish Theatre Magazine is a quarterly giving in-depth coverage of theatre nationwide.

Newspapers

The Irish devour newspapers, and have no fewer than five morning newspapers to serve the island's population of 5 million. The Irish Times and the Irish Independent are published in Dublin. The Irish Examiner is published in Cork.

The Irish Times, the most serious and comprehensive, is best for foreign news, arts and business, and has a great letters page. The Independent broadly supports the Fine Gael party and aims for a hard-hitting style. The Examiner is the staple diet of business and farming people in the southwest. Two morning papers are published in Belfast: the Unionist/Protestant Newsletter and the nationalist/Catholic Irish News; it can be fascinating and instructive to compare their treatments of a controversial story.

There are three evening papers: the Evening Herald (from the Independent stable in Dublin),

All bars are now smoke-free.

the *Echo* (Cork) and the *Belfast Telegraph*, which also publishes a tabloid Saturday morning edition. All contain lots of sport and showbiz.

The *Independent* has a Sunday version; also published from Dublin are the *Sunday World*, a lurid tabloid (pin-ups, shocks, scares, scandals, etc.) and the *Sunday Business Post*, which concentrates on business and politics. The London *Sunday Times* Irish edition is published in Cork and distributed nationally. From Belfast, there is *Sunday Life* from the Telegraph stable.

Since all the British dailies and Sundays are readily obtainable on both sides of the border, even the most news-hungry visitor should be satisfied. UK readers can expect an 'Irish edition' of their usual paper, with a focus on Irish topics.

There are nearly 100 local papers, which may be entertaining and informative if you are interested in a particular region, or interested in newspapers themselves.

Radio
RTE1 is the main station for news, current affairs and drama; 2fm has a staple output of pop music and the recently launched Lyric FM is for lovers of classical music. There are also a number of independent local radio stations. In Northern Ireland the commercials-free BBC Radio Ulster has full local coverage, as do the advertising-funded Downtown Radio and Cool FM.

Television
The national broadcasting service, Radio Telefis Éireann (rté) has three TV channels (one of them, TG4, broadcasting exclusively in the Irish language). Ireland's first

independent television network TV3, was launched in 1998 to provide an alternative to rté – 'a middle-of-the-road service aimed at Middle Ireland'.

In addition, the British TV channels (both BBC and commercial channels) can be received by satellite, as can many satellite channels including Sky, ESPN, Setanta Sports and Eurosport. In Northern Ireland, BBC1 includes local coverage, as does its commercial counterpart, UTV.

Money
In 2002 Ireland became one of the first 12 countries to adopt the euro (€). It is divided into 100 cents. The coins used are 1¢, 2¢, 5¢, 10¢, 20¢, 50¢, €1, €2. The notes are €5, €10, €20, €50 and €100.

In Northern Ireland, the British pound (£) is used. Exchange rates vary but many shops in border areas will accept either currency.

In the Irish Republic, banks are open 10am–4pm, Mon–Fri. Branches in small towns may close from 12.30pm to 1.30pm. Most Dublin banks are open until 5pm on Thursday. In Northern Ireland, bank opening hours are 9.30am–4.30pm, Mon–Fri.

Traveller's cheques are accepted at all banks.

MasterCard and Visa are the most commonly acceptable credit cards, followed by American Express and Diners Club. But many small guesthouses and bed-and-breakfast places will expect payment to be made in cash.

O

Opening Hours
Shops and department stores usually open at 9.30am and close at 6 or 7pm, Mon–Sat. In smaller towns, some shops close for lunch between 1pm and 2pm. **Supermarkets** and convenience stores generally open until 9pm, seven days a week, and some until much later. In many towns and smaller cities, shops close one day a week or observe early-closing (1pm, usually on Wednesday or Thursday); Dublin has a number of 24-hour shops. **Post Offices** open 9am–5.30pm, Mon–Fri, and 9–1 Sat; some of the smaller ones close for lunch. **Government offices** are open to the public Mon–Fri, 9am–5pm.

Museums and other tourist sights are often closed on Monday, and outside Dublin and Belfast most have restricted opening hours between November and Easter or late May.

In hotels and B&Bs, **breakfast** is generally served from 8–10am, and in restaurants and pubs until noon. **Restaurants and pubs** generally serve a lunch menu between 12.30 and 2.30pm, and dinner from 6 to 9.30pm.

P

Postal Services
At the time of writing, letters, postcards and airmail weighing less than 50 grams (approximately the weight of an envelope containing up to three regular A4 sheets of paper) cost €0.60 within Ireland, €0.90 to the UK, all European Union countries, and the rest of the world.

In Northern Ireland, British postal rates apply.

Most newsagents and postcard outlets also sell stamps.

Philatelists may obtain information on Irish stamps from the Controller, Philatelic Section, gpo, Dublin 1.

Public Holidays
1 January, 17 March (St Patrick's Day), Good Friday (Northern Ireland only), Easter Monday, First Monday in May, Spring Holiday (last Monday in May in Northern Ireland, first Monday in June in Republic), 12 July (Northern Ireland only), Summer Holiday (first Monday in August in Republic, last Monday in August in Northern Ireland) last Monday in October (Republic only), Christmas Day and 26 December.

R

Religious Services
All hotels and B&Bs will have details of nearby Roman Catholic and Church of Ireland services.

Roman Catholic
Dublin's principal Catholic cathedral is the place to hear the Palestrina Choir, which showcases the best Irish male voices. Latin Mass is sung here every Sunday morning at 11am. Pro-Cathedral, Marlborough Street, off O'Connell Street.

Church of Ireland

At 6pm on Wednesday and Thursday you can enjoy a choral evensong in Dublin's oldest church. Christchurch Cathedral, Christ Church Place.

Muslim

The Islamic Cultural Centre at the Dublin Mosque provides services and information for Ireland's rapidly growing Muslim population, now the third largest congregation after the Church of Ireland. Dublin Mosque, 163 South Circular Road, Dublin 8, tel: 01-453 3242, www.islamireland.ie.

Presbyterian

The Presbyterian Church of Ireland serves the whole island, north and south, and has a membership of about 300,000 in over 560 congregations, 527 of which are in Northern Ireland. The Information Office, Presbyterian Church in Ireland, Assembly Buildings, 2–10 Fisherwick Place, Belfast BT1 6DW, Northern Ireland, tel: 028-9032 2284, www.presbyterianireland.org.

Methodist

There are about 250 Methodist congregations in Ireland. See website for contact details and meeting times. Secretary of Conference, 1 Fountainville Avenue, Belfast, BT9 6AN, tel: 028 9032 4554, www.irishmethodist.org.

Other churches

Unitarian
A lively congregation meets on Sundays at 11am in this handsome 19th-century church in the centre of Georgian Dublin to share a bond of religious sympathy rather than a creed-bound faith. There are also lunchtime talks series. Contact Rev. Bridget Spain, Minister, Unitarian Church, 112 St Stephen's Green West, Dublin 2, tel: 01-478 0638, www.dublinunitarian.org.

Quaker
There are meetings every Sunday at 11am at the Quaker Meeting House, Frederick Street, Off York Street, Belfast. In Dublin meetings are held at 11am on Sundays and 6.15pm on Thursdays at the Quaker Meeting House, 4–5 Eustace Street, Temple Bar, Dublin 1. There are about 30 other meeting houses in Ireland. For details tel: 01-499 8003, or see www.quakers-in-ireland.ie.

Jewish
The Terenure Hebrew Congregation welcomes visitors to join them for daily, Shabat (8.30am) or Yom Tov services conducted according to the Ashkenazi tradition. Rathfarnham Road, Dublin 6, tel: Or contact The Jewish Community Office, Herzog House, 1 Zion Road, Rathgar, Dublin 6, tel: 01492 3751, www.jewishireland.org (website is common to both organisations).

Smoking

Since 2004 smoking has been banned in all enclosed places of work in Ireland, including public transport, airport terminals, cinemas, banks, offices, shops, pubs, restaurants and cafés. Exceptions include hotel and B&B bedrooms and private rented accommodation. Hotels and B&Bs may choose to allow smoking in some bedrooms, or may opt to have smoke-free bedrooms. Ask about their policy when booking. Most pubs and some restaurants have adapted existing beer gardens or patios to cater for smokers.

Telephones

The international dialling code for the Republic of Ireland is **353**. Northern Ireland's code is **44**. If you are calling the North from the Republic, just substitute the code 028 with 048, rather than using the international dialling code.

There are several telecommunications companies operating in Ireland – the largest one being Eircom (www.eircom.ie). A local call from a public telephone costs 40 cents. Public telephones mainly use phone cards, which are widely available from post offices, newsagents and supermarkets. Phonecards cost from €5 up. Telephone boxes are gradually disappearing, as the mobile (cell) gains dominance.

International calls can be dialled direct from private phones, or dial 11818 for the international operator. To contact the local operator, dial 11811. The long-distance services of AT&T, Sprint and MCI are also available.

Telephone services in Northern Ireland are operated by British Telecom; dial 100 for the operator.

Mobile (Cell) Phones

Only mobile phones with GSM will work in Ireland. If your phone is non-GSM, consult with your provider before travelling. It may be cheaper to buy a local SIM card and top up with prepaid calls. Local providers include 3, Meteor, O2, Tescomobile and Vodafone.

If you are coming from the UK, your mobile should work in Northern Ireland, but you will need international roaming in the Republic.

Time Zone

Ireland follows Greenwich Mean Time. In spring, the clock is moved

Tourist Information Centres are a good source of free local maps.

one hour ahead for Summer Time to give extra daylight in the evening; in autumn it is moved back again to GMT. At noon according to GMT, it is: 4am in Los Angeles; 7am in New York; 1pm in Western Europe; 8pm in Singapore; 10pm in Sydney; midnight in New Zealand.

Tourist Information

Irish Tourist Board (Fáilte Ireland)

General enquiries: Fáilte Ireland, 88–95, Amiens Street, Dublin 1, tel: 01-884 7700; (0808-234 2009 in UK, in Ireland 1800-363 626; www.ireland.com). Within the Republic see www.discoverireland.ie
Dublin City: Dublin Tourism, Suffolk Street, (near Grafton Street) Dublin 2, tel: 01-605 7700 (0800-039 7000 in UK); www.visitdublin.com.
For tourist information within Ireland tel. 1890 324 583, for information on Northern Ireland within Ireland tel: 1850-230 330. For accommodation offers visit www.ireland.com.

Regional Offices

Local tourist offices can be found throughout Ireland. A number are mentioned in the Places chapters. For details see www.discoverireland.ie.

Northern Ireland Tourist Board

www.discovernorthernireland.com
Belfast: 59 North Street, Belfast BT1 1NB; tel: 028-9023 1221.
Dublin: 16 Nassau Street, Dublin 2; tel: 01-679 1977, or 1890-230 330.

Tourism Ireland Offices Abroad

For information on the whole island.
Australia: 5th level, 36 Carrington Street, Sydney 2000, NSW; tel: 02-9299 6177; www.ireland.com.
Britain: Nations House, 103 Wigmore Street, London W1U 1QS; tel: 020-7518 0800, fax: 020-7493 9065, www.ireland.com.
Canada: 2 Bloor Street West, Suite 3403, Toronto, ON M4W; tel: 800-223 6470/416-925 6368; www.ireland.com.
New Zealand: Level 6, 18 Shortland Street, Private Bag 92136, Auckland 1; tel: +649-977 2255,; www.ireland.com.
US: 345 Park Avenue, New York, NY 10154; tel: +1 800 2223 6470/212-418 0800; www.ireland.com.

Websites

General

(For regional tourist information, see list above.)

www.ireland.com The official marketing website of Tourism Ireland, it covers both the Republic of Ireland and Northern Ireland, and is designed to help you plan your holiday.
www.discoverireland.ie This is the website to use in the Republic of Ireland to plan your day-to-day activities, book accommodation and find out about festivals and other events.
www.discovernorthernireland.com Information on Northern Ireland.
www.irishabroad.com celebrates all things Irish, and has some quirky stories.
www.ireland-information.com is a free information service covering everything from genealogy to Irish jokes.
www.irelandofthewelcomes.com carries extracts from Tourism Ireland's excellent magazine, *Ireland of the Welcomes.*
www.overheardindublin.com Genuine vox pops. Prepare for the capital by familiarising yourself with its famous wit. Not for the prudish.

Accommodation

Accommodation can be booked though Ireland.com, discoverireland. ie and discovernortherieland. com above, all of which are run by government-funded official Irish tourism organisations.
www.goireland.com You can reserve accommodation online anywhere in Ireland, north and south, and also book ferries, flights and car hire.
www.irelandhotels.com Book a hotel online at the website of the Irish Hotels Federation.
www.nihf.co.uk The Northern Ireland Hotels Federation.
www.irelandbluebook.com contains Ireland's most upmarket country house hotels and restaurants.
www.hostels-ireland.com Book a Tourist Board-approved holiday hostel online.

Eating Out/Food

www.bordbia.ie to locate the nearest farmers' market.

Genealogy

www.nli.ie. The Genealogy Office of the National Library in the best starting place.

Heritage

www.heritageireland.ie gives details of the National Monuments, historic houses, parks and gardens in State care. Buy a Heritage Card on day one for great savings on admission fees.

The website www.dublinbus.ie will help you find your way around.

www.heritageisland.com introduces over 80 places to visit, with a map to download and a discount scheme to join.

Leisure and Sport

www.irishgolf.ie All that golfers need to know.
www.isasurf.ie Surfing updates.
www.irishtrails.ie Information on walking in Ireland from long-distance waymarked trails to a stroll in the park
www.gaa.ie To track down a game of hurling or Irish football.
www.discoverireland.ie/activities has a wealth of information on walking, cycling, angling, golf, horse riding and cruising the Shannon and the canals.

Transport

www.aaireland.ie Driving advice, time and distance between cities, etc.
www.irishrail.ie Get timetables and book tickets on Ireland's railways.
www.buseireann.ie for local and intercity bus services outside Dublin.
www.dublinbus.ie for bus services within Dublin.
www.dublinairport.com live flight information and links to all airlines.

Weather

www.met.ie for the latest forecast.

What's On

www.entertainment.ie will tell you what's on in theatres, cinemas, clubs and at festivals.
www.comhaltas.com for news of the Irish traditional music scene.

FURTHER READING

IRISH CLASSICS

Easons, the Dublin book retailer and wholesaler, compiled a list of the top Irish classics of all time. It serves as a useful introduction to the key figures from the past:

Gulliver's Travels by Jonathan Swift (1667–1745). The Dean of Dublin's St Patrick's Cathedral was also great satirist, the original book is a savage indictment of mankind's folly, far removed from the many children's adaptations.

The Vicar of Wakefield by Oliver Goldsmith (1728–74). A graduate of Trinity College, Dublin, like many others he headed for London where his comic novel about a hapless vicar, and his hilarious play *She Stoops to Conquer* gave him enduring fame.

Castle Rackrent by Maria Edgeworth. Published in 1800, Edgeworth's novel uses pointed humour to question Anglo-Irish identity and absentee landlords.

The Complete Works of Oscar Wilde (1854–1900). Besides his sparkling drawing room comedies, Wilde also wrote, poetry, essays, charming children's stories and a novel.

The Complete Works of W.B. Yeats (1865–1939). Winner of the 1923 Nobel Prize for Literature, beside his achievements as poet and dramatist, he played a key role in the struggle for Irish independence, was a founder of the National Theatre and a Senator.

Dracula by Bram Stoker (1847–1912). The only novel of Dublin-born Stoker's large output still read.

The Playboy of the Western World by J.M. Synge (1871–1909). The masterpiece of a multi-faceted writer who invented a new language using the poetry inherent in the Irish vernacular. Its earthy realism caused riots at its Abbey premiere.

Portrait of the Artist as a Young Man; Dubliners; Ulysses by James Joyce (1882–1941). His coming-of-age novel and the collection of Dublin stories will help you decide whether to tackle his magnum opus, *Ulysses*.

Shadow of a Gunman; Juno and the Paycock; The Plough and the Stars by Sean O'Casey (1880–1964). His trilogy of tragicomedies are set in the Dublin tenements, and deal with the problems of ordinary families caught up in historic events.

CONTEMPORARY FICTION AND POETRY

Fiction

More Pricks than Kicks by Samuel Beckett. People are often surprised at how funny the Nobel Laureate's first story collection is, with its cast of outrageous Dublin characters.

Murphy by Samuel Beckett. Aspiring authors may be encouraged to know that this comic first novel was rejected by 41 publishers.

The Third Policeman by Flann O'Brien. Straight-faced novel of absurdist humour.

An Old Woman's Reflections by Peig Sayers. Memoir written in Irish by a natural storyteller about life on the Great Blasket Island.

The Islandman by Tomás O Crohan. Vivid memoir of a Great Blasket Island farmer-fisherman, written originally in Irish.

The Ginger Man by J.P. Donleavy. Exuberant, often hilarious, account of post-war Dublin, as seen by a hard-living American.

Langrishe, Go Down by Aidan Higgins. The last great Irish 'big house' novel, chronicling its decline, championed by Samuel Beckett and Harold Pinter.

The Country Girls; A Fanatic Heart: Selected Stories, Saint and Sinners by Edna O'Brien. While Ireland's leading female author's first novel is a witty picture of Dublin in the 1950s, the stories are darker and deeper.

Troubles by J.G. Farrell. Wry, atmospheric account of sitting out the Civil War in a crumbling hotel.

The Book of Evidence and **The Sea** by John Banville. A leading intellectual as well as a novelist, his 1989 novel is the disturbing story

of a sleazy Dublin murderer, while his 2005 Booker Prize-winner is a tender account of lost love.

The South by Colm Toibín. Now an internationally known novelist and travel writer, his first novel about an Irishwoman's love affair with Spain remains one of his best.

Collected Short Stories; The Last September by Elizabeth Bowen. One of the last writers in the Anglo-Irish tradition, her compelling novel is set in the Troubles.

Collected Short Stories by William Trevor. Set in both England and Ireland, among the plain people. Trevor is a master of the quiet epiphany.

Creatures of the Earth: New and Selected Stories by John McGahern. One of the most understated and highly rated chroniclers of rural Ireland.

There are Little Kingdoms; Dark Lies the Island by Kevin Barry. Short stories that use anarchic comedy to skewer the absurdities of post-Celtic Tiger rural Ireland. A name to watch.

All Names Have Been Changed by Claire Kilroy. A wry look at 1980s Ireland and its literary culture by an up-and-coming young novelist, set at Trinity College Dublin in a tight-knit group of creative writing students.

Poetry

Penguin Book of Contemporary Irish Poetry edited by Peter Fallon and Derek Mahon. Well-balanced selection of today's poets.

Collected Poems by Louis MacNeice. A major 20th-century poet, born in Ulster and educated in England, where he lived.

Collected Poems and **Finders Keepers** by Seamus Heaney. Superbly crafted lyric poems by Ireland's latest winner of the Nobel Prize for Literature, and a collection of his incisive literary essays and lectures.

Collected Poems by Derek Mahon. A major 20th-century poet in the metaphysical mode, his more

sophisticated œuvre is considered by many to be superior to Heaney's.
Collected Poems by Michael Longley. At his best, his perceptive lyrics, often nature-inspired, can stand beside fellow Ulster poets, Heaney and Mahon.
A Snail in My Prime by Paul Durcan. Popular, readable poet, known for his quirky humour and often agonising honesty.

HISTORY

Luck and the Irish: A Brief History of Change, 1970–2000 by Roy Foster. An enjoyable analysis of how the Celtic Tiger came to growl and how everyday life was transformed.
Modern Ireland 1600–1972 by R.F. Foster. Readable academic history with many new insights.
The Course of Irish History edited by T.W. Moody and F.X. Martin. General narrative history, by established experts in each period, revised and updated.
The Story of Ireland: In Search of a New National Memory by Neil Hegarty. Book of the 2012 RTE TV series in which journalist Fergal Keane takes a fresh look at Irish history.
Ireland – A History by Robert Kee. Readable illustrated history, good on disentangling the Troubles.
How the Irish Saved Civilization by Thomas Cahill. A humorous look at Irish achievements down the years, with a serious core.
The Great Hunger: Ireland 1845–1849 by Cecil Woodham Smith. The classic account of the Famine is a harrowing but compelling narrative.
Atlas of the Great Irish Famine edited by John Crowley, William J. Smith and Mike Murphy. Computer generated graphics and authoritative essays elucidate the causes of the Great Famine and its effects.
Twilight of the Ascendancy by Mark Bence Jones. Well-informed social history documenting the demise of the 'big house'. Wonderful old photos.

BIOGRAPHY

James Joyce by Richard Ellman. One of the finest literary biographies.
W.B. Yeats, a Life by R.F. Foster. Definitive two-volume life of the poet by leading historian.
Damned to Fame: A Life of Samuel Beckett by James Knowlson. The official biography.

Michael Collins by Tim Pat Coogan. The life of the pro-Treaty politician on which Neil Jordan's 1996 film was based.

MEMOIRS AND JOURNALISM

Angela's Ashes by Frank McCourt. Bestselling account of a miserable childhood in Limerick, subsequently filmed in 1999.
Are You Somebody by Nuala O'Faolain. The 200-page introduction to the late author's collected journalism is admirably candid about her problems with alcohol and sex.
To School Through the Fields by Alice Taylor. A quiet account of a rural childhood in the 1940s, which became an international bestseller.
McCarthy's Bar by Pete McCarthy. Humorous account of an Englishman's discovery of his Irish roots. Excellent on pubs.

CURRENT AFFAIRS

A Place Apart by Dervla Murphy. Her 1978 account of Northern Ireland is still first-rate.
After the Ball by Fintan O'Toole. One of Ireland's sharpest cultural commentators on the legacy of the Celtic Tiger.
Ship of Fools – How Stupidity and Corruption Sank the Celtic Tiger by Fintan O'Toole. All you need to know about Ireland's economic catastrophe presented as a tightly argued polemic.
Wasted – A Sober Journey through Drunken Ireland by Brian O'Connell. An interesting look at the human cost of Ireland's famous love of alcohol-fuelled partying.

Bookshop at the Dublin Writers Museum.

GENEALOGY

Surnames of Ireland by Edward McLysaght. There are numerous pocket books, but this is the standard work.

ARCHITECTURE

The Architecture of Ireland by Maurice Craig. An early account of the uniqueness of Irish architecture and still one of the best.
Georgian Dublin by Desmond Guinness. Enduring illustrated study of Dublin's 18th-century architecture.
The Irish Round Tower by Brian Lalor. Scholarship at its most readable.

ART AND DECORATIVE ARTS

A Concise History of Irish Art by Bruce Arnold. The definitive account, updated to include more on Irish modernism.
Art in Ireland since 1910 by Fionna Barter. Up-to-date survey of contemporary Irish art at home and in the diaspora.
Irish Country Furniture by Claudia Kinmoith. Interesting insights into Ireland's underestimated decorative arts.
Irish Gardens by Olda FitzGerald. Lavishly illustrated guide to the best gardens in the land.

COOKERY

Irish Traditional Cooking by Darina Allen. Authentic recipes.
Wild Food by Biddy White Lennon. Tips on foraging in the Irish countryside and plenty of recipes for Irish wild goods, including seaweed.

Browsing at The Hugh Lane's bookshop.

DRAMA

The Complete Dramatic Works by Samuel Beckett. Includes the famous *Waiting for Godot*.
Plays: One and **Plays Two** by Brian Friel. Includes *Dancing at Lughnasa* and *Translations*.
McPherson: Four Plays by Conor McPherson. Eerie dramas, including *The Weir*, set in the west of Ireland.

FOLKLORE

In Ireland Long Ago by Kevin Danaher. A highly readable account of the fast-disappearing old ways.
Irish Folk Ways by Estyn Evans. Pioneering ethnographical study.
Irish Trees – Myths, Legends and Folklore by Niall MacCoitir. From the Celts onwards, trees have had a special place in Irish folklore.

MUSIC

Irish Traditional Music by Ciaran Carson. Complete guide to playing techniques, singing and instruments, including pub etiquette.
Bringing It All Back Home by Nuala O'Connor. Updated account of the history of Irish traditional music at home and abroad.
Irish Rock by Tony Clayton-Lea and Richard Taylor. The growth of the Irish rock scene, strong on punk and new wave, including U2.

TRAVEL

Belfast: A Pocket History by Jonathan Bardon and David Burnett. Bestselling account of 13 centuries.
Dublin edited by Peter Somerville Large. History of the city, rich in anecdote.

In Search of Ireland by H.V. Morton. Wallow in nostalgia as an Englishman gets to grips with 1938 Ireland.
The Aran Islands by J.M. Synge. Published in 1907, it is the best book to read on a first visit.
A Place Near Heaven by Damien Enright. A calendar year in west Cork as observed by an amiable nature lover.
The Height of Nonsense by Paul Clements. Light-hearted account of climbing the highest peak in each of Ireland's counties.
Connemara: Listening to the Wind and **Connemara: The Last Pool of Darkness** by Tim Robinson. Magisterial and mesmerising two-

Send Us Your Thoughts

We do our best to ensure the information in our books is as accurate and up-to-date as possible. The books are updated on a regular basis using local contacts, who painstakingly add, amend and correct as required. However, some details (such as telephone numbers and opening times) are liable to change, and we are ultimately reliant on our readers to put us in the picture.

We welcome your feedback, especially your experience of using the book "on the road". Maybe we recommended a hotel that you liked (or another that you didn't), or you came across a great bar or new attraction we missed.

We will acknowledge all contributions, and we'll offer an Insight Guide to the best letters received.

Please write to us at:
Insight Guides
PO Box 7910
London SE1 1WE
Or email us at:
hello@insightguides.com

volume exploration of Ireland's great wilderness landscape, from polymath mathematician and artist turned mapmaker and author.
Eating Scenery: West Cork, the People and the Place by Alannah Hopkin. A close look at a scenic corner of rural Ireland, concentrating on the huge social changes of the past 30 years.

LANDSCAPE AND TOPOGRAPHY

The Shell Guide to Reading the Irish Landscape by Frank Mitchell and Michael Ryan. Explaining the natural, historical and geological factors that have shaped the Irish landscape.
Atlas of the Rural Irish Landscape edited by F.H.A. Allen, Kevin Whelan, Matthew Stout. Case studies of the effects on the landscape of changes in land use from prehistoric times to the present day, revised edition 2012.
Farming and the Burren by Brendan Dunford. Analyses the impact man's activities have had on this strange limestone landscape from Neolithic times to the present.
Handbook of the Irish Seashore by Matt Murphy. What lurks in the rock pool.
The Blasket Islands – Next Parish America by Joan and Ray Stagles. The moving story of the hardy inhabitants of a small island off the coast of Dingle who persisted in the old way of life until 1953.

OTHER INSIGHT GUIDES

More than 180 **Insight Guides** and **Insight City Guides** cover every continent, providing information on culture and all the top sights, as well as superb photography and detailed maps. In addition, a companion series of **Insight Guides Great Breaks** provides a selection of clearly timed walks and tours within UK locations, while **Insight Smart Guides** present comprehensive listings in a snappy, easy-to-find way, held together by an A–Z theme and with a street atlas showing major attractions, hotels and public transport.

Titles that highlight destinations in this region include *Great Breaks: Belfast, Explore Ireland, Insight Guide Pocket Dublin, Insight Guide Pocket Ireland* and *Insight Guide Great Britain*.

CREDITS

Insight Guide Credits

Distribution
UK, Ireland and Europe
Apa Publications (UK) Ltd;
sales@insightguides.com
United States and Canada
Ingram Publisher Services;
ips@ingramcontent.com
Australia and New Zealand
Woodslane; info@woodslane.com.au
Southeast Asia
Apa Publications (SN) Pte;
singaporeoffice@insightguides.com
Hong Kong, Taiwan and China
Apa Publications (HK) Ltd;
hongkongoffice@insightguides.com
Worldwide
Apa Publications (UK) Ltd;
sales@insightguides.com
Special Sales, Content Licensing and CoPublishing
Insight Guides can be purchased in bulk quantities at discounted prices. We can create special editions, personalised jackets and corporate imprints tailored to your needs.
sales@insightguides.com
www.insightguides.biz

Printed in China by CTPS

All Rights Reserved
© 2017 Apa Digital (CH) AG and Apa Publications (UK) Ltd

First Edition 1986
Tenth Edition 2017

www.insightguides.com

Editor: Kate Drynan
Author: Alannah Hopkin
Head of Production: Rebeka Davies
Update Production: AM Services
Picture Editor: Tom Smyth
Cartography: original cartography Berndtson and Berndtson, updated by Carte

Contributors

This new edition of Insight Guide: Ireland was updated by Mary Conneely, a Dublin-based travel writer. It builds on the edition written by Alannah Hopkin and Brian Bell. Other contributors include Biddy White Lennon for the Food chapter, Maxmedia Communications for the chapters on Sport, Golf and Angling, John Daly, Paul Clements, Jane Powers and Tina Neylon.

The chapters on Northern Ireland and Belfast were reworked by Seth Linder, editor of a listings magazine in Belfast.

Thanks also go to Penny Phenix who indexed the guide.

About Insight Guides

Insight Guides have more than 45 years' experience of publishing high-quality, visual travel guides. We produce 400 full-colour titles, in both print and digital form, covering more than 200 destinations across the globe, in a variety of formats to meet your different needs.

Insight Guides are written by local authors who use their on-the-ground experience to provide the very latest information; their local expertise is evident in the extensive historical and cultural background features. All the reviews in **Insight Guides** are independent; we strive to maintain an impartial view. Our reviews are carefully selected to guide you to the best places to eat, go out and shop, so you can be confident that when we say a place is special, we really mean it.

Legend

City maps

	Freeway/Highway/Motorway
	Divided Highway
	Main Roads
	Minor Roads
	Pedestrian Roads
	Steps
	Footpath
	Railway
	Funicular Railway
	Cable Car
	Tunnel
	City Wall
	Important Building
	Built Up Area
	Other Land
	Transport Hub
	Park
	Pedestrian Area
	Bus Station
	Tourist Information
	Main Post Office
	Cathedral/Church
	Mosque
	Synagogue
	Statue/Monument
	Beach
	Airport

Regional maps

	Freeway/Highway/Motorway (with junction)
	Freeway/Highway/Motorway (under construction)
	Divided Highway
	Main Road
	Secondary Road
	Minor Road
	Track
	Footpath
	International Boundary
	State/Province Boundary
	National Park/Reserve
	Marine Park
	Ferry Route
	Marshland/Swamp
	Glacier Salt Lake
	Airport/Airfield
	Ancient Site
	Border Control
	Cable Car
	Castle/Castle Ruins
	Cave
	Chateau/Stately Home
	Church/Church Ruins
	Crater
	Lighthouse
	Mountain Peak
	Place of Interest
	Viewpoint

INDEX

Main references are in bold type

A

abbeys. *See* monasteries
accidents and emergencies 326
accommodation 326
  contacts 333
Achill Island 232
Achill Sound 233
activities 328
Adare 206
  Adare Heritage Centre 206
  Adare Manor and Golf Resort 206
  Augustinian Friary 206
  Desmond Castle 207
Afro-Celt Sound System 70
agriculture 161
Ahern, Bertie 62
Ahern, Cecilia 75
Aillwee Cave 216
air travel 324
  Aran Islands 229
Allenwood 149
Allihies 190
  Allihies Copper Mine Museum 190
Allingham, William 262
Altar 188
amusement parks
  Gillighan's World 255
  Leisureland (Salthill) 226
  Waterworld and Seaweed Baths (Bundoran) 262
Ancient Order of Hibernians 290
ancient sites 253. *See also* Craggaunowen Project
  Altar Rock 188
  Beaghmore 280
  Beltany Stone Circle (Raphoe) 267
  Carrowkeel Cemetery 253
  Céide Fields 233
  clocháns 196
  Corlea Trackway 244
  Dowth 147
  Drombeg Stone Circle 185
  Dún Aengus (Inishmore) 230
  Dunbeg Fort (Ventry) 196
  Gallarus Oratory 197
  Grange Stone Circle 206
  Grianán of Aileach 268
  Hill of Tara 145
  in Connemara 229
  in Rossmore Forest Park 250
  Janus statue (Boa Island) 283
  Kilfinane Moat 168
  Megalithic cemetery (Carrowmore) 255
  Navan 286
  near Blacklion 247
  Newgrange 147
  of The Burren 218, 217
  Poulnabrone 218, 215
  Staigue Fort (Castlecove) 195
  stone circle (Ahakista) 188

Struell Wells (Downpatrick) 292
White Island statues 282
Andrew Jackson Cottage 297
angling. *See* fishing
Annalong 289
  corn mill 289
Annals of the Four Masters 263
Annamakerrig House 250
Annestown 159
An Spidéal 227
  Spiddal Craft & Design Studios 227
An Taisce 251
Antrim 303
  Antrim Castle Gardens 303
  Clotworthy Arts Centre 303
  Steeple Park 303
Antrim, County 273
Aosdána 80, 81
Aran Islands 229
  tourism 229, 231
architecture 102
  Cahers 215
  contemporary 130
  Georgian 103, 117, 122, 124
  in Belfast 307
  Palladian 239
  religious 167
  round towers 157
  rural bungalows 251
Ardara 265
  Heritage Centre 265
Ardfert 198
Ardglass 291
Ardmore 160
Ardress House 287
Ards Peninsula 293
Argory 287
Arigna Mining Experience 261
Arklow 153
  Arklow Maritime Museum 154
Armagh 285
  County Museum 285
  Mall 285
  Market Place Theatre and Arts Centre 286
  Palace Demesne 286
  Planetarium 285
  St Patrick's cathedrals 285
  St Patrick's Trian 286
Armagh, County 273, 285
art and crafts
  Bennettsbridge craft trail 165
  Celtic Revival 79
  glass and crystal 158, 165
  illuminated manuscripts 78, 119, 157
  Impressionism 80
  Kilkenny Design Centre (Kilkenny) 164
  lace 250
  pottery 283
  prehistoric and Celtic 78
  stained glass 80
  weaving 263

art galleries. *See* museums and galleries
Arvagh 247
Ashford 144
  Mount Usher Gardens 144
Asquith, Herbert 46
athletics 93
Athlone 246
  Athlone Castle 246
Atlantic Drive 233
Auld Sod 162
Autograph Tree (Gort) 217
Avoca 144

B

Bailieborough 248
Ballina 234
Ballinamore 261
Ballinasloe 237
  horse fair 239
Ballinskelligs Bay 194
Ballybunion 94, 198
  Lady's Strand 198
Ballycastle 299
  Auld Lammas Fair 299, 329
  Ballycastle Museum 299
  Bonamargy Friary 299
Ballycopeland Windmill 295
Ballycotton 161
Ballydehob 187
Ballydonegan 190
Ballygalley 298
Ballyhack 156
  Ballyhack Castle 156
Ballyhalbert 295
Ballyholme Bay 296
Ballyjamesduff 248
  Cavan County Museum 248
Ballyliffin 94
Ballymacarbry 167
Ballymena 303
Ballymoney 303
Ballymote 253
Ballynahow 194
Ballyshannon 262
  Rory Gallagher International Tribute Festival 263
Ballyvaughan 216
Ballywalter 295
Baltimore 187
Banagher 240
  Cloghan Castle 240
Banbridge 288
Bandon, River 183
Bangor 295
  North Down Heritage Centre 295
Banna Strand 198
Bann, River 302
Bansha 168
Bantry 188
  Bantry House and Gardens 71, 188
Bantry Bay 38, 188
Banville, John 81

Barnacle, Nora 141
Barnesmore Gap 267
Barrow, River 165, 166
Barry, Commodore John 154, 155
Barry, James 79
Bateman, Colin 316
beaches 10
  around Dublin 144
  Galway and the West 226, 233
  Limerick and the Shannon Region
    210, 211
  Northern Ireland 291, 293, 295,
    296, 297, 299, 302
  Northwest Ireland 255, 258, 262,
    265
  Southeast Ireland 153, 154, 159,
    160
  Southwest Ireland 181, 187, 190,
    193, 195, 196, 198
Beaghmore 280
Béal na Blath 185
Beara Peninsula 97, 182, 190
Bearna 227
Beatty, Sir Alfred Chester 128
Beaufort, Francis 146
Beckett, Samuel 74
bed-and-breakfasts.
  See accommodation
beehive huts. See cloch_ns
Belfast 62
  Albert Memorial Clock 312
  Alfred Street 309
  An Cultúrlann McAdam Ó Flaich
    320
  Aunt Sandra's Candy Factory 319
  Belfast Castle 321
  Belfast Central Library 311
  Belfast City Cemetery 320
  Belfast Exposed 317
  Belfast Harbour 313
  Belfast Metropolitan College 309
  Belfast Print Workshop 319
  Belfast Waterfront Hall 313
  Belfast Zoo 321
  Big Fish 312
  Black Box 318
  Cathedral Quarter 316
  Cave Hill Country Park 321
  City Hall 307
  Clifton House 321
  Clonard Church 320
  Conway Mill 320
  Cotton Court 318
  Craft NI 318
  Creative Writers' Network 74
  Crescent Arts Centre 316
  Crown Liquor Saloon 86, 310
  Crumlin Road 321
  Crumlin Road Gaol 321
  Custom House 312
  Donegall Quay 312
  East Belfast 319
  Elmwood Hall 315
  Europa Hotel 310
  Exhange and Assembly Rooms
    316
  Falls Road 320
  First Presbyterian Church 311
  Gaeltacht Quarter 320
  Grand Opera House 309

  Great Victoria Street 309
  Harland and Wolff 308
  High Street 312
  history 308
  Home Front Exhibition 317
  Kelly's Cellars 311
  Linen Hall Library 310
  Lyric Theatre 315
  Malmaison Belfast hotel 314
  McHugh's bar 312
  Merchant Hotel 318
  Metropolitan Arts Centre (MAC)
    317
  Naughton Gallery 314
  nightlife 316
  Odyssey Arena 312
  Parliament Buildings 319
  Pirates Adventure Golf Course
    319
  political murals 321
  Presbyterian Assembly Rooms
    310
  Provincial Masonic Hall 311
  pubs 86, 310, 311, 314, 317
  Queen's Film Theatre 315
  Queen's Quarter 314
  Queen's University 314
  restaurants 316, 318
  Rosemary Street 311
  Royal Belfast Academical
    Institution 309
  Royal Courts of Justice 313
  Royal Ulster Rifles Museum 317
  Seamus Heaney Centre 315
  Shaftesbury Square 310
  Shankill 321
  Sinclair Seamen's Church 321
  St Anne's Cathedral 317
  St George's Church 312
  St George's Market 313
  St Malachy's Church 309
  St Mark's Church 319
  St Matthews church 321
  Stormont 55, 319
  St Patrick's Cathedral 318
  St Peter's Cathedral 320
  Streamvale Open Farm 320
  taxis 316
  Ten Square hotel 307
  Titanic Belfast 312
  Titanic Dock and Pump House
    313
  Titanic Quarter 312
  tourist information 307
  tours 312, 319
  transport 305
  Ulster Hall 309
  Ulster Museum 315
  Victoria Square 314
  W5 312
  Wellington Place 310
Bellaghy Bawn 281
Belleek 283
  Belleek Pottery 284
Belvedere House and Gardens
  243
Bennettsbridge 165
  Moth to a Flame 165
  Nicholas Mosse Pottery 165
Berkeley, Bishop George 120

Best, George 319
Bettystown 148
bicycle hire 122, 135, 325
  Aran Islands 229
  Burren, The 216
Binchy, Maeve 75
birdlife 184, 260, 303
  birds of prey 216, 284
  corncrakes 266
  eagles 192
  migrations 145
  observatories 187
  of The Burren 216
  of the peat bogs 280
  puffins 212
  sea birds 156, 161, 212, 299
  waders 233
  waterfowl 292
bird sanctuaries. See nature
  reserves and bird sanctuaries
Birr 240
  Birr Castle and Demesne 240
  Dooly's Hotel 241
  Emmet Square 241
  Ireland's Historic Science Centre
    240
  Oxmanton Mall 241
Black Bog 278
Black Books 24
Blacklion 247
Blackshaw, Basil 79
Blackwater, River 159
Blarney 176
  Blarney Castle 176
  Blarney Stone 177
Blasket Islands 197
Blessington 143
  Russborough 143
Blue Raincoat Theatre Company
  256
Boa Island 283
  Janus statue 283
boat and ship building 44
  Asgard II 153
  at Baltimore 187
  currachs 187
  Gypsy Moth III 153
  in Belfast 308
  St Brendan 208
  Titanic 305, 312
boat trips. See also cruising, whale
  and dolphin watching
  Belfast 313
  Galway and the West 226, 227
  Inland Ireland 246
  Limerick and the Shannon Region
    210, 215
  Northern Ireland 281, 287, 295,
    302
  Northwest Ireland 257, 259, 262,
    266
  Southwest Ireland 186, 190, 191,
    193, 194, 197
Bog of Allen 149
Böll, Heinrich 23, 233
Bonaparte, Napoleon 39
Bono 25
Book of Armagh 286
Book of Ballymote 253
Book of Durrow 78

Book of Kells 36
Boole, Professor George 174
Borrisokane 241
boxing 92
Boycott, Captain Charles 233
Boyne, River 146
Boyzone 69
Brandon Bay 195
Brandon Mountain 98
Bray 137
Brian Ború, King 36
Bricklieve Mountains 253
Brittas Bay 144
Broderick, John 281
Brontë, Charlotte 240
Brontë Homeland 288
Brontë, Patrick 288
Brosnan, Pierce 146
Buncrana 268
    Fort Dunree Military Museum 268
Bundoran 262
    Tullen Strand 262
    Waterworld and Seaweed Baths
        262
Bunmahon 159
Bunratty 207
    Bunratty Castle and Folk Park 207
    Durty Nelly's pub 208
Burke, Edmund 120
Burren, The 214, 214
Burtonport 266
Bushmills 301
business hours. See opening hours
bus travel 325
    from England and Wales 325
Butler, Hubert 99
Butlersbridge 247

C

Caha Mountains 190
Caherconnell Visitor Centre 215
Caherdaniel 195
    Derrynane House 194
Cahersiveen 193
    Barracks, The 193
Cahir 167
    Cahir Castle 168
    Swiss Cottage 168
Caiseal 227
Caledon 57
canals 281, 289
    Grand Canal 101
Cape Clear Island 187
Cappoquin 159
    Mount Melleray 159
Carlingford 148
Carlingford Lough 148
Carnlough 298
Carrauntoohil 100, 101
car rentals 325
Carrick 264
Carrick-a-Rede Rope Bridge 299,
    300
Carrickfergus 297
    Carrickfergus Museum & Civic
        Centre 297
    Castle 297
    Flame, The Gasworks Museum
        297

Carrickkildavnet Castle 233
Carrickmacross 250
Carrick-on-Shannon 261
    Costello Memorial Church 261
Carrigaholt 210
Carrigallen 261
Carron 215
    Burren Perfumery & Floral Centre
        215
    Michael Cusack Centre 215
Carrowkeel Cemetery 253
Carrowmore 255
Carruth, Michael 92
Carson, Ciaran 315
Carson, Sir Edward 46, 47
Casement, Roger 198
Cashel 167
    Cashel Palace Hotel 167
    Cormac's Chapel 167
    Rock of Cashel 167
    St Patrick's Cathedral 167
Casino Marino 138
Casla 227
Castle Archdale Country Park 282
Castlebar 234
    National Museum of Country Life
        234
Castleblayney 250
    Hope Castle leisure park 250
Castle Caldwell 283
Castlecaulfield 279
Castle Coole 285
Castlecove 195
    Staigue Fort 195
Castle Espie 292
Castle Leslie hotel 250
Castlepollard 243
castles and fortifications 36, 207
    at Easky 255
    Athlone 246
    Bagenal's Castle (Newry) 289
    Ballyhack 156
    Ballymote 253
    Blarney 176
    Bunratty Castle and Folk Park
        (Bunratty) 207
    Cahir 168
    Carrickfergus 297
    Carrickkildavnet Castle (Achill
        Island) 233
    Castle Cauldwell 283
    Charles Fort (Kinsale) 183
    Cloghan Castle (Banagher) 240
    Cloughoughter 247
    Dalkey 137
    Derry City Walls 275
    Desmond Castle (Adare) 207
    Desmond (Kinsale) 183
    Donegal 263
    Dublin 127
    Dún Aengus (Inishmore) 230
    Dunbeg Fort (Ventry) 196
    Dundrum 291
    Dunguaire Castle (Kinvarra) 217
    Dunluce 301
    Enniskillen 281
    Greencastle 289
    Johnstown (Wexford) 155, 157
    Kilkenny 157, 164
    King John's Castle (Limerick) 202

Knappogue Castle (Quin) 208
Leamaneh 214
Lismore 160
Lynch's Castle (Galway) 223
Malahide 139
Monea 284
Nenagh 241
Parke's Castle 257
Reginald's Tower (Waterford) 157
Roscommon 245
Ross Castle (Killarney) 193
Rossmore 250
Staigue Fort (Castlecove) 195
Thoor Ballylee (Gort) 217
Trim 146
Tully 284
Waterford 157
Castletownbere 190
    MacCarthy's Bar 190
Castletownshend 186
    St Barrahane's Church 186
Castlewellan 291
Castlewellan Forest Park 291
cathedrals
    Christ Church (Dublin) 128
    Christ Church (Waterford) 158
    Christ the King (Mullingar) 243
    Collegiate Church of St Nicholas
        (Galway) 222
    Kildare 162
    Our Lady Assumed into Heaven
        and St Nicholas (Galway) 225
    St Anne's (Belfast) 317
    St Canice's (Kilkenny) 163, 164
    St Carthage's (Lismore) 160
    St Colman's (Cobh) 178
    St Columb's (Derry) 275
    St Fachtnan's (Kilfenora) 214
    St Feithlimidh's (Cavan) 247
    St Fin Barre's (Cork) 173
    St Macartan's (Monaghan) 250
    St Mary's (Dublin) 132
    St Mary's (Limerick) 203
    St Patrick's (Armagh) 285
    St Patrick's (Belfast) 318
    St Patrick's (Cashel) 167
    St Patrick's (Dublin) 128
    St Peter's (Belfast) 320
Causeway Coastal Road 298
Cavan 247
    St Feithlimidh's Cathedral 247
    tourist information 248
Cavan, County 274
Cavendish, Lord Frederick 44
Céide Fields 233
Celbridge 148
    Castletown House 148
Celtic Tenors, The 71
Charles II 37
Charleville Forest Castle 243
Chichester, Arthur 308, 310
Chieftains, The 69
children 327
churches. See also cathedrals
    Augustinian Friary (Adare) 206
    Church of Ireland (Timoleague)
        184
    Clonard (Belfast) 320
    Coolbanagher 242
    Costello Memorial Church 261

Duiske Abbey (Graiguenamanagh) 166
First Presbyterian (Belfast) 311
French (Waterford) 158
Layde Old Church (Cushendall) 299
Our Lady's Nativity (Timoleague) 184
Sinclair Seamen's (Belfast) 321
St Anne's (Cork) 176
St Anne's (Dublin) 123
St Audoen's (Dublin) 129
St Barrahane's (Castletownshend) 186
St George's (Belfast) 312
St Malachy's (Belfast) 309
St Mark's (Belfast) 319
St Mary's (Dublin) 133
St Matthews (Belfast) 321
St Michan's (Dublin) 118, 133, 134
St Multose (Kinsale) 183
Temple Connor (Clonmacnoise) 240
Churchill, Sir Winston 46
Cill Chiarain 227
cinemas
Belfast 315
Irish Film Institute (Dublin) 126
Claddagh Records 68
Claddagh Ring 224
Clane 149
Clannad 69
Clare Island 232
Clarke, Darren 93
Clifden 230
Cliffs of Moher 211, 212, 213
New Visitor Experience 211
O'Brien's Tower 212
climate 327
Galway and the West 233
Gulf Stream, effects of 181, 195
Southeast Ireland 153
Southwest Ireland 181, 189
clocháns 41, 196
Clogheen 167
Clogher 280
Cloghmore 289
Clonakilty 184
Emmet Square 184
General Post Office 184
Michael Collins Centre 185
West Cork Model Railway Village 184
West Cork Regional Museum 185
Clonea 159
Clones 249
Wee Abbey 249
Clonmacnoise 40, 237, 239
Clonmel 167
clothing 327
Cloughoughter Castle 247
Coagh 280
Coalisland 280
Craic Theatre Company 280
Coalisland Enterprise Centre 280
coal mining 260
Cobh 178
Cobh Heritage Centre 178
St Colman's Cathedral 178

Titanic Experience Cobh 178
Coleraine 302
Collins, Michael 48, 185
Collins, Patrick 80
Collins, Steve 92
Collooney 253
Colmcille Heritage Centre 267
Columbus, Christopher 222
Comber 292
comedy 72
Comeragh Mountains 167
Comhaltas Ceoltóiri Éireann 68
concert halls. See theatres and performance venues
Cong 227
Ashford Castle hotel 229
Connemara 226
Connemara Heritage & History Centre 230
Connemara National Park 230
Connolly Cleary 79
Connolly, James 46
Conor Pass 197
Coogan, Amanda 81
Cooke, Barrie 79, 80
Cookstown 280
Cooley Peninsula 148
Coote, Charles 248
Cootehill 248
Bellamont House 248
Copeland Island 295
copper mining 159, 190
Corcomroe Abbey 216
Cork 171
Cork Butter Museum 176
Cork City Gaol 176
Cork Public Museum 176
Crawford Municipal Art Gallery 175
English Market 174
Firkin Crane Centre 176
Fitzgerald Park 176
Grand Parade 173
history 171
Munster Literature Centre 73
Opera House 175
pubs 89
Radio Museum 176
Rory Gallagher Piazza 175
Shandon Bells 176
Shandon Craft Market 176
shopping 175
South Mall 174
St Anne's Church 176
St Fin Barre's Cathedral 173
St Patrick's Street 175
tourist information 173
University College 173
Washington Street 173
Corlea Trackway Visitor Centre 244
Corrib, River 221, 225
coursing 92
Courtmacsherry Estuary 184
Courtown 154
Coyle, Gary 81
Craggaunowen Project 208
Craigavon 287
Crawfordsburn 296
Old Inn 296

Crawfordsburn Country Park 296
Creggan 279
crime and safety 201, 327
drugs trade 61
Croagh Patrick 98, 101, 231
Cromwell, Oliver 37, 147, 157, 163, 206
Cronin, Anthony 81
Cross Border Orchestra of Ireland 71
Cross, Dorothy 79
Crossmaglen 287
cruising. See also boat trips
Inland Ireland 240, 241, 246, 247
Northern Ireland 281
Northwest Ireland 260, 261
Cuilcagh Mountain Park 285
Cultra 296
Ulster Folk and Transport Museum 296, 297
culture and society 19, 59
Curracloe Strand 154
Curragh Racecourse 162
Curragh, The 149, 162
Cusack, Michael 90, 215
Cushendall 299
Curfew Tower 299
Layde Old Church 299
Cushendun 299
customs and entry regulations 327
cycling 325. See also bicycle hire
competitive 92
Dublin 122, 135
Northern Ireland 287, 291

D

Dalkey 137
Dalkey Castle 137
Dalkey Island 137
Daly, Willie 213
Danby, Francis 79
dance
Riverdance 19, 68
traditional 68, 209
Davitt, Michael 45, 74
Deane, Michael 309
Defenders, The 38
de Lorean, John 59
Derreen Gardens 191
Derry 57, 274
Bogside 275
Craft Village 277
Derry City Walls 275
festivals 274
Guildhall 276
Millennium Forum 277
Museum of Free Derry 275
Nerve Centre 277
Peace Bridge 274
Peoples' Gallery 275
Playhouse 277
Roaring Meg 275
Siege of 1689 57, 275
St Columb's Cathedral 275
tourist information 276
tours 276
Tower Museum 276

Verbal Arts Centre 73, 276
VOID 276
Derry, County 273
Derrymore House 289
Dervock 303
Deserted Village 233
de Valera, Eamon 48, 55, 47
Devenish Island 282
Diamond Hill 101
Diarmuid, King of Leinster 157
Dillon, Gerard 80
Dingle 196
An Diseart 196
Dingle Peninsula 97, 182, 195
disabled travellers 328
Doagh Island Famine Village 268
Donaghadee 295
Donard Forest Park 291
Donegal 263
Donegal Craft Village 263
Franciscan abbey 263
Donegal, County 262, 274
Donleavy, J.P. 25
Dooagh 233
Doolin 213
Doolin Cave 211
Doo Lough Pass 100, 231
Down, County 273
Downhill Demesne 302
Downpatrick 292
Down County Museum 292
Downpatrick and County Down
Steam Railway 292
Inch Abbey 292
St Patrick Centre 292
Struell Wells 292
Dowra 247
Dowth 147
driving 325
Dublin ring road 148
Galway ring road 221
Drogheda 147
Beaulieu House 147
Boyne Suspension Bridge 147
Millmount Museum 147
Dromahair 257
Drombeg Stone Circle 185
Dromineer 241
Drowse, River 259
Drumcliff 257
Drum Hills 160
Drumlane Abbey 247
Drumshanbo 260
Drumsna 261
Dublin 25
Abbey Theatre 130
American Embassy 136
architecture 103
Ark 126
Aviva Stadium 93
Ballsbridge 136
Bank of Ireland 118
Belvedere College 133
bicycle hire 122, 135
Blackrock 136
Bloomsday 73
Buswell's Hotel 123
Chester Beatty Library 127
Christ Church Cathedral 128
City Hall 126

Clarence, The 126
Cow's Lane Designer Mart 126
Croke Park 91
Curved Street 125
Custom House 129
docklands development 130
Dublin Castle 127
Dublin City Gallery The Hugh Lane
80, 132
Dublinia 128
Dublin Writers Museum 132
Dublin Zoo 136
Fishamble Street 126
Fitzwilliam Square 124
Four Courts 134
Garden of Remembrance 132
Gate Theatre 132
General Post Office 47, 131
Government Buildings 124
Grafton Street 121
Grand Canal Theatre 131
Gravity Bar 129
Guinness's Brewery 129
Guinness Storehouse 129
Ha'penny Bridge 125
history 50, 118
Irish Film Institute 126
Irish Museum of Modern Art 80, 135
Irish Writers' Centre 73
Iveagh House 122
James Joyce Centre 133
Kilmainham Gaol 135
Kilmainham Royal Hospital 134
Leinster House 123
Liberties 128
Little Museum 122
Mansion House 123
Marsh's Library 128
Merrion Square 123
Molly Malone statue 121
Moore Street Market 131
National Concert Hall 122
National Gallery of Ireland 124
National Library 123
National Museum 123
National Museum of Decorative
Arts and History 136
Natural History Museum 124
Newman House 122
Number 29 124
O'Connell Bridge 118, 129
O'Connell Street 53, 130
O'Connell Street statues 131
Old Jameson Distillery 134
Olympia Theatre 126
Parnell Street 133
Peacock Theatre 130
Phoenix Park 135
Powerscourt Centre 121
pubs 86
Rotunda Hospital 132
Rotunda Rooms 132
Royal Dublin Society 136
Samuel Becket Bridge 131
Shelbourne Hotel 122
Spire of Dublin 131
St Anne's Church 123
St Audoen's Church 129
St Mary's Church 133

St Mary's Pro-Cathedral 132
St Michan's Church 118, 133, 134
St Patrick's Cathedral 128
St Stephen's Green 121
Tailor's Hall 129
Temple Bar 19, 125
tourist information 119
Trinity College 119, 120
West Dublin 134
Writers' Museum 73
Dublin, County 145
Dubliners, The 69
Dugort 233
Dunbrody Abbey 157
Dundalk 148
Dundalk Bay 148
Dundonald Ice Bowl 319
Dundrum 291
Dunfanaghy 266
Art Gallery 266
Dunfanaghy Workhouse 266
Dungannon 279
Linen Green 279
Dungarvan 159
Dungloe 266
Dun Laoghaire 136
Dunlap, John 277
Dunlewey Visitor Centre 266
Dunluce Castle 301
Dunmore East 159
Dunne, Ben 60
Dunquin 197
Durcan, Paul 75
Dzogchen Beara Retreat Centre 190

E

Easky 255
eating out 82. See also restaurants
economy 19, 56, 57, 221
2008 financial crisis 62
Northern Ireland 59
Republic 59
eco-tourism 239, 266
education 199
Egan, Felim 78
electricity 328
Elizabeth I 36
embassies and consulates 328
Emo Court 242
England
relations with 35
Ennis 209
Clare Museum 209
Ennis Friary 209
Enniscrone 94, 253
Kilcullen's Bath House 253
Enniskerry 145
Powerscourt House and Gardens
145
Enniskillen 281
Cole's Monument 282
Enniskillen Castle 281
Ennistymon 211
environmental issues 63
Enya 25, 69
Erne, River 260, 281
source 247

Erne-Shannon Waterway 260
Errigal Mountain 98, 101, 266
European Union 19, 60
Eyeries 191

F

Falcarragh Visitor Centre 267
Farrell, J.G. 188
Fastnet Rock Lighthouse 187
Father Ted 24, 231
Fenians 43
Fermanagh, County 273, 281
ferries
  Aran Islands 215, 229
  Arranmore Island 266
  Ballyhack–Passage East 157
  Buncrana–Rathmullan 268
  Cape Clear and Sherkin islands
    187
  Clare Island 232
  Devenish Island 282
  from Britain 297
  Greencastle–Magilligan Point
    268
  Rathlin Island 300
  Strangford–Portaferry 293
  Tarbert–Killimer 198, 207
  Tory Island 266
  Valentia Island 194
  White Island 282
festivals and events 8, 328
  An Tóstal (Drumshanbo) 260
  arts festivals 76
  Auld Lammas Fair (Ballycastle)
    299, 329
  Baltimore Seafood and Wooden
    Boats Festival 187
  Belfast Festival at Queens
    (Belfast) 330
  Bloomsday (Dublin) 73, 328
  Blues in the Bay (Warrenpoint)
    289
  Burren in Bloom (Ballyvaughan)
    216
  City of Derry Jazz and Big Band
    Festival (Derry) 274
  Connemara Pony Show (Clifden)
    230
  Cork Jazz Festival (Cork) 171,
    329
  Cruinniú na mBád (gathering of
    the boats) (Kinvarra) 217
  Cúirt International Festival of
    Literature (Galway) 73, 224
  Dublin Writers Festival (Dublin) 73
  East Cork Early Music Festival 71
  Fleadh na gCuach (Kinvarra) 217
  Fleadh Nua (Ennis) 209, 210
  Galway Arts Festival (Galway) 77,
    221, 224, 329
  Galway Races (Galway) 77, 224,
    329
  Great Music in Irish Houses
    Festival 69
  Halloween Carnival (Derry) 274,
    329
  Immrama (Lismore) 73
  International Choral Festival
    (Cork) 171

Joe Mooney Summer School
    (Drumshanbo) 260
  Listowel Writers' Week (Listowel)
    73, 198, 328
  Maiden of the Mourne
    (Warrenpoint) 289
  Matchmaking Festival
    (Lisdoonvarna) 213, 329
  Orangemen's Day parades
    (Northern Ireland) 37, 290,
    329
  Puck Fair (Killorglin) 193, 329
  Rory Gallagher International
    Tribute Festival (Ballyshannon)
    263
  Rose of Tralee Festival (Tralee)
    198, 329
  Shannon International Music
    Festival (Limerick) 71
  Sligo Baroque Music Festival 71
  St Patrick's Day 292, 328
  Tedfest (Inishmore) 231
  walking festivals 99
  West Cork Chamber Music
    Festival (Bantry) 71
  West Cork Literary Festival
    (Bantry) 73
  Wexford Festival Opera (Wexford)
    71, 155, 329
  Yeats International Summer
    School (Sligo) 256, 329
Field, John 71
film industry and locations 26,
    134, 143, 146, 154, 160, 165,
    196, 229
  Ardmore Studios (Bray) 26
  Galway and the West 230
fish farming 267
fishing 96, 196
  Galway and the West 227, 234
  Inland Ireland 237, 241, 247
  Northern Ireland 283, 287, 295,
    302
  Northwest Ireland 258, 259, 260,
    261, 262
  regulations and licences 97
  sea fishing 96
  Southwest Ireland 194
fishing industry 161, 187, 190,
    229, 264, 303
Florence Court 285
Foley, John Henry 79
food and drink 82, 86. See
    also eating out, pubs, restaurants
  cheeses 181
  cider 167
  contemporary Irish cuisine 83
  Euro-Toques 83
  farmers' markets 85
  Féile Bia programme 85
  fish and shellfish 182
  fuchsia branding 185
  Guinness 89, 129
  Irish coffee 208
  liqueurs 243
  liquor laws 330
  local produce 181
  poteen 298
  whiskey 161, 301
football, Gaelic 91

football, soccer 92, 93
forest parks. See parks and
  gardens
Forkhill 287
Forsyth, Frederick 59
Fota Arboretum 177
Fota Estate 177
Fota Island 177
Fota Wildlife Park 177
Foyle, River 274
Foynes 207
  Foynes Flying Boat Museum 207
Frames, The 70
French, Percy 295
friaries. See monasteries
Friel, Brian 75
further reading 334

G

Gaelic Athletic Association 90,
    215
Gaelic League 45
Gaeltachts 72, 199, 227
Gale, Martin 79
Gallagher, Rory 175, 263
Gallarus Oratory 197
gallowglass 245
Galway 221
  An Taibhdhearc 224
  Ballybrit Racecourse 224
  Browne's Gateway 222
  Cathedral of Our Lady Assumed
    into Heaven and St Nicholas
    225
  Claddagh 224
  Claddagh Museum 224
  Collegiate Church of St Nicholas
    222
  Corrib Princess cruises 226
  Druid Theatre Company 224
  Eyre Square 222
  farmers' market 223
  festivals 77, 224
  Fishmarket 225
  Galway City Museum 224
  Galway Races 77, 224, 329
  history 221
  Long Walk 225
  Lynch's Castle 223
  Music for Galway 224
  National University of Ireland 223
  Quincentennial Fountain 222
  Salmon Weir Bridge 225
  shopping 223
  Spanish Arch 225
  Thomas Dillon's 224
  tourist information 222
Galway Bay 216, 221, 226
Galway, James 290
Gandon, James 118, 129, 242
Gap of Dunloe 100, 193
Garinish Island 189
Garron Tower 298
Gartan Lough 267
gay and lesbian travellers 330
Geldof, Bob 19, 25
genealogy resources 123, 164,
    261, 268, 277, 278, 279, 280,
    333

geography and geology 143, 153, 159, 212, 215, 237, 250, 300
of The Burren 214
Tetrapod footprints (Valentia Island) 194
Giant's Causeway 300
Gibson, Mike 93
Gillighan's World 255
Gladstone, William Ewart 43
Glandore 186
Glasnevin 137
Botanic Gardens 137
Glasnevin Museum and Cemetery Tour 138
Glasson 245
Glebe House Gallery 267
Glenaan 298
Glenariff 298
Glenariff Glen 298
Glenarm 298
Glenballyeamon 298
Glencloy 298
Glencolumbkille 265
Folk Village Museum 265
Glencorp 298
Glendalough 144
Glendun 298
Glendun Viaduct 299
Glengarriff 189
Glengarriff Bamboo Park 189
Ilnacullin Gardens 189
Glenmacnass Waterfall 144
Glen of Aherlow 168
Glenshesk 298
Glens of Antrim 98, 298
Glentaisie 298
Glenveagh National Park 267
Glenview Folk Museum 261
Gold Coast 296
Goldsmith, Oliver 120, 245
golf 94, 206
competitive 93
dress codes 95
Dublin 139
Galway and the West 227
golf resorts 94
Limerick and the Shannon Region 211
Northern Ireland 291, 293
Northwest Ireland 266, 267
Southwest Ireland 194, 198
Gore Booth, Constance 257
Gore Booth, Eva 257
Gort 217
Autograph Tree 217
Coole Park 217
Thoor Ballylee 217
Gougane Barra 189
St Finbar's Oratory 189
Graiguenamanagh 166
Duiske Abbey 166
Grange Stone Circle 206
Grattan, Henry 37
Great Blasket 197
Great Blasket Centre, The 197
Great Island 177
Greencastle 289
Inishowen Maritime Museum and Ianetarium 268
Greenisland 297

Gregg, John 250
Gregory, Lady 130, 217, 258
Greyabbey 294
greyhound racing 92, 267
Grianán of Aileach 268
Griffith, Arthur 46, 48, 47
Guerin, Veronica 61

H

Handel, George Frideric
Messiah 127
statue 127
Hansard, Glen 70
Harrington, Padraig 93
Harris, Richard 202
Harry Clarke Studios 80
Haughey, Charles 60, 81
health and medical care 330
Healy Pass 190
Heaney, Seamus 25, 74, 281
Helen's Bay 296
Henry, Paul 80, 232
Henry VIII 36
Hewitt, John 298
Higgins, Alex 92
Higgins, Michael D. 63
hiking. See walking and hiking, long-distance footpaths
Hill of Slane 146
Hill of Tara 145
historic houses 9, 102
Ardress House 287
Argory 287
Avondale (Rathdrum) 144
Bantry House and Gardens (Bantry) 71, 188
Beaulieu House (Drogheda) 147
Belfast Castle (Belfast) 321
Bellamont House (Cootehill) 248
Belvedere House and Gardens 243
Casino Marino 138
Castle Coole 285
Castletown House (Celbridge) 148
Castle Ward House (Strangford) 293
Charleville Forest Castle 243
Derrymore House 289
Derrynane House (Caherdaniel) 194
Downhill Demesne 302
Drewsborough House (Tuamgraney) 208
Emo Court 242
Florence Court 285
Georgian House and Garden (Limerick) 204
Iveagh House (Dublin) 122
Lissadell House 256
Mansion House (Dublin) 123
Mount Stewart 294
Muckross (near Killarney) 192
Newman House (Dublin) 122
Number 29 (Dublin) 124
Powerscourt House and Gardens (Enniskerry) 145
Rothe House (Kilkenny) 163
Russborough 157

Russborough (Blessington) 143
Shanagarry House (Shanagarry) 161
Slane Castle 146
Springhill House 280
Strokestown Park House 244
Tullynally Castle 243
Westport House & Country Park (Westport) 232
history 30, 157
ancient times 35
Anglo-Normans 36, 118, 157, 221
Battle of Clontarf 36, 118
Battle of the Boyne 37, 290
British Empire 38
Celtic era 118
Celts 35
civil war 50, 52, 131
Confederation of Kilkenny 163
Easter Rising of 1916 46, 257
emigration 42, 54, 56, 178, 276
English rule 36, 118, 157
Flight of the Earls 267
Great Famine of 1845 42, 166, 187, 245, 259
Great Rebellion of 1798 38, 39, 118, 149, 157, 253
Home Rule movement 44
independence and partition 48, 49, 46
independence movement 42
Industrial Revolution 44, 308
Irish Free State 118
medieval Golden Age 35
Northern Ireland Troubles 20, 57, 61, 273, 275, 283, 287
partition 273
Rising of 1916 118, 131
Treaty of Limerick 203, 206
Vikings 36, 118, 157
War of Independence 118
World War I 47, 183
World War II 55
Hollywood 143
Holy Island 209
Holywood 296
Hone, Evie 80
Hone, Nathaniel 80
Hook Head Peninsula 156
Hook Lighthouse 156
horse-drawn caravans 169
horse racing 150
Ballybrit Racecourse (Galway) 224
Curragh Racecourse 162
Galway Races 224
Laytown 148
horses 148, 163
gigs 204
horse fairs and trading 193, 210, 239
Irish Horse Museum (Kildare) 163
National Stud (Kildare) 163
Horslips 69
hotels. See accommodation
Howth 139
Howth Head 139
hurling 90

I

ice hockey 312
Ilen, River 187
Inch 196
industry and commerce
technology 172
industry and technology 60
Inisheer 229
Inishkeen 250
Patrick Kavanagh Centre 250
Inishmaan 229
Inishmore 229
Dún Aengus 230
Inishowen Peninsula 268
Inis Saimer 263
Inistioge 165
Woodstock Gardens and
Arboretum 165
Inland Ireland 237
Innisfallen Island 193
Innishmurray Island 259
Inny, River 97
Ireland's Eye 139
Irish Linen Centre and Lisburn
Museum 288
Irish National League 44
Irish National Volunteers 46
Irish Republican Army (IRA) 43, 49,
61, 55
Irish Republican Brotherhood 43
Irish-speaking areas 72, 182, 187,
196, 199, 227, 230, 266
place names 197
Irish Tenors, The 71
Irish Volunteers 37
Island Magee 297
Iveragh Peninsula 97, 191

J

Jackson, President Andrew 297
James I 37
James II 37
Jellett, Mainie 80
Jennings, Pat 93
Jerpoint Abbey 165
Jerpoint Glass 165
Jordan, Neil 190
Joyce, James 26, 74, 120
Ulysses 140

K

Kavanagh, Patrick 249, 250
kayaking 139
Kealkil 189
Keane, John B. 73
Keating, Sean 80
Keel 233
Kelly, Cathy 75
Kelly, Sean 92
Kenmare 94, 191
Kenmare Heritage Centre 191
Kenmare River 191
Kennedy Homestead 157
Kennedy, President John F. 157,
222
Kenny, Enda 62
Kesh 283

Keyes, Marian 75
Kila 69
Kilbeggan 243
Locke's Distillery 243
Kilcar 264
Kilcock 149
Larchill Arcadian Garden 149
Kildare 149, 162
Irish Horse Museum 163
Irish National Stud 149
Japanese Gardens 163
National Stud 163
Round Tower 162
St Fiachra's Garden 163
Kildare, County 148
Kilfenora 213
Burren Centre 214
St Fachtnan's Cathedral 214
Kilfenora Ceilí Band 213
Kilfinane 168
Kilkee 210
Kilkeel 289
Kilkenny 163
Black Abbey 163
Kilkenny Castle 157, 164
Kilkenny Design Centre 164
Kytler's Inn 164
Rothe House 163
Round Tower 164
Shee Alms House 163
St Canice's Cathedral 163, 164
Tholsel 163
Killala 39, 234
Killarney 182, 191
jaunting cars 192
Muckross Park, House and
Traditional Farms) 192
Ross Castle 193
Killarney lakes 191
Killarney National Park 192
Killary Harbour 231
Killerig 94
Killeshandra 247
Killorglin 193
Glenbeigh Woods 193
Killybegs 264
Maritime & Heritage Centre 264
Killykeen Forest Park 247
Killynether Wood 295
Kilmore Quay 156
Kilronan 229
Kilrush 209
Vandeleur Walled Garden 210
Kilrush Forest Park 210
King, Cecil 80
Kingscourt 248
Kinsale 183
Charles Fort 183
Desmond Castle 183
Kinsale Regional Museum 183
Old Courthouse 183
restaurants 183
St Multose Church 183
Kinvarra 216
Dunguare Castle 217
Murphy Store 217
Kircubbin 293
Kirkistown Circuit 294
Knightstown 194
Knock 234

Knock Folk Museum 234
Kylemore Abbey 231
Kytler, Dame Alice 164

L

Lagan, River 312
Laghy 263
Lahinch 94, 211
Lake Isle of Innisfree 257
Langan, Clare 79, 81
language 45, 168, 199
local dialects 298
Ogham 253
regional accents 173
Lanyon, Sir Charles 307, 308
Laragh 143
Larne 297
Lavery, John 80, 315
Lawlor, John 79
Laytown 148
Leamaneh Castle 214
Le Brocquy, Louis 80
Leenane 231
Sheep & Wool Centre 231
Lee, River 171
Leitrim, County 259
Lemass, Sean 57
Letterkenny 267
Lewis, C.S. 319
Liffey, River 118, 143
Lifford 267
Lifford Greyhound Stadium 267
lighthouses
Black Head 297
Donaghadee 295
Fastnet 187
Hook 156
Loop Head 210
Mizen Head 188
Limerick 201
Bishop's Palace 202
bookshops 205
Crescent, The 204
Georgian House and Garden 204
history 206
Hunt Museum 204
King John's Castle 202
Limerick City Gallery of Art 204
Limerick City Museum 203
Milk Market 205
Newtown Pery 204
People's Park 204
shopping 205
St John's Square 204
St Mary's Church of Ireland
Cathedral 203
tourist information 201
tours 201, 202
Treaty Stone 203
University of Limerick 205
linen 44, 280, 288, 292, 308
liquor laws 330
Lisdoonvarna 213
Matchmaking Festival 213, 329
Lismore 160
Lismore Castle 160
St Carthage's Cathedral 160
Lissadell House 256
Lissavaird 185

Listowel 198
Listowel Writers' Week 73, 198
Seanchaí 73
literature 72, 45. See also individual
writers' names
Dublin Writers Museum (Dublin)
132
illuminated manuscripts 36
James Joyce Centre (Dublin) 133
James Joyce Museum
(Sandycove) 136
Limericks 203
Little Island 177
Lloyd George, David 48
Londonderry. See Derry
long-distance footpaths 11
Beara Way 191
Brandy Pad 101
Burren Coastal Walk 101
Burren Way 212
Cavan Way 99, 248
Dingle Way 101
Grand Canal Way 101
Kerry Way 99
North Antrim Coast Path 302
Sheep's Head Way 188
Slieve Bloom Way 101, 241
Ulster Way 302
Loop Head Lighthouse 210
Lough Allen 97, 259, 260
Lough Corrib 225, 226, 227
cruises 227
Lough Derg 97, 209, 241, 264
St Patrick's Purgatory 264, 265
Lough Derg Drive 241
Lough Derravaragh 244
Lough Ennel 243
Lough Erne 281
Loughgall 286
Dan Winter Ancestral Home 286
Dispensary House Gallery 287
Lough Gara 96
Lough Gill 257
Lough Gur 206
Lough Navar Forest Park 284
Lough Neagh 303
Lough Ree 245
Lough Rynn Castle hotel 261
Louisburgh 231
Lower Lough Erne 281
Lullymore 149
Irish Peatland Conservation
Council Nature Centre 149
Lurgan 287
Lusitania 178, 183

M

MacCarthy, Pete 190
Macgillicuddy's Reeks 193
MacGillycuddy's Reeks 99
Maclise, Daniel 79
Macnas 224
MacNeice, Louis 24
Madden, Anne 79
Magdalen laundries 27, 63
Mahee Island 293
Nendrum Abbey 293
Malahide 139
Malahide Castle 139

Malin Head 268
Mamturk Mountains 226
maps 100, 330
Marble Arch Caves 284
Marconi, Guglielmo 299
markets
Cow's Lane Designer Mart
(Dublin) 126
English (Cork) 174
farmers' market (Galway) 223
farmers' markets 85
Milk Market (Limerick) 205
Moore Street (Dublin) 131
Shandon Craft Market (Cork) 176
St George's (Belfast) 313
Markievicz, Countess 257
Martin, Violet 186
Maskey, Alex 307
Maynooth 149
Mayo, County 233
McAleese, Mary 61
McAuley, Dave 92
McBride, John 46
McCabe, Patrick 249
McCourt, Frank 201
McCracken, Henry Joy 311
McDonagh, Martin 75
McDowell, Graeme 94
McGahern, John 74, 259
McGuigan, Barry 92, 249
McGuinness, Martin 62
McGuinness, Norah 80
McIlroy, Rory 93
McKenna, Barney 69
McKiernan, Catherina 93
McKinley, President William 303
Meath, County 145
Mebh of Connaught 255
media 330
Irish-language media 199
Mellifont Abbey 147
Midleton 161
Old Midleton Distillery 161
Mizen Head 188
Mizen Head Visitor Centre 188
Mizen Peninsula 188
mobile (cell) phones 332
Mohill 260
Monaghan 250
County Museum 250
Garage Theatre 250
Market House 250
St Macartan's Cathedral 250
tourist information 248
Monaghan, County 274
monasteries 36
abbey (Innisfallen Island) 193
An Diseart (Dingle) 196
Ardmore 160
Black Abbey (Kilkenny) 163
Bonamargy Friary (Ballycastle)
299
Cistercian (Greyabbey) 294
Cistercian monastery
(Multyfarnham) 244
Clonmacnoise 40, 237, 239
Corcomroe Abbey 216
Drumlane Abbey 247
Duiske Abbey (Graiguenamanagh)
166

Dunbrody Abbey 157
Ennis Friary (Ennis) 209
Franciscan abbey (Donegal) 263
Franciscan Friary (Timoleague)
184
Glendalough 144
Inch Abbey (Downpatrick) 292
Jerpoint Abbey 165
Mellifont Abbey 147
Mount Melleray (Cappoquin) 159
Nendrum Abbey (Mahee Island)
293
Roscommon Abbey (Roscommon)
245
Scattery Island 210
Skellig Michael 41, 194
Sligo Abbey (Sligo) 255
St Mary's (Devenish Island) 282
St Molaise's (Innishmurray Island)
259
Monea 284
money matters 19, 331
budgeting for your trip 326
euro 61
euro, acceptance in Northern
Ireland 274
money-saving tips 11
Moneymore 280
Moore, Christy 70
Moran, Dylan 146
Morrison, Van 69, 319
motor racing 294
Mountaineering Ireland 98
Mountbatten, Lord Louis 258
Mount Gabriel 188
Mount Juliet estate 165
Mountshannon 209
Mount Stewart 294
Mourne Mountains 98, 289
Moving Hearts 70
Mullaghmore 258
Mullingar 243
Cathedral of Christ the King 243
Multyfarnham 244
Cistercian monastery 244
Murphy, Dervla 73
Murrisk Abbey 231
museums and galleries 9
Allihies Copper Mine Museum
(Allihies) 190
Arklow Maritime Museum (Arklow)
154
Art Gallery (Dunfanaghy) 266
Avondale (Rathdrum) 144
Ballycastle Museum (Ballycastle)
299
Belfast Exposed (Belfast) 317
Carrickfergus Museum & Civic
Centre (Carrickfergus) 297
Cavan County Museum
(Ballyjamesduff) 248
Claddagh Museum (Galway) 224
Clare Museum (Ennis) 209
Cobh Heritage Centre (Cobh)
178
contemporary art galleries 78
Cork Butter Museum (Cork) 176
Cork Public Museum (Cork) 176
County Museum (Armagh) 285
County Museum (Monaghan) 250

Crawford Municipal Art Gallery (Cork) 175
Dispensary House Gallery (Loughgall) 287
Down County Museum (Downpatrick) 292
Dublin City Gallery The Hugh Lane (Dublin) 80, 132
Dublinia (Dublin) 128
Dublin Writers Museum (Dublin) 132
Dunfanaghy Workhouse (Dunfanaghy) 266
Famine Museum (Strokestown Park House) 244, 245
Folk Village Museum (Glencolumbkille) 265
Fort Dunree Military Museum (Buncrana) 268
Foynes Flying Boat Museum (Foynes) 207
Galway City Museum (Galway) 224
Glasnevin Museum (Glasnevin) 138
Glebe House Gallery 267
Glenview Folk Museum 261
Great Blasket Centre (Great Blasket) 197
Hunt Museum (Limerick) 204
Inishowen Maritime Museum and Planetarium (Greencastle) 268
Ireland's Historic Science Centre (Birr) 240
Irish Agricultural Museum (Wexford) 156
Irish Horse Museum (Kildare) 163
Irish Linen Centre and Lisburn Museum 288
Irish Museum of Modern Art (Dublin) 80, 135
Irish National Heritage Park (Wexford) 155
James Joyce Centre (Dublin) 133
James Joyce Museum (Sandycove) 136
Kerry County Museum (Tralee) 198
Kilmainham Gaol (Dublin) 135
Kinsale Regional Museum (Kinsale) 183
Knock Folk Museum (Knock) 234
Limerick City Gallery of Art (Limerick) 204
Limerick City Museum (Limerick) 203
Lismore Castle gallery (Lismore) 160
Little Museum (Dublin) 122
Locke's Distillery (Kilbeggan) 243
Maritime & Heritage Centre (Killybegs) 264
Metropolitan Arts Centre (MAC) (Belfast) 317
Michael Collins Centre (Clonakilty) 185
Millmount Museum (Drogheda) 147
Model (Sligo) 256

Museum of Free Derry (Derry) 275
National Gallery of Ireland (Dublin) 124
National Museum (Dublin) 123
National Museum of Country Life (Castlebar) 234
National Museum of Decorative Arts and History (Dublin) 136
Natural History Museum (Dublin) 124
Naughton Gallery (Belfast) 314
Nenagh Heritage Centre 241
Nicholas Mosse Pottery Museum (Bennettsbridge) 165
North Down Heritage Centre (Bangor) 295
Old Jameson Distillery (Dublin) 134
Peoples' Gallery (Derry) 275
Radio Museum (Cork) 176
Rothe House (Kilkenny) 163
Royal Ulster Rifles Museum (Belfast) 317
Skibbereen Heritage Centre (Skibbereen) 187
Sligo County Museum (Sligo) 256
Sligo Folk Park 259
Titanic Belfast (Belfast) 312
Tower Museum (Derry) 276
Ulster-American Folk Park 278
Ulster Folk and Transport Museum (Cultra) 296, 297
Ulster Museum (Belfast) 315
Verbal Arts Centre (Derry) 276
VOID (Derry) 276
W5 (Belfast) 312
Writers' Museum (Dublin) 73
music 67. *See also* individual musicians and bands
Celtic fusion 69
classical 70
country 250
Handel's Messiah 127
marching bands 290
musical instruments 67
Music for Galway 224
opera 71
popular and club music 69
rock 263
séan nós singing 67, 69
showbands 69
singing 69
traditional 67, 88, 183, 209, 213, 260
mythology and legends 45
Children of Lir 244
connected with St Patrick 167, 293
Deirdre of the Sorrows 287
Fionn MacCool 289, 303
Queen Medb and the brown bull of Cooley 148

N

Nairn 265
Dolmen Centre 266
National Land League of Ireland 45

national parks
Burren, The 214
Connemara 230
Glenveagh 267
Killarney 192
National Symphony Orchestra of Ireland 70
National Trust for Ireland. *See* An Taisce
nature reserves and bird sanctuaries
Carlingford Lough 148
Cliffs of Moher 212
Coole Park (Gort) 217
Copeland Island 295
Dalkey Island 137
Dundalk Bay 148
Ireland's Eye 139
North Bull Island 139
Peatlands Park 280
Rathlin Island 300
Saltee Islands 156
Strangford Lough 293
Wexford Wildlife Reserve 154
Navan 146
Navan Centre 286
Neeson, Liam 316
Nenagh 241
Governor's House 241
Nenagh Castle Keep 241
Nenagh Heritage Centre (Nenagh) 241
Newbliss 250
Newbridge 149
Newcastle 291
Newgrange 147
Brú na Bóinne Visitor Centre 147
New Ross 166
Dunbrody Famine Ship 166
Newry 288
Bagenal's Castle 289
newspapers and magazines 330
Newtownards 294
Movilla Abbey 294
Scrabo Tower 295
Nire Valley 167
Nire Valley Drive 167
Nore, River 165
North Bull Island 139
Northern Ireland 52, 273
border 53, 273
Northwest Ireland 253

O

O'Brien, Edna 56, 209
O'Carolan, Turlough 68
O'Casey, Sean 130
O'Connell, Daniel 42, 195
O'Connor, Joseph 75
O'Conor, John 71
O'Conor, Roderic 80
O'Doherty, Brian 79
O'Doherty, Ken 92
O'Donnell, Daniel 263
O'Donoghue, Hughie 80
O'Flaherty, Liam 230
O'Flanagan, Sheila 75
Ogham Stones 173
O'Hara, Dan 230

Ó Lionáird, Iarla 70
Omagh 61, 277
O'Malley, Grace 232
O'Malley, Tony 80
O'Neill, Captain Terence 57
O'Neill, Hugh 37, 308
opening hours 331
Opera Theatre Company 71
Orangemen 38, 290
Ó Riada, Sean 68
Orpen, William 80
Osborne, Walter 80
O'Shea, Kitty 45
O'Sullivan, Sonia 93
O'Toole, Fintan 260
O'Toole, St Lawrence 128
Owen, Enoch Trevor 194
Oxford Island 303
    Lough Neagh Discovery Centre
    303

P

Paisley, Reverend Ian 57, 62
Pale, The 36, 118, 147
Parke's Castle 257
parks and gardens. See
    also historic houses
    Antrim Castle Gardens (Antrim)
    303
    Ballymaloe Cookery School
    gardens (Shanagarry) 161
    Birr Castle and Demesne (Birr)
    240
    Botanic Gardens (Glasnevin) 137
    Castlewellan Forest Park 291
    Cave Hill Country Park (Belfast)
    321
    City Hall Gardens (Belfast) 307
    Crawfordsburn Country Park 296
    Derreen Gardens 191
    Donard Forest Park 291
    Fitzgerald Park (Cork) 176
    Fota Arboretum 177
    Garden of Remembrance (Dublin)
    132
    Glengarriff Bamboo Park
    (Glengarriff) 189
    Ilnacullin Gardens (Glengarriff)
    189
    Japanese Gardens (Kildare) 163
    Johnstown Castle Gardens
    (Wexford) 155
    Killykeen Forest Park 247
    Kilrush Forest Park 210
    Larchill Arcadian Garden (Kilcock)
    149
    Lismore Castle Gardens (Lismore)
    160
    Lough Navar Forest Park 284
    Merrion Square (Dublin) 123
    Mount Usher Gardens (Ashford)
    144
    Palace Demesne (Armagh) 286
    People's Park (Limerick) 204
    Phoenix Park (Dublin) 135
    Powerscourt House and Gardens
    (Enniskerry) 145
    Rossmore Forest Park 250
    Silent Valley Mountain Park 291

    Slieve Gullion Forest Park 287
    Steeple Park (Antrim) 303
    St Fiachra's Garden (Kildare) 163
    St Stephen's Green (Dublin) 121
    Tollymore Forest Park 291
    Vandeleur Walled Garden (Kilrush)
    210
    Woodstock Gardens and
    Arboretum (Inistioge) 165
Parnell, Charles Stewart 43, 144
Patterson's Spade Mill 303
Pearse, Pádraic 46
Peatlands Park 280
Peel, Sir Robert 42
Peep o' Day Boys 38
Penn, William 161
people 22
    African community 205
    Brazilian community 217
    immigrants 60, 171
    of Belfast 305
    Polish community 205
    travellers 53, 169
Pettigo 283
Pitt, William 38
plantlife 181, 195
    fuchsias 185
    of The Burren 214
    rare species 234
    spring gentian 214
Planxty 70
politics and government 60
    Anglo-Irish Agreement 60
    Catholic Emancipation Bill 42
    constitution 54
    Dáil Eireann 48
    Fianna Fáil 46, 54
    Fine Gael 54
    Labour Party 54
    Land Act of 1881 44
    Northern Ireland 20, 307, 308
    Republic 20
    Sinn Féin 47, 48
Pomeroy 280
Port 265
Portadown 287
    Lough Neagh Discovery Centre
    287
Portaferry
    Exploris 293
Portavogie 295
Portlaoise 242
Portmagee 194
    Skellig Experience 194
Portmarnock 139
Portrush 301
    Portrush Countryside Centre 302
Portstewart 302
postal services 331
Poulnabrone 218, 215
Powerscourt Waterfall 145
Priests, The 71
Prosperous 149
public holidays 331
pubs 9, 86
    Belfast 86, 310, 311, 314
    Dublin 86
    Inland Ireland 246
    Northern Ireland 282
    Northwest Ireland 255, 268

    pub food 83
    traditional music pubs 88
Purple Mountain 193
Purser, Sarah 80

Q

Quin 208
    Knappogue Castle 208
Quinlan, Linda 81

R

radio 331
rail travel
    Giant's Causeway and Bushmills
    Railway steam train 301
Raleigh, Sir Walter 161
Ramelton 268
    Donegal Ancestry 268
Raphoe 267
    Beltany Stone Circle 267
Rathdrum 144
    Avondale 144
Rathfriland 291
    Brontë Interpretive Centre 288
Rathlin Island 300
Rathmullan 267
    Flight of the Earls Heritage Centre
    268
Redmond, John 46
Reid, Nano 80
religion 20
    Christianity, arrival of 36
religious services 331
restaurants 83
    Belfast 309
    Euro-Toques 83
    medieval banquets 208, 209,
    217
Rineen 186
Ring of Beara 190
Ring of Kerry 182, 193
Ritchie, William 308
road bowling 93, 286
Roaringwater Bay 187
Robertson, Daniel 145
Robinson, Mary 60
Roche, Stephen 92
Roche, Vivienne 79
Rockcorry 250
Ros a'Mhil 229
Roscommon 245
    Roscommon Abbey 245
    Roscommon Castle 245
Roscrea 241
    Damer House 242
    Roscrea Heritage Centre 241
Rossbeigh 193
Rosscarbery 185
Rosse, 3rd Earl of 240
Rosses Point 257
Rossinver 260
Rossmore Castle 250
Rossmore Forest Park 250
Rossnowlagh 262
Rostrevor 289
Roundstone 227
    Roundstone Music, Craft &
    Fashion 227

round towers 36. See
    also monasteries
    Antrim 303
    Clones 249
    Devenish Island 282
    Kildare 162
    Kilkenny 164
Roundwood 144
Rower, The 166
rugby 93, 205, 328
Russborough
    Russborough House 157
Ryanair 19, 62

S

Saltee Islands 156
Salthill 226
    Atlantaquaria 226
    Leisureland 226
Sandycove 136
    James Joyce Museum 136
    The Forty Foot 136
Sawel 101
Scarriff 208
Scarva Visitor Centre 289
Scattery Island 210
Schull 188
Scott, Patrick 80
Scrib 227
Scully, Sean 78, 79
Severin, Tim 208
shamrock 162
Shanagarry 161
    Ballymaloe Cookery School, Farm
        Shop and Gardens 161
    Ballymaloe House hotel 161
    Shanagarry Design Centre 161
    Shanagarry House 161
Shannonbridge 239
Shannon Harbour 101, 240
Shannon, River 96, 201, 207, 209,
    237, 239, 245, 260
    source 247
Shaw, George Bernard 24, 74
    statue (Dublin) 124
Sheep's Head Peninsula 188
Shercock 248
Sheridan, Richard Brinsley 74
Sherkin Island 187
ship building. See boat and ship
    building
shopping. See also markets
    antiques 206
    art and crafts 11, 161, 164, 176,
        227, 277
    outlet shopping 288
Silent Valley Mountain Park 291
Simnel, Lambert 128
Sion Mills 277
Sitric, King 128
Skellig Michael 41, 194
Skellig Rocks 191
Skibbereen 186
    Skibbereen Heritage Centre 187
Slane 146
    Slane Castle 146
Slea Head 197
Slieve Anierin 260
Slieve Bloom Mountains 99, 241

Slieve Bloom Way 241
Slieve Donard 291
Slieve Gullion 287
Slieve Gullion Forest Park 287
Slieve League 265
    Slieve League Cultural Centre
        265
Slievemartin 289
Slieve Miskish Mountains 190
Slievemore Mountain 233
Slieve-na-Calliagh 98
Sligo 255
    Factory Performance Space 256
    Hargadon's pub 255
    Hawk's Well Theatre 256
    Model 256
    Sligo Abbey 255
    Sligo County Museum 256
    Yeats Memorial Building 255
Sligo, County 253
Sligo Folk Park 259
smoking 63, 87, 332
Sneem 195
snooker 92
soccer 92, 93
social issues 62
Society of United Irishmen 38
Somerville and Ross 186
Somerville, Edith 186
Southeast Ireland 153
Southwest Ireland 181
Spanish Armada 258, 276, 301
Spelga Pass 100
Sperrin Mountains 101
sports 90, 205. See also by name
    Gaelic Athletic Association 215
Springhill House 280
St Brendan 208
St Brigid 162
St Canice 163
St Cormac 167
St Declan 157, 160
Stephens, James 43
St Finbar 171, 189
Sting 69
St Kevin 144
St Kieran 239
St Oliver Plunkett 147
storytellers 72
St Patrick 36, 146, 167, 286, 292,
    293
Strabane 277
    Gray's Printing Press 277
Straffan 149
Strangford 293
    Castle Ward House 293
Strangford Lough 292, 293
    Strangford Lough Wildlife Centre
        293
Streedagh Strand 258
Strokestown Park House and
    Famine Museum 244
Strongbow 36, 128, 157
Suck, River 97, 237, 239
surfing 195, 196, 211
    Northwest Ireland 253, 262, 263
Swanlinbar 247
Swift, Jonathan 74, 128
swimming
    The Forty Foot (Sandycove) 136

Synge, John Millington 74, 130,
    230

T

Tarbert 198, 207
Taylor, Dennis 92
telephones 332
television 331
Termon, River 283
Terryglass 241
Thatcher, Margaret 59, 60
theatres and performance venues
    Abbey Theatre (Dublin) 130
    An Taibhdhearc (Galway) 224
    Belfast Waterfront Hall (Belfast)
        313
    Black Box (Belfast) 318
    Clotworthy Arts Centre (Antrim)
        303
    Corn Mill (Carrigallen) 261
    Craic Theatre Company
        (Coalisland) 280
    Elmwood Hall (Belfast) 315
    Factory Performance Space (Sligo)
        256
    Firkin Crane Centre (Cork) 176
    Garage Theatre (Monaghan) 250
    Gate Theatre (Dublin) 132
    Grand Canal Theatre (Dublin)
        131
    Grand Opera House (Belfast) 309
    Hawk's Well Theatre (Sligo) 256
    Lyric Theatre (Belfast) 315
    Market Place Theatre and Arts
        Centre (Armagh) 286
    Meeting House Square (Dublin)
        125
    Metropolitan Arts Centre (MAC)
        (Belfast) 317
    Millennium Forum (Derry) 277
    National Concert Hall (Dublin)
        122
    Nerve Centre (Derry) 277
    Odyssey Arena (Belfast) 312
    Olympia Theatre (Dublin) 126
    Opera House (Cork) 175
    Peacock Theatre (Dublin) 130
    Playhouse (Derry) 277
    Rotunda Rooms (Dublin) 132
    Siamsa Tire (Tralee) 198
    Slane Castle (Slane) 146
    St Anne's Church (Dublin) 123
    Ulster Hall (Belfast) 309
    Wexford Opera House (Wexford)
        155
Thomastown 165
Three Jolly Pigeons pub 246
Tiernan, Tommy 146
time zone 332
Timoleague 184
    Church of Ireland 184
    Church of Our Lady's Nativity
        184
    Franciscan Friary 184
Titanic 178. See also boat and ship
    building
Tollymore Forest Park 291
Tone, Wolfe 38, 39
Toome 303

Torc Waterfall 192
Tory Island 266
tourism 61
  eco-tourism 239, 266
  fuschsia branding 185
tourist information 333
tours. *See also* boat trips
  Burren, The 216
  Moher Rangers (Cliffs of Moher) 212
  Ring of Kerry 193
Tralee 197
  Denny Street 198
  Kerry County Museum 198
  Rose of Tralee Festival 198, 329
  Siamsa Tíre 198
  Town Park 198
Tramore 159
transport 324
Trawmore 233
Trim 146
Trollope, Anthony 240, 261, 262
Tuamgraney 209
  Drewsborough House 208
Tullamore 243
  Tullamore Dew Heritage Centre 243
Tully 284
Tullynally Castle 243
Tulsk 245
  Cruachan Aí Visitors Centre 245
Twelve Pins (or Bens) 98, 226
Tyrone, County 273
Tyrone Guthrie Centre 250
Tyrrell, Charles 81

U

U2 19, 69, 126
Ulster 37, 45, 273. *See also* Norhern Ireland
Ulster-American Folk Park 278
Ulster Defence Association 58
Ulster Orchestra 70
Ulster Volunteer Force 46
Unesco Global Geopark 285
Unesco World Heritage Site 301
Union Hall 186
  Keelbeg Pier 186
United Irishmen 311
United States
  influence of 19
  presidential connections 157, 278, 297, 303
Upper Lough Erne 281

V

Valentia Island 194
Vee Gap 159
Ventry 196
  Dunbeg Fort 196
Vinegar Hill 157

W

Walker, Sarah 81
Walker, William Hall 163
walking and hiking 11, 98
  Inland Ireland 237, 241, 248
  Limerick and the Shannon Region 212
  Northern Ireland 287, 289
  Northwest Ireland 265
  Southeast Ireland 159, 168
  Southwest Ireland 188, 194
  walking festivals 99
Walsh, Louis 69
Warrenpoint 289
waterfalls
  Glenmacnass 144
  Powerscourt 145
  Torc 192
Waterfoot 298
Waterford 157
  Bishop's Palace 158
  Christ Church Cathedral 158
  City Hall 158
  French Church 158
  Reginald's Tower 157
  The Mall 158
  Waterford Castle 157
  Waterford Crystal Experience, The 158
  Waterford Treasures 158
Waterville 94, 194
Wavertree, Lord 163
websites 100, 333
Wellbrook Beetling Mill 280
Wells, H.G. 139
West Cork 182
Westlife 69
Westport 231, 232
  Clew Bay Heritage Centre 232
  Westport House & Country Park 232
Wexford 155, 157
  Irish Agricultural Museum 156
  Irish National Heritage Park 155
  Johnstown Castle 157
  Johnstown Castle Gardens 155

Wexford Festival Opera 71, 155, 329
Wexford Opera House 155
Wexford Wildlife Reserve 154
whale and dolphin watching 186, 196, 210, 262
Whiteabbey 297
White Bay 298
Whitehead 297
White Island 282
Whiterock Bay 293
Wicklow, County 143
Wicklow Mountains 143
Wild Atlantic Way 7, 181
Wilde, Oscar 74
wildlife. *See also* birdlife, national parks, nature reserves and bird sanctuaries
  butterflies 216
  deer 192, 284
  dolphins 186, 196, 207, 210, 262
  insects 280
  of the peat bogs 280
  pine martens 216
  porpoises 262
  salmon 225, 227
  seals 137, 139, 186, 190, 262
  trout 227
  whales 186, 262
wildlife parks. *See* zoos and aquariums
William of Orange 37, 147, 206, 275, 290
Wilson, President Woodrow, ancestral home 277
windsurfing 195
Wolfe Tones 39, 70

Y

Yeats, Jack B. 80
Yeats, John Butler 80
Yeats, W.B. 25, 45, 54, 74, 130, 217, 255, 256, 258
Youghal 160

Z

zoos and aquariums
  Atlantaquaria (Salthill) 226
  Belfast Zoo (Belfast) 321
  Dublin Zoo (Dublin) 136
  Exploris (Portaferry) 293
  Fota Wildlife Park 177